The Walker's Handbook

Hugh Westacott was born in 1932 and has been an enthusiastic walker all his life. For many years he was a librarian, but following the success of *The Walker's Handbook* he left the profession in 1980 to devote himself to full-time writing. He is the author of numerous footpath guides and is currently writing *The Walker's Encyclopaedia*. Among his other interests are the history of walking, landscape history, and the relationship between walking and literature. He is the proprietor of Footpath Publications, which specialises in publishing footpath guides to out-of-the-way places, and Rucksack Holidays which brings Americans on walking tours of Britain. Hugh Westacott is married to an American and they have one son. He has two daughters by a previous marriage. He divides his time between England and San Antonio, Texas.

Also by Hugh Westacott

Footpaths and Bridleways in Buckinghamshire No. 1: Winslow Area,
   Footpath Publications, 1974.
Footpaths and Bridleways in Buckinghamshire No. 2: Buckingham Area,
   Footpath Publications, 1975.
Walks around Buckingham and Winslow, Footpath Publications, 1976.
A Practical Guide to Walking the Devon South Coast Path, Footpath
   Publications, 1976.
Walks and Rides on Dartmoor, Footpath Publications, 1977.
A Practical Guide to Walking the Ridgeway Path, Footpath Publications,
   4th Ed., 1978.
Discovering Walking, Shire Publications, 1979.
A Practical Guide to Walking the Dorset Coast Path, Footpath
   Publications, 1982.
The Devon South Coast Path (with Mark Richards), Penguin Books,
   1982.
The Dorset Coast Path (with Mark Richards), Penguin Books, 1982.
The Ridgeway Path (with Mark Richards), Penguin Books, 1982.
The Brecon Beacons National Park (with Mark Richards), Penguin
   Books, 1983.
Dartmoor for Walkers and Riders (with Mark Richards), Penguin Books,
   1983.
The North Downs Way (with Mark Richards), Penguin Books, 1983.
The Somerset and North Devon Coast Path (with Mark Richards),
   Penguin Books, 1983.
Walking: an Annotated Bibliography, Footpath Publications, 1991.
*The Illustrated Encyclopaedia of Walking & Backpacking: Places, People
   & Techniques*, Oxford Illustrated Press, 1991.

THE WALKER'S HANDBOOK

The Complete Guide to Walking in the UK

Hugh Westacott

PAN BOOKS
London, Sydney and Auckland

For my son Dorian, born 26 July 1988

First published in 1978 by Penguin Books
New edition published 1989 by Oxford Illustrated Press
This edition published 1991 by Pan Books Ltd
Cavaye Place, London SW10 9PG
9 8 7 6 5 4 3 2 1
© Hugh Douglas Dyer-Westacott 1989
ISBN 0 330 31177 8

Printed in England by Clays Ltd, St Ives plc

Contents

List of Figures

Acknowledgements

The scope of this book is so large that I have had to rely on many people to provide me with information on aspects of walking that are outside my experience. So many people have helped so willingly, that it is difficult to know where to start expressing my thanks, and how to do it adequately.

My thanks are due to the national park officers and their staff for much of the information contained in Chapter 13; to the Countryside Commission and the Countryside Commission for Scotland for information about long-distance paths; to the directors and staff of the national tourist offices listed in Chapter 18 who provided me with information about walking in their countries; to the directors, secretaries and staff of all the organisations listed in Appendix 2; and to the Controller of Her Majesty's Stationery Office for permission to reproduce the Ordnance Survey Maps (Crown copyright reserved).

Everybody was helpful, but a few deserve particular mention for advice and assistance over and above what could reasonably be expected of them. In particular, Mr K. E. Foster of the Ordnance Survey Information Branch for unfailing patience and courtesy in replying to my nitpicking questions; Mr Wilfred Capper of the Ulster Preservation Society, whom I am tempted to call the Mr Walking of Northern Ireland; Michal Bucholz of the State Tourist Office in Warsaw who compiled a very detailed dossier of information about walking in Poland; Neil Venter of Satour who replied to my letter of enquiry by actually writing the section on South Africa for me; Mark Richards for general advice and encouragement; John Trevelyan of the Ramblers' Association who read the section on the legal aspects of walking in manuscript and made helpful comments; and Roger Smith, editor of *Scottish World,* who read the manuscript and made many valuable suggestions that greatly improved the final version.

And finally, as a former member of the profession, I should like to pay tribute to those indefatigable and knowledgeable librarians, the hewers of wood and drawers of water in the field of information retrieval, whose efforts we too readily take for granted and to whom I am so deeply indebted: Adele Brazier and the staff of the Amersham Library; Clive Bostle and the staff of the County Reference Library, Aylesbury; Peter Brown and the staff of the Palmers Green Library; and the staff of the Enfield Reference Library.

Preface to the Third Edition

Nine years have passed since the last edition of *The Walker's Handbook* appeared. The success of the two previous editions has encouraged me to undertake a complete revision of the text and to rearrange some of the material. After much heart-searching I have abandoned imperial measures in favour of their metric equivalents. A whole generation has been educated using the metric system, Ordnance Survey maps are largely metric and it seems sensible for we old fogies to move with the times.

To convert metric measures to imperial:

Multiply metres by 3.28 to convert to feet.

Divide kilometres by 1.6093 to convert to miles.

Divide centimetres by 2.54 to convert to inches.

The following quick conversions will give acceptably accurate results:

Metres to feet: multiply by 3 and add 10%.

Kilometres to miles: multiply by 5 and divide by 8.

Centimetres to inches: multiply by 2 and divide by 5.

Preface to the Fourth Edition

The text of this edition is substantially the same as that of the third edition. However, the opportunity has been taken to update the bibliographies and lists of organisations; to expand and revise the chapter on long-distance paths; and to correct a few minor inaccuracies and clear up a few ambiguities pointed out by correspondents and reviewers.

Introduction

In the *Introduction* to the second edition of *The Walker's Handbook* published in 1980 I commented on the revival of interest in walking for recreation. During the last nine years that interest has quickened with more and more people seeking the peaceful solace of the countryside as a balm to the pressures of modern life. Several new magazines about walking have appeared (two have ceased publication), some of the quality newspapers regularly publish articles about the subject, footpath guides and books about walking pour from the printing presses, and almost every High Street now has an outdoor shop where walking and backpacking gear can be purchased.

Despite the huge numbers of people who regularly take to the hills and dales, few well-researched, accurate and comprehensive books about walking have been published, and mine seems to be the only one that has remained in print for a significant length of time. Far too many 'how to' books are written by authors who do not bother to obtain their material from original sources and are content to copy bibliographies and the addresses of organisations from other books. As I write, I have recently-published books on my desk that contain information that is *several years* out of date. The climbing fraternity is much better served by its authors who exhibit a standard of scholarship and elegance of writing that we walkers should try to emulate.

The Walker's Handbook is about all kinds of walking; from ambling through lowland pastures in high summer to tramping the tops of the Lake District and Scotland in the depths of winter; from exploring the rolling bocage of Normandy to backpacking the alpine Haute Route and the

3000-metre ridges of the GR20 in Corsica. It is about walking only; it does not cover any aspect of climbing and those who want to know about anything that involves ropes, karabiners or pitons must look elsewhere. Whenever the term 'climbing' is used in this book it means 'ascending'.

The Walker's Handbook is written with the newcomer to walking in mind, but should also prove to be a useful work of reference for the more experienced, as it contains a great deal of information not readily available elsewhere. In particular, the extensive bibliographies and the information given about Ordnance Survey sheet numbers and footpath guides for the long-distance paths, National Parks, Areas of Outstanding Natural Beauty, Scotland, Ireland and foreign countries should prove useful.

Walkers tend to be individualists and we all have our fads, fancies and prejudices, likes and dislikes. Let me declare mine now so that those who read on may make allowances for them. For many years my particular love has been for the mountains and fells of the Lake District, the Pennines and Scotland, and even though I have extended my walking experience considerably since the first edition of this book appeared, my feet still instinctively turn northwards. I have explored some of the lonely wastes of Iceland; walked the Kaibab/Bright Angel Trail which descends more than 1500 metres from the South Rim of the Grand Canyon to the Colorado River; climbed from below sea-level to the summit of Telescope Peak which soars for 3367 metres above Death Valley; learned, under the tutelage of my American wife, to appreciate the harshly vivid colours of the mountains of Texas and the San Antonio hill country; climbed some of the highest Alpine routes accessible to walkers, and marched across the spiny ridges of Corsica. Yet despite these experiences, I remain faithful to my original loves and their only rival in my affections is the Southwest Coast Path that I have walked six times and am inclined to believe is, mile for mile, the most rewarding walk in Britain.

I am delighted that more people are discovering the gentle pleasures of walking, but I am uneasy about some of the activities of bodies like the Countryside Commission and the National Parks that are supposed to look after the interests of walkers. The provision of rangers, nature trails, picnic sites, car parks and toilets may seem perfectly reasonable but they smack of regimentation and nannying. I deeply resented being stopped by a National Park ranger, however well-meaning, who wanted to satisfy himself that I was properly equipped for the hills and produced a checklist of essential items. The current buzzword is 'interpretation', and it now seems *de rigueur* to be able to interpret everything one sees; I prefer to attempt to understand, experience, and above all, to love the landscape.

Fortunately, there will always be people who want to follow their own paths and this book is written specially for them. Much of it contains guidance and suggestions only, based on a lifetime of wandering in the hills. In the course of time, the reader may wish to follow his own inclinations and walk in the manner that suits him; that is all to the good, for there are only three rules from which the walker should never depart:

1. Follow the Country and Mountain Codes.
2. Obey the law.
3. Be properly equipped for the mountains and fells.

This book is a distillation of information about walking and at the end of every chapter will be found a bibliography of recommended books chosen for their quality and usefulness so that the reader can pursue in greater detail subjects of particular interest. Most of them have been written within the last ten years and a significant number are still in print and obtainable from bookshops and libraries.

I am conscious that *The Walker's Handbook* is a pedestrian work. I hope it communicates my enthusiasm for walking, but a book crammed with facts and information intended to instruct, cannot convey my passion for the incomparable variety and beauty of the British countryside. The description of the joy, sometimes bordering on ecstasy, that I experience when I tread the secret ways through pasture and copse, moor and mountain must wait for another, more self-indulgent book.

I have tried to ensure that the information contained in this book was correct at the time of going to press.

The Pleasures of Walking

After breathing, walking is probably the most basic human activity, and a person who is unable to walk is regarded as severely handicapped. Almost everybody *can* walk, but the way in which each person walks varies enormously. There is all the difference in the world between the businessman hurrying tensely and purposefully to the station fearing that his train might have left and the walker slowly ascending a mountain path filling his lungs with unpolluted air and revelling in the magnificent scenery around him. Yet both are putting one foot in front of the other.

Already we have hit on one of the clues to walking for pleasure. Many people delight in beautiful scenery and there is no doubt that the best way to enjoy and experience the countryside is to walk in it. Those who see the countryside from the inside of a car miss so much. Roads rarely follow the most scenic routes, but footpaths nearly always do. Roadside verges always stink of petrol fumes, whereas two hundred metres away over the stile it is possible to smell the wild fragrance of the countryside.

Walking combines well with other interests. The naturalist has to walk quietly through the landscape to avoid disturbing wildlife and even the casual walker is likely to see things he will remember for a long time. Some of my special memories are of watching buzzards soaring effortlessly from the Cheviots, seeing a vixen carrying a rabbit back to her cubs, almost stepping on a fox in a ditch very early in the morning, and watching three young weasels playing tag around an oak tree. One walk near Malham in Yorkshire was made memorable by a botanist friend showing me tiny Alpine flowers growing in the clefts of the limestone.

The landscape itself is a fascinating study. Although the shape of the mountains, hills, streams and valleys pre-dates man, yet man has largely created the British landscape. He has cut down the primeval forest, drained the land and enclosed the fields with a complicated pattern of hedges, walls and ditches. The animals that he has grazed, the crops he has sown, the trees he has felled, the valleys he has drained or flooded for reservoirs—all have an effect on the ecology of the landscape.

In the course of moulding the landscape, man built towns and villages. Discovering the reasons for siting settlements in particular places makes an interesting detective puzzle for the curious to unravel. The walker has time to admire the natural taste and eye for beauty shown by our ancestors in building even the humblest dwellings. It is hard to pass by Thwaite in Swaledale, for instance, and not remark on the number of exceptionally elegant stone barns, with built-in dovecots to be seen in the fields. Evidence of change, decay and renewal are there for the inquiring walker to discover and interpret. A few kilometres from where I once lived is a pleasant village that I have driven through many times, but it was not until I walked through it and in the surrounding fields that I noticed that the church stood in an isolated position outside the village. This so intrigued me that I went over to investigate. In the fields around the church were numerous shallow depressions where once houses had stood. I discovered from a visit to the local history library that much of the village had been moved a few hundred yards to a new site and only the church had been left untouched.

It is exciting to discover for oneself traces of the past. A piece of rough land fenced off from an otherwise fertile pasture turns out to be the remains of a motte and bailey castle built by the Normans; a circular barn on a slight bluff is all that is left of an old windmill; that remarkably broad path with a pronounced crown and evidence of ditches on both sides is obviously an old road which may turn out to be prehistoric or Roman, or a forgotten drove road. It is fun, too, to follow old Roman roads from Ordnance Survey maps and it is surprising how many there are for the diligent searcher to find. Those interested in antiquities marked on the Ordnance Survey maps will find that accurate use of the compass is invaluable in pin-pointing the exact location of sites.

There is now a great deal of interest in industrial archaeology and the walker will often observe traces of past industry. The Pennines are particularly rich in old mine workings where lead, iron, silver and other metals and minerals were extracted. Because the workings are often some distance from the nearest settlement, they have frequently remained remarkably intact and it is possible to come across not only mine shafts and levels, but also engine sheds and bits of rusting machinery. The industrial revolution started in the valleys of northern England, where there was abundant water both for power and for cleaning, and some of these early factories still exist as fine buildings in lovely settings. Disused canals, railways and tramways can be found all over the country and are well worth exploring.

Investigating places connected with writers and their work can add an extra dimension to walking. One thinks of the Hardy country in Dorset or, as he called it, Wessex; the Brontë country near Keighley in West Yorkshire, and the Shakespeare country in Warwickshire. Top Withens, the ruined house generally believed to be the inspiration of *Wuthering Heights* in Emily Brontë's novel, actually lies on the Pennine Way. Arthur Ransome set his books in the Lake District and at Beatrix Potter's home at Far Sawrey near Windermere it is possible to see the vegetable garden where Mr MacGregor chased Peter Rabbit and the chimney that Tom Kitten explored. One can have a good long walk over the Berkshire Downs following the journey of the rabbits in Richard Adams's novel, *Watership Down*.

Walking as described in this book is not a competitive sport and is done purely for pleasure. It is an excellent way of keeping fit and can be continued until late into life. There are many seventy-year-olds who regularly go into the mountains and who can surprise younger, less experienced walkers with their strength and stamina.

The novice walker should proceed with some caution, especially if he has a sedentary job and is unused to exercise. Make a start by toning up the muscles of the legs and feet by going barefoot about the house and garden. Take purposeful strolls along quiet roads, parks and canal paths, covering a specific distance—say five or six kilometres, working up to about ten. Once you are able to cover ten kilometres without discomfort, you are ready for some real walking and can plan some circuits on local footpaths. No special clothes or equipment are necessary for walking in lowland areas, though most people will find comfortable stout shoes a help, together with a small rucksack, to carry sandwiches, a drink and a plastic raincoat. Before trying more ambitious walks on moor and mountain it is essential to have the proper equipment.

Where to go? One of the United Kingdom's greatest glories is its amazing variety of scenery packed into such a small area. It is possible to go to any rural area and have a splendid holiday exploring the local footpath and bridleway network. As we have seen, walking combines very well with other interests and walkers will have the venue of their holiday dictated by the location of their interest. Chapters 13 and 14 describe all the National Parks and Areas of Outstanding Natural Beauty for those interested primarily in walking in beautiful scenery. In Chapter 15 are described all the long-distance paths created by the Countryside Commission, all of which are suitable for walking holidays, and one can stay at different places every night. But some of them—especially the Southern Upland Way and Pennine Way—are very arduous and suitable only for the experienced fell-walker.

On winter evenings it is fun to examine Ordnance Survey maps to plan new walks and to remember old ones. The place names of Britain are so musical and exciting that they positively invite investigation— Rough Tor, Brown Willy, Sutton Thorn, Downhayne Brake, High Cup Nick, Dollywaggon Pike, Glaramara, Pike o' Stickle, Ringing Roger, Thunacar Knott, Chanctonbury Ring, Ivinghoe Beacon, Black Sail Pass, Wildboarclough, Cader Idris, Pen-y-Ghent, Great Whernside, Langstrothdale . . .

Select Bibliography of Inspirational Books

Birkett, Bill, *Classic Walks in Great Britain,* Oxford Illustrated Press, 1987.

Brown, Hamish, *Hamish's Groats-End Walk,* Gollancz, 1981.

Brown, Hamish, *Hamish's Mountain Walk,* Gollancz, 1978.

Hillaby, John, *Journey through Britain,* Constable, 1968.

Hillaby, John, Editor, *Walking in Britain,* Collins, 1988.

Smith, Roger, Editor, *The Winding Trail; a Selection of Articles and Essays for Walkers and Backpackers,* Paladin, 1986.

Unsworth, Walt, Editor, *Classic Walks of the World,* Oxford Illustrated Press, 1985.

Wainwright, A., *Ex-Fell-Wanderer,* Westmorland Gazette, 1987.

Wainwright, A., *Fell-Wanderer; the Story Behind the Guidebooks,* Westmorland Gazette, 1966.

Wilson, K., and Gilbert R., *Classic Walks,* Diadem, 1983.

Wilson, K. and Gilbert R., *The Big Walks, Challenging Mountain Walks and Scrambles in the British Isles,* Diadem, 1980.

Wilson, K., and Gilbert R., *Wild Walks,* Diadem, 1987.

SECTION 1: EQUIPMENT AND WALKING SKILLS

1 Clothing, Boots and Equipment

Before choosing clothes and equipment for walking it is as well to have a clear idea of the sort of terrain you are likely to explore. Unless the conditions were to be exceptionally severe, it is unlikely that anyone would ever be in any danger in any lowland part of the southern counties, or far from a place from which help could readily be obtained. It is quite different in the mountains and on the moors. Even in the summer months, conditions above 600 metres can be appalling and help unobtainable. The novice, sitting in a café in the valley watching the rain gusting in, cannot imagine what it is like on top of the fells. Once, early in September, I was walking the Pennine Way and left Dufton to walk the thirty-two kilometres to Alston. It was raining gently and there was a strong breeze in the valley, but the higher I climbed the more the wind blew and visibility became poorer. At the top of Great Dun Fell (834 metres) is a radar station with several huge masts, but so bad were the conditions that I could see them only when I was within twenty metres of them. I had to walk the ten kilometres from Knock Hush to Cross Fell navigating entirely by compass. The wind was so strong that at times I had to bend almost double to force my way along. The local Helm Wind was blowing and it would have been wiser to retreat, but there was plenty of shelter along the way and as I had a tent, sleeping bag, survival bag and three days' supply of food, so I decided to continue.

Cairns mark the path, but in the thick mist it was impossible to see from one to the next and the rain was drumming on my fell-jacket like hail stones. On the north face of Cross Fell, which is almost 900 metres high, the path makes a 90° turn to meet the old corpse road to Garrigill. There is a trig point on the top of Cross Fell and I hoped to find it so that I could use it to take a bearing. Although I knew I was on the summit of Cross Fell because I had passed through the girdle of rocks which form its outer edge, I was unable to locate the trig point even though I quartered the summit in a grid pattern counting my steps so as not to get lost. In the end, I had to take my compass bearing and walk down the fellside until I picked up the path. When walking in such conditions one loses all sense of direction and it is essential to rely on the compass even though one's instincts may tell one that the compass points in the wrong direction. If these were the conditions in early September, imagine what they are like in the depths of winter!

I have described this walk as it illustrates very clearly the weather any walker is likely to meet, sooner or later, on mountains or moorland. Unless properly clad and equipped, the walker will be in serious danger of dying of exposure. From time to time, tragic incidents are reported of walkers and climbers who have succumbed to the rigours of the weather. Practically all these incidents would not have happened if those involved had been properly equipped. Less than a week after walking over Cross Fell I was in Borrowdale in the Lake District near Sprinkling Tarn, some 600 metres up, when I came across the body of a camper dead beside his collapsed tent. The police were able to reconstruct the sad story. He had left Seathwaite on a Saturday afternoon in early September in driving rain and a howling gale. A shepherd had stopped him and warned him that he should not go onto the fells in such conditions. Nevertheless, he carried on and by the time night fell he was soaked to the skin. He pitched his tent in the most sheltered spot he could find, took off all his wet clothes and got into his sleeping bag. During the night the wind rose to tremendous force (one shepherd said they were the worst autumn gales he could remember) and his tent blew down. He was now without any protection except for a heap of stones behind which he tried to shelter. It was too late; although the weather was not cold, the wind and the rain soon sapped his strength and he died of exposure. Had he had with him a survival bag, which is merely a plastic bag large enough to get inside, he would almost certainly have lived to tell the tale.

Exposure occurs when the body temperature cools down to a point where it can no longer support life. It is obvious that this will happen if the body is not protected against extremely low temperature, but it is often not appreciated that exposure can occur in comparatively mild temperatures if the body is not adequately protected against wind and rain. The temperature of the body is controlled by the pores of the skin. Under normal conditions the pores excrete water vapour. When the body is cold, the pores close, and in an attempt to increase warmth by stimulation the body will start to shiver; when too hot, the skin will be flooded by moisture which cools the body by evaporation. Both sweating and shivering are to be avoided whenever possible because in these conditions the body is not at its most efficient and valuable energy is being wasted in an attempt to regulate the temperature.

The properly clad walker, therefore, must wear clothes which will protect him from the elements and at the same time keep him at an efficient temperature. There are fashions and fads in walking as there are in all sports, and personal preferences play a part, too. I do not like anoraks because I think they are too short in the body and ventilation cannot be controlled adequately. Nevertheless, a good anorak will have all the weatherproof qualities which make it a suitable garment for walking on the fells. Providing that clothing is chosen on the correct principles, you will still have a choice of gear to suit your own needs. Warmth is induced by trapping layers of air all round the body. Still air is an excellent insulator and it is essential to wear clothes that will trap the air and hold it in place. At the same time it is important that the water vapour given off by the body can escape easily and that is provided to provide sufficient ventilation to prevent sweating.

In foul weather, rainproof outer garments are required. These may be an anorak, a cagoule (which is really a knee-length anorak), or jacket. I favour the knee-length jacket as it gives the best control over ventilation and can be undone and worn open in between showers. When buying equipment always go to a specialist walkers' and climbers' shop—advice will be obtainable from the staff, who are likely to be enthusiasts themselves and have a great deal of practical experience. Avoid chain and army surplus stores.

Outdoor leisure clothing is now both big business and high fashion with a multi-million pound turnover. Many of the expensive clothes designed to withstand the rigours of the Himalayas are bought by people who are unlikely to wear them in climatic conditions more demanding than those to be found in Sloane Square and Hampstead Heath. Competition is intense and it seems that every year a new miracle fabric or revolutionary style is introduced at the annual Camping and Outdoor Leisure Trade Exhibition. This exhibition, which is not open to the public but is widely reported in outdoor magazines, is the most important British market-place for manufacturers and the retail trade. It is possible to sympathise with the efforts of salesmen to sell their products but the prudent walker will assess his needs carefully before succumbing to glossy blandishments. Remind yourself that walking for pleasure became popular in the early nineteenth century but it was not until well into the present century that specialised clothing for walking was developed.

Those for whom economy is a prime consideration will probably find most of their walking clothes already in their wardrobe. Everyday cotton or woollen shirts, sweaters, and underwear are perfectly satisfactory for all but the most extreme conditions. Breeches can be made from old worsted or tweed trousers. Cut off the legs eighty centimetres below the knee and open up the leg seam so that the bottom of the leg can be secured below the knee by a Velcro fastening. The off-cuts from the legs can be used to make a double seat and knee reinforcements.

Jeans are not for walking as they are cut too tight for comfort and are miserably cold when wet. More than one walker has died from exposure because his wet jeans could not keep him warm.

Outdoor clothing manufacturers are at last waking up to the fact that women account for half of the walking market and are beginning to design boots and clothing especially for them rather than treating them as small men. Women not only have a different general configuration but often have relatively shorter arms and legs. Every lady walker who has ever had to disappear behind a hedge knows that God must be a man. In the United States female walkers can buy diaper rain pants—waterproof overtrousers that unsnap like a baby's disposable nappy thus making calls of nature much easier. American ladies can also buy a dinky little instrument ('as supplied to national park rangers') that will convert them to men thus avoiding the unpleasant feeling of long wet grass brushing against the bare bottom. For the truly fastidious the complete outfit comes with a convenient carrying case and a portable tank!

Essential Clothing

There is no doubt that British clothing and equipment for walkers is as good as any manufactured anywhere in the world, and British-made rucksacks, tents, sleeping bags and specialised clothing are sought eagerly by foreign visitors. There is such a range of materials and designs on the market that walkers can be forgiven if they are deluded by advertising into buying gear that they do not really require. Before buying a great deal of expensive clothing and equipment it is wise to consider very carefully the use to which you will put it. For example, the walker who is content with day trips to the mountains and fells during the more temperate months of the year does not really require breathable waterproof clothing (see pp25-28), and will find conventional shell garments (rain-proof outer clothing, see p25) perfectly satisfactory because he will be able to dry his clothes at the end of every day. The same is true of those who spend their walking holidays at bed and breakfast establishments. If money is not a prime consideration then you might as well buy breathable waterproofs; they are better and you will be more comfortable. Information about the properties of the materials used will be found on pages 26-28.

The fell-walker who returns home every night needs only to buy four items of specialised clothing:

Boots (see pp28-29)
Woollen stockings (see p28)
Anorak or cagoule (shell clothing, see below)
Overtrousers (shell clothing, see below)

Everything else can probably be found in the wardrobe at home. There are now specially made synthetic materials with properties superior to natural fibres, but anyone planning to use old sweaters, shirts, and trousers converted into breeches should make sure that they are made of the appropriate *natural* fibre. An acrylic sweater has only a fraction of the warmth of a lambswool sweater. Polyester trousers are not suitable for converting to breeches as they are not warm enough, but many a fine pair of breeches has been made from a discarded pair of worsted trousers.

Shell Clothing

Rain-proof outer garments are often referred to as shell clothing and come in various styles:

Anorak A hip-length hooded garment with a short zip from the chest to the neck which opens a gusset through which the anorak is pulled over the head. There is often a kangaroo pocket across the front of the chest. The main disadvantage of anoraks is that they cannot be opened fully to allow ventilation between showers.

Cagoule A knee-length anorak.

Jacket The most versatile shell garment is a thigh- or knee-length jacket with a full front two-way zip which allows the garment to be opened and ventilated between showers thus helping to disperse condensation. They usually have two large patch pockets at the front and often a useful map pocket inside the front storm flap covering the zip, which can be reached without undoing the whole jacket.

Overtrousers These are needed to keep the lower half of the body dry. The best designs have large zipped gussets extending from the ankle to halfway up the leg so that they can be pulled on over boots. Often there are openings in the side to allow access to pockets in the breeches.

Gaiters These are attached to the boots by means of hooks and straps, and zip up the back as far as the knee. They are not essential but are useful to protect the legs from mud and wet vegetation. Although there is a gap between the bottom of the skirt of the cagoule or knee-length jacket and the top of the gaiter they offer sufficient protection to obviate the need to use overtrousers between showers.

The best gaiter currently available is the Yeti, made by Berghaus Ltd., which completely encloses the boot and is secured to the sole by a rubber rand that provides an effective waterproof seal. The best version is the Trionic which is designed to be used with specially made Scarpa boots that have a groove around the sole, into which the rand fits, and there is a universal fitting designed for use with any reasonably stiff boot.

Shell clothing is made from materials that are classified either as *impermeable, non-porous fabrics* or as *porous fabrics*.

Impermeable, Non-Porous Fabrics

These are totally waterproof but prevent water-vapour emitted by the body from escaping allowing condensation to form on the inside of the garment.

Nylon comes in several weights per square metre and can be made waterproof by treating it with a standard polyurethane (PU) finish.

Advantages: Nylon is relatively inexpensive, strong, virtually tearproof unless snagged, and light in weight. It requires no particular care and can be packed wet without adverse effects. It is waterproof and windproof and leaking seams can be cured by the application of clear Bostik or a special seam-sealant obtainable from outdoor shops.

Disadvantages: Eventually the waterproof coating will crack and the garment will leak but to some extent its waterproofing qualities can be restored by the application Texnik which is available from outdoor shops.

Cordura A special weave of abrasive resistant nylon ideal for use in gaiters. It is usually coated with polyurethane. For advantages and disadvantages *see* nylon above.

Oiled or waxed cotton Properly designed waxed cotton shell garments are completely wind and waterproof.

Advantages: Any tears can be patched and sewn at home and the whole garment can be reproofed by the application of more wax. Note that the wax is not greasy and is quite pleasant to the touch. Waxed cotton can be packed wet for several hours without adverse effects.

Disadvantages: Heavier than most other materials, and in cold weather tends to be stiff until warmed by the body.

Porous Fabrics

These are waterproof but allow water vapour emitted by the body to escape (known as moisture vapour transmission or MVT) thus preventing condensation forming on the interior of the garment.

Porous fabrics fall into three separate categories:

Ventile A high-quality material woven by Thomas Ashton from Egyptian cotton was developed during the war and is currently enjoying some popularity. The fibres absorb water and swell thus forming a very efficient waterproof barrier.

Advantages: Excellent wind and waterproof qualities that last the lifetime of the garment, pleasant feel and can be repaired at home with needle and thread.

Disadvantages: Relatively heavy, especially when wet and takes a long time to dry.

Poromeric or micro-porous fabrics work on the principle that a molecule of water is twenty thousand times larger than a molecule of water vapour. A poromeric fabric has millions of tiny holes per square centimetre, each large enough to allow water vapour to escape, but far too small to allow water to penetrate. It should be noted that the amount of condensation that forms inside the garment depends to some extent on the metabolic rate of the wearer and how clean the garment is kept as the tiny pores can become clogged with dirt and body oils.

Aquatex manufactured by Phipps-Faire Ltd uses a micro-porous membrane laminated to the shell fabric.

Cyclone manufactured by Carrington Performance Fabrics has a shell that is coated with a poromeric polymer and then bonded to a nylon layer.

Entrant manufactured by Toray Industries uses a micro-porous coating applied to the inside of nylon twill.

Gore-Tex manufactured by W. L. Gore & Associates uses a PTFE (polytetrafluoroethylene) membrane laminated between an inner and outer breathable fabric.

Hydrophyllic fabrics get their waterproof and moisture vapour transmission properties from two entirely different yet compatible molecular chains. One chain is hydrophyllic (from the Greek meaning water-loving) and the other is hydrophobic (water-hating). Molecules of water vapour from inside the garment are attracted to the hydrophyllic molecules in the coating and pass through to the outside. Rain strikes the hydrophobic molecules on the outside of the fabric and is repelled. There are no pores so contamination by body oils or dirt cannot occur.

Sympatex is manufactured by Akzo (formerly Enka) and is made from a non-porous membrane laminated to a shell fabric. Its MVT properties are similar in performance to the best of the poromeric fabrics.

Breathable polyurethane coatings All such products are manufactured in Britain by the Baxendale Chemical Company Ltd and are sold to a number of cloth and garment manufacturers who market the finished product under their own labels. Some, like Peter Storm Ltd modify them to suit their own purposes. The Baxendendale breathable polyurethane is only fractionally more expensive to manufacture than non-porous polyurethane yet the garments made from it are considerably more expensive as the manufacturers make the most of the novelty value of the product. Breathable polyurethane coatings reduce condensation considerably but not so much as Sympatex and the poromeric fabrics.

It is generally accepted that the fabrics of shell garments for use in the mountains should be capable of withstanding a hydrostatic head of 150 centimetres. The British Standard 'Method of test for the resistance of fabrics to penetration by water' requires a sample of the fabric, 50 millimetres in diameter, to be placed in a sealed clamp. One face of the fabric is then subjected to a steadily increasing pressure of water at a rate of 1 centimetre per minute. When the water penetrates, the pressure (expressed as a height in a vertical tube) is measured and this is known as the hydrostatic head of that sample of material. Note that the weakest part of any garment is at the seams and it is quite normal for the best shell clothing to have entry pressures of only 5 – 20 centimetres at the seams.

Good-quality shell garments should be designed so that there are no seams at the shoulders, and all exposed zips and pockets should be protected by storm flaps. Seams should be welded, doped or taped to make them as waterproof as possible.

Footwear

Socks The most comfortable socks and stockings are knitted in loopstitch which on the inside looks like towelling and completely covers the seams, thus making blisters less likely. Some walkers like to wear two pairs of socks as this gives a pleasant cushioned effect. Woollen hose with nylon reinforced toes and heels are the most popular, but stockings made from synthetic fibres are available for those allergic to wool.

Boots and shoes The only advantages that boots have over shoes is that the higher cuff gives more protection from mud and surface water. The padded cuff of a boot will also protect the sensitive ankle bone from painful contact from rocks and other obstacles in rough country.

There has been a revolution in the design of walking boots in the last few years with the almost universal adoption of lightweight styles. Gone are the clumsy, old-fashioned clodhoppers that had to be worn for many miles before they became comfortable, and in their place there is a wide choice of beautifully made lightweight boots that feel snug as soon as fitted and that require very little breaking in. The lighter the boot the less energy you will expend. For every kilogram on your feet you will have to lift approximately one tonne every kilometre that you walk.

Modern walking boots have a patterned sole made of hard moulded rubber that is very wear-resistant. The uppers are usually made of soft leather (some models are available in tough fabrics such as Cordura but they are not very suitable for the wet conditions found in Britain as they take so long to dry) with a bellows tongue to prevent the ingress of water, and hook lacing for speed and maximum adjustment.

Some boot manufacturers fit Sorbothane footbeds to their more expensive ranges. Sorbothane absorbs shock and disperses the energy slowly so that the footbed cushions the heel without springing back immediately.

Each boot size is usually made on a standard last so that there is no choice of width but the lacing system allows some adjustment. Those with narrow feet should lace their boots tightly to reduce the width and provide a good fit. If you have broad feet either lace the first few hooks loosely or start threading the laces halfway up the boot.

When buying boots try them on over your normal walking socks. There should be just enough room to poke a forefinger down the back of the heel and when you lift your foot behind you and tap the toe smartly on the floor you should not be able to feel your toes touch the front of the boot. This should allow sufficient room for your feet to swell when they are hot and when you descend a steep hill you are less likely to bruise your toenails.

Dress your boots *sparingly* with one of the proprietary brands such as Nikwax. After every walk clean your boots by gently washing away the mud with plenty of water and a washing-up brush. Stuff the boots with rolled-up newspaper and leave for a few hours in a warm room well away from direct heat. If the dressing appears to have leached apply another coat but do not allow the leather to become clogged with oil or wax or your boots will deteriorate rapidly.

Leather is not waterproof although it can be made water resistant if properly dressed. Some manufacturers are now incorporating Gore-Tex or Sympatex linings into their more expensive ranges and it is possible to buy detachable Gore-Tex linings and Gore-Tex socks.

There are three main types of construction employed in the manufacture of walking boots:

Veldtschoon This is one of the most expensive methods of boot construction. The upper is lasted separately from the sole and is then turned outward (as opposed to inward in the conventional shoe) and sewn onto the inner sole, which in turn is cemented or sewn onto the through-sole. This method prevents the ingress of water at the welt.

Blake sole This is the traditional method of constructing boots and shoes in which the upper is sewn between two leather through-soles.

Injection-moulded through-sole This is a new process which relies upon cement to bond the sole to the upper and inner sole thus forming a waterproof bond. PVC is injected in liquid form into the upper which effectively seals the soles from water penetration.

Other Clothing

Manufacturers have gone to great lengths to develop materials to keep walkers warm in winter, cool in summer, and dry and comfortable at all times.

Underwear Everyday underwear is satisfactory (except in the coldest conditions), providing that it is made from wool, cotton or a suitable synthetic material. Men will probably find boxer shorts more comfortable than briefs and some women favour old-fashioned gym-knickers for walking. Those who require additional warmth in winter should try wearing an old pair of ladies' tights (with the feet cut off) under their breeches.

The most comfortable materials are the synthetics that do not absorb moisture but wick it away from the body (known in the trade as vapour transmission or VT). If you wear a conventional cotton shirt on a hot day the back soon gets soaked with perspiration and if you take a short break you will experience an unpleasant cold and clammy feeling when you shoulder your rucksack again. This is because cotton absorbs moisture too efficiently and quickly becomes sodden. Even in the hottest weather you would keep more comfortable if you wore a thin polypropylene vest or T-shirt under your cotton shirt. Polypropylene will not absorb moisture but will transmit it to the next layer of clothes so you remain dry and cool at all times.

Breeches The best winter-weight breeches are made from Helenca (see p32) or tweed. Helenca may not be quite so warm as tweed but it has the advantage of two-way stretch, and it will not absorb water so it dries much more quickly. For summer, use a special material of terylene and cotton which is both water-repellent and quick-drying. There are moleskin, corduroy and needlecord breeches on the market but they have the great disadvantages of feeling cold when wet and of taking a long time to dry.

Well-designed breeches should have plenty of pockets secured by zips or Velcro flaps. They should fasten at the knee and have a double seat and knee pieces.

Shirts and Sweaters Clothing worn between underwear and shell garments is often known as midwear. Shirts and sweaters should be made of wool, cotton or one of the synthetic materials. Shirts with breast pockets are particularly useful for carrying such items as pens and a compass. In winter, several thin layers will be found to be warmer than one heavy sweater and will also allow the wearer to adjust his body temperature by removing and adding layers as necessary.

Jackets and Duvet Clothing There is a huge range of jackets on the market ranging from cotton for summer wear to down, Hollofil and pile fabrics for the most arctic conditions. Although useful, none are really essential except perhaps for winter walking in Scotland. I have often walked in sub-zero temperatures wearing windproof shell clothing and layers of woollens underneath.

Hats In winter conditions a woollen or fibre-pile balaclava helmet is very useful as up to 40 per cent of body heat is lost through the head. Modern balaclavas can be rolled up above the ears to serve as an ordinary woollen hat when conditions do not warrant covering the ears, neck and mouth.

Gloves Gloves or mitts are necessary in cold conditions. They are often made from felted, oiled wool which helps to keep them waterproof. Excellent inexpensive thermal gloves are made by Damart Ltd., Bingley, West Yorkshire BD97 1AD. In really arctic conditions windproof over-mittens are required.

Those who walk in lowland areas, especially if they intend to do some serious walking, will find the outfit described above will suit their needs very well, but none of it is essential. If you want to walk in canvas boots, or shoes, or wellington boots and carry a plastic mac then do so. You will come to no harm and your walking will cost you very little. In wet weather an indefatigable walking friend of mine wears a cloth cap, riding mac and wellington boots. It would not suit me but he is perfectly happy.

Other equipment likely to be required is a small rucksack for carrying spare items, a map case which allows the map to be protected yet read, first-aid kit, secateurs and a stick. Secateurs are useful for cutting back overgrown vegetation on stiles and a stick is invaluable for fending off inquisitive animals, testing the depth of mud and jumping over boggy patches. I never take either item in mountainous country, as there is no call for secateurs and a stick can be dangerous amongst rocks—it can easily trip the unwary. In mountainous country, a whistle should always be carried round the neck on a lanyard so that the international mountain distress signal can be given if the walker gets into difficulty. The signal is six consecutive blasts on the whistle repeated at minute intervals. A large plastic bag or space blanket should always be kept in the rucksack for use in mountainous country, as should a torch, a compass and pocket-knife.

Specialised equipment for use in the mountains in winter is described in Chapter 7.

In recent years manufacturers of kit and clothing for walkers and backpackers have experimented with many new materials and there is now a bewildering variety on the market. The following non-technical guide may be found helpful.

Synthetic Materials

Cholorofibre is a material in various weights that has the ability to wick moisture away from the skin leaving the wearer feeling dry. Needs frequent washing to keep it sweet-smelling.

Uses: underwear.

Climaguard manufactured by Rotofil is a microfibre fabric, which, when woven, forms a windproof and water-repellent material that breathes.

Uses: jackets.

Cordura is a special weave of nylon, developed by Du Pont, which is similar in appearance to cotton duck but is lighter, stronger, has a much greater resistance to abrasion and does not absorb water.

Uses: gaiters and rucksacks.

Dunova made by Bayer is an acrylic fibre similar in feel to cotton. It has an inner absorbent fibre surrounded by a non-asborbent, porous sheath. Moisture is wicked from the skin by capillary action leaving the wearer feeling dry.

Uses: underwear.

Fibrepile was originally developed by Du Pont and looks somewhat like artificial fur. It is warm to the touch even when wet but is often plagued by 'pilling' in which the fur tends to go into little balls.

Uses: midwear and sleeping bags.

Field Sensor manufactured by Toray Industries is a fabric that wicks moisture away from the skin by capillary action.

Uses: underclothes and midwear.

Fleece is a brushed woven polyester fabric with a warm, comfortable feel.

Uses: midwear.

Helenca is a special weave of nylon that has two-way stretch. It will not absorb water, remains warm when wet and dries quickly.

Uses: breeches.

Hollofil is a resilient synthetic fibre made by Du Pont. Each filament has a hole throughout its length that not only reduces weight but gives added insulation because of the air that is trapped. It will not absorb water, dries quickly and remains warm when wet.

Uses: insulation for sleeping bags and duvet clothing.

Isodry manufactured by Neidhart is a thin insulating wadding that the manufacturers claim improves with washing.

Uses: insulation for warm clothing.

KS 100 developed for Karrimor is a tough, highly-resistant nylon fabric similar in appearance to cotton duck. It comes in various weights denoted by a suffix.

Uses: rucksacks and gaiters.

Libond is a low-loft fibre wadding insulation with a soft feel.

Uses: insulation for winter clothing.

Lotus is a synthetic fabric with irregular shaped microfibres that feels like cotton and is inherently water-repellent.

Uses: jackets.

Nylon is a generic term used to describe a man-made fabric that can be made into a yarn and woven into fabrics which have widely differing properties depending on their weaves. Nylon fabrics do not absorb water and therefore dry quickly, but they are not rendered water-repellent until treated with silicone, neoprene or polyurethane. Silicon-proofed nylon will still breathe but is not fully waterpoof. Nylon treated with conventional polyurethane or neoprene is absolutely waterproof, but as it is totally impervious to water vapour, condensation forms on the inside of the garment or tent.

Pertex made by ICI is a close woven, non-waterproof nylon useful for dispersing water by capillary action.

Uses: lightweight towels, clothing, sleeping bag covers and lining fabrics.

Polypropylene is a synthetic fibre that wicks water away from the skin. It needs frequent washing to prevent it becoming smelly and contaminated by body salts.

Uses: underwear and midwear.

Quallofil made by Du Point and similar to their Hollofil except that it has four holes in each individual fibre thus increasing the insulation.

Uses: insulation for sleeping bags and duvet clothing.

Ripstop nylon is made from a special weave that is highly resistant to tearing.

Uses: tents, rucksacks and shell clothing.

Sorbothane is an exceptionally dense material that feels like rubber. It can absorb shock without immediately rebounding and it disperses the energy slowly.

Uses: footbeds.

Thinsulate is a microfibre insulating wadding from 3M.

Uses: insulation for winter clothing.

Cotton Materials

Cotton is a natural fibre which can be woven into a variety of cloths. Cotton breathes and will absorb water and perspiration and is thus suitable to be worn next to the skin. When wet, cotton loses its warmth and becomes unpleasantly cold and clammy. It can be made water-repellent by coating with silicones, and totally waterproof by applying paraffin wax (it will then lose the capacity to breathe and condensation will form on the inside of the material).

Corduroy A cut-weft pile fabric in which the cut fibres form the surface of the material. It is very soft to the touch but will absorb large quantities of water which makes it feel very cold and unpleasant. Wet corduroy takes a long time to dry. Corduroy is occasionally made from materials other than cotton.

Uses: breeches.

Cotton duck A heavy material used where strength is required. It will absorb water but can be made water-repellent by proofing with silicones.

Uses: rucksacks and gaiters.

Gaberdine The name given to a weave which produces a smooth, fine cloth. Not all gaberdines are made entirely of cotton.

Uses: breeches and lightweight showerproof jackets.

Moleskin or **molecord** A thick, heavy cotton fabric which will absorb a lot of water.

Uses: breeches.

Needlecord A material very similar to corduroy, but finer.

Uses: breeches.

Polycotton A mixture of polyester and cotton used in varying proportions. It gives the pleasant feel of cotton but absorbs less water and dries more quickly.

Uses: jackets and trousers.

Stormbeta is a waterproof, breathable polycotton fabric developed by Berghaus.

Uses: shell clothing and jackets.

Woollen Materials

Wool is a natural fibre obtained from sheep which can be spun into a yarn and woven or knitted into a great variety of cloths, all of which breathe. Wool has the remarkable property of absorbing large quantities of water and yet still retaining its warmth. It takes a very long time to dry. Woven cloths can be made water-repellent by treating with silicones.

Knitted Woollens Very fine wools, such as lambswool, are used in winter-weight underwear and for lightweight sweaters. Providing that you are not allergic to wool, lambswool is non-irritating and can be worn next to the skin. The coarser, heavier woollens may irritate the skin but make excellent warmth-inducing garments. Some walkers wear oiled wool sweaters under shell clothing as these wools will not absorb so much condensation.

Uses: underwear, sweaters, socks, gloves and hats.

Flannel A soft fabric which, if mixed with another material (usually cotton), is more properly known as *union flannel*.

Uses: heavy shirts and breeches.

Tweed There are a great number of tweeds in a variety of weights and degrees of softness. All tweeds are very hard-wearing and can be made water-repellent by the application of silicones. Derby tweed is a mixture of cotton and wool. Some tweeds are described as thornproof which indicates that the fibres will not be torn or broken if snagged by vegetation.

Uses: breeches.

Other Materials

Down Down comes from the breasts of geese and ducks and is the lightest and warmest insulation known, but it has the disadvantage of losing most of its insulating properties when wet. It takes a long time to dry.

Uses: fillings for sleeping bags and duvet clothing.

Silk is the warmest, strongest, most absorbent, lightest and most expensive of all natural fibres. It can absorb moisture up to 30% of its own weight and still feel warm and dry to the touch.

Uses: underwear and glove linings.

Testing of Materials and Clothing

Most makers of outdoor clothing make up their garments from materials supplied by textile manufacturers. The quality of the garment depends not only on the excellence of the design of the finished article but also the intrinsic merits and suitability of the material used.

Textile manufacturers are constantly upgrading their materials and striving to develop new fabrics to fulfil particular needs. Probably the most famous example of an entirely new material is Gore-Tex which was introduced to overcome the problem of condensation in waterproof garments. Following Gore's lead, a number of manufacturers have attempted different solutions to the same problem.

All textile manufacturers check their products rigorously. First they are tested in the laboratory using a number of British Standards tests for abrasion resistance, hydrostatic head (waterproof qualities), flammability, burst strength, permeability, pilling, seam failure, tear strength, thermal resistance etc. Then the material is made up into the products for which it was designed and tested in the field, often by several manufacturers, so that by the time it appears on the market, all the problems should have been solved. Laboratory testing is invaluable but it is often not until thousands of the products have been used by consumers that the real problems appear. One well-known textile manufacturer introduced a waterproof material that had proved successful in other parts of the world but in the particular weather conditions in Britain it did not always work. The problems were solved eventually but it cost the company a great deal of money. The British Textile Technology group (see p294) is an independent company that specialises in working with manufacturers to develop and test materials.

Bibliography
Constance, Hazel, *Gear for the Outdoors and How to Make it,* Robert Hale, 1982.

2 Walking Techniques

The serious walker knows that there is a good deal more to walking than being able to put one foot in front of the other. Technique is unimportant to the ambler who is content to do ten kilometres, but the person who enjoys a forty-kilometre tramp, especially if it is repeated day after day, as it would be on a walking holiday, will tend to develop his own style and subconsciously learn the techniques of good walking. If the neophyte is aware of the techniques before he starts walking seriously, he will learn more quickly.

Great physical strength is not necessary but stamina is important. I am below average height, am slightly built and weigh sixty-three kilograms yet I have often walked forty kilometres in a day; the furthest I have walked in one day is fifty-two kilometres and the hardest day's walking of my life was the last stage of the Pennine Way when, carrying a fifteen kilogram pack, I walked the forty-four kilometres in driving rain and gale-force winds, sinking up to my knees at times in peat bogs.

On level ground use your natural stride and resist any temptation to lengthen it. On a gradient the stride should be shortened but the legs should move at the same speed, maintaining the rhythm of walking. Perhaps the best analogy is that of a motor car driven by an engine maintaining a constant speed, with the road speed controlled by infinitely variable gearing. When the hill is exceptionally steep, some walkers find it worthwhile to adopt a zig-zag route, moving one or two steps at an angle of 45° to the slope and then 45° in the opposite direction, rather like a yacht tacking against the wind. This makes the route longer but less arduous.

Whenever possible, put the whole of the sole of the foot down on firm ground and avoid toe and heel holds. The experienced walker always chooses the easiest route along an uneven path and rarely stumbles or loses his balance. If one route on a path becomes unwalkable, retrace a few steps and seek an alternative, as this is much less tiring and dangerous than jumping down or scrambling up. It is very dangerous to jump even from small heights with a heavy pack—the weight can easily unbalance the unwary and can cause compression fractures and spinal injury.

The novice may be surprised to learn that it is usually more tiring to descend a steep hill than to climb it, especially with a heavy pack. A long descent puts great strain on the muscles at the front of the thighs and unless the walker is fit these muscles can become very tender. The secret of walking down steep hills is to allow the legs to bend slightly at the knee so that the body is not jarred when each foot is put on the ground. If the ground is not too rough it is a good plan to run downhill in a skipping motion taking very short steps and turning 45° every few yards. In one or two places on steep and rocky paths it may be helpful to turn round and come down backwards, especially with a heavy pack.

It is important to conserve energy as much as possible and to avoid unnecessary exertion. Therefore, do not swing the arms in an exaggerated fashion as soldiers do on a route march. The arms can help the walker to maintain his balance, but an expert walker will be quite happy to clasp his hands behind his back or lightly grasp the bottom of his rucksack while walking on level, even ground.

When setting out on a long walk, start off slowly, well within your normal walking pace, and gradually work up to your usual speed and stride. This is particularly important in mountainous country, when the walk usually starts from the valley with a long climb. It is a sure sign of the novice to rush up the first hill, sink down at the top to regain his breath and then gallop down the other side. The experienced walker will climb up slowly, perhaps pause for a minute at the top to admire the view and regain breath and then continue steadily and rhythmically down the other side, soon leaving our novice far behind.

Speed and Distance

It is important to be able to calculate the length of time that a walk will take. This information is often required in order to catch a bus or train, or rendezvous with a car at a suitable pick-up point, or to avoid being caught out after dark on a winter's afternoon.

Many walkers believe that they can cover ground faster than they actually can and confuse the speed of their pace on level ground with their average speed. They may well walk at five kilometres per hour across a flat, firm field but they ignore the slowing effect of boggy areas, hills, the time taken to climb stiles and to pass through gates, take photographs and refer to the map so that their average speed is considerably slower. I once met a backpacker in the Highlands of Scotland who assured me that he averaged eight kilometres per hour, but I watched him when he left me and his pace did not appear to be significantly faster than mine which is five kilometres per hour, although I cannot maintain that as an average speed. As an experiment, I plotted a thirty-two kilometre gently undulating circuit on minor roads around my home in San Antonio, Texas and set out to walk it as fast as I could wearing running shoes, T-shirt and cotton shorts and carrying a small day-sack containing water and food. At the time I was very fit and I completed the circuit in five hours and twenty minutes which included a stop for lunch of exactly thirty minutes. My actual walking time was four hours fifty minutes which is 6.62 kilometres per hour (or a fraction over four miles per hour).

It is a good plan to keep records of the time taken to complete walks making notes of variable factors such as the terrain, the weather and the number in the party as this will provide useful data for calculating the time required to complete a range of walks in different kinds of country. It is widely believed that a good average walking pace is five kilometres (three miles) per hour. This speed is easy enough to maintain on roads, but there are not many walkers who can sustain this speed, excluding meal breaks, on paths.

The generally accepted method of calculating the time required to complete a walk in mountainous country is by using Naismith's rule, which states *allow one hour for every five kilometres (three miles) measured on the map plus an additional half hour for every three hundred metres (one thousand feet) climbed.* The distance climbed is the sum total of all the ascents *not just the highest point reached* (see Fig. 1). *Example:*

Total distance measured on the map	10 km
Total height climbed	870 m
Time required to walk 10 km	2 hours
Time required to climb 870 m	1.5 hours
	Total 3.5 hours

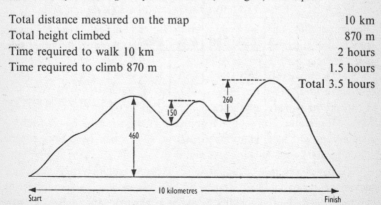

Fig. 1 Naismith's formula

Note that the average speed is 2.9 kph but if the walk were level the average speed would be 5 kph.

Naismith's rule assumes average fitness and good conditions, and extra time should be allowed for bad weather, difficulties in route-finding, heavy packs, meals and other stops. Remember, too, that a party tends to be slower than an individual because time is wasted by queuing for stiles and the need to wait for those who have taken advantage of a convenient stone wall.

In order to take account of these variable factors Tranter's variation to Naismith's rule has been formulated (see Fig. 2). To use it, it is first necessary to establish your fitness level or, in the case of a group, the fitness level of the weakest member of the party which is done by calculating the time taken to climb 300 metres (1000 feet) in 800 metres ($^1/_2$ a mile) when fresh, with no rests and at a normal pace. If this takes 30 minutes then your fitness level is 30.

	TIME TAKEN IN MINUTES ACCORDING TO NAISMITH'S RULE									
FITNESS LEVEL	60	120	180	240	300	360	420	480	540	600
15	30	60	90	120	165	210	270	330	405	465
20	40	75	135	195	270	330	390	465	525	600
25	50	90	180	255	330	420	510	600	690	795
30	60	120	210	300	405	510	630	750	870	
35	70	145	230	320	425	540	660			
40	80	165	255	345	450	570	690			
45	90	180	270	365	480	TOO MUCH TO BE ATTEMPTED				
50	100	195	285	390	510					

Fig. 2 Tranter's variations to Naismith's rule

Example: a walk of 12 kilometres with a total height gain of 800 metres will, according to Naismith's formula, take 4 hours and 6 minutes.

Applying Tranter's variation to our fitness level of 30 we get an estimated time of 5 hours.

Tranter's variation can be applied in other ways:

weight of rucksack: drop one fitness line for every 13 kilograms
weather: drop one fitness line for poor visibility or strong winds
conditions underfoot: drop one fitness line for waterlogged or slippery conditions and up to four fitness lines for snow.

As a rule of thumb, in lowland country allow three kilometres (two miles) per hour plus time for meal stops. A large party is likely to require considerably longer because of the extra time taken to climb stiles and negotiate ploughed fields. Probably the fastest walking is on chalk downs where the paths tend to be well marked. In such conditions a fit walker may average five kilometres per hour.

I find that the secret of walking long distances—say thirty kilometres and more—is not so much walking at top speed but to keep going with the minimum of stops. Study the map carefully beforehand, fill out a route card (see pp72-79) and make a note of any likely difficulties. Train yourself to walk for two or three hours at a stretch without stops. Do not waste time by stopping to put on and take off sweaters but do it on the march by releasing your rucksack from one shoulder, easing your arm out of your sweater and sliding it through the rucksack strap. Repeat the process with the other strap and pull your sweater up to your neck. When the rucksack is secured normally, pull the sweater over your head and then tie it round your waist. When stopping for a meal or a rest, choose a comfortable, sheltered spot, take off boots and rucksack and after eating and drinking lie flat on your back for several minutes and relax completely. Any slight stiffness in the legs will disappear a few minutes after starting to walk again. Do not overlook the psychology of the early start, for every hour of walking before lunch seems worth two of those after lunch. A walk that may seem hard if started at nine in the morning can seem relatively easy if begun at seven.

Path Surfaces

The soil which forms the surface of a path has certain qualities and it is as well to know the different characteristics of each type as they affect the walker. It is assumed that hard moulded-rubber soles are worn.

Rock Dry rock of all kinds, from sandstone to granite, provides a good surface on which the boots will not slip. Rubber soles grip reasonably well on clean (i.e. lichen- or mud-free) rock but when rock is covered with lichen or mud (usually known as greasy rock) great care is necessary as it is easy to slip. Ice-covered rock is lethal.

Scree Scree is loose pieces of rock, about the size of large pebbles, on a steep mountain slope. It is very fatiguing to climb because when advancing one step you slip back half a step, rather like climbing steep shingle on the beach. However, scree can be fun to descend. Run down the slope boldly, digging in the heels at each step. The loose rock will move under your feet, as shingle would, but it is very bad for the boots.

Peat Peat is formed by decomposing vegetation, usually heather and bracken, and is a dark chocolate colour. Dry peat provides a good surface, pleasantly springy underfoot. Wet peat is slightly slippery, but as it tends to be covered with heather it causes difficulties only when deep and free from vegetation. In wet weather on some fells, such as Kinder Scout in the Peak District, it is possible to sink to one's knees in peat bogs. With a little experience it is possible to see firmer footing provided by clumps of sphagnum grass, heather and bog cotton which will help to keep you from sinking too deeply into the bog.

Heather Heather is found throughout the upland areas of Britain. It will not grow on well-used paths as it cannot withstand constant trampling, but it often borders paths. Heather is very abrasive and tiring to traverse in pathless country, especially when wet. It will not grow in standing water and provides a firm foothold in boggy areas.

Grass Grass provides pleasant walking though it is slippery on slopes when wet.

Clay Clay is dreadful stuff. If frozen or baked hard, it becomes rutted and one fears for one's ankles at every step. When waterlogged, it is as slippery as a skating rink. Clay, when ploughed, clings tenaciously to the boots in great lumps, increasing the weight on the feet several-fold. It is very difficult to remove, but the worst can be got off with the aid of a stick and plenty of thick wet grass. It is often helpful to kick an imaginary football as this will loosen the largest lumps.

Chalk The finest and most springy turf grows on chalk. With heavy use the grass is worn away exposing the chalk which can then erode badly. This happens frequently at the most popular beauty spots in the chalk country of southern England. It provides a good firm surface when dry, although it makes the boots dusty, but it is treacherous when wet as it becomes very slippery. Wet escarpments should be avoided whenever possible.

Sand Sandy soils always drain exceptionally well and are pleasant to walk on in all weathers.

Stiles and footbridges are often very slippery when wet and great care must be taken when negotiating them.

Fell-Walking in Winter

After the walker has gained some experience, he may wish to venture onto the fells in winter. Even though there may be no snow about, the conditions on the tops are likely to be arctic, with very cold winds, and it is absolutely essential to go properly dressed and equipped. Wear windproof clothing in the form of anorak, cagoule or fell-jacket and overtrousers together with extra woollen sweaters and woollen long johns. Head and hands should be protected with a balaclava helmet or woollen hat which will cover the ears and woollen gloves or mitts with windproof over-mitts in the severest weather. It is much better and warmer to wear layers of thin woollen clothing rather than one heavy sweater. Carry a rucksack large enough to contain all the spare clothing, take plenty of food and a hot drink, a survival bag and first-aid kit. Do not go alone unless very experienced, and leave word of your route with someone responsible, not forgetting to report your safe return. Be sure to check the local weather forecast before setting off and do not go if bad conditions are expected.

If snow is lying on the ground, special precautions and equipment are necessary. Snow makes even familiar paths and routes look different and often obscures cairns and other features useful for route-finding. There are many varieties of snow, depending on the weather conditions. Fresh snow is the easiest and safest to negotiate but it can be very annoying if more than ankle-deep. Snow that has been lying some time is likely to have been subjected to alternate freezing and thawing which puts a crust on it which makes for much firmer footholds. If the snow lasts long enough the constant thawing and freezing will make it very hard or perhaps turn it into ice. Rocks are likely to be covered in ice crystals and streams will be surrounded by large areas of ice.

Rubber soles do not give a good grip on hard snow and ice, so crampons must be worn. The best crampons are 'lobster claws' and consist of ten or twelve spikes on a frame which is strapped to the soles of the boots (see Fig. 3). There are two forward-projecting spikes which are extremely useful for kicking steps in encrusted snow. Crampons have to be adjusted so that they fit the boot tightly and this will probably entail bending the frame slightly so that when pressed into position without the bindings attached they will not drop off when the boot is shaken. Care must be taken when handling

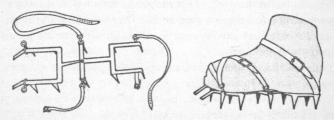

Fig. 3 Lobster-claw crampons

crampons as they can tear stockings and inflict lacerations if the wearer stumbles. With ordinary crampons (ones without the front lobster claw) it is necessary to walk with all the points in contact with the snow, and on a slope this can be cumbersome and uncomfortable. With lobster-claw crampons, it is possible to walk up slopes using only the front four points, which makes for easier and speedier progress.

Walkers who are likely only to require crampons occasionally should consider buying instep crampons. These are much smaller than ordinary crampons and are attached to the instep of the boot. They have four points and are quite satisfactory for all but the most rugged conditions.

If conditions warrant the wearing of crampons, an ice axe (see Fig. 4) should be carried for step-cutting in ice. An ice axe has a head consisting of an edge for cutting steps in hard snow and brittle ice and a pick for use on hard ice. The handle is wood or metal with a metal spike in the end which can be used for belaying. Handles come in various lengths and it is important to choose one that matches your height. The correct length can be determined by holding the axe by the head with the shaft downwards.

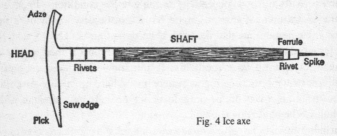

Fig. 4 Ice axe

The tip of the spike should be about two centimetres off the ground. Ice axes should be carried with the spike pointing forwards and downwards. When not likely to be required, the axe can be attached head upwards to the shoulder straps of the rucksack or inside the rucksack with the handle resting on the bottom of the pack. It is advisable to cover the spike to prevent damage.

All fell-walkers who venture out in snowy conditions should know how to use an ice axe as a brake in the event of a fall on snow-covered slopes (see Fig. 5). It is wise to practise the technique on a safe slope until you can do it properly every time. As soon as you start to fall, roll over onto your chest keeping your feet up so that your crampons do not catch in the snow and cause you to somersault. Get the shaft of your ice axe under your armpit and, leaning on the head, force the pick end into the snow. If done properly, it will effectively bring you to a stop on slopes up to an angle of 40°.

Ice axes can also be used for cutting steps if the surface is too hard for

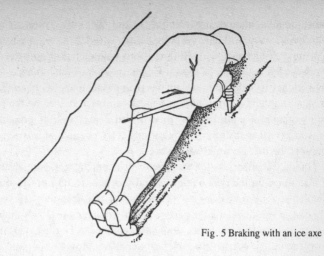

Fig. 5 Braking with an ice axe

steps to be kicked. Hold the axe with both hands on the spike end of the handle and allow the weight of the axe to drive it into the snow and through the ice. With practice it should be possible to learn to cut a step in two or three blows, because the fewer blows struck, the quicker will be the progress and the minimum possible amount of energy will be expended.

On steep ascents, where the walker intends to take the most direct route, the steps should point inwards to the slope and they should be cut so that the sole of the boot can be accommodated. When descending steep slopes, traversing a slope of zig-zagging, long flat steps should be cut to take the whole of the boot. You should cut your steps nearest to you and then work further away so that you can take advantage of the first cut made.

It cannot be emphasised too strongly that you should be taught ice and snow techniques by an expert.

Leading Walks

Experienced walkers are sometimes approached by rambling clubs, schools and local organizations to lead walks. Before consenting, it is wise to agree on the following points:

(a) the length of the walk in the light of the experience of those taking part
(b) the type of terrain to be covered
(c) the conditions under which you are prepared to lead
(d) the number in the party

It is absolutely essential for the leader to survey the walk a month or so before it takes place. Make a note of any particular problems such as missing footbridges, overgrown stiles etc., and take steps to see that the more serious matters are rectified before the walk takes place or an alternative route will have to be arranged. A tactful letter or phone call to a farmer telling him you are leading a walk will often get a stile put in across a barbed-wire fence. County Councils have been known to erect footbridges speedily and they are worth approaching, but unless the stream is very wide and deep, a little ingenuity can often overcome the problem. For example, if a stream has to be forded it may well be possible to get reasonably close to the point by car and take a couple of breeze blocks to the ford before the walk takes place.

Having satisfied yourself that the route is practicable, issue instructions, if necessary, on the type of clothes and footwear to be worn together with details of food and drink to be taken and the time the walk will take, keeping in mind that a large party will move much more slowly than a small group. When the walk starts, designate someone to be the gate shutter and to bring up the rear so that the party does not straggle too much. Before moving off, it is a good plan to mention briefly the need to obey the Country Code and, in particular, to walk through growing crops in single file.

Leading walks in the mountains and on the fells is a much more serious business. It is essential for the leader to insist on every member of the party being properly dressed and equipped with foul-weather gear, large plastic bag and food and drink (including an emergency supply). The leader should have an inspection before moving off and refuse to take anyone without the necessary kit and equipment. It is generally accepted that one leader should not be in charge of more than ten walkers and so, for a large party, several leaders may be required. It is much better for each group of ten to move off separately rather than attempt to keep together. Each leader must have a first-aid kit and a list of the names, addresses and telephone numbers of everyone in his party. Details of the route and estimated time of arrival must be left with a responsible person.

In view of some of the appalling accidents that have happened in recent years to school parties in the mountains, many education authorities now insist that group leaders must have undertaken the Mountain Walking Leadership Training scheme (see pp303-4).

Bibliography

Hunter, Rob, *Winter Skills,* Constable, 1982
Information for Leaders of Rambles compiled and published by the Ramblers' Association.
Langmuir, Eric, *Mountaincraft and Leadership; a Handbook for Mountaineers and Hillwalkers in the British Isles,* Scottish Sports Council in association with the Mountainleader Training Board, 1984.

3 Ordnance Survey Maps

The United Kingdom is probably the best-mapped country in the world. The Ordnance Survey was first established after it was discovered that royal troops were at a great disadvantage during the Jacobite uprising because of a lack of accurate maps. When peace was established, it was decided to map the whole of the country at a scale of 1 inch to the mile. The first map was published in 1801 and the Ordnance Survey has been busily mapping ever since. The maps range in scale from 1:63360 (the famous 1 inch to the mile with which most walkers are familiar, which have now been replaced by the 1:50000) to 1:1250 or 50 ins. to the mile. In practice, walkers are likely to use the 1:63360, the 1:50000 (2 cm to the kilometre) and the 1:25000 (4 cm to the kilometre), although occasionally it may be useful to consult the larger-scale maps for particular purposes. The Ordnance Survey also publish special maps such as historical and geological maps which can be useful and interesting to those pursuing a particular hobby. Keen map-users can obtain free from the Ordnance Survey, Maybush, Southampton SO9 4DH, a copy of their current map catalogue.

In one brief chapter it is quite impossible to give an adequate description of the riches contained in Ordnance Survey maps. They are wonderful mines of information, works of art in themselves, and repay careful study.

Most walkers are familiar with the *folded* Ordnance Survey maps which come complete with a cover. However, many people prefer to buy the flat *unfolded* versions as they can be cut or folded to fit map cases. If a lot of walking is done in one particular area, it is a good plan to buy two copies of the required map and to cut each one in a different way so that each section of one map overlaps a section of the other. If two sections are placed back to back in a transparent map case a wide area of country will be covered and, when the edge of one map is reached, by turning over the map case your position on the second map will be some way from the edge of the map. This is a great advantage when route-finding.

Certain considerations have to be borne in mind when using any of the Ordnance Survey maps. Pay particular attention to the date of the survey, which will be found somewhere on the map, for a map can only be accurate at the time of the survey. The countryside is constantly if only imperceptibly changing; new roads are built, old roads are re-aligned, canals are filled in and reservoirs created, building development takes place, farmers grub hedges and erect new barns, woods are felled and forests planted. The map-user must always think of the possible changes which may have happened since the date of the survey, especially if the map apparently does not agree with the terrain!

The reputation of the Ordnance Survey is such that many people believe all their maps to be absolutely accurate. A little reflection will show that this cannot be the case because the scale itself prevents it. For example, on the 1:50000 map, unclassified roads with a minimum width of 4.3 metres are represented by a yellow line 1 millimetre wide. Yet strictly speaking 1 millimetre represents 50 metres on the ground on a map of this scale. If the roads were drawn exactly to scale they would be almost invisible.

The National Grid

All Ordnance Survey maps with a minimum scale of 1:63360 show the full national grid. Each map has been divided into squares with the lines running almost exactly due north to south and east to west. The grid lines are spaced at one kilometre intervals and are used for providing an exact reference to any given point on any edition of the map, and for compass work, described later in this chapter. To give a full grid reference:

1. Establish from the map the letters which designate the 100-km. square in which the map falls, SP in Figure 6.

2. Find the km. square which contains the feature to which you wish to assign a grid reference.

3. Identify the horizontal grid line immediately south of the feature.

4. From the *western* edge of the map follow this line until you meet the vertical grid line immediately to the *west* of the feature.

5. Follow this vertical grid line to the bottom of the map where a number will be found. This should be written down.

6. Follow the grid line back to near the feature and estimate the number of tenths of a grid square along the horizontal line the feature lies, and write down this number.

7. You now have half of your grid reference known as an *easting*. Repeat

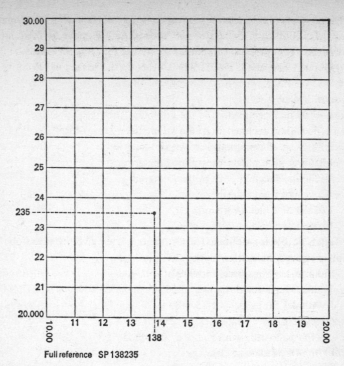

Full reference SP 138235

Fig. 6 Grid references

the process on a vertical plane to establish your *northing* and you will end up with a six-figure reference which occurs only once in every 100 km. If the letters for the 100-km. square are used, the reference is unique. The reference for the point in Figure 8, for example, is SP 138235.

Always find your eastings before your northings and remember it by imagining the squirrel which runs along the grass and then up the tree. There is an excellent explanation of the national grid on most copies of Ordnance Survey maps.

Grid references are invaluable for establishing meeting places. It is much better to agree to meet at SP 707212 than at 'the gate on the right-hand side of the road about a kilometre beyond the railway bridges on the Quainton to Edgcott Lane'.

Scale

The easiest way of grasping the concept of map scale is to appreciate that it is expressed as a proportion. In the example 1:50000, the first figure represents the unit on the map and the figure after the colon represents the number of units on the ground. Most Ordnance Survey maps are now metric so it is useful to express the scale of the 1:50000 map as 1 centimetre to 50000 centimetres (which is 500 metres) or, to make it even more convenient, 2 centimetres to 1 kilometre. (Note that imperial measure *can* be used but 1 inch on the map is 50000 inches on the ground which converts to 0.7891413 miles which is not a convenient fraction!)

Metric scales are:
1.50000 or 2 centimetres to the kilometre
1:25000 or 4 centimetres to the kilometre
1:10000 or 10 centimetres to the kilometre
1:2500 or 40 centimetres to the kilometre
1:1250 or 80 centimetres to the kilometre

Imperial scales are:
1:63360 or 1 inch to the mile
1:10560 or 6 inches to the mile

Maps suitable for walkers The Ordnance Survey gives its most popular map series distinctive titles:
Landranger Maps (scale 1:50000)
Tourist Maps (various scales 1:258545, 1:126720, 1:63360 and 1:50000)
Pathfinder Maps (scale 1:25000)
Outdoor Leisure Maps (scale 1:25000)

Landranger Maps

The Second Series of Landranger Maps covers the whole country in 204 sheets each covering an area measuring 40 km x 40 km. Most maps in this series are now metric but until metrication is completed in the 1990s some sheets will show contours based on imperial contours of 50 feet converted to the nearest metre. As 50 feet is 15.24 metres the sequence of contours is 15, 30, 46 which looks odd, but for the purposes of counting contours to estimate height gain (see p58) the interval should be regarded as 15 metres. On the great majority of Second Series maps height is indicated by contours at 10 metre intervals with metric spot heights. The Second Series is a considerable improvement on both the First Series and the old 1:63360 (1 inch to the mile) which they replace. Minor revisions of significant changes, especially new roads, are often incorporated whenever the map is reprinted. Every sheet is identified by a sequential number which starts at 1 for the northerly tip of the Shetland Isles and ends at 204 at The Lizard in Cornwall. Note that Northern Ireland, which has its own Ordnance Survey (see p306), and the Channel Islands are not included in the Landranger series.

Landranger maps show public rights of way (except in Scotland), distinguishing between roads, footpaths, bridleways, roads used as public paths and byways open to all traffic, and designate long-distance paths by name. They distinguish between deciduous, coniferous, mixed woodland, orchards and parkland; show rock features; information centres; car parks; picnic sites; viewpoints; camp sites; caravan sites; youth hostels; public telephones; golf courses; public toilets; footbridges; level crossings; towpaths; streams; marshes; weirs; lakes; canals; fords; slopes; cliffs; lighthouses; beacons; high and low water marks; sand; mud and shingle; pylons; buildings; quarries; spoil heaps; TV masts; churches (distinguishing between those with tower; spire or with neither); chimneys and towers; glasshouses; heliports; triangulation pillars; windmills (with or without sails); windpumps; national, county and district boundaries; National Trust properties distinguishing between those always open and those with restricted hours; national park and forest park boundaries; post offices; public houses; milestones; mileposts; clubhouses; town halls; coastguard lookouts; Roman villas; castles; battlefields; tumuli and other antiquities; ferries distinguishing between passenger and vehicular; and a wide range of railway features. The only significant feature essential for walking in lowland areas that is lacking are field boundaries. These maps are suitable for navigating in mountainous and moorland regions and are useful for the initial planning of routes in lowland areas.

The Ordnance Survey Landranger Gazetteer; a Gazetteer of all Names Shown on Ordnance Survey 1:50000 Scale Landranger Maps contains 250,000 names and identifies them by the map sheet number and a four-figure grid reference. It is a useful reference tool, available in book form or microfiche, for all who love maps and place-names.

Tourist Maps

These maps cover some of the most popular areas but vary somewhat in style and scale from map to map. Unlike the Landranger and Pathfinder maps they are tailored to cover a specific area and it is always cheaper to buy one Tourist map of, say, the Lake District rather than the several Landranger maps that cover the same area.

The following maps are non-metric and based on the old seventh series 1:63360 (1 inch to the mile) survey.

    T1 Dartmoor
    T2 North York Moors
    T3 Lake District
    T4 Peak District
    T5 Exmoor
    T6 New Forest
    T7 Ben Nevis and Glen Coe
    T8 Cotswolds
    T9 Loch Lomond

Relief is indicated by contours at 50 feet intervals and also by shading. Rights of way are shown and updated from time to time and camp sites, car parks, viewpoints and other tourist information are included. All these maps are suitable for navigation except T8 Cotswold and T11 The Broads which covers enclosed country where the lack of field boundaries on the map make route finding difficult.

T10 Snowdonia is a useful map for route-planning as it shows public rights of way, but the small scale (1:126720 or $^1/_2$ inch to the mile) does not give sufficient detail for navigation.

The West Country map has no number and as it has a scale of 1:258545 (approximately 3 miles to the inch) it cannot be used for navigation.

Pathfinder Maps

These are superb maps that show the countryside in great detail and are essential for walking in lowland, pastoral areas. Most of the country is now covered by this series, which replaces the First Series 1:25000 maps, and the remaining sheets will be issued in 1990. Note that Northern Ireland, which has its own Ordance Survey (see p306), the Isle of Man and the Channel Islands are not included in the Pathfinder series. Each sheet covers an area measuring 20 kilometres by ten kilometres, and shows rights of way (except in Scotland). The most important feature for navigating in lowland areas is the field boundary (hedge, wall or fence) which allows the walker to follow the true line of the path with great confidence and to recognise immediately the field he or she is in. Oddly enough, there is no mention of field boundaries on the key to these maps.

An indication of the amount of detail shown can be gained by comparing the keys of the Landranger and Pathfinder series. Here is a comparison of some of the features listed (symbols omitted).

Landranger	Pathfinder
Rock features	
outcrop	outcrop
scree	scree
cliff	vertical face
	loose rock
	boulders
Quarries & Pits	
quarry	chalk pit, clay pit or quarry
spoil heap, refuse tip or dump	refuse or slag heap
	gravel pit

coniferous wood

non-coniferous wood

mixed wood

orchard

park or ornamental grounds

marsh or salting

coniferous trees

non-coniferous trees

mixed wood

orchard

not shown

marsh

saltings

reeds

coppice

scrub

bracken

rough grassland

heath

Contours

10 metres (fully metric maps) or 15 metres (maps based on converted imperial survey with contours at 50 feet)

Lowland areas: 5 metres (fully metric maps) 8 metres (maps based on converted imperial survey with contours at 25 feet) Upland areas: 10 metres (fully metric maps) 8 metres (maps based on converted imperial survey with contours at 25 feet)

There is a useful and simple method of determining the Pathfinder maps required for a given area from the appropriate Landranger or Tourist map. Each 10-kilometre grid square (delineated by bold blue lines) on these maps delineates *half* the area of a Pathfinder map. Check the key to the map and find the two letters that identify the 100-kilometre square in which the map falls. This is given in blue in the section showing how to give a grid reference. If there are two sets of figures it means that the map overlaps two 100-kilometre squares and you must refer to the map to discover which square you want. These numbers are printed on the map on each of the four corners and wherever two 100-kilometre squares meet. Find and write down the *first* digit of the double figures in the bold north-south grid of the 10-kilometre grid square (see Fig. 6) on the western side of the area in which you are interested. Next, write down the *first* digit of the double figures of the bold 10-kilometre east-west grid line on the southern side of the area in which you are interested. This gives half the sheet number. In the great majority of cases the first digit of a sheet number begins with 0 or an even numbered digit and 10 must be added or subtracted in order to get the other half. *Example:*

100-kilometre grid square found on map key   SP

First digit of the double figures on the bold grid line on the western side of the north-south grid   8

First digit of the double figures on the bold grid line on the southern side of east-west grid   2

Therefore, *half* the sheet number is SP82. The first digit, 8, is an even number, so 10 should be *added* to the number for the second half of the map giving the complete sheet number as SP82/92. If half of the sheet number had been SP72 then, as the first digit, 7, is an odd number, 10 should be *subtracted* giving a sheet number of SP62/72.

Maps covering coastal areas sometimes have sheet numbers beginning with an odd numbered digit but in these few cases establishing half of the number required will be sufficient to identify the sheet.

A sequential numbering system for Pathfinder maps is currently being introduced and an index may be obtained free from the Ordnance Survey.

Outdoor Leisure Maps

Like the Tourist Maps, these cover popular areas of the country. The scale is 1:25000 but each map covers a much larger area than the Pathfinder maps. Some are totally metric, but some are still using a survey based on imperial measures with contours at 25 feet intervals. They include tourist information such as the location of camping and caravan sites, information centres, viewpoints, golf courses, car parks, picnic sites, youth hostels and mountain rescue posts.

Outdoor Leisure maps are available for the following areas:

OLM 1	The Peak District—Dark Peak area
OLM 2	Yorkshire Dales—Western area
OLM 3	Aviemore and the Cairngorms
OLM 4	The English Lakes—NW area
OLM 5	The English Lakes—NE area
OLM 6	The English Lakes—SW area
OLM 7	The English Lakes—SE area
OLM 8	The Cuillin and Torridon Hills
OLM 9	Brighton and Sussex Vale (now discontinued)
OLM10	Yorkshire Dales—Southern area

OLM11	Brecon Beacons—Central area
OLM12	Brecon Beacons—Western area
OLM13	Brecon Beacons—Eastern area
OLM14	Wye Valley and the Forest of Dean
OLM15	Purbeck
OLM16	Snowdonia—Conwy Valley area
OLM17	Snowdonia—Snowdon area
OLM18	Snowdonia—Harlech and Bala areas
OLM20	South Devon
OLM21	South Pennines
OLM22	New Forest
OLM23	Snowdonia—Cadair Idris area
OLM24	The Peak District—White Peak area
OLM25	Isles of Scilly
OLM26	North York Moors—Western area
OLM27	North York Moors—Eastern area
OLM28	Dartmoor
OLM29	Isle of Wight
OLM30	Yorkshire Dales—Northern and Central areas
OLM31	Teesdale
OLM32	Mountainmaster of Ben Nevis

Other Maps

Two other maps are useful for occasional reference. The 6 ins. to the mile (1:10580), now gradually being replaced by the 1:10000 (1 centimetre to 100 metres), can be very useful for establishing the true line of the path where it is not entirely clear on the smaller-scale maps. The 1 centimetre to 25 metres map (1:2500) gives Ordnance Survey field numbers which are often referred to in planning applications and proposals for diverting and extinguishing paths. Large public libraries, estate agents and surveyors usually have these maps for their area.

Map-Reading

A map gives a representation of the area it covers by using symbols. In order to understand and use the map properly it is necessary to be able to interpret the symbols used, which will be found in the key somewhere on the map. These symbols vary slightly depending on the scale and series map being used. The most common can be quickly learned, but do be aware that some symbols have variants which, in some cases, can provide vital information, especially if you are lost. For example, there are three symbols used on the 1:50000, 1:63360 and 1:25000 maps to indicate churches and chapels:

+
■   church or chapel with tower
+
●   church or chapel with spire

+   church or chapel without either

This means that it may be possible to identify a village from a hillside by the kind of church it has. Note that some symbols look very similar. On the 1:50000 map these very similar symbols are used to delineate different things and it is necessary to check the key constantly until the map reader is thoroughly familiar with all the symbols. For example:

+   church or chapel without spire
+   site of antiquity
− + − + − National boundary

Contours

Contour lines indicate three dimensional features (length, width and height) on the two dimensional (length and width) surface of a map. This feature of Ordnance Survey maps is the most confusing and difficult for beginners to grasp but once understood, it is easy to visualise the shape of the land from the configuration of the contour lines. A contour is a line drawn at uniform height eg 200 metres, 210 metres, 220 metres etc. A walker who was able to follow the exact line of contour would remain at exactly the same height for the duration of his walk. Figure 7 shows a hill with contours sketched in. Imagine that the three-dimensional model is

Fig. 7 Contours

made of ice and that the contours are made of thin wire. If it were possible to melt the ice without disturbing the relative position of the wire contours they would sink to the base-board on which the model stands and look

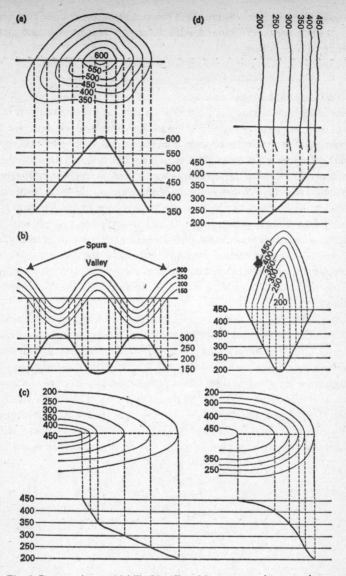

Fig. 8 Contour shapes: (a) hill; (b) valley; (c) concave and convex slopes; (d) escarpment

exactly like the contours of a map (see Fig. 8). The shape of hills and valleys can be reconstructed by projecting the contours as shown in the examples above.

No two features in the country have identically shaped contour lines, but some fall into certain categories that it is helpful to be able to recognise and these are shown in Figure 8.

Note that the height of contour lines is shown only at intervals and it is often necessary to trace the line of the contour for some distance to establish the height. Unless the heights are traced it is sometimes difficult to decide whether the contours indicate a hill or a valley as the patterns are the same as can be seen by examining Figure 8 (b). However, if a stream is shown it *must* be a valley and if there is no stream it is *likely* to be a hill (but beware—dry valleys are quite common in limestone country). In such cases it is essential to trace the contour lines to find a height. The figures indicating the height of contour lines *always* read *up* the slope so if the figures on the contours can be read you must be looking up the slope.

Every fifth contour is shown as a thicker line and the quickest way of calculating height gained is to establish the contour interval from the map key, count the thicker contour lines and multiply by the distance between the thick lines, count the number of thin lines at each end, multiply these by the contour interval and add to the figure obtained from the thick lines.

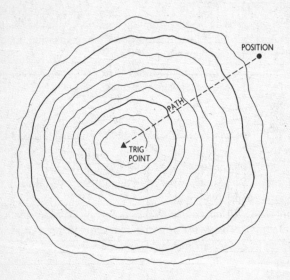

Fig. 9 Counting contours

Example: Figure 9 shows contours taken from the 1:25000 map. According to the key the distance between thick contour lines is 25 metres and there is a 5-metre interval between the thin lines. Therefore the height is:

2 thick lines x 25	=	50 metres
3 thin lines x 5	=	15 metres
		———
Height gained		65 metres

Note that a magnifying glass is an indispensable tool for map reading. If one is not incorporated into your compass it is well worth buying an inexpensive plastic lens which can be carried in the map case or pocket.

Many walkers use an opisometer, or map measurer, which is a device comprising a small wheel linked to a counter. It is useful for measuring distances when planning walks but it is usually not sufficiently accurate for the precise needs of foul weather navigation where a romer is to be preferred (see p60).

Maps are expensive and need protection from the elements. Many walkers use map cases which can be purchased from outdoor shops but in my experience these soon tear. They are designed to be worn round the neck, but quite apart from looking odd, they are a nuisance in a strong wind and I prefer to carry my maps in a self-sealing freezer bag that I can slip into the pocket of my cagoule or breeches. When on a walking tour I waterproof my maps by painting them on both sides with the cheapest clear matt varnish from the local hardware store. The maps take on a slightly brown tinge but become highly water-resistant and can still be marked with a lead pencil. This method is much less expensive than buying document sprays from stationers, or laminating between plastic sheets.

Bibliography

Harley, J. B., *Ordnance Survey Maps: a Descriptive Manual*, Ordnance Survey, 1975.

Ministry of Defence, *Manual of Map Reading*, HMSO, 1973.

Neve, Richard, *Simply Map-reading*, Ordnance Survey in conjunction with Telegraph Maps, 1988.

Seymour, W. A., *History of the Ordnance Survey*, Dawson, 1980.

Wilson, John G., *Follow the Map; the Ordnance Survey Guide*, published jointly by A & C Black and the Ordnance Survey, 1985.

4 Navigation

In the following pages are described a number of techniques to assist in route-finding. Many who walk only in lowland areas never use a compass and rely entirely on their map-reading skills, but anyone who walks in mountainous or moorland country must be competent in the use of both, and understand the many ways in which they can be employed. Theoretical knowledge obtained from reading manuals like this is no substitute for practical skills and every opportunity should be taken to practise and master these techniques. Some of them can be useful in lowland countryside, too. For example, if walking in an area where paths are poorly defined on the ground, the use of a compass as described below will enable the route to be followed with pin-point accuracy. I have navigated at night through unfamiliar fields using this technique and had no trouble in finding the stiles and gates on the line of the path.

The best compass for walkers is an orienteering compass made by the Silva company. There are various models but they all have the same essential features. The type 4S illustrated in Figure 10 is typical. The compass is mounted in a transparent perspex base containing a small magnifying glass. On the base of the compass housing is engraved an arrow which points to the north on the edge of the housing. Parallel to the arrow are engraved lines. The whole of the compass housing can turn on the perspex base.

Somewhere on the base plate will be found romer scales for 1:63360, 1:50000 and 1:25000 maps, which are used for measuring short distances and for giving grid references (see Fig. 6). The lanyard is used for attaching the compass to a rucksack shoulder strap or shirt. Silva also manufacture

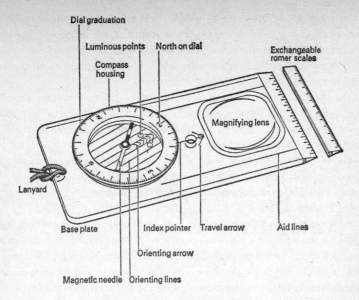

Fig. 10 Silva compass type 4S

prismatic, sighting, thumb and wrist compasses as well as plastic romers that are useful to keep handy in the pocket. Some walkers attach tachometers to their compasses as an aid to pace counting, a technique used in foul weather navigation (see pp71-2).

Before using a compass, it is necessary to grasp certain fundamental principles. On every Ordnance Survey map three norths are shown (see Fig. 11):

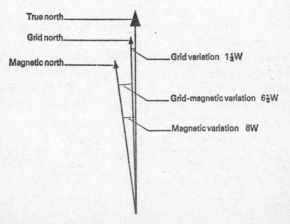

Fig. 11 The three norths

Magnetic north: the north to which the compass needle always points and which changes slightly from year to year.

Grid north: the north pointed at by the grid lines on the map.

True north: the actual north pole, which is of no interest at all to the walker and which may be ignored.

The various norths are shown in diagramatic form somewhere on the map together with a statement of the variation of magnetic north from grid north; for example 'Magnetic north about $8^1/2°$ west of grid north in 1974 decreasing by about $^1/2°$ in eight years'.

The Silva compass can be used in a number of ways, each one of which should be mastered by practising the techniques in familiar surroundings before venturing into unknown territory where your very life may depend upon its accurate use.

How to Stay on Course (see Fig. 12). Let us suppose you are on a fell following an indistinct path. You know your position on the map and your destination is a mountain peak that you can see some miles ahead of you. You notice some low cloud coming down which will obscure your destination. Take your compass and point the direction-of-travel arrow at the peak you wish to reach. Turn the compass housing until the arrow on the base of the housing points in the same direction as the north (red) end of the compass needle. Keep the compass needle and the arrow on the base of the housing in line and follow the direction-of-travel arrow. Rather than keeping the eye glued to the direction-of-travel arrow it is easier and more accurate to find an object such as a cairn, tree or boulder on the line of the path somewhere near the limit of visibility and walk towards it repeating the process until the destination is reached.

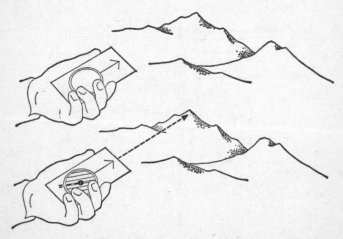

Fig. 12 How to stay on course

Plotting a Course from the Map (see Fig. 13). Very often paths follow straight lines between well-defined features. A path rarely curves across a field and even in mountainous country they are often straight unless following a natural feature such as a stream.

Using an Ordnance Survey map and a Silva compass it is possible to plot your course beforehand by noting down the compass bearing at each point the path changes direction. The method is as follows:

1. Place the map on a flat surface. It is *not* necessary to orientate it (i.e. position it so that the northern edge faces north).

2. Place the straight perspex base of the compass along the line of the path to be followed making sure that the direction of travel arrow is pointing in the direction you want to go (see Fig. 13a).

3. Without moving the base, turn the compass housing until the arrow points towards the north (top) edge of the map and is exactly parallel to the north-south grid lines (see Fig. 13b).

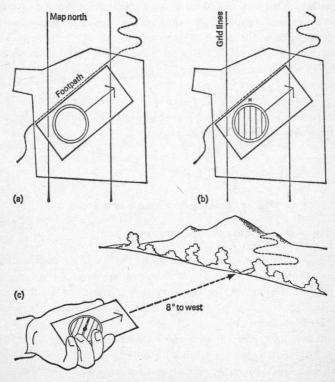

Fig. 13 Plotting a course from the map

4. In order to get the arrow in the compass housing to point to grid north it is necessary to *add* the magnetic variation found at the bottom of the map by moving the compass housing the appropriate number of degrees.

5. Read off the bearing from the point indicated on your compass and note it down. When reaching that point in the walk set the compass for that bearing and, holding it in your hand, turn your body until the red arrow in the compass housing is in line with the north-pointing needle.

6. The line of the path runs where the direction-of-travel arrow on the base plate of the compass is pointing (see Fig. 13).

The above method illustrates the principles of using the Silva compass and the relationship between grid north and magnetic north. Once these principles are grasped, it is possible to make a short cut in the method. Instead of adding the magnetic variation (in this example 8°) to the grid bearing, point the compass needle to 352° instead of 360° or magnetic north (see Fig. 14). Many walkers stick a strip of sticky paper to the underside of the compass to mark the difference between grid north and magnetic north (some compasses have an adjustable pointer or scale known as an inclinometer).

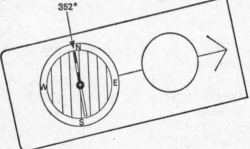

Fig. 14 Correcting for magnetic variation

The method of plotting a course now becomes:

1. Place a straight edge of the base along the line of the path with the direction of travel arrow pointing in the direction you want to go.

2. Without moving the base, turn the compass housing so that the arrow in the housing points towards the north end of the map and exactly parallel to the north-south grid lines.

3. Remove the compass from the map and holding the compass in front of you turn your body until the north (top) edge of the compass needle points to 352° (or the appropriate magnetic variation, as it varies slightly in different parts of the country and from year to year).

4. The line of the path runs where the direction-of-travel arrow is pointing.

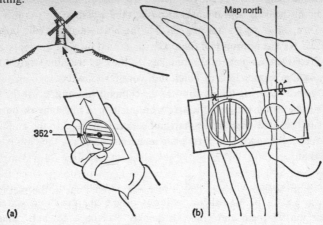

Fig. 15 Finding your exact position on the map

Finding your exact position on the map (see Fig. 15). Very often you may be walking along a path and although you are not lost you wish to know your precise position on that path. Your position can be found as follows:

1. Select a prominent landmark which can be identified both on the ground and on the map.

2. Point the direction-of-travel arrow at the landmark.

3. Turn the compass housing so that the arrow on the base lines up with the north-facing needle.

4. *Subtract* the difference between magnetic north and grid north by moving the compass housing the correct amount.

5. Place the base plate of the compass on the map with the straight edge touching the landmark from which the bearing was taken.

6. Without altering the position of the compass housing, turn the base plate on the map until the arrow on the base of the compass housing points to the north (top) edge of the map and is exactly parallel to the grid lines.

7. Where the edge of the base plate intersects the line of the footpath is your exact position.

It is obvious that another short cut can be made. Instead of subtracting the magnetic variation, just point the direction-of-travel arrow to the landmark and then turn the compass housing until the north-facing compass needle is pointing at 352° instead of 360°. The procedure then becomes:

1. Select a prominent landmark which can be identified on the ground and on the map.

2. Point the direction-of-travel arrow at the landmark.

3. Turn the compass housing so that the north-facing needle lines up with 352° (or the appropriate figure).

4. Place the base plate of the compass on the map with the straight edge touching the landmark from which the bearing was taken.

5. Without altering the position of the compass housing, pivot the base plate on the landmark until the arrow on the base of the compass housing points to the north edge of the map and is exactly parallel to the grid lines.

6. Where the edge of the base plate intersects the line of the path is your exact position.

The three situations outlined above are fundamental to the use of compass and map. All other conditions of use are variations on these themes; master them and you will quickly become adept and come to regard your map and compass as your best friends which will never let you down. The examples which follow have dispensed with the cumbersome add or subtract for magnetic variation.

Finding your Position when Completely Lost No walker should ever be completely lost unless he has behaved exceptionally foolishly. Being lost usually means that you know your position to within a kilometre or so, but you need to identify exactly where you are.

Examine the map and note carefully the last time you were absolutely certain of your position. This can usually be done by some physical feature such as a road, stream, church or hill, but do make certain that you crossed the road or stream at the right point and that it was the right hill and the right church. Assuming that you can mark on the map your last known position, mark off the direction in which you travelled, if necessary by taking a bearing with your compass. Next, estimate the time taken and/or the distance covered since your last known position and mark this estimated position on the map. You should now have a fairly clear idea of where you are.

Orientate the map by setting the compass at 360° and placing the base plate on the north-south grid lines. Next turn the map and the compass without disturbing the position of the compass until the north-facing arrow points to 352° or the appropriate figure (see Fig. 16). The map is then set exactly and it should be possible to recognise certain features such as hills (from the shape of their contours) or buildings such as churches. Select two features and take a bearing from each of them as described on pages 65-66 above. Where the two lines intersect is your exact position. You will then be able to take another compass bearing to rejoin the path at some

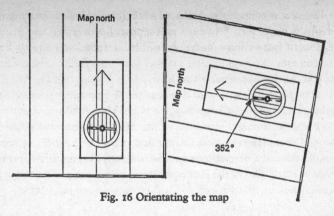

Fig. 16 Orientating the map

appropriate point. If it proves impossible to locate your position, there is nothing to be done but to retrace your steps until you reach a point which you can definitely identify.

Resections (backbearings or 'cocked hats') This is the most accurate way of pinpointing your position when traversing pathless country. Take bearings on at least two, and preferably three, known physical objects that can be identified on the map. Convert these to the map as described in *Finding your exact position on the map* and draw intersecting lines (see Fig. 17). However hard you try you will be unable to be accurate enough to get the three lines to intersect at one point and will end up with a 'cocked

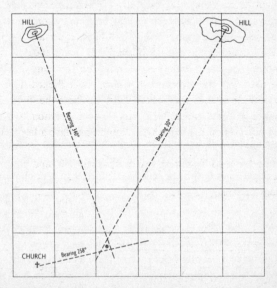

Fig 17 Resections showing position in centre of 'cocked hat'

hat'. The most accurate fix is the centre of the 'cocked hat'. In practice, this technique is rarely used because it presupposes fine weather, and in those conditions, if two or three landmarks can be identified you already know where you are!

How to Make a Diversion and Remain on Course (see Fig. 18). This is a very useful technique when a diversion has to be made in poor visibility to avoid, for example, a large boggy patch. When following a compass bearing and the route is obstructed, turn 90° to the right and count the number of paces taken to clear the obstacle. Turn 90° parallel to the path and walk along the original compass bearing until it is possible to make another 90° turn. Count the same number of paces that you made before, then take another 90° turn and you will be on your original course.

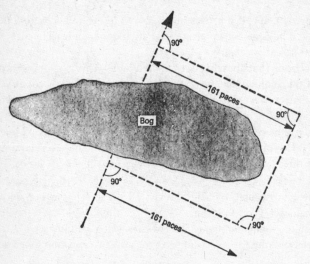

Fig. 18 How to make a diversion and remain on course

Bearing Errors (see Fig. 19). Even the most experienced cannot expect to navigate in bad visibility with an accuracy better than 4°. An error of 4° means that for every kilometre covered the navigator will be 70 metres off course. If the error is 6° then he will be 105 metres out which is an error of approximately 10%.

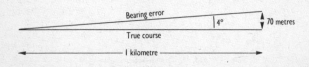

Fig. 19 Bearing errors

Aiming Off There are some circumstances when it is helpful to build in a deliberate error when navigating over pathless country. For example, in Figure 20, the navigator is making for the footbridge over the stream but due to the lie of the land (or poor visibility) he will be unable to see it until almost at the river bank. If he aims exactly for the bridge and cannot find it when he gets to the river he will not know whether it lies to the left or right (it may even be missing!). But if he chooses a bearing that will bring him to the river bank 200 metres to the left of the bridge he will know that he must turn right in order to find it. This technique is known as *aiming off* and is used frequently in mountainous country.

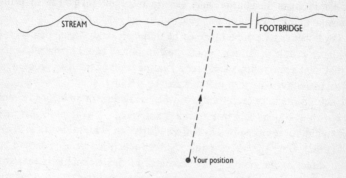

Fig. 20 Aiming off

Taking the Aspect of the Slope Knowledge of this technique can occasionally be useful. Imagine that the navigator is either on a long mountain ridge or following a path that follows a route somewhere between the summit of a long ridge and the valley bottom (see Fig. 21). He has been walking for some time and wishes to establish his exact position

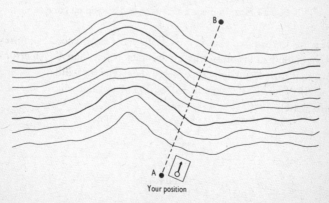

Fig 21 Taking the aspect of the slope

but there is no readily identifiable feature from which to take a bearing. He should stand upright with his feet together making sure that he is in exactly the same plane as the slope and point the direction of travel arrow on the compass at his boots, then carefully raise the compass until it is pointing down the slope and take a bearing. (The purpose of pointing the compass at his boots before taking the bearing is to ensure that the direction of travel arrow is at 90° to the valley bottom.) Convert to a grid bearing and put the compass on the map keeping the lines in the compass housing parallel with the grid lines on the map and the arrow pointing to map north. The compass is gently pushed along the route until the long side of the compass base plate crosses the contour lines exactly at a right angle. This indicates the position.

An even better fix can be obtained by finding a small stream descending the ridge. Straddle the stream, point the direction of travel arrow along the line that the stream follows and take a bearing. Follow the map procedures above and obtain a fix that will include the stream.

Attack Points In poor visibility, or when searching for an inconspicuous object such as a small tent in featureless moorland, it is often quicker and easier to aim for a more obvious feature nearby known as the attack point (see Fig. 22). Once the attack point has been reached a bearing should be plotted direct to the object. The advantage of this technique is that the attack point can be used as a marker and returned to if the objective cannot be found at the first attempt.

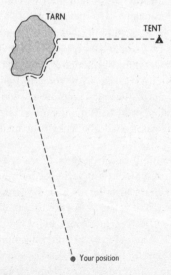

Fig 22 Attack points

Foul Weather Navigation

Mastery of the techniques described above will make a competent fair weather navigator but additional skills are required when visibility is poor. In some moorland areas of the country, such as Dartmoor and the Pennines, paths that are easy to follow in good visibility tend to disappear during heavy rain when the peaty ground becomes waterlogged. When it is raining on the moors visibility is usually much reduced and if there is mist or low cloud it may not be possible to see for more than 25 metres. In such conditions it is very easy either to lose or mistake the line of the path and the same skills are required as when navigating over pathless country.

It is important that everyone who walks in the upland areas of Britain should be familiar with the arcane techniques used in foul weather navigation. In bad weather, when visibility may be as low as 25 metres and in the winter conditions of a whiteout down to less than 5 metres, it is obvious that the only possible method of navigation where there is no path is a combination of compass bearing and distance covered.

The first essential is to get an accurate fix *before* the bad weather sets in. Next examine the map carefully and decide whether it is wise to alter the original route to the destination. Consider the following points:-

1. Is the route dangerous in poor visibility? If it follows a knife-edge ridge or runs close to an escarpment an alternative route should be selected to obviate the risk of falling.

2. Is it possible to make a diversion that will follow an obvious feature such as a stream, wall or well-drained track? This is the attack point principle described on page 70.

Let us assume that you are returning to your tent that has been pitched beside a clump of rocks that is marked on the map but is in the middle of featureless moorland exactly one kilometre from the last identifiable feature which is a small tarn. How are you going to find the tent?

A compass alone is not sufficiently accurate to find a tiny object in conditions of poor visibility, wind and driving rain because, as we have seen even an experienced navigator would be lucky if he made an error of less than 4°.

In Chapter 2 consideration was given to methods of estimating the time required to cover a specific distance in various conditions, but we need a much more accurate method in order to find the tent. If you know the length of your stride you can do it. (It is easy to establish the number of paces taken to cover 100 metres, and every hill-walker should write this information on the back of his compass.) I prefer to count each double pace made by my right foot. Let us assume that it takes you 64 double paces to cover 100 metres, therefore to cover one kilometre you must count 640 double paces. The easiest way to do this is to use a tachometer (see p61) or find six pebbles and carry them in the left hand transferring one to the right hand whenever you count to 100 (this is a safer method than throwing one away for every 100 metres covered because, should one set be accidentally dropped, it will still be possible to calculate the distance covered). When the last pebble has been transferred you know that you have to count to 40. You are now as close to your tent as you can get by dead reckoning and must use another technique, known as a spiral search, to locate it because you do not know in which direction it lies. Using your compass, walk:

 north for 10 paces
 east for 10 paces
 south for 20 paces
 west for 20 paces
 north for 30 paces
 and so on until the tent is found (see Fig. 23).

Fig. 23 Spiral search

If there are several people in the party a sweep search can be made (see Fig. 24). Members of the party should walk parallel to the navigator just below the limit of visibility always keeping their neighbour in sight.

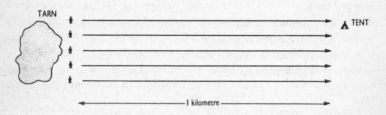

Fig 24 Sweep search

Route Cards

Many walkers prepare route cards, especially when walking in pathless country and particularly in bad weather. They serve at least two useful purposes. First, the discipline of examining the map carefully, calculating distance, height gained, estimating time, aiming off and attack points is useful and may reveal problems that might otherwise be overlooked.

Second, route cards save time by obviating frequent reference to the map and are invaluable in bad weather when the map can reveal nothing useful and the wind may be too strong even to consult it, let alone take an accurate compass bearing from it.

Here is my foul weather route card, based on the 1:25000 Outdoor Leisure Map, from my campsite at Conies Down Water in the centre of Dartmoor to the road at Batworthy a distance of 14 kilometres (see Figs. 25 and 27).

1. Path E for 1.75 km to West Dart river easy undulating   20 mins
2. Bearing 76° for 1.3 km 60 m height gain to wall ....   16 mins
3. Follow indented wall generally N & NW for 3.4 km with 120 m height gain to East Dart river ....   40 mins
4. N for 800 m to boulders & cross river at W loop ....   9 mins
5. Bearing 56° for 500 m level to path* ....   6 mins
6. N through 2 walls for 2.6 km gentle climb to forest ....   30 mins
7. Leave path & follow forest boundary for 1.4 km level to 2nd wall ....   16 mins
8. Aim off 38° to wall 1.5 km level ....   17 mins
9. Turn right at wall & follow to road at Batworthy 600 m level ....   7 mins

Total *walking* time	161 mins
Departure:	1000
ETA:	1300

*If the path cannot be found:

10. Continue on bearing for 1.8 km from river with 70 m gentle climb to forest boundary ....   20 mins
11. Turn left & follow forest wall through 4 walls for 3.2 km undulating to 8 above ....   35 mins

NB: the difference between the walking time and the estimated time of arrival is accounted for by the time to cross the stream, taking bearings and a short stop. I was fit and in a hurry. Had the weather been fine and the walk longer the pace would have been more leisurely.

It is instructive to compare the above route card with one for the same journey based on the 1:63360 Tourist Map (see Fig. 27).

1. Path E for 1.75 km to West Dart river ....   20 mins
2. Bearing 96° for 800 m & 70 m height gain to Longaford Tor ....   10 mins

Fig. 25 1:25000 Outdoor Leisure map of Dartmoor

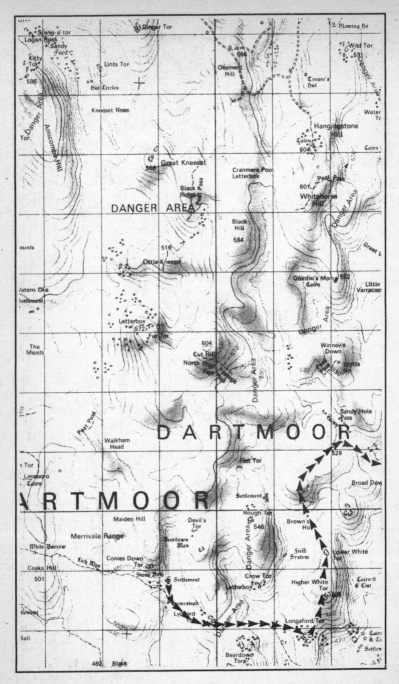

Fig. 27 1:63360 Tourist map of Dartmoor

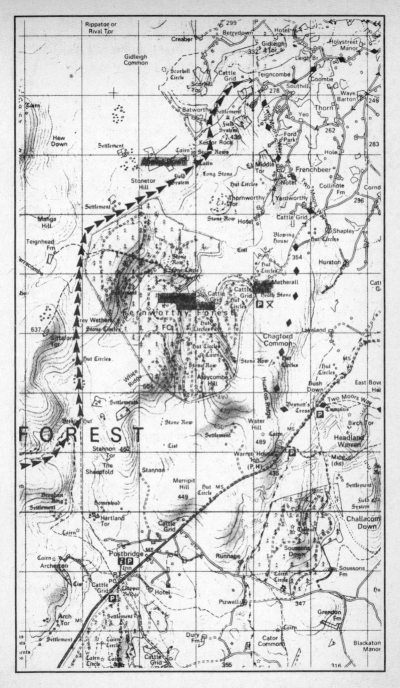

77

3. Bearing 26° for 800 m across saddle to High White Tor   9 mins
4. Bearing 4° for 500 m level to Lower White Tor .... 6 mins
5. Bearing 335° for 700 m 30m height loss to Brown House (ruin) Make spiral search to locate Brown House (see p68) .... 10 mins
6. Bearing 335° for 500 m with 65 height gain to unnamed tor .... 6 mins
7. Bearing 32° for 1.5 km with 45 m height gain to West Dart river .... 18 mins
8. Turn right & follow West Dart river for 1.5 km to south loop .... 20–25 mins
9. Cross river bearing 56° for 500 m level to path* .... 5 mins
10. N on path for 2.6 km gently climbing to entrance of Fernworthy forest .... 27 mins
11. Follow forest boundary N & NE for 1.6 km level to end of forest .... 18 mins
12. Bearing 55° for 1.9 km (no objective) .... 23 mins
13. Bearing 3° to 700 m level to road .... 9 mins

Total *walking* time   186 mins

Departure: 1000
ETA: 1320

*If the path cannot be found

14. Continue on bearing for 1.8 km from river with 80 m gentle climb to forest boundary .... 20 mins
15. Turn left & follow forest boundary for 3.4 km undulating to end of forest .... 38 mins

Notes When compared with the 1:25000 route card it will be seen that a different route is followed using heights (stone walls could not be used because they are not marked on Tourist Maps).

Step 8: it is difficult to estimate the time required for this section because the map indicates that the river flows through a narrow, steep-sided, boulder-strewn valley.

Step 12: it is unusual to walk on a bearing without a definite objective but it is justified in this case because of the close proximity of enclosed country which forms an enclave around this part of Dartmoor. Even a significant navigational error at this point of the journey would not lead me into danger and I would have no difficulty in getting off the open moor and locating the road.

Bibliography

Cliff, Peter, *Mountain Navigation,* Cordee, Rev. Ed., 1986.

Langmuir, Eric, *Mountaincraft and Leadership; a Handbook for Mountaineers and Hillwalking Leaders,* Scottish Sports Council in association with the Mountainwalking Leader Training Board, 1984.

Walker, Kevin, *Mountain Navigation Techniques,* Constable, 1986.

5 Planning a Walk and Map-Reading

In this chapter a short walk in lowland country is described to illustrate some of the problems likely to be encountered when map-reading. It is extremely expensive to reproduce Ordnance Survey maps and so an imaginary route on non-existent maps has been used using only those features to be found on Ordnance Survey maps omitting only grid lines and contours. Note that contours are not often used for navigation in lowland country but they are very important in upland areas.

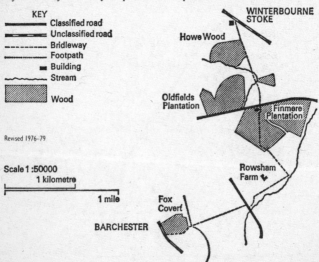

Fig. 28 The 1:50000 map used for route-planning

This walk is from Barchester to Winterbourne Stoke. The Landranger 1:50000 map (see Fig. 28) was used for route-planning and the Pathfinder 1:25000 map (see Fig. 29) will be used for navigation. We have never walked these paths before, and as the region is not a popular walking area and is farmed intensively, the paths are unlikely to be clearly defined on the

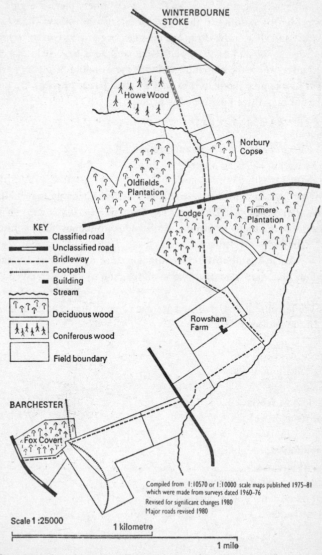

Fig 29 The 1:25000 Pathfinder map used for route-finding

ground and reliance must be placed on natural features to pinpoint the route.

As field boundaries are not shown on the Landranger map we can only rely on walking in the right general direction, whereas when using the Pathfinder map it is possible to progress from field to field, thus ensuring that the line of the path is followed exactly.

The walk starts from the road at Fox Covert where there is a gate and bridleway sign. According to the map, the bridleway follows the edge of Fox Covert and so we walk down the outside edge of Fox Covert to a gate in the hedge at the end of the wood. Here we find a huge field of gently waving barley where the map indicates that there should be a very narrow field. Let us examine the map to work out what has happened.

There are only three possible explanations:

1. The map is wrong.
2. We have misread the map and are lost.
3. The terrain has been altered.

Each possibility must now be considered. It is very unlikely that the map was wrong *at the date of the survey*. The Ordnance Survey is not infallible but its errors are usually in minute details and it would not make a mistake of this magnitude.

Are we lost? Again, this is very unlikely, as Fox Covert is readily identifiable and there is no other wood on the map which we could confuse with it.

Has the terrain altered? Let us consider some of the changes man can make on the landscape. He can:

erect buildings
demolish buildings
realign roads
build new roads
construct reservoirs
fill in canals
abandon railway lines
divert streams
plant new plantations and woods
fell plantations and woods
plant hedges
grub hedges

In this case the most likely explanation is that a hedge or hedges have been

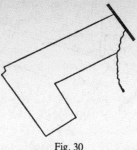

Fig. 30

grubbed and we have to consider which ones have gone. As far as we can tell from a not very good vantage point, the field now looks roughly the shape shown in Figure 30. The long hedge which runs towards the road is still there, as is the hedge at which we are standing, although we are suddenly struck by doubts when we realise that the edge of Fox Covert does not project beyond our hedge as shown on the map. Let us consider the possibilities again:

1. The map is inaccurate (this possibility can be discounted).
2. The hedge has been moved.
3. Part of the wood has been felled.

An examination of the hedge shows that it is old, containing many varieties of shrubs and some well-established trees. This proves fairly conclusively that part of Fox Covert has been felled and the 1:50000 map, based on a much later survey, shows the footpath crossing the bridleway running outside Fox Covert, whereas the 1:25000 map shows the footpath emerging from the wood.

We have now identified two hedges and from the size of the field we can deduce that the hedge which formed the boundary of the narrow enclosure has been grubbed. But even if we imagine our map without that hedge the shape of the field is still wrong, so we have to consider whether any other hedges have been removed. We can see that the field is L-shaped and this gives us the clue, for we can now see that another hedge running at right angles to the bridleway has been removed.

Although we do not plan to follow it, let us turn our attention to the map-reading problems involved in following the footpath which crosses the bridleway (see Fig. 31).

Using the 1:25000 map anyone travelling in a southerly direction would expect to pass the edge of Fox Covert and then to walk up the right-hand headland of a now non-existent hedge (a headland is a path that follows a

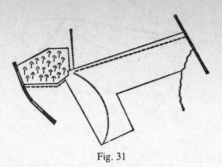

Fig. 31

field boundary). When the hedge was grubbed the farmer should have applied to divert the path along the other headland because the path makes for the corner of the field, and his own, as well as recreational, interests would be better served by a sensible diversion. Without accurate surveying instruments it would be impossible to follow the true line of the path, so in these circumstances it would be better to follow the headland route.

To return to our bridleway. We can now walk down the left-hand headland to a gate at the bottom of the field. After passing through the gate we see that according to the map the path moves slightly away from the headland. However, there is a tractor trail running to the road and following the left-hand headland so, as the field is full of wheat and the true line of the path not restored, we follow the tractor trail to the road.

At the road we turn right and look for a bridleway sign on the left-hand side. There is no signpost but we can see a gate which must be the one we want because it is roughly halfway between the point from where we emerged onto the road and the little bridge which carries the road over the stream. We pass through the gate and walk diagonally across the field to a gate we can see in the hedge opposite. The path now heads across the field to the junction of the hedge and stream, where we find a wide gap leading into the next field. The fields on each side of the gap are pasture and there is no sign on the ground of the route of the bridleway. Anyone using the 1:50000 map would be quite unable to determine which side of the hedge to follow.

However, we are using the 1:25000 map and so we confidently follow the left-hand headland to a gate which leads into the next field, where the bridleway follows the right-hand headland. At the top of this field we reach Finmere Plantation. Here again we notice some changes. The map shows this as a deciduous wood, but changes have taken place, as shown in Figure 32.

We find there is no proper access through the fence which forms the boundary of the plantation. We manage to scramble over, but a horse

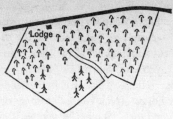

Fig. 32

would not get through. At this point we pause to establish that we are on the line of the path and, having satisfied ourselves that we are, we make a note of the grid reference and the circumstances so that we can report the matter to the County Engineer of Barsetshire.

We follow the left-hand headland of the clearing in the plantation and note that some young conifers have been planted. At the end of the clearing we come to another fence with no access, so we make another note to inform the County Engineer and then reach a broad forest track on the other side of the fence. As this track appears to be about the right distance from the edge of the wood we think it must be the path, so we turn right and follow it. A number of forest tracks not marked on the map cross the path, but as the path we are following seems to be going in the right direction we do not trouble to confirm it by a compass bearing. After a few hundred yards our confidence is confirmed when we reach a clearing around the Lodge. We keep the Lodge on our left and find a gate and bridleway sign on the main road.

On the other side of the road we see a gate and bridleway sign, so we follow the path down the headland to a gated culvert which crosses the stream and then follows it. According to the map the path crosses the stream again at a footbridge and sure enough we come to a wide farm bridge solidly constructed of sleepers laid on stout timbers and obviously designed to accommodate tractors. We cross the bridge and find a farm track curving away to the far right-hand corner of the field (see Fig. 33).

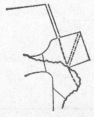

Fig. 33

Before automatically following the farm track our natural caution asserts itself. On checking the map we find that the path runs along the edge of Howe Wood and we can now see a gate on the edge of the wood. We ignore the farm track and make for the gate, entering a narrow lane bordered by hedges which leads into a field. The path continues in the same direction to the corner of the field to a gate in the hedge bordering the road. Beside the gate is a house, which causes us some confusion as it is not marked on the map, and for a moment or two we wonder if we have gone wrong. However, we can now see that it is a modern house, probably built after the survey for the 1:25000 map, and reference to the 1:50000 map confirms that a house should be there. We are now on the outskirts of Winterbourne Stoke and walk down the road into the village.

This imaginary walk illustrates many of the problems of map-reading likely to be encountered in lowland country. There is no doubt that the thousands of miles of hedges that have been grubbed in recent years to enlarge the fields to make them more convenient to farm causes route-finding problems for walkers. Those described on the walk above are a comparatively simple exercise in deduction. The following real-life example is much more complicated. Figure 34 shows some fields and the

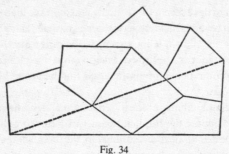

Fig. 34

path crossing them as they were at the time they were surveyed. Figure 35 shows the modern field pattern with eight hedges removed. It is very

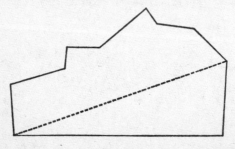

Fig. 35

difficult to cope with situations like this. Sometimes by standing on the top of a stile or a gate it is possible to work out what has happened, but in the absence of any feature such as a building or road which can be used as a point of reference, the only thing to do is to take a compass bearing and march across the field.

Fortunately, this path goes in a straight line. Had it changed direction at each of the old hedges the problem would have been very much more difficult (see Fig. 36). It would have been necessary to take a compass

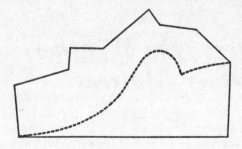

Fig. 36

bearing to where the hedge used to be, then, using the romer on the edge of the Silva compass, to measure the distance to the non-existent hedge. Four millimetres on the 1:25000 map represents 100 metres on the ground, so if you know the number of paces you take to cover 100 metres (see p71) you will be able to count the appropriate number of paces and be able to arrive at the point where the hedge used to be with reasonable accuracy. If this process of taking a compass bearing, measuring the distance on the map and then counting the appropriate number of paces to cover the required distance is repeated at every field boundary you will, sooner or later arrive at a feature that you will recognize from the map. If you follow this procedure carefully you will be surprised at how well you can stay on course.

6 Safety, the Weather and Other Matters

In Chapter 1, discussing clothing and equipment for walking in the high places, I wrote about the dangers of exposure and how quickly one can die if not properly equipped. I described the case of a man who had died in a few hours after his tent had blown down on a mild night in early September. By contrast, there was a case in the winter of 1974-5 when a fifteen-year-old schoolboy got lost on the fells above Grassington in Yorkshire. Fortunately, he was properly equipped with plenty of food, a stove and plastic survival bag. He survived no less than four freezing February nights before being found none the worse for his experience. Undoubtedly, he should not have set out on such a walk alone in winter, but when things went wrong he kept his head and remembered all the survival techniques he had been taught.

Everyone venturing onto the fells must be aware that there is an element of danger. It is the height of folly to go unless properly dressed and equipped with map and compass. Only the experienced should walk alone. Careful note should be taken of the weather forecast and, if visibility is likely to be poor it is better not to go. Even with the most careful preparations things can still go wrong. An ankle can be twisted, a compass can be broken or lost, a map blown away in the wind. If misfortunes like these happen in fog, the lone walker can be in real trouble. All fell-walkers should have some knowledge of survival techniques so that if they do get into trouble they know exactly what to do. In every rucksack should be carried a spare woollen sweater, woollen gloves, a large plastic survival bag or 'space blanket', plenty of spare food, a torch and first-aid kit containing Elastoplast for blisters and a couple of dressings. If you have a first-aid certificate add six triangular bandages and you will be able to cope with most emergencies.

If trouble does occur, the first thing to do is try to find a sheltered spot such as a shepherd's hut, the lee of a stone wall, a sink hole or some deep depression in the heather. Put on all the clothes in the rucksack, cut a mouth hole in the plastic survival bag and pull it over the head, first pulling up the anorak hood. Try to find something to act as an insulator to sit on, such as a thick mattress of heather. Empty the rucksack and put your feet, with your boots still on, into it, carefully arranging the rucksack under the skirt of the survival bag. Lastly, slip your arms out of the sleeves of your anorak as this will help to keep you warm. Stay like this until conditions improve or help arrives. If you really need help, blow your whistle using the international mountain distress signal of six consecutive blasts repeated at minute intervals.

A group of people should huddle together and, if very cold, take it in turns to sit on the outside of the circle. Only if someone is injured should the group break up and attempt to go for help and, ideally, at least three of the party should set out together.

Exposure

Exposure or hypothermia is probably the greatest danger in the mountains. It is caused by the body surface being chilled sufficiently long for the body core temperature to be lowered to a point where it can no longer maintain the vital organs. When the skin and the tissues immediately below it become cold, blood rushes to the surface to warm the affected area. If it is very cold, the blood itself is cooled and returns to the body core to be warmed again. If this process goes on for long it will quickly sap the energy of the patient and result in death. One of the most significant factors in exposure is the strength of the wind, which causes what is known as the 'wind-chill factor' shown diagramatically in Figure 37.

Line 1 indicates when the temperature feels cold
Line 2 indicates when the temperature feels bitterly cold
Line 3 indicates when flesh exposed to the air is likely to freeze
Line 4 indicates when flesh exposed to the air is liable to freeze in one minute
Line 5 indicates when flesh exposed to the air is liable to freeze in thirty seconds
The shaded area indicates when conditions are dangerous to survival.

It will be appreciated from the diagram that a person standing in still air at

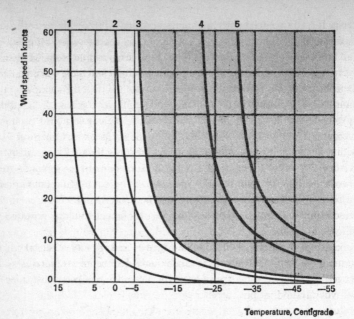

Fig. 37 Wind-chill scale

−25°C is no more at risk than someone wearing similar clothes standing in a 30-knot wind when the temperature is −10°C.

Exposure can be avoided in most weather conditions by wearing the proper clothing. The risk is accentuated by fatigue and hunger. Unfortunately, the symptoms of the onset of exposure are not very striking, and difficult to diagnose in oneself. The danger signals are stumbling, a sense of unreality and difficulty in making decisions. The patient must be given rest, warmth and food. Warmth is essential and serious cases should be treated by wrapping them in sleeping bags or blankets, preferably with another member of the party whose body heat will help the patient. Never attempt to warm by rubbing or administering alcohol, for although spirits make a person feel warm they achieve this by encouraging the blood to go from the recess of the body to the surface, which has the effect of sending the cool surface blood into the body, thus reducing even further the body core temperature. Rubbing has a similar effect.

Mountain Rescue

Should you ever be in the position of having to get help for someone in trouble, it is essential to make the patient as comfortable as possible. Next mark your map as accurately as you can, showing the position of the patient. Examine the map carefully to work out the quickest way of getting help. It might be quicker to head across country to the nearest road to stop a car, or there might be a farm at the head of a nearby valley, although not all farm buildings marked on the map are necessarily inhabited. Make your plan and reassure the patient by telling him of your intentions. Get to a telephone as soon as possible, dial 999 and ask for the police, as they normally co-ordinate rescue services. Keep calm, give details of the patient together with a description of his position, including a grid reference. Answer carefully and precisely all the questions the police put to you. It is quite likely that you will be asked if you are willing to accompany the rescue party in order to show them the exact position of the injured person. Most people want to go immediately, but you should consider very carefully whether you are in a fit condition. Remember that mountain rescue teams are made up of very fit men and women and they will want to travel fast. Note carefully any instructions the police may give you and obey them meticulously. Naturally you will be very concerned about the patient and very conscious of the passing of time. It takes some time to get together the eight or ten members of the mountain rescue team, as they are all volunteers and have to be called from their place of work. If you do return with them, it is quite likely that you will have to take your turn on the stretcher party. Handling a stretcher in mountainous country is very hard work. Six stretcher-bearers are needed—one at each end and two on each side. The front and rear bearers have a full harness and the four side bearers have a webbing strap which passes over the shoulders. One hand holds the stretcher and the other holds the strap so that much of the weight is taken on the shoulders. On narrow rocky mountain paths the language tends to be picturesque!

Mountain rescue services are provided free in Great Britain and are often made up of volunteers who undertake such work for love of their fellow men. They have to spend hours, sometimes even days, searching, often in bad weather, for walkers and climbers who, more often than not, have got into difficulties because of their own foolhardiness. Some of these volunteers actually lose wages as a result of their rescue activities. Remember, then, if ever you have to be rescued to make a handsome donation to the work of the rescue team who perhaps saved your life.

Blisters

Fortunately, comparatively few people have to be rescued each year, but probably thousands of others require some simple first aid. Blisters are the commonest cause of discomfort in walkers. Prevention is better than cure and the point has to be made that blisters would not develop if the proper precautions were taken. At the first hint of a blister, stop and examine the foot. If there is a small blister, sterilize a needle in a match flame and gently push the needle through the blister from one side to the other. Take a clean tissue and gently squeeze the blister until all the fluid is out. From the first-aid kit select a suitable-sized cushioned plaster and cut away the medicated gauze (this is to prevent the hard gauze aggravating the trouble). Gently press the plaster into place and smooth it into position. Try to establish the cause of the blister by examining socks and boots for any foreign matter. More severe blisters should be protected by thick adhesive moleskin. Carefully cut a hole in the moleskin large enough to contain the blister. Apply the moleskin after piercing the blister, then cover the hole with an ordinary plaster with the gauze removed. This technique will effectively remove all further pressure from the blister.

Sunburn and Windburn

A hot summer's day brings with it the risk of sunburn. On the fells it is not often that the wind is still enough for the walker to want to expose much of his body except perhaps his arms, but in the lowland country there is a temptation to bare the arms and legs. Exercise increases the risk of sunburn because perspiration tends to irritate the skin made tender by the sun. The damage is often done before the sufferer realises that he is being affected and therefore it is advisable to be aware of the danger and to keep the limbs covered by light clothing.

Windburn is more common than sunburn in the high places and usually makes the face tender and cracks the lips. It is sensible to carry a soothing cream and some lip salve.

Lightning

An electrical storm in the mountains will make ice-axes and pack frames hum and cause the skin and hair to tingle. A flash of lightning is caused by electrical activity ionising the air allowing electricity to arc to earth. Lightning takes the shortest route to earth and will usually strike the nearest prominent feature. A useful analogy to help appreciate the effects of lightning is to liken it to water. A quantity of water dropped from a height will splash in all directions. Like water, electricity will follow the line of least resistance through gullies and cracks, and along the surface of wet rock. If a human body offers the line of least resistance to the path of the current then electricity will be attracted to it. A direct strike is the most dangerous and is often fatal, but ground currents which occur as the electricity is dispersing itself into the earth can also be dangerous.

If caught in an electrical storm, the walker should try to find a prominent feature such as a large rock at least ten metres high. The area immediately around the rock, formed by a radius equivalent to the height of the rock, is an area of relative, but not absolute, safety. Having protected yourself from the risk of a direct strike it is now necessary to take precautions against injury from ground currents. Try to find a small boulder or stone to sit on well away from any cracks, crevices or gullies along which electricity might travel, insulate yourself as well as possible by placing a rucksack on the boulder and wait for the storm to pass. Avoid being caught on ridges and the summit of mountains and hills during an electrical storm. If in a forest, shelter under trees that are lower than their fellows. Do not shelter in caves or recesses in the rock as these are likely to attract a lightning strike.

Avalanches

An avalanche is a mass of falling rock, snow or ice, or a combination of all three. In Britain, most avalanches are caused by ice and snow melting on steep slopes, or fresh snow being disturbed by walkers and climbers. Most British avalanches are comparatively minor affairs when compared with alpine avalanches and rarely involve damage to property. Nevertheless, even in Britain, and especially Scotland, avalanches are serious hazards that claim a number of victims every year, and those who enjoy walking in winter in the upland areas should be aware of the dangers.

The causes of avalanches are extremely complex and depend upon the structure of the snowflake, the temperature of the ground and surrounding air, windspeed, turbulence, humidity and lapse rate (for definition see Glossary). Snowflakes are unstable and the structure is liable to change (known as metamorphism—see Glossary for definition) and in certain conditions this can result in an avalanche.

Avalanches are most likely to occur immediately after heavy snowfalls on slopes with an angle of 30° – 45° though they can occur on slopes of 20° – 60° (they do not normally occur on steeper slopes because the angle prevents snow accumulating). The best way of avoiding avalanches, which are often set off by human activity, is to avoid snow-covered slopes as much as possible and to keep to the ridge.

Emergency Rations

All walkers should carry a reasonable supply of food and drink. It is unwise to rely on pubs even in lowland areas because there is always the risk of being delayed, or the food being sold out before arriving. It is extremely foolish not to carry food and water on the fells. In addition to the food needed for the day, emergency rations must be carried. Take what you enjoy eating but ideally it should be rich in carbohydrates. I always take crispbread and cheese, dates and apples. The emergency rations should include more crispbread and cheese, dates, fruit, Kendal Mint Cake and chocolate. Probably the most refreshing drink is lemon or lime squash, but avoid all carbonated drinks or you will find that you will regret drinking them for several hours afterwards. Find room in the rucksack for a tube of water-purifying tablets so that in an emergency, mountain water can be drunk.

The Weather

The weather is an unfailing topic of conversation in all parts of Great Britain. Owing to its location in a great ocean off a very large landmass, our country experiences very unsettled weather and surprising variations in the amount of rainfall. The wettest place is Styhead Tarn in Cumbria, with a mean average rainfall of 439 cm per year, and the driest is Great Wakering in Essex, with a mean average rainfall of 48.8 cm per year.

As most of our rain is brought by westerly and south-westerly winds and because there is much high land in the western part of the country it follows that the eastern parts of the country are much drier than the western parts. For example, Edinburgh's mean average rainfall is 69.8 cm compared with 99 cm for Glasgow. There can be enormous variations locally; for example Grasmere has 241.3 cm of rain each year whereas Windermere, which is only 13 kilometres away, has only 172.7 cm and Seathwaite, 11 kilometres from Grasmere, has 332.7 cm each year.

Generally speaking, the walker is more interested in the absence of adverse conditions than in sunny weather. Firm rules cannot be laid down for selecting the best time to take a walking holiday but the weather records show that June and September are often the driest months, with a good chance of fine sunny spells at the beginning of both months. July and August are usually wetter than the other summer months.

The country is well covered by the national weather forecast which is broadcast on radio and television. In addition, local forecasts are available by telephone and details will be found in all telephone directories. When camping it is not always possible or convenient to telephone the weather service and many campers use a small transistor radio for receiving forecasts.

It is very useful to be able to anticipate changes in the weather and to interpret correctly what the wind and clouds are signalling. Providing they are understood properly, there is truth in some of the old-fashioned weather proverbs.

'Red sky at night, shepherd's delight' is nearly always true if the red sky is caused by the rays of the setting sun reflected on clouds very high in the sky, indicating that a cold front has just passed and that there will now be a period of settled weather.

'Red sky at morning, shepherd's warning' is usually true when the sun's rays are shining on high clouds which signal the approach of a warm front which will bring rain with it.

'Rain before seven, fine by eleven' is very often found to be correct because, unless the depression is very deep, indicated by very thick, fast-moving, low-lying stratus clouds; it rarely rains for more than four hours at a stretch in Great Britain.

In summer time if the day dawns crystal clear with the hardness of a sapphire then the weather is certain to deteriorate within a few hours.

There is one virtually foolproof method known as the 'cross-wind rule' of establishing whether the weather will deteriorate or improve within a few hours. It is often not appreciated that weather conditions cause winds to blow in different directions at certain heights. Thus the clouds may move in a direction different from that of the surface wind which the observer can feel on his face.

Rule 1: Stand with your back to the surface wind and if the clouds come from the *left*-hand side then the weather will usually deteriorate in the next few hours.

Rule 2: Stand with your back to the surface wind and if the clouds come from the *right*-hand side then the weather will usually improve within the next few hours.

Rule 3: Stand with your back to the surface wind and if the clouds move on a parallel course the weather will not change very much during the next few hours.

(The walker must ensure that his back is turned towards the true surface wind and that the direction has not been distorted by natural features such as mountains and hills.)

The Mountain Code

In this chapter and throughout the book great emphasis has been laid on the need to follow a safe code of conduct when walking in the high places. It must not be thought that there is danger lurking behind every cairn or in every mountain stream, but as with almost any sport or recreation there is an element of risk which is greatly increased by foolhardiness. Always follow the mountain code.

Be Prepared

Do not tackle anything which is beyond your training and experience.
Ensure that your equipment is sound.
Know the rescue facilities available in the area you are in and the procedure in case of accidents.
Know first aid.
Avoid going into the mountains alone unless you are very experienced.

Leave word of your route and proposed time of return. Always report your return.

Make sure your map and compass skills are well practised.

Rely on your compass.

Consider Other People

Avoid game-shooting parties.

Lead only climbs and walks which you are competent to lead.

Enjoy the quiet of the countryside; loud voices and radios do disturb.

Do not throw stones and dislodge boulders.

Do not pollute water.

Choose a climb which will not interfere with others, or wait your turn.

Be Weather Wise

Know the local weather forecast.

Weather conditions change rapidly. Do not hesitate to turn back.

Know the conditions on the mountain; if there is snow or ice only go out when you have mastered the use of ice axe and rope.

Respect the Land

Keep to footpaths through farm and woodland. If in doubt, ask.

Camp on official sites or obtain permission of the landowner.

Dig a hole to make a latrine and replace the turf.

Remember the danger of starting a fire.

Take all your litter home.

Avoid startling sheep and cattle.

Help Conserve Wild Life

Enjoy the plants, flowers and trees but never remove or damage them.

Avoid disturbing wild life.

Professional Instruction in Hill-Walking

The best way to learn about safety in the hills is under professional guidance. A number of outdoor pursuit centres provide courses in hill-walking and there are three National Outdoor Training Centres all of which provide courses for the general public:

National Outdoor Training Centre: Glenmore Lodge, Aviemore, Inverness-shire PH22 1QU. Tel. 047986-256.

National Outdoor Training Centre: Plas-y-Brenin, Capel Curig, Betws-y-Coed, Gwynedd LL24 OET. Tel. 06904-214.

National Outdoor Training Centre: Plas-Menai, Llanfairisgaer, Caernarfon, Gwynedd LL55 1UE. Tel. 0248-670964.

The British Mountaineering Council (see pp293-4) arranges courses in various parts of the country, and there are a number of privately owned establishments but these vary greatly in quality and there is no system of licensing or inspection. Their addresses may be obtained from the advertising pages of the outdoor magazines listed in Appendix One. Note that some organisations offer 'survival courses' which teach the participants how to survive in adverse conditions by building shelters, snaring animals and eating berries; such skills are of little value to the British hill-walker.

Bibliography

Barton, R. D., and Wright, D. S. B., *A Chance in a Million; Scottish Avalanches for Climbers and Skiers,* Scottish Mountaineering Club, 1985.

Daffern, Tony, *Avalanche Safety; for Skiers and Climbers,* Diadem, 1983.

Epp, Martin, and Lee, Stephen, *Avalanche Awareness,* Wild Side, 1987. (Distributed in UK by Cordee).

Fraser, Colin, *Avalanche and Snow Safety,* John Murray, 1978.

Jepson, Tim, and Barry, John, *Safety on Mountains,* British Mountaineering Council, Rev. Ed., 1988.

Lachappelle, Edward R., *The ABC of Avalanche Safety,* Cordee, 1979.

Langmuir, Eric, *Mountaincraft and Leadership; a Handbook for Mountaineers and Hillwalking Leaders,* published jointly by the Scottish Sports Council and the Mountainwalking Leader Training Board, 1984.

McInnes, Hamish, *International Mountain Rescue Handbook,* Constable, 2nd Rev. Ed., 1972.

Ministry of Defence, *Royal Air Force Mountain Rescue Handbook,* HMSO, 1972.

Mountain and Cave Rescue with Lists of Official Rescue Teams and Posts; the Handbook of the Mountain Rescue Committee. Published annually by the Mountain Rescue Committee.

Mountain Hypothermia, compiled and published by the British Mountaineering Council, 1973.

Pedgley, D. E., *Mountain Weather; a Practical Guide for Hillwalkers and Climbers in the British Isles,* Cicerone Press, 1979.

Renouf, Jane, and Hulse, Stewart, *First Aid for Hill Walkers and Climbers,* Cicerone Press, 1982.

Unwin, D. J., *Mountain Weather for Climbers,* Cordee, 1978.

7 Backpacking

Backpacking is the craft of carrying in a rucksack the essentials with which to support life for several days. Modern technology has produced reliable lightweight materials which ensure that the walker's load does not have to be unduly heavy. He will be warm, comfortable and dry, and his evening meal can be prepared cleanly on a tiny stove in a few minutes. There is no need to be dirty, uncomfortable, wet or cold in order to enjoy the great outdoors, and cooking over an open fire is not only unpleasant but anti-social and contrary to the Country Code. Although the modern backpacker does not rough it, he does live much closer to nature than any other holidaymaker. There is a very special quality about a sunset seen from the door of a tent high up on a fellside, and only the most prosaic will not respond to the changing pattern of light in a mountain valley as the sun comes up. No food tastes better (even if it is dehydrated) than the meal cooked by a beck at the end of an exhilarating day's walking in the mountains.

Weight is something to be considered very carefully when selecting equipment. It is possible to be too fanatical about saving grams but it is surprising how quickly they can mount into kilos. It is perfectly possible, and indeed desirable, to ensure that the total weight of equipment does not exceed fourteen kilograms.

The solo backpacker has to carry everything himself. Two or more persons backpacking together can share certain items of equipment such as tent, stove, fuel and canteen thus reducing the weight carried by each walker.

Rucksack

Modern rucksacks are carried high on the back and are so designed that the weight is distributed down the body, so that the walker can walk in a natural posture without the need to lean forward to counterbalance the load. The better rucksacks have a wide padded hip belt which is tightened after the pack is lifted onto the shoulders. The shoulder straps are then slackened and most of the weight is carried on the hips. It is quite astonishing how comfortable this type of rucksack can be, and I have often walked forty kilometres in a day carrying a fifteen-kilogram pack in mountainous country.

There are two distinct styles of rucksack giving a choice between an external and an internal frame.

External Frame An external-framed rucksack has a frame separate from the pack or sack. The pack frame comes in several lengths to suit persons of different back lengths and is fitted with a padded hip-belt so that about 70 per cent of the weight is carried on the pelvic girdle. Pack frames allow sacks of different sizes to be fitted to the same frame according to the capacity required, and keep the sack well away from the body so that air can circulate and thus keep the back cool. The main disadvantage of an external-framed rucksack is that it does not lie close to the body and there tends to be a certain amount of movement between the sack and the frame which can occasionally catch the unwary off balance. They are awkward to lift into the boots of cars and the luggage racks of trains and coaches, and the frames often catch on bushes and low branches.

Internal Frame The internal framed rucksack is the most popular style. The frame is inside the padded back of the sack keeping the rucksack as close to the body as possible so that the centre of gravity is near the spine. Most of the weight is carried on the hips by means of a padded belt. Internal-framed sacks have none of the sloppiness often associated with external-framed sacks but they tend to be warmer in hot weather and it is not possible to fit different-sized sacks to one frame. Some models have adjustable back lengths.

Sacks Sacks come in a bewildering variety of shapes, sizes and designs. There are models with many separate compartments, detachable pockets, fittings for skis, crampons and ice axes and a wide variety of pockets.

When choosing a rucksack it is essential to go to a reputable retailer who knows and understands what he is selling. Rucksacks have to be fitted as carefully as a suit to ensure maximum comfort and performance. Make sure that the rucksack is of the correct size for your needs and that it has all the pockets and fittings required. Generally speaking, there should not be more than two compartments in the main body of the rucksack or it will not be possible to use the space available to maximum advantage. All zip fasteners should be protected by flies to prevent the ingress of water. It is advisable to line the inside of the rucksack with a large polythene bag as most sacks leak slightly at the seams. The buckles on modern rucksacks are made from plastic and are enormously strong despite their flimsy appearance.

The size and capacity of rucksacks is expressed in litres. Rucksacks with a capacity of 20–40 litres are day sacks designed to carry food, drink and foul-weather gear for a day's outing. The larger sizes will enable a parent to carry all the family's needs. 40–60 litre sacks are suitable for backpackers who prefer to bed and breakfast or who walk with others and are able to share certain items of equipment. 60–80 litre sacks are large enough to carry a complete backpacking outfit. Most rucksacks are made of 7-oz. polyurethane-coated nylon, Cordura, KS-100e or occasionally in traditional cotton duck.

In order to achieve maximum comfort and convenience, rucksacks must be packed properly. The basic principle is to keep heavy items towards the top of the sack and as close to the spine as possible. In practice this has to be modified a little to ensure that everything is packed in a convenient order. Carry in the outside pockets those items such as foul-weather clothes, food, drink and maps which are likely to be required while walking as this obviates the need to open the main sack. It is usual to put the sleeping bag inside a stuff-sack at the bottom of the rucksack. Next come clothes in two stuff-sacks or polythene bags (one for clean clothes and one for soiled linen). On top of the clothes put food and cooking equipment in two polythene carrier bags and at the very top goes the tent with the poles pushed down the length of the rucksack. The insulating mat can be carried under the rucksack, at the very top under the flap, or coiled loosely inside the main sack. If it is readily available it is useful to sit on during rest periods. This method of packing a rucksack ensures that the tent can be pitched in wet weather without unpacking the rucksack and if the tent has to be struck when wet it is separated by the cooking equipment from dry clothes and the sleeping bag.

Tent

Modern one-man tents for backpackers can be as light as 1.3 kg. They are made of polyurethane-coated nylon, which is 100 per cent waterproof and will only let in water if damaged. But because the fabric is impermeable, there are problems of dampness inside the tent due to condensation. Various ingenious methods are employed to overcome condensation, including foam lining and permeable but waterproof inner tents which allow water vapour to pass through the inner tent, to condense on the underside of the impermeable skin. If water falls back on the inner tent the silicone proofing will prevent it coming through and it will roll harmlessly down the edge of the tent where it can be shaken out before the tent is struck.

There are now a number of Gore-Tex tents on the market. This is an interesting development in the use of single-skin materials but although Gore-Tex is a considerable advance on totally impermeable fabrics it requires a certain amount of body heat to drive the water vapour through the pores. When it is realized that the purpose of a sleeping bag is to prevent the loss of body heat into the tent it will be seen that Gore-Tex is not necessarily the complete answer.

Practically all tents will suffer from condensation to a greater or lesser degree when the weather is cold and the atmosphere is damp. In such circumstances it is important to keep sleeping bags and clothes as dry as possible and to mop up any condensation as soon as it forms.

Ultra-lightweight tents suitable for backpackers should not be used in high altitudes except in settled conditions in temperate weather. It is much better to seek the shelter of the valley rather than try to ride out bad weather high in the mountains. Proper mountain tents designed to withstand gale-force winds in exposed places are much heavier than tents normally used by backpackers.

Sleeping Bags

Sleeping bags are graded for their seasonal suitability. A four-season bag is for winter use anywhere in the British Isles. A three-season bag is for spring, summer and autumn use. A one-season bag is for summer use only. Some firms manufacture their sleeping bags so that two bags can be used together to convert a three-season bag into a four-season bag. Over the years a number of designs have evolved to conserve the heat of the body, ranging from the simple tapered bag with a draw cord at the neck to tulip- and mummy-shaped bags which contour the figure and are fitted with hoods.

Design and Construction Bags which rely on filling for insulation need to be so constructed that the filling is contained and does not move about.

Simple quilting: This is the simplest form of quilting which has the disadvantage of allowing the cold to enter wherever the bag is stitched. See Figure 38(a).

Double quilting: Two layers of simple quilting are sewn together thus effectively eliminating cold spots. See Figure 38(b).

Box wall quilting: This is an improvement on simple quilting but the upright wall sections allow the filling to fall away from the dividing sections. See Figure 38(c).

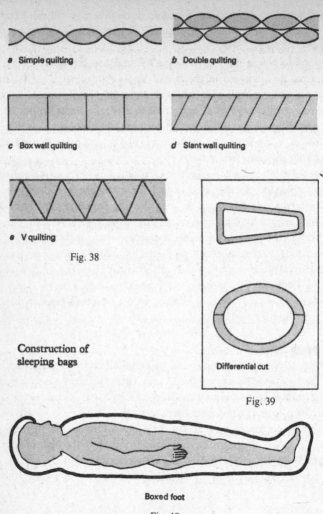

a Simple quilting

b Double quilting

c Box wall quilting

d Slant wall quilting

e V quilting

Fig. 38

Construction of sleeping bags

Differential cut

Fig. 39

Boxed foot

Fig. 40

Slant wall quilting: By constructing the sections on the slant the filling cannot fall away and makes for a warm bag. See Figure 38(d).

V quilting: This is the most expensive and complicated construction. It is the most effective method of holding the filling in place and is found on the best bags. See Figure 38(e).

Differential cut: The outer shell of the bag is cut larger than the inner shell to allow the filling maximum room in which to loft. See Figure 39.

Boxed foot: A panel is put into the bottom of the bag to provide more room for the feet. See Figure 40.

Fillings

The material that provides the insulation to keep the sleeper warm is known as the filling. The cheapest bags, such as those often favoured by family campers, are filled with terylene (dacron) but this material is now seldom used in bags designed for backpacking because the more sophisticated design and expensive manufacturing process makes it pointless to economise on the filling.

Down is the most expensive filling and is still found in the best and lightest bags (see p35). The resilience of down is called loft and the springy nature of the material allows air to be trapped which is largely responsible for its insulating qualities. Unfortunately, not only does down lose all its heat retaining properties when wet but it takes a long time to dry and it is of the utmost importance to keep down sleeping bags dry. Down bags can be made waterproof without affecting their insulating qualities by treating them with TX10 manufactured by Nikwax, Durgates Industrial Estate, Wadhurst, East Sussex TN5 6DF. To keep them sweet and clean they should be washed occasionally in a special preparation called Loft, also manufactured by Nikwax, or dry cleaned. Fumes from dry-cleaning fluids become trapped in the down and are lethal, so it is essential to air the bag thoroughly after dry-cleaning by hanging it on a washing line for several hours.

Hollofill and **Quallofil** are synthetic fillings (see pp32-3) that have a pleasant, resilient feeling and although heavier than down and not such good insulators, they have the advantages of remaining warm when wet and dry very quickly because they do not absorb water. They can be laundered in a washing machine.

Fibrepile sleeping bags are cut to shape from the insulating material itself (see p32) and do not require baffles to contain a loose filling thus making them cheaper to manufacture. They remain warm when wet and can be laundered in a washing machine.

Insulating Mats

An insulating mat which goes under the floor of the tent should always be used with a sleeping bag. These are made of a non-porous closed-cell flexible material which completely insulates the sleeping bag from the ground thus preventing the loss of body heat, which could be considerable.

Cooking Equipment

Backpackers require the following qualities in a cooking stove. It must be light in weight, compact, efficient and clean, and fuel must be readily available. The most commonly used fuels are butane gas, solid fuel tablets, methylated spirits, paraffin and petrol. With any stove using liquid fuel there is a real risk of contaminating food. Methylated spirit and petrol are highly volatile, and petrol is difficult to obtain in small quantities. Solid fuel is very expensive and inefficient, and the heat cannot be controlled accurately. Bottled gas is widely available, easily handled and probably the safest fuel to use. With careful planning one 500 gram container will last one person a week assuming that the stove is used only twice a day.

Stoves and fuel containers must always be left outside the tent at night to obviate the risk of lethal fumes leaking.

There are a number of compact light cooking pans which nest together. They usually have a frying pan, plate and saucepan, and with properly prepared menus this kit will be perfectly adequate. A polythene mug, a knife, fork and spoon set, which fit neatly together with a clip, an aluminium pot holder to remove saucepans from the stove, a tiny plastic condiment set, water-purifying tablets, non-safety matches individually sealed in candle wax against dampness and then kept in a 35-mm. film case with a piece of nail file on which to strike them, a small piece of green nylon scourer, and a minute baby can-opener complete the equipment. Some backpackers carry a disposable butane cigarette lighter as this will always work in damp conditions.

Food and Menus

Backpackers require a balanced diet of a high calorific value. All food should require the minimum of preparation and only a few minutes' cooking time. There is a wide variety of convenience food on the market which meets these requirements and accelerated freeze-dried meals may be obtained from specialist outdoor shops. A great deal of time can be saved if the food is packed into individual portions for each meal and the food for one day contained in a plastic bag. Consider a menu for one day; there is no need to cook breakfast as it can consist of a large plate of muesli (Alpen, Familia etc.) to which has been added sugar and dried milk to taste before the trip started. This individual portion can be poured from its plastic bag into a plate and water added. Fill the saucepan with water and put it on the stove. When the water boils, pour from another previously prepared tiny plastic bag a mixture containing a tea or coffee bag, dried milk and sugar. This makes a marvellous breakfast which will keep the walker going for two or three hours, and washing-up is kept to a minimum. Lunch consists of crispbread, cheese and dates or dried apricots. I have the same lunch every day and so have a special plastic bag kept at the top of my pack which contains all I need. Water is drunk straight from the container.

Dinner may consist of an accelerated freeze-dried complete meal or if supplies are bought from a village shop, a can of meat heated in boiling water. Pour some dehydrated potato from an individual plastic bag into a plate and then add boiling water to make whipped potato mash. Remove the can of meat from the saucepan, and while keeping the water boiling pour in an individual portion of accelerated freeze dried peas which will cook in two minutes. Dessert can consist of dried fruit. Tea or coffee can be made before retiring for the night. Other dinner menus are a can of meat dropped into one of the quick soups such as Chef or Batchelor's Cup-a-Soup. If a shop can be visited late in the afternoon it would be worth buying a can of Irish stew or some cooked meat and fresh fruit but it is not wise to carry heavy items like this very far. In my view, cooking should be kept as simple as possible, with a minimum of washing up. There are a number of firms specializing in lightweight foods suitable for backpackers, but unfortunately these are available only from outdoor shops far from the place they are to be eaten. Some backpackers mail small parcels of dehydrated foods to post offices along their route so that they can collect them as required.

One of the secrets of keeping warm while backpacking in winter is to eat well. Hot soups and stews will be found very appetizing, and muesli made from hot milk is much nicer and more sustaining than porridge.

Personal Hygiene

No one likes to be dirty for long and at the end of a day's walking most of us are not nice to know at close quarters. A good wash at the end of the day can do wonders for morale and bestow a sense of well-being. On commercial camp sites, washing presents no problems, but it is difficult if camping wild with no wash basins available. It must be remembered that each person needs about two litres of water (weighing 2 kilograms) to cover evening meal, breakfast and essential washing. If there is any doubt about the availability of water at a camp site, water must be obtained beforehand. There is usually no difficulty in finding water in mountainous country. It can be carried conveniently in a two litre plastic jerrycan in which some supermarkets sell liquids or a collapsible plastic water-carrier. Drinking water in lowland areas must be obtained only from a reliable household supply, but in the mountains and on the fells, water from fast-running streams is usually fairly safe to drink, though water-purifying tablets available from a chemist's shop must always be used.

A small washing-up bowl can be made by cutting off the top of a two litre plastic container. This bowl is large enough to contain sufficient water for an elementary wash. Deodorants should not be used as it is unwise artificially to restrict sweating when exercising hard. Carry a small quantity of talcum powder, which will make you smell sweet and is useful for powdering the feet.

A compact toothbrush which has a detachable handle into which the brush fits when not in use, toothpaste, flannel and towel and a partially used bar of soap carried in a freezer bag are all the toilet articles that are required.

Socks and underwear can be washed in the washing-up bowl. A small container of soap powder or mild detergent should be carried and this can also be used for washing-up. Clothes can be dried by hanging them from the back of the rucksack in dry weather, but as heavy woollen stockings take a long time to dry even in good weather, they should be washed as soon as used. When passing through towns it is worth looking for laundrettes so that wet clothes and sleeping bags can be put in the drying machines.

Many backpackers find that they become constipated during the first few days of a walking holiday. Two or three Beechams pills carried in the first-aid box will be found useful and a small pack of tissues carried in the breast pocket will be found invaluable as handkerchiefs, tea towel and toilet tissue.

Proper sanitary arrangements must be made well away from any streams. Make a shallow pit about 8 cm. deep with a stick or the heel of your boot and then cover the stools with a thin layer of earth. Rubbish which will break down and rot may also be buried but tins and plastic bags must be disposed of properly in a litter bin even if this means carrying them a considerable distance.

Kit and Equipment

To give some idea of the kit and equipment required for a solo backpacking trip I have listed below my own outfit together with the weight of each item. It does not include those items that are being worn but only those that are actually carried in the rucksack.

Summer Outfit	*Weight in Grams*
Rucksack	1500
Tent	1500
Sleeping bag	1100
Insulating mat	250
Butane stove	180
Butane fuel cartridge	500
Canteen	300
Cutlery	100
Panhandle	30

Cup	30
Nylon scourer	25
2-litre water carrier	60
Washing-up bowl	60
Water-sterilising tablets	24
Matches	30
3 pairs of socks	225
2 pairs of underpants	120
1 light woollen sweater	350
2 cotton shirts	300
Pyjamas (long-johns and thermal sweater)	300
Lightweight trousers	300
Trainers	500
Toilet kit	400
Pertex towel	100
Torch	120
Survival bag	100
Food for 3 days	2500
Water	1000
First-aid kit*	150
Sundries (pen, paper, toilet tissue, J-cloths, plastic bags etc)	1000
Weight of packed rucksack	**13154**

Equipment not carried in the rucksack: Clasp knife, whistle, Silva compass, map & guidebook, camera, binoculars, miniature radio, sunglasses.

*See p88 for a description of what the kit should contain.

Winter Outfit

	Weight in Grams
Rucksack	1500
Mountain tent	3500
Four-season sleeping bag	2500
Insulating mat	250
Petrol stove	750
Fuel	600
Canteen	300
Cutlery	100
Panhandle	30
Cup	30

Nylon scourer	25
2-litre water carrier	60
Washing-up bowl	60
Water-sterilising tablets	24
Matches	30
3 pairs of socks	225
Thermal underwear	500
2 woollen sweaters	1000
Pyjamas (long-johns and thermal sweater)	300
Lightweight trousers	300
Trainers	500
Toilet kit	400
Pertex towel	100
Torch	120
Survival bag	100
Food for 3 days	2500
Water	1000
First-aid kit	150
Candles	180
Ice-axe	1500
Crampons	500
Sundries (pen, paper, toilet tissue, J-cloths, plastic bags etc)	1000
Weight of packed rucksack	20134

Equipment not carried in the rucksack: Clasp knife, whistle, silva compass, map & guidebook, camera, binoculars, miniature radio, snow goggles.

Apart from the heavier pack carried, the winter backpacker will carry extra weight in the form of winter-weight boots, breeches, sweater and shirt, and will also wear gloves, overmitts and a balaclava.

Camp Sites

Permission should normally be sought from the landowner before camping in open country. However, in some mountainous areas of Great Britain a tradition of tolerating *bona fide* backpackers has grown up, though notices forbidding camping must always be respected.

The essentials of a good camp site are a sheltered level spot, preferably on grass, and easy access to fresh water. Idyllic-looking sites near mountain streams should be viewed with caution as becks and ghylls can rise with surprising rapidity in heavy rain with the risk of flooding the tent. Choose a site into which rainwater will not drain and avoid areas where mist is likely to form.

The tent should be pitched with the entrance facing away from the prevailing wind. Many tents for backpackers are shaped so that the occupants have to sleep with their heads near the door, so unless the ground is level it is important that the site should slope gently away to the feet. Having selected the site, remove any stones and hassocks of grass so that there are no bumps underneath the floor of the tent.

Wet clothes, boots, rucksacks and cooking equipment should be kept in the porch of the tent. If your tent lacks a porch, store these items in a large plastic bag weighted with stones outside the tent. Camping is much more pleasurable if everything is kept scrupulously clean and tidy and has its allotted place in the tent. This will help the backpacker to strike camp and make an early start. Before leaving the site look round carefully to ensure that you have left no trace of your passing.

When pitching a tent in the rain the following technique will ensure that all kit is kept as dry as possible. Erect the tent while still wearing foul-weather gear making sure that the rucksack is closed as soon as the tent has been removed from it. Once the tent is erected bring the rucksack as close to it as possible. Remove overtrousers and gaiters and put them under the tent porch. Next, take off your cagoule as quickly as possible and sit on the groundsheet just inside the tent doorway but with your feet and legs in the porch. Remove your boots and place them under the flysheet, pull your rucksack into the porch and unpack it as neatly as possible putting the contents in their allotted place in the tent or porch. When striking camp in wet weather follow the same procedure in reverse.

Winter Backpacking

Many enthusiastic backpackers continue camping throughout the winter months. A four-season sleeping bag and, in mountainous areas, a heavier tent, ice axe and crampons are required. These items together with extra clothing make for a considerably heavier load. The shorter days and a heavier pack mean that the distance walked each day is likely to be less than during the summer months. Most backpackers get into their sleeping bag as soon as the tent is pitched in order to remain warm and snug. In summer, most walkers are content to retire at sunset when camping in remote areas, but it is a dismal prospect to go to bed at 5 p.m. in the depths of winter. There are a number of battery-operated and butane lamps available, but the cheapest and lightest (and the most dangerous) forms of illumination are nightlights and candles. They must be used with extreme care as tents are very inflammable, but they provide a cheerful and satisfactory light which is good enough to read by and they generate a surprising amount of warmth. Stearine candles are the best as they last a long time and provide more light than conventional candles. If the tent has an upright pole, place the candle in the plastic top from an aerosol can which has been filled with water and secure it to the pole with a rubber guy-line. A reflector and draught excluder can be made from a small piece of aluminium foil which will direct the light to fall where required. If the tent has angled poles then the candle will have to go in a suitable container on the floor.

Bibliography

Constance, Hazel, *Gear for the Outdoors and How to Make it*, Hale, 1982.

Constance, Pat, and Hazel, *Modern Lightweight Camping*, Hale, 1985.

Hunter, Rob, *Winter Skills*, Constable, 1982.

McNeish, Cameron, *The Backpacker's Manual*, Oxford Illustrated Press, 1984.

Walker, Kevin, *Wild Country Camping*, Constable, 1989.

8 *Walking Holidays*

The walker who has gained some experience and pleasure in exploring local paths, and has become proficient in the use of map and compass, may wish to venture on a walking holiday. There are many kinds of walking holiday, some of them suitable for families. Children are tough little creatures and providing they have been used to walking from an early age they should get a great deal of enjoyment from a walking holiday, especially if some days are set aside for visits to the beach and places of interest.

Walking holidays fall into two main categories; centre-based where the entire holiday is spent at one location; or a tour, usually following a long-distance path, which involves moving on every so often to new accommodation. One significant advantage that a centre-based holiday has over a tour is that it is easy to take a full day off from walking if the weather is inclement or fancy dictates. Also, it is easier to keep up to date with laundry and to dry clothes. On a tour, especially if accommodation has been reserved in advance, the walker has little choice but to continue.

Some walkers like to plan and organise their own holidays whilst others prefer to buy a package from one of the many tour companies specialising in walking holidays. Planning your own holiday can be great fun and can be tailored precisely to your own needs. It involves poring over maps, guides, timetables and accommodation directories which on long winter evenings can be almost as enjoyable as the holiday itself.

On no account plan a walking holiday for which you do not have the requisite experience. However alluring it may seem, do not attempt to backpack the Pennine Way or undertake a strenuous Alpine walk if you have never tackled anything more demanding than day walks in the

Cotswolds. Even if you are young and strong the chances are that you will have a miserable time because you will lack the requisite stamina and experience, and if in a group, suffer the humiliation of being left behind by much older walkers. On the other hand, a centre-based holiday in the Lake District or in an Alpine village offering easy mountain paths should prove very enjoyable and extend your walking experience.

Packaged walking holidays offer several advantages. First you have only to decide which one you want, book it and follow the instructions on how to join the party; all the planning is done for you. Second, you should get like-minded, friendly people as companions (this appeals particularly to single persons). Third, on many walking tours the luggage is taken by van and walkers only have to carry day packs. Fourth, the party should have a leader who is experienced, knowledgeable and know the area well. Some organisations like the Holiday Fellowship and the CHA actually own the premises used for their holidays. They are often similar to country hotels and as they can accommodate a large number of people, there is a wide range of activities and a choice of walks of varying degrees of difficulty. Thus it is possible to start the holiday with easy walks and gradually progress to more difficult routes. The Youth Hostels Association (see Youth Hostels Association, Scottish Youth Hostels Association and Youth Hostels Association of Northern Ireland in Appendix 2) which, despite their names, cater for persons of all ages, provide inexpensive and not too spartan accommodation, as well as organising walking holidays. It should be noted that some of these organisations are 'dry' and do not permit alcoholic drinks on their premises. There are now many organisations and businesses that offer courses on hill-walking, survival and related subjects and as these are always located in upland areas it is possible not only to enjoy a good holiday but also to extend your walking experience and improve your skills (see pp96-7).

The leader can make or break a holiday especially on a tour where it is difficult to escape from him. Many leaders are unpaid and recruited by the tour company with the offer of a free holiday. Sometimes leaders do not know the area, because they are only interested in visiting new places, and rely on their map-reading skills, itineraries issued by the tour operator and reports of previous leaders. Some leaders are very good indeed but a few are dreadful and there have been cases where a party has deposed an incompetent leader and appointed another from among themselves. The duties of a leader can be onerous. Not only must he be a knowledgeable and experienced walker and navigator familiar with the kind of terrain in which he is leading, but he must also be a diplomat, a linguist (if leading foreign tours), and at all times be cheerful and encouraging. He must know the signs that indicate that a person is concealing distress, set a reasonable pace suitable for the experience of the party, and be possessed of sound judgement and good social skills. A leader should command by example and be strong-minded enough not to be persuaded into a course of action that he knows is unwise, and have sufficient tact and moral authority to carry the party with him.

These are formidable qualities for which, in most cases, he will receive neither training, guidance nor reasonable recompense from the tour company. It is likely that he will be interviewed briefly by somebody in the company and if he appears suitable, and is free on the dates that a leader is required, he will be appointed. I have led tours for many years and I have had to watch helplessly as other leaders have taken their innocent charges into considerable danger. In Switzerland, I once saw a party organised by a well-known tour company being led over a dangerously steep snowfield. The line taken by the leader was wrong, nobody in the party had ice-axes or crampons, and even after three people had fallen and slid fifty metres until stopped by rocks, the leader was still calling for the rest of the party to follow.

A common failing, especially in younger leaders, is a tendency to look down on their clients. All leaders should remember that members of the party have paid for their holiday and are entitled to be treated with dignity and respect. One leader is notorious in the tour business for humiliating his clients by making them ford a waist-deep icy river despite there being a perfectly good bridge 400 metres upstream. He believes it is good for their souls to be uncomfortable.

A good leader must sometimes be firm. If a member of the party has chosen a holiday that is beyond his physical ability, then it would be wrong for the leader to tailor the routes to suit the convenience of the weak member. Those who have chosen their holiday correctly are entitled to expect the holiday that they bought. In such cases, it is the duty of the leader to take action and it is usually possible to put the matter tactfully and in such a way that the client suggests the solution himself. On the few occasions that I have had to intervene I have invariably found the decision greeted with relief and the client has been content to explore some easier routes on his own.

The leader should be aware of the social side of the holiday and must do his best to keep everybody happy. A good way of breaking the ice on the first night of the tour is for the leader to say a few words about himself and invite each member to introduce themselves by giving their name, where they come from, occupation etc. The leader should try to avoid petty antagonisms developing, and if a member of the group seems unpopular, then it is the leader's responsibility to do his best to prevent him from becoming isolated. Single ladies often feel vulnerable, and the leader should see that they are not subjected to unwelcome advances, but if the attraction is mutual then it is not the leader's concern. At least two of the holiday romances on tours that I have led have blossomed into marriage (including my own!).

The brochure issued by the company should describe the holidays offered accurately and in detail. Most have their own grading system that describes the degree of difficulty and should include not only the average distance covered and the total height gained each day, but also the kind of terrain and whether the paths are clearly defined or any scrambling is involved. It should also state the maximum number in each party (which should not, for the more demanding walks, exceed ten, plus the leader), the meal plan and the type of accommodation.

Generally speaking, a domestic do-it-yourself walking holiday is cheaper than a comparable package deal (but remember that you don't have a leader), but companies operating overseas tours can save so much of the scheduled air fare by using charter flights that it would be difficult for an individual to plan a similar holiday at comparable cost.

In 1980 there were relatively few companies in the package walking tour business, but since then the number has mushroomed, more appear every year and it seems doubtful whether the market is large enough to keep them all in business. Some of them are very small and run as part-time ventures. As there are no laws or regulations covering this kind of business anybody can operate walking tours from his home. The only outlay required is money for a brochure and advertising. In response to the unregulated growth of outdoor-activity tour operators, the British Activity Holiday Association (see p293) was founded in 1986. It requires its members to abide by the Association's *Code of Practice* which has been approved by the Office of Fair Trading. The *Code of Practice*, with its emphasis on learning and education, seems particularly applicable to those organisations that cater for young people. In 1988 the Association had one hundred members, of which four could be classed as specialising in walking tours. Note that BAHA only concerns itself with holidays in the United Kingdom and does not monitor overseas tours.

The best sources of information about firms offering walking holidays are listed in the bibliography at the end of the chapter and the advertisements carried by the walking magazines listed in Appendix 1. *Country Walking* carries an annual Holiday Supplement in the January issue. Some of the more up-market companies advertise in the quality Sunday newspapers.

After you have written for and received the brochures that interest you, examine them carefully and make a shortlist of possible holidays. Before making the final choice do not hesitate to make further enquiries of the company. Most of them are small organisations and are usually happy to answer your questions by letter or telephone. If in doubt, question them carefully especially about the leaders they recruit, and their qualifications!

Bibliography

Activity and Hobby Holidays, published annually by James of Fleet Street Ltd., in association with the English Tourist Board. (NB this directory covers England only.)

Nineham, Gillian, Editor, *Adventure Holidays,* published annually by Vacation Work.

Shales, M., Editor, *The Traveller's Handbook,* Heinemann in association with Wexas, 5th Rev. Ed., 1987.

SECTION 2: THE LEGAL ASPECTS OF WALKING

9 Behaviour in the Countryside

Every square centimetre of this beautiful country of ours is owned by someone. There is no such thing as waste ground; there is only land that is not well kept and thus becomes derelict. Whenever you are out walking you are crossing land that belongs to someone. He will have a great interest in it, as it probably provides his livelihood. Because this is so, there is sometimes a conflict of interests between the farmer or landowner, who is naturally interested in the efficient use of the land, and those who seek their recreation in the countryside. These interests are not always easy to harmonise. Matters would be less difficult if more walkers had some understanding of modern farming methods and the ways of the countryside and if farmers paid more attention to their legal obligations towards footpaths and bridleways.

Beauty is said to be in the eye of the beholder, and the sight of a field of golden corn or a herd of fat bullocks is more pleasing to a farmer than a barren fellside or inhospitable mountain. A farmer wants to improve the land until it will bear crops and he has little sympathy with those conservationists who want to leave certain areas in their wild state.

Barbed Wire and Electric Fences
Barbed wire is a perennial problem for walkers, yet it is the farmer's friend. He uses wire because farm animals like to push against obstacles in the hope of breaking through; barbed wire and electric fences prevent them from pushing. Farmers with attested herds of cattle have to prevent the possibility of infection from a neighbouring herd by double fencing, and barbed wire provides the ideal answer. Nevertheless, barbed wire without

proper access through it constitutes an obstruction and is illegal on the line of a path. The problem can be overcome by the provision of a stile or gate through the fence or by a 'hoosier'. In this device, the fence has a movable post with a loop of wire on it which drops over a fixed post, thus allowing the walker to undo the wire and fasten it again behind him. Electric fences and single-strand barbed-wire can be sleeved with rubber hose.

Damage

Farming is very capital-intensive and there is often a lot of expensive machinery lying around unattended. This makes some farmers feel very vulnerable and they fear that large groups of people crossing their land may damage machinery, crops and stock. In my experience, most farmers are friendly towards individual walkers but suspicious of large groups. It is one of the curiosities of human nature that people in groups tend not to behave quite as well as each one of them would individually. Large numbers of people walking together can cause considerable damage unless they walk considerately. Forty people climbing over a field gate rather than bothering to open it will not improve it, especially if it is climbed at the latched end so that the full weight is taken on the hinges. A 63 kilogram person climbing a gate 3 metres long with hinges 0.75 metres apart will exert a leverage of 500 kilograms on the hinges. No gate can stand this kind of misuse for long. The same group walking carelessly four or five abreast will damage wet pasture; for too many walkers fail to recognize that grass is a valuable crop.

Dogs

The legislation covering paths does not include any mention of dogs, but in the case of *Regina* versus *Matthias* in 1861 it was held to be legal to push a pram on a public footpath, providing the path was physically capable of accommodating the pram, on the grounds that a pram was a 'natural accompaniment' of a pedestrian. Presumably, the argument could be extended to include dogs. But dogs can be a menace to stock, for it is a natural instinct in most dogs to chase anything that is nervous of them. Apart from the obvious danger that this will encourage the dog to worry sheep and perhaps eventually kill, there is a serious risk of dairy cows going dry and of pregnant animals aborting. Even the best-behaved dog must be kept on a leash when there is stock about. Under the Farm Animals Act, 1971, farmers have a right, under certain circumstances, to shoot dogs found worrying animals if that is the only way to prevent it happening. I know of one case where a farmer found a pedigree dog chasing his sheep and warned the owner that the dog would be shot if found worrying stock again. The owner indicated that only a barbarian would shoot such a valuable animal and he would have no hesitation in suing if the farmer were to be so foolish. A few days later, a Landrover drew up at the owner's home and the bodies of a sheep, horribly mutilated, and the shot dog were deposited on the front doorstep. No legal action was taken because the farmer was acting within his rights.

Fires

In many people's minds there is a romantic view of backwoodsmen sitting round a camp fire cooking their evening meal. This indeed is common practice in the wilderness areas of the United States and is perfectly proper there, but make a golden rule *never* to light fires in this country. It is a practice fraught with danger practically anywhere except perhaps on the beach. Lighting fires in cultivated country is unforgivable and is done only by the ignorant and stupid. A farmer finding anyone lighting fires on his land is likely to hand out a tongue lashing which will not easily be forgotten. Irresponsible behaviour will quickly alienate sympathetic farmers. As we have seen, if hot food is needed there are many lightweight portable stoves on the market which can be used in complete safety. All modern stoves burn clean fuel so they have the added advantage over camp fires in that they do not soil the outside of the cooking utensils.

Litter

The litter sometimes to be found in popular walking areas is a disgrace to the walking fraternity. A civilised person never deposits litter.

Pubs

Part of the pleasure of walking is the occasional visit to a country pub. Walkers are likely to arrive travel-stained, with muddy boots and perhaps soaking wet, for a friendly pub is a pleasant haven in the rain. Some landlords welcome walkers but others prefer not to have them as they are trying to attract a different clientele. It is their privilege to do this as they are not obliged to serve anyone if they do not wish to. Most landlords insist that large rucksacks must be left outside. Groups of walkers are likely to be high-spirited and noisy, which may not matter in a bar frequented by walkers but would not be popular in a quiet country pub where the locals are likely to resent any hint of rowdyism.

Farm Animals

It is surprising how many people are nervous of cattle. Apart from bulls, and cows with newly-born calves, cattle are normally absolutely harmless but very inquisitive. Heifers and bullocks in particular are skittish and will come galloping across the field to investigate strangers, but they will come skidding to a halt a few yards away and will then follow at a safe distance. Dogs can be an embarassment because cattle will often form a defensive ring and attempt to menace the dog. Very occasionally horses may kick or bite, pigs are reputed to be able to inflict a savage bite, rams and billy goats can be belligerent and geese noisy and aggressive, but I have never heard of a walker being attacked by these animals.

Bulls are the most dangerous animals to be found on farms. No bull is to be trusted, but the most dangerous are the dairy breeds, particularly Friesians, Jerseys and Guernseys. Bulls usually signify their annoyance by a roaring or bellowing noise which is quite different from the lowing of cows. The safest thing to do if a bull is encountered is to get out of the field fast without attracting the attention of the animal. All cattle are interested in humans and it does not follow that a bull is threatening merely because it comes towards you, but the wise take no chances! Fortunately, the bull is a clumsy animal and, providing you keep calm, it should be possible to dodge if it does charge. Walkers should take comfort from the fact that in the past twenty years no one, other than farm workers, has been killed by a bull.

Occasionally, the walker will discover farm animals in trouble. Unless it is easy to do something for them, like releasing them from a wire fence, it is better to inform the nearest farm. Make a note of the exact position of the animal and of any identification marks so that a clear description can be given to the farmer. If it is not his animal he will know to whom it belongs and will telephone him. Sometimes lambs appear to be lost and will be found bleating piteously, but do not touch them because the mother is almost certain to be nearby and if her lamb is moved she may never find it.

Sheep sometimes get onto their broad flat backs and are unable to regain their feet. To right the animal, kneel beside it and seize one front leg and pull it across its chest. This will bring the animal onto its side and it will be able to get to its feet.

Diseases of Animals

All farm animals are subject to disease. The most virulent and feared are brucellosis, foot and mouth disease, fowl pest, and swine vesicular disease. Under the Animal Health Act, 1981, temporary orders extinguishing rights of way may be made, but in any case considerate walkers will avoid areas known to be affected and respect notices forbidding entry because of disease. Unless there is an outbreak of disease there is no likelihood of walkers spreading infection except by inexcusable behaviour such as leaving gates open. Rational arguments that no order has been made forbidding the use of paths during an outbreak of disease are unlikely to convince a farmer desperately worried about losing his stock and livelihood. Farmers grow attached to their animals and have enormous justifiable pride in the splendid pedigree animals that they rear; never put them at risk.

Brucellosis or contagious abortion is a disease which affects cattle, causing cows to abort, and it may be responsible for undulant fever in humans if the untreated milk of infected cows is drunk. The disease can be carried by dogs, by wild animals and by boots which have come into contact with an infected foetus or afterbirth. A government scheme exists for the eradication of brucellosis which registers herds which are free from the disease and which are constantly tested to ensure their continual freedom. Attested herds have to be separated from other cattle by double fencing and this is one of the main reasons for refraining from cutting barbed wire obstructing paths. It is much better to take the matter up with the farmer, County Council or Parish Council as detailed in Chapter 10.

Foot and mouth disease is a highly infectious disease of cattle, sheep and pigs. Infected animals become feverish, develop blisters in the mouth and on the feet, readily salivate and become lame. It is a notifiable disease and is controlled by the wholesale slaughter of cattle, sheep and pigs on the premises, whether or not they are infected, and the movement of animals for a very wide area around the infected herd is prohibited. The speed with which the disease can spread is frightening and during the bad outbreak of 1967–8 thousands of beasts were destroyed and their carcasses burned in huge funeral pyres. The virus is very tenacious and can be spread by wind, rain and snow. Walkers should be aware that it can be spread by clothing, especially by boots, and paths in infected areas should never be used during the outbreak.

Fowl pest is a disease of poultry spread by a highly infectious virus. Since vaccination against the disease is now widespread, it is much less common than once it was. Fowl pest can be spread by clothing and walkers should avoid infected farms and broiler houses.

Swine vesicular disease is very similar to foot and mouth disease but is peculiar to pigs and first occurred in this country in 1972. The only way to control an outbreak is to slaughter all pigs on the premises and to control the movement of pigs. It is considered possible to transmit the disease on clothing, so walkers should avoid infected areas.

Trespass

In many parts of England and Wales, it is quite normal for some villagers to roam at will through the fields. They have no right to do this except with the permission of the landowner, but they are tolerated because they are country folk who would never walk where they would cause damage. Walkers sometimes meet them in the fields and may be puzzled when informed that they go where they like, for it must be a fundamental rule, strictly adhered to by all walkers, *never* to stray from the right of way without the express permission of the farmer or landowner. Few farmers are likely to object to picnicking in pasture near the line of the path but the considerate person will leave no trace of his meal behind him. Animals may die if they swallow plastic bags and be severely injured by tin cans and broken bottles. Keep a plastic bag in your rucksack so that you can carry your litter home and dispose of it properly.

Anyone who strays from the line of the path is trespassing unless it is necessary to circumvent an obstruction caused by the landowner, but this does not entitle a walker to trespass on the property of another landowner. Trespassing is not normally an offence punishable at law but is a civil wrong or 'tort', and anyone causing damage in the course of trespassing can be sued. It is also possible for a landowner to obtain an injunction to prevent trespass and sue for damages even if no harm has been done. Landowners have a right to insist that trespassers leave their land, or return to the right of way, and may use any reasonable and necessary force to compel them.

It is comparatively rare for walkers using rights of way to be approached by landowners and told that they are trespassing. Providing you are absolutely sure of your facts, and especially if you have a copy of the Definitive Map with you (see pp124-5) and have checked with the local authority that there has been no extinguishment or diversion, you should discuss the matter courteously and, if agreement cannot be reached, politely but firmly insist on using the public path. But if the situation gets out of hand, it is probably better to ask for the name and address of the landowner and of the person who actually stops you and report the matter in detail to the local authority.

In Scotland the law of trespass is different. It is not possible for a landowner to sue for trespass unless he can prove that damage has occurred, that the trespass took place in the pursuit of game, or that some other offence was committed. The only remedy available to the landowner is to require the trespasser to leave his land or return to the right of way, and if necessary, may use reasonable force to compel him. The practical result is that walkers in Scotland have much greater freedom to roam than they do in England and Wales, and are unlikely to be challenged either when using a path or track, or when traversing pathless, uncultivated country.

Wild Flowers and Fruits

Wild flowers must never be picked, but it is permissible to take wild fruits under certain conditions. Mushrooms etc. which grow on the line of the path may be taken, but you can be sued for damages by the landowner if you take anything from his land that is not on the line of the path. However, it is apparently not stealing to take wild mushrooms and fruits even if they are not on the path unless you sell them for gain or reward. In practice, of course, it is customary for blackberries to be picked from hedgerows, sometimes in large quantities, and very few landowners would object, but some farmers get very cross if the mushrooms they were expecting for their own breakfast are taken. Never, under any circumstances, pick anything cultivated, not even a single ear of corn.

The Country Code

The guide to good behaviour is the Country Code which, unfortunately, is curiously worded and needs some explanation.

1. *Enjoy the countryside and respect its life and work*.

2. *Guard against all risks of fire*. Never light fires and always break your dead matches in half to make certain that they are out.

3. *Fasten all gates*. Unless you find an open gate secured. Never swing on gates and if they will not open climb them only at the hinge end.

4. *Keep your dogs under close control*. Exceptionally obedient dogs may not need to be on a leash when there is no stock about but *all* dogs *must* be on a leash in the presence of farm animals and game.

5. *Keep to public paths across farmland*. Always keep to the path unless walking in an area where access agreements have been negotiated.

6. *Use gates and stiles to cross fences, hedges and walls*. Dry stone walls are very vulnerable. Never climb them or remove any stones from them. Building and repairing dry stone walls is a highly skilled craft.

7. *Leave livestock, crops and machinery alone*.

8. *Take your litter home*. Cans and bottles can injure the feet of animals and plastic bags can be fatal if swallowed. The Americans sum it up in a great phrase: 'Pack your trash'. You brought the rubbish, so take it home again!

9. *Protect wild life, wild plants and trees*. Never pick flowers or dig them up. Never damage trees or carve into the bark and never interfere with nests or take eggs.

10. *Take special care on country roads*. Drive carefully and if on foot always keep in single file facing oncoming traffic.

11. *Make no unnecessary noise*.

10 Rights of Way in England and Wales

There are about 217,000 kilometres of public paths in England and Wales forming a dense network that covers the two countries (Scotland, too, is criss-crossed by public paths but as that country has a different legal system, the subject is dealt with in Chapter 11). John Hillaby in his book *Journey through Britain* and Hamish Brown in *Hamish's Groats End Walk* have shown that it is possible to walk the length and breadth of our beautiful land almost entirely on public paths. The path network is a priceless historical and recreational heritage that must always be safeguarded. Anyone who has lived in the United States knows that there is nothing comparable there, and city-dwelling American walkers often have to drive eighty kilometres and more to a state or national park in order to find a network of trails. In some cases they may have to pay an entrance fee and even obtain a permit if they wish to backpack.

Paths were established in prehistoric times long before the Romans built our first proper road system. They were used for trading purposes and linked centres where the essentials of prehistoric life were to be found—salt, flint, pottery etc. Normally, they follow high-level routes—travelling was easier on hills because the low-lying land had not yet been drained. The long-distance Ridgeway Path follows a prehistoric trading route for part of its length, from Avebury in Wiltshire to Ivinghoe in Buckinghamshire. During the Middle Ages, the land was drained and reclaimed from the forest which, to a large extent, covered the country and then paths were used as a means of getting about the countryside by the shortest route. Most walkers will have observed that paths usually provide the more direct route from village to village and often are considerably shorter than the road route.

From the nineteenth century onwards, paths were also used for recreation. The novels of Jane Austen and Thomas Hardy abound in references to walks being taken for recreational purposes on public paths. During those dreadful years between the two world wars, thousands of the unemployed left the industrial cities of the north each weekend to forget their unhappy lot for a while by walking the hills of Yorkshire, Derbyshire and Northumbria. Many of the battles to gain access to the moors were won at this time by men being prepared to go to prison rather than be excluded from some of the fells.

Definitive Maps

In the immediate post-war years, the government decided to tidy the jungle of case law which largely governed the use of paths. The National Parks and Access to the Countryside Act, 1949 laid upon the County Councils a statutory duty to compile and publish Definitive Maps showing all public paths on a scale not less than 1:25000. The County Council normally invited each parish council to survey the paths in its parish and from this information the Draft Map was compiled and published.

At this stage, it was possible to assert that a path shown on the Draft Map was not a right of way and had only been used by the public with the permission of the landowner. In some cases, the exact line of the right of way was disputed. Did it go one side or the other of a hedge? It was possible, also, to get paths not shown on the Draft Map included as rights of way, for the person who had supplied the information about paths in the parish perhaps had been unaware that this particular path had been used by the public as a right of way.

The evidence was then sifted and negotiations took place between the interested parties on any points in dispute. If it was not possible to resolve any dispute by negotiation, a public inquiry was held by an Inspector appointed by the Minister of Town and Country Planning. The Inspector submitted the results of his inquiry to the Minister, who made a decision in the light of the evidence. The Provisional Map was then published incorporating all the decisions made resulting from the publication of the Draft Map.

After the publication of the Provisional Map, a period of twenty-eight days was allowed for landlords and tenants to object to the inclusion on the map of paths which crossed their land. Any objections were heard at the Quarter Sessions with the highway authority defending the case.

After any objections had been determined the County Council then published the Definitive Map.

The importance of the Definitive Map cannot be exaggerated. It provides conclusive evidence in law of the existence of a right of way at the time the map was made. A path that appears on the Definitive Map is always a right of way, even if it was included by mistake, unless an extinguishment or diversion is granted, which can only be done by due legal process. Even though a path may be overgrown with vegetation, obstructed by barbed wire, have houses built across it and be ploughed up, there is still a right to use it, and the local authority, which has a statutory duty 'to assert and protect the rights of the public to the use and enjoyment of all highways and to prevent, as far as possible, the stopping-up or obstruction of those highways', can use its powers to have the path opened for public use.

The Definitive Map can be seen at the County Council offices, usually in the Surveyor's Department. The local public library may well have a copy and in any case will be able to tell you where a copy may be seen.

Some counties use the 1:25000 map, others prefer the 1:10560 or 1:10000 map. Whichever map is used, footpaths and bridleways are drawn in and allocated a number which is usually done parish by parish. Thus, each path can be readily identified—for example, Aylesbury 7. Counties which use the 1:25000 map often publish copies for sale to the public. Unfortunately, with a map of this scale it is not always entirely clear exactly where the path runs unless the rights of way have been drawn meticulously. If the Definitive Map is based on the 1:10560 or 1:10000 map, there should never be any doubt of the true line of the path, but it is more difficult to publish that map for sale to the public.

When local government was re-organised in 1974, County Councils were allowed to enter into agreements with District Councils to delegate some or all of their functions. It is possible to establish the practice in any given authority by inquiring from the County Surveyor or at the public library. Details of diversion and extinguishment orders made since the Definitive Map was made can usually be obtained from the County Council.

Rights of way are shown on the following Ordnance Survey maps: 1:25000 Pathfinder, 1:50000 Landranger and 1:63360 Tourist. In cultivated country where diversions and extinguishments are much more common, it is essential to use the 1:25000 map for walking.

Rationalisation of Public Paths

The National Farmers' Union is committed to a rationalisation of the footpath and bridleway network which would result in far fewer paths especially in lowland cultivated areas. It is argued that the existing pattern of paths is not necessary, as few people use them and they are inimical to efficient agriculture. The problem needs to be considered carefully, and the natural instinct of most walkers to reject out of hand the concept of rationalisation is probably unwise. Walkers with an intimate knowledge of paths in an intensively farmed area know that where fields are crossed by two or more paths, as sometimes happens (I know of one five hectare field with no less than five paths across it!), a slight re-arrangement can often be made without detriment to recreational interests. The claim that paths should be extinguished if nobody uses them cannot be taken seriously if the paths concerned are not restored after ploughing, are obstructed by barbed wire and growing crops, and have bulls loose on them. Experience shows that paths are well used in those parts of the country where farmers observe the law meticulously and fulfil their legal obligations towards public paths.

There are varying and often exaggerated opinions as to how much farming land is 'lost' to public paths. At the 1974 Annual General Meeting of the Commons, Open Spaces and Footpaths Preservation Society, the then Vice President of the NFU stated that public paths in England and Wales occupy 200,000 hectares of good land and that the production of food must take priority over public paths. This statement was later admitted to be inaccurate. It is generally agreed that there are about 200,000 kilometres of public paths in England and Wales, so according to NFU arithmetic, assuming that all land occupied by paths were capable of being cultivated, every path, on average, would have to be 12 metres wide! The true figure is difficult to calculate accurately because many paths cross non-productive land such as moorland, fell and common, and some paths are used as tractor trails by the farmer himself. An estimate of 12,000 hectares of productive land 'lost' to public paths is probably much nearer the truth, which is the area covered by one hundred medium-sized farms—a small price to pay for such a valuable amenity which can be used by the whole population.

Definitions

The terms *highway* and *public right of way* are roughly synonymous and denote a route over which the public have the right of passage. Where the terms are used without qualification they include all highways and public rights of way from footpaths to motorways.

The following terms are defined in the Wildlife and Countryside Act, 1981:

Footpath: means a highway over which the public have the right of way on foot only, other than such a highway at the side of the road.

Bridleway: means a highway over which the public have the following, but no other, rights of way, that is to say, a right of way on foot and a right of way on horseback or leading a horse, with or without a right to drive animals of any description along the highway. (Note that the Countryside

Act, 1968 Section 30 allows the riding of bicycles on bridleways providing that they give way to horse riders and pedestrians. The local authority has the power to make bye-laws prohibiting the riding of bicycles on any particular highway.)

Byway open to all traffic: means a highway over which the public have a right of way for vehicular and all other kinds of traffic, but is used mainly by the public for the purpose for which footpaths and bridleways are so used.

Public path: means a highway being either a footpath or a bridleway.

Road used as a public path (RUPP): this was defined under the National Parks and Access to the Countryside Act, 1949 as a highway, other than a public path, used by the public mainly for the purpose for which footpaths and bridleways are so used. Under the Wildlife and Countryside Act, 1981 every RUPP must be reclassified either as a byway open to all traffic, or as a bridleway, or as a footpath.

Rights of Way Maps

Under the provisions of the National Parks and Access to the Countryside Act, 1949 County Councils were required to prepare Definitive Maps of footpaths and bridleways. If a public path is shown on the Definitive Map, that is conclusive evidence in law (even if the path was included in error) of the existence of that right of way unless a diversion or extinguishment has been granted by due legal process (see below). The Wildlife and Countryside Act, 1981 placed a duty on surveying authorities to bring their Definitive Maps up to date and to maintain them as changes occur.

Diversion and Extinguishment of Paths

It is necessary from time to time for paths to be diverted or extinguished to allow development to take place, or for the land to be used more efficiently. In order to maintain the path network it is essential that any attempt to divert or extinguish a path without authority should be vigorously opposed, otherwise the changes will not appear on maps and a great deal of ill-will and confusion will be caused. Paths may only be diverted or extinguished by due legal process, the most important of which, are set out below:

Highways Act, 1980, Section 118: This enables a local authority (including a National Park) to close a public path if it is not necessary for public use.

Highways Act, 1980, Section 119: This enables a local authority (including a National Park) to divert a public path in the interests of the owner, lessee, or occupier of land crossed by a public path or way, or the public.

Highways Act, 1980, Section 116: This section of the Act is used primarily for downgrading a bridleway to a footpath or for removing vehicular rights from a public road. It is rarely used for straightforward extinguishments or diversions because interested parties have the power of veto. Under this section of the Act, a Highway Authority may make an application to a magistrates court for an order:

(a) to extinguish a highway, other than a classified road, on the grounds that it is unnecessary.

(b) to divert a highway, other than a classified road, so as to make it more commodious for the public.

The Highway Authority must inform the District Council, the Parish Council, Community Council, or the Chairman of the Parish Meeting, of its intention to apply for an order. If any of the above bodies object to the application, then the Highway Authority cannot proceed. Any objectors must appear personally before the magistrates to state their case.

Town and Country Planning Act 1971, Section 211: This section of the Act allows the Secretary of State to authorise the stopping up or diversion of any highway that crosses or enters the route of the highway under construction.

Town and Country Planning Act, 1971, Section 214: allows the Secretary of State to extinguish any public right of way and a local authority to extinguish a footpath or bridleway on land held by a local authority for planning purposes. The Secretary of State has to be satisfied that an alternative right of way has been, or will be, provided.

The actual procedures for diverting and extinguishing paths vary a little according to particular circumstances but usually conform to the following general pattern:

1. If the County Council makes the order it must consult the District Council.

2. If the District Council makes the order it must consult the County Council.

3. If the path is within a National Park the body making the order must consult the Countryside Commission.

4. The order must be advertised in at least one local newspaper and at the ends of the sections of the path affected and in certain circumstances in the *London Gazette.*

5. The advertisement must state the general effect of the order and must indicate where a map showing the path in question can be inspected and allow at least twenty-eight days for objections to be filed.

6. A copy of the order must be sent to the Parish or Community Council within whose area any part of the path affected lies and also to any interested parties including certain specified amenity bodies such as the

Ramblers' Association and the Open Spaces Society.

7. If no objections are received within the twenty-eight days allowed or if any objections made are subsequently withdrawn, the authority making the order can confirm the order.

8. If objections are made, the matter is referred to the Secretary of State for the Environment who may appoint an inspector and hold a public enquiry or may deal with the matter in other ways.

9. The inspector will then announce his decision.

Creation of Paths

Although England and Wales are blessed with a very dense network of footpaths and bridleways, it is sometimes necessary to create paths. The most usual cases are short stretches to link existing rights of way for long-distance paths and occasionally, where the changing pattern of land use makes it desirable, for a new path to be created either by agreement or order to link with existing paths and thus preserve the path network.

The authority making the creation agreement or order, which may be a County Council, District Council or a National Park Board, must bear the following considerations in mind: (a) the extent to which the path would add to the convenience or enjoyment of a substantial section of the public, or to the convenience of local residents; (b) the effect the path will have on the rights of persons interested in the land.

As far as possible new paths are created by agreement and the number of creation orders is very small. Compensation must be paid to the landowner if a path is created.

If a path is created by order, the procedure for advertising and objecting is similar to that for extinguishing and diverting paths.

Gates and Stiles

Under Section 146 of the Highways Act, 1980, landowners have a legal duty to maintain in good condition all gates and stiles crossed by public paths. The highway authority is under an obligation to contribute at least 25% of the approved cost of the work. If the work is not done, the highway authority can do what is necessary and charge the cost to the landowner. All gates on bridleways must be capable of being opened by a rider without dismounting, and stiles must not be built across bridleways.

Obstructions

There is no statutory definition of an obstruction but there are two useful judicial definitions. In *Seekings v Clarke (1961)* Lord Chief Justice Parker remarked 'It is perfectly clear that anything which substantially prevents the public from having free access over the whole of the highway which is not purely temporary in nature is an unlawful obstruction.' Mr Justice

Byles in *R v Matthias (1861)* stated 'A nuisance to a way is that which prevents the convenient use of the way by passengers.'

Highway authorities have a statutory duty to prevent obstructions. Under the Highway Act, 1980, section 130 (1) they have a duty to protect and assert the rights of the public to the use and enjoyment of the highways for which they are the highway authority. Under section 130 (3) they must prevent the stopping up or obstruction of those highways. Highway authorities may enforce the law through the courts or, after serving notice and getting no response, they may do what is necessary themselves and recover the cost from the landowner.

In certain circumstances walkers may remove obstacles from the line of the path providing they remove no more than is actually necessary and also providing that they did not undertake the journey with the specific intention of dealing with the obstruction. Walkers are advised to use this right with great circumspection.

Ploughing

Under section 134 of the Highways Act 1980 as amended by section 61 of the Wildlife and Countryside Act 1981 a farmer may, in the interests of good husbandry, plough footpaths and bridleways (except headland paths) but not paths with vehicular rights over them. The surface must be made good within two weeks of ploughing or, if the weather makes that impossible, as soon as practicable.

In certain circumstances farmers may have a common law right to plough headland paths, but if this is not recorded in the statement accompanying the definitive map, then the onus of proof lies with the farmer.

Highway authorities, district and local councils have the right to prosecute farmers who fail to restore the surface of the path after ploughing. Alternatively they may, after serving notice on the farmer, restore the surface of the path themselves and charge the cost to the offender.

The law on ploughing and obstruction has been strengthened by the Rights of Way Act, 1990. The surface of any path that has been disturbed (e.g. by ploughing of harrowing) must be made good for the reasonable convenience of users. Cross-field footpaths must be at least 1 metre wide; cross-field bridleways must be at least 2 metres wide; headland footpaths must be at least 1.5 metres wide; and headland bridleways at least 3 metres wide. Crops, except grass, must be prevented from growing or falling over the line of the path. Local authorities have the right to restore the line of the path after giving the landowner 24 hours notice and to charge him for any costs incurred.

Bulls

Under section 59 of the Wildlife and Countryside Act 1981 farmers may pasture beef breed bulls that are accompanied by cows or heifers in fields crossed by public paths. It is illegal to pasture bulls more than ten months old of recognised dairy breeds such as Ayrshire, British Friesian, British Holstein, Dairy Shorthorn, Guernsey, Jersey and Kerry in fields crossed by public paths.

Dangerous Animals

It is an offence to have an animal known to be dangerous (including beef breed bulls) in fields crossed by public paths. Under section 2 of the Animals Act 1971 the keeper of a bull is liable for damages if it injures a path user and the keeper knew that it was dangerous. Section 3 of the Health and Safety at Work Act 1974 requires employers and employees not to put third parties at risk.

Waymarking and Signposting

Waymarking may be defined as marking the course of the route at points along it. Waymarking is complementary to signposting, which is normally reserved for the points where a path makes a junction with a road. Signposts advertise a path and its initial direction; waymarks enable users to follow the path accurately at points where they might otherwise have difficulty.

Under Section 27 of the Countryside Act, 1968 as amended by Section 65 of the Wildlife and Countryside Act, 1981 a highway authority has the duty to erect and maintain a signpost where a footpath, bridleway or byway leaves a metalled road and must indicate the classification of the right of way. Should the highway authority not wish to erect a signpost it must first obtain the consent of the parish council (or the chairman of the parish meeting if there is no council). If the parish insists on the provision of the signpost then the highway authority is required to provide one.

The highway authority has a duty to erect signposts along the route of a path if it thinks them necessary. Before doing so, it must consult the owner or occupier of the land concerned and obtain his consent.

The Countryside Commission has issued recommendations on the design of waymarks which have been widely accepted and adopted (see Fig. 41). The colours from British Standard range 4800 should be:

yellow 08 E 51 for footpaths

blue 20 E 51 for bridleways

red 06 E55 for byways open to all traffic

It should be noted that the permission of the landowner and the highway authority should be obtained before undertaking waymarking because it is

Fig. 41 The waymark symbol

an offence under Section 132 of the Highways Act, 1980 to inscribe, paint or affix without lawful authority any picture, letter, sign or other mark upon the surface of a highway or upon any tree, structure or works in the highway.

Footbridges

Under section 328 (2) of the Highways Act, 1980 the highway authority has a general duty to maintain most bridges. However, if another authority such as Britrail or British Waterways is responsible for the bridge then the duty of maintaining it falls on them.

Misleading Notices

Under section 57 of the National Parks and Access to the Countryside Act, 1949, it is an offence to display a notice containing a misleading statement likely to deter the public from using a public path. Thus it is an offence to erect a notice warning 'Beware of the bull' if there is never a bull in that field. Notices such as 'Trespassers will be prosecuted' and 'Private road' are more difficult to deal with. The walker who strays from a path *is* trespassing and the road *may* be private but have a right of way on foot over it. One possible solution is for the County Council to erect a footpath sign near the notice.

Enforcement of the Law

As can be seen from the above outline, much of the law relating to public paths is clear, unambiguous and fairly easily comprehended. Unfortunately, the mere existence of a law does not carry the guarantee that it will be obeyed, and there is no doubt that, in many parts of the country, path law is largely ignored. How, then, can pressure be brought to bear on those who are not carrying out their legal obligations?

The following authorities have a statutory duty to assert and protect the rights of those who use public paths. In Greater London it is the London

Borough Councils; in the former Metropolitan Counties it is the District Councils; and everywhere else in England and Wales it is the County Councils. A stranger or occasional visitor has little choice but to write to the council concerned giving details of the problem quoting, if possible, the parish and path number and certainly giving the grid reference (see pp48-9). Sooner or later, the council will take some kind of action, but it must be remembered that in most counties the paths section of the Highways Department is likely to be very understaffed.

A local person can do a lot more, and there are several lines of action which can be taken. If a farmer or landowner is at fault, he can be approached direct by telephone or letter. If it is not known to whom the land belongs an intelligent guess can be made by relating gates and farm tracks to a particular farm and establishing the name of the farm from the map. The local public library will provide you with the name of the occupier of the farm from the electoral roll. A polite and carefully worded letter or telephone call suggesting that the problem may be on their land will often produce results. Parish Councils can also be very helpful. The name of the Parish Clerk can be obtained from the public library or the Chief Executive of the District Council. Many Parish Councils are very jealous of their local paths and can often get results quickly.

Private Prosecutions

The local rambling club or footpath society will probably take up the matter, if asked, but if all else fails, there are legal remedies. These should be used only as a last resort and only after repeated efforts have failed to produce results. It is much better to use persuasion rather than alienate the local farming community by rushing into hasty legal action. Nevertheless, if somebody proves to be recalcitrant, the only certain remedy will be to invoke the law.

The citizen, either as an individual or on behalf of an organisation, can invoke Section 56 of the Highways Act, 1980 to compel the highway authority to repair a highway. First establish from the Chief Executive of the County Council whether it admits responsibility for that particular highway (quote the parish and path number from the Definitive Map). Once responsibility is admitted, and after a reasonable time has elapsed for the work to be put in hand, it is possible to get an order from the magistrates compelling the authority to carry out the necessary work. This tactic is extremely useful when dealing with missing footbridges and minor obstructions arising from lack of maintenance.

If a local authority is in breach of its statutory obligations, then the local Ombudsman may be able to help. He has no powers to force the authority to act but his opinion is likely to carry great weight and there are several

133

examples where his intervention has resulted in getting obstructed paths opened. The procedure for approaching the Ombudsman is set out in a booklet which may be obtained from the Commission for Local Administration in England, 21 Queen Anne's Gate, London SW1H 9BU and the Commission for Local Administration in Wales, Derwen House, Court Road, Bridgend, Mid-Glamorgan CF31 1BN.

An individual can prosecute for obstruction under Section 137 of the Highways Act, 1980 'If a person, without lawful authority or excuse, in any way wilfully obstructs the free passage along a highway he is guilty of an offence and liable to a fine not exceeding level 3 on the standard scale.' The procedure to be followed is described in detail in *Rights of Way: a Guide to Law and Practice* by Paul Clayden and John Trevelyan.

An individual may take certain steps to remove physically an obstruction on a path providing that he is on a *bona fide* journey and not setting out with the sole intention of removing the obstruction and also providing that only enough of the obstruction is removed to allow free passage along the path. Great caution should be used in removing obstructions for, if stock strays or becomes infected from neighbouring animals, it may result in thousands of pounds' worth of damage. It is probably kinder to initiate a private prosecution and if persuasion fails to have the obstacle removed and the resulting publicity in the local press may have a salutary effect.

Improvement of Paths

If there are many path problems in your area and no organisation for their protection exists, you might consider forming one. Such organisations take many forms. They may be rambling clubs, riding clubs (whose members are likely to be interested only in bridleways) or rights of way societies which can bring riders and walkers together for their mutual benefit. A letter to the local paper announcing a public meeting to discuss path problems is likely to bring a surprisingly large audience and often representatives from the highway authority will attend, if invited, and answer questions. An active society can in three of four years improve the condition of local paths and people will find that they are usable again.

Some Parish Councils hold an annual walk of all the paths in their parish. Unfortunately, they do not always take up the problems they discover with the landowner or relevant authority. If your Parish Council does not walk its paths, encourage them to do so and, if necessary, offer to lead them and try to ensure that the Parish Clerk takes any necessary remedial action.

A local rambling club or right of way society can improve local paths by bridging ditches and clearing excessive growth. Officials of the highway authority will often be only too pleased to supply materials such as old railway sleepers and deliver them to the site. They will negotiate with the landowner for permission to erect bridges and agree on the exact line of the path so that vegetation can be removed.

Ditches up to about four metres wide are best bridged with old railway sleepers. Carefully measure the length of the sleeper required and the highway authority will have them cut to size and delivered as close to the site as they can get a vehicle. A four-metre sleeper can be carried for a kilometre or so by four men taking the weight on two lengths of iron piping. If the ditch is not liable to flood, the bank should be dug out so that the sleeper lies flush to the surface. Wooden pegs hammered into the ground on each side of the sleeper and then nailed to it will hold it in position (see Fig. 42). For lengths over two metres, it is better to use two sleepers side by side.

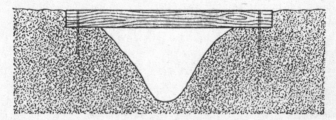

Fig. 42 Ditch-bridging

For clearing undergrowth from the surface of a path the following equipment will be found useful:

billhooks
slashers
toggle-loppers (fearsome secateurs with 50-cm handles which will remove branches 4 cm thick with one snip)
axes
saws
secateurs

Remove from the line of the path all vegetation including saplings and any branches hanging over the path less than two metres from the ground. It is as well to agree beforehand with the landowner about the disposal of hedge trimmings. He may want them burnt in a special area or he may prefer them to be heaped at intervals and allowed to rot. Under no circumstances allow them to fall into ditches as they will block them and may cause flooding.

Many highway authorities are prepared to make token payments to club funds for work of this kind. Do not hesitate to ask, for you are saving the ratepayers' money by doing the work of the highway authority for them.

Once a path has been cleared of obstructions it is a good plan to encourage the general public to use it by seeking permission from the owners of the land which it crosses to waymark it. The principles of waymarking are described on pages 131-2.

Bibliography

Agate, Elizabeth, *Footpaths, a Practical Handbook*, British Trust for Conservation Volunteers, 1983.

Clayden, Paul, and Trevelyan, John, *Rights of Way: a Guide to Law and Practice*, published jointly by the Open Spaces Society and the Ramblers' Association, 1983.

Garner, J.F., *Garner's Rights of Way*, Longmans, 5th Rev. Ed., 1989.

Garner, J. F., and Jones, B. L., *Countryside Law*, Shaw and Sons, 1987.

11 The Law Relating to Footpaths and Bridleways in Scotland

The law relating to rights of way in Scotland is quite different from the law in England. There are no Definitive Maps of rights of way, since 'user' right by the public is based upon custom around which much case law has been built up. It is as well to remember that Scotland has a small population of five million, concentrated for the most part in the Lowlands, and there are not the same pressures from recreational interests. There is much wild countryside in its 80,000 square kilometres, which supports only hill-farming, forestry, shooting, deer-stalking and fishing and, provided that these interests are not disregarded, walkers enjoy tremendous freedom.

It is useful for walkers to have some knowledge of the legal position of rights of way in Scotland, and an outline of the most important provisions will be found below. However, the legal status of rights of way is of less practical importance than it is in England and Wales because the law of trespass is different (see p121). Providing that the legitimate interests of sportsmen and foresters are respected (see pp241-2) virtually all paths and tracks in open country may be used. Nor, in practice, are walkers confined to paths in open country as there is widespread toleration of general roaming and camping wild.

Definitions

In the Countryside (Scotland) Act, 1967 and the Town and Country Planning (Scotland) Act, 1972 the following definitions occur:

Bridleway: A way on which the public have the following but no other rights of way, that is to say, a right of way on foot and a right of way on horseback or leading a horse, with or without a right to drive animals of any description along that way.

Footpath: A way over which the public have the following but no other rights of way, that is to say, a right of way on foot with or without a right of way on pedal cycles.

Public path: A way which is a footpath or bridleway or a combination of those.

Acquisition at Common Law

The majority of public rights of way have been acquired at common law. The criteria for acquiring such rights are as follows:

1. The path must have been used by the general public for a continuous period of not less than twenty years. The amount of use depends upon local circumstances and a path in thinly populated areas will need less use than a path in a well-populated area.

The use must be by the general public not just by a privileged group such as tenants, employees and postmen. The use must not have been prevented at any time by the landowner such as by closing and locking gates unless it can be shown that the users refused to accept such limitations.

2. The use must be as a matter of right and not just of toleration or generosity on the part of the landowner.

3. The beginning and the end of the path must be public places or places where the general public may lawfully resort such as public roads, churches, cemeteries and ferries. It probably includes the summits of the more popular mountains and places on the seashore where the public habitually resort to bathe or for boating.

4. The path must have a reasonably defined route, though this does not necessarily mean that the track must be visible; but the general public must have always followed approximately the same route and the path must be capable of being used along its whole length.

Acquisition by Statute

Paths may be acquired by statute in a number of ways.

1. A local planning authority may enter into an agreement with a landowner to create a public path. If it proves impossible to reach agreement, a path may be created by order. A local planning authority has the power to divert a public path providing that the diversion is not substantially less convenient to the public. Any diversion or creation order has to be confirmed by the Secretary of State for Scotland after objections have been invited. (Countryside (Scotland) Act, 1967, Sections 30, 31 and 38.)

2. To enable the path network to be maintained the Secretary of State for Scotland may, when making an order extinguishing or diverting a highway to enable development to take place, create or improve other highways. (Town and Country Planning (Scotland) Act, 1972, Sections 198 and 200.)

Similarly, under Section 199 of the same Act, local planning authorities may create or improve other rights of way when making an order extinguishing or diverting public paths to allow development to take place.

Under Section 201 of the Act, orders may be made by the Secretary of State for Scotland if requested by the appropriate local authority to prevent or limit vehicles using a particular highway. There is provision under all these Sections for objections to be made and, if the Secretary of State for Scotland thinks fit, for a local inquiry to be held.

The Secretary of State for Scotland has to confirm all orders made by local authorities unless the order is unopposed.

Enforcement

The Countryside (Scotland) Act, 1967 makes clear provision for the enforcement of the law relating to footpaths and bridleways. Section 46 (i) states: 'It shall be the duty of a local planning authority to assert, protect and keep open and free from obstruction or encroachment any public right of way which is wholly or partly within their area, and they may for these purposes institute and defend legal proceedings and generally take such steps as they may deem expedient.'

Any member of the public may bring an action to vindicate a right of way and this right of vindication includes societies and organisations as well as several persons binding together for this particular purpose.

The legal procedure is by action of declarator that a right of way exists raised in the Sheriff Court or the Court of Session and presenting suitable evidence to prove his point. The kind of evidence required is proof of use as of right for the prescriptive period of twenty years, such as maps, guidebooks and the statements of elderly persons with personal knowledge of the path.

If judgement in favour of the existence of the right of way is given then the question cannot be reopened, but if the judgement is against the existence of a right of way the matter can be reopened if more evidence comes to light.

Maintenance of Public Paths

The landowner of ground crossed by a public right of way has no responsibility for maintaining or repairing the route. The public may repair a right of way providing that no damage is caused to the landowner's property. Under Section 46 of the Countryside (Scotland) Act, 1967 local planning authorities have a duty to assert, protect, keep open and free from obstruction or encroachment any public right of way within their area. This section gives local planning authorities power to maintain paths if they so wish but they are under no obligation to do so. However, under Section 33 of the same Act, local planning authorities have a duty to maintain public paths which have been created by agreement or order or diversion orders. The Secretary of State for Scotland has the power to order local planning authorities to carry out necessary work if he thinks they have failed in their duty.

Guideposting

Guideposts may be erected by local authorities upon any right of way and, under Section 46 of the Countryside (Scotland) Act, 1967, by any person with the consent of the local planning authority. Section 53 of the same Act permits local authorities to make a financial contribution to anyone carrying out such work.

Diversion of Paths

A landowner has no right to alter the route without due legal process, although there is usually no difficulty if the public using the route accept any minor changes as reasonable.

The procedure to divert the path is for the landlord, tenant or occupier of the land crossed by the path to apply to the local planning authority for a diversion order. The planning authority must invite objections to the diversion and then make a diversion in the light of the circumstances. (Countryside (Scotland) Act, 1967, Section 35.)

1. A local planning authority may make a diversion order extinguishing a right of way and substituting a new right of way providing that the new path is not substantially less convenient for the public. Any such orders have to be considered in the light of objections made and the order has to be confirmed by the Secretary of State for Scotland. (Countryside (Scotland) Act, 1967, Section 38.)

2. A bridleway, which includes public paths, may be diverted by the Secretary of State for Scotland to allow development after objections have been invited. (Town and Country Planning (Scotland) Act, 1972, Section 198.)

3. Local planning authorities may divert paths to allow development to take place after inviting objections and obtaining confirmation, if necessary, by the Secretary of State for Scotland. (Town and Country Planning (Scotland) Act, 1972, Section 199.)

Extinction of Paths

1. Paths acquired by common law may be extinguished if they have not been used for twenty years providing that the general public have acquiesced in this disuse. Common-law extinguishment needs no positive action on the part of the landowner, but of course it is possible to challenge the extinguishment in the courts.

2. All public paths, whether acquired by statute or at common law, may be the subject of extinguishment orders.

3. Local authorities and certain statutory bodies such as Electricity Boards have the power to acquire land free of all rights of way.

4. Local planning authorities may extinguish a right of way on the grounds that it is not needed for public use by means of a public path extinguishment order, which must then be ratified by the Secretary of State for Scotland. (Countryside (Scotland) Act, 1967, Section 34.)

5. The Secretary of State for Scotland may issue an order extinguishing any right of way if the land crossed by the right of way has been acquired for planning purposes by the local authority. He must be satisfied that an alternative right of way has been provided, will be provided or is not necessary.

A local authority may extinguish a footpath or bridleway on the same grounds and conditions. (Town and Country Planning (Scotland) Act, 1972.)

Obstructions

Obstructions of any kind that are likely to impede the person using the path are not permitted on rights of way. Such obstructions include barbed wire, electric fences, walls and fences unless provided with proper access such as a gate or stile. Bridleways must not have stiles placed on them and it is illegal to lock a gate on a public bridleway.

Anyone wishing to erect a stile or gate across a public right of way must apply to the planning authority for permission to do so. If the planning authority refuses permission the applicant may appeal to the Secretary of State for Scotland. (Countryside (Scotland) Act, 1967, Section 45.)

The remedy for a walker meeting an obstruction on a public right of way is to remove as much of it as is necessary to allow him to pass. The law recognises this right providing that the action is taken within a reasonably short time of the erection of the obstruction. Obstructions which cannot be dealt with in this manner should be brought to the notice of the local planning authority for action as described above under 'Enforcement'.

Ploughing

Landowners and tenants have a right to plough public paths unless this right has been excluded by a public path creation agreement or order or a diversion order. The landowner or tenant must inform the local planning authority within seven days of ploughing the right of way and must reinstate the surface as soon as may be. The public has the right to continue to use paths that have been ploughed (Countryside (Scotland) Act, 1967, Section 43).

Bulls

The law concerning bulls on public paths is confused. It is an offence to permit a bull of a recognised dairy breed over ten months old to be at large in a field crossed by a public path unless cows or heifers are also at large in the same field (Countryside (Scotland) Act, 1967, Section 44). However, it is believed that under common law it is illegal to have any bull running free in a field crossed by a public right of way, although to prove the point a case would have to be heard in the courts.

Maps

Although there are no Definitive Maps in Scotland, local authorities have, in some cases, prepared lists of rights of way and maps, but although these may be challenged their publication helps towards the establishment of rights of way by use by the public.

Local planning authorities have a duty to prepare and keep up to date maps showing details of any land which has been acquired for public access or which has been made subject to access agreements (Countryside (Scotland) Act, 1967, Section 26). Local planning authorities must record details of all orders for access, creation, diversion and extinguishment of paths on maps.

Access to the Countryside

Under the provisions of the Countryside (Scotland) Act, 1967, various authorities are empowered to establish right of access in the countryside. A right of access is not the same as establishing a right of way—it can be better compared to the enjoyment of a public park. It also produces a negative right in that one cannot be treated as a trespasser when acting lawfully. Access agreements are not usually applied to 'excepted land', which includes agricultural land.

Local planning authorities may establish country parks or pleasure grounds and administer them for the benefit of the public. (Countryside (Scotland) Act, 1967, Section 48.)

The Forestry Commission may establish recreational facilities, including nature trails and paths. (Countryside (Scotland) Act, 1967, Section 58.)

The Secretary of State for Scotland may establish recreational facilities, including nature trails and paths on land owned by the government and may appoint the Countryside Commission for Scotland as his agent. (Countryside (Scotland) Act, 1967, Section 60.)

A local planning authority may, with the approval of the Secretary of State for Scotland, negotiate access agreements with landowners and others having interest in the land such as holders of fishing and shooting rights. Rights of way shall not be affected by the terms of access agreements. If it proves impossible to conclude an agreement, the planning authority may make a compulsory access order, which has to be approved by the Secretary of State after hearing objections before the order can become effective. (Countryside (Scotland) Act, 1967, Sections 13 and 14.)

If it proves impossible to provide access either by agreement or by making an order, the planning authority may with the consent of the Secretary of State for Scotland acquire the land either by agreement or compulsorily. (Countryside (Scotland) Act, 1967, Section 24.)

The Secretary of State for Scotland may acquire land by agreement, or compulsorily, if it has proved impossible to provide access either by agreement or by order. (Countryside (Scotland) Act, 1967, Section 25.)

How to Preserve Rights of Way

The body most active in the preservation of rights of way is the Scottish Rights of Way Society Limited (see p309), which will offer advice and, where necessary, approach the proper authorities. An individual who comes across problems should take up the matter with the landowner, or if this produces no result with the local planning authority, asking them to take action under Section 46 of the Countryside (Scotland) Act, 1967 'to assert, protect, and keep open and free from obstruction or encroachment any right of way'. Should these approaches fail, the Scottish Rights of Way Society should be informed, giving a clear description of the problem together with a grid reference.

Members of the public can help, too, just by walking paths which are in danger of falling into disuse. This will help prevent losing those paths subject to common law under the prescriptive period of twenty years.

The philosophy behind the preservation of rights of way in Scotland is quite different from the English concept. The law is dynamic and paths that have fallen into disuse because they no longer serve a useful purpose are replaced by new paths which may become rights of way in twenty years' time.

Bibliography

Rights of Way; a Guide to the Law in Scotland. Scottish Rights of Way Society Ltd., 1986.

12 Footpath Guides and How to Write Them

Footpath guides serve a number of purposes. Firstly, it is reasonable to assume that the author knows the area well and has chosen the best routes. Secondly, they supplement maps and in many cases provide more detailed information than the Ordnance Survey map, though experienced walkers usually like to have the appropriate Ordnance Survey map with them even when using a footpath guide. Thirdly, they are extremely useful to the many people who enjoy a walk in the countryside but to whom the Ordnance Survey map is something of a mystery. Footpath guides are usually devoted to a particular area, but in recent years a number of guides to long-distance footpaths have been published, some of which cover considerable stretches of contrasting countryside.

There are two distinct categories of footpath guides. Illustrative, where the main emphasis is on drawing maps sufficiently detailed for the walker to follow the path, and descriptive, where the author gives a description of the route supplemented either by sketch maps or by superimposing the line of the path on the Ordnance Survey map.

Illustrative Guides

The best-known examples of illustrative guides are A. Wainwright's seven *Guides to the Lakeland Fells*. These contain superb maps on a scale of 1:25000, giving details not found on Ordnance Survey maps such as gates, stiles, cairns and individual trees for all routes to the summit of every mountain and fell in the Lake District. In addition, they contain delightful line drawings and an entertaining, but erudite, commentary on things to be seen along the route. Mr Wainwright has set a standard that few can emulate, although the principles that he used can be applied to any area. Mark Richards has written a number of guides, adopting the methods used by Mr Wainwright in his *Pennine Way Companion*.

An interesting development in footpath guides is the Automobile Association's *No Through Road*. This is a large coffee table item with a separate book of walks in a ring binder. These selected walks cover the whole country but are very short. What is so interesting is that the routes are shown by means of coloured aerial photographs. This method seems very effective but is so expensive that the technique can be used only for books which will have a huge sale.

Descriptive Guides

Descriptive guides vary greatly in quality and usefulness. It is very difficult to write accurate descriptions of a route and only the most skilful writer will manage to avoid ambiguities. The countryside is constantly changing and if, for example, a farmer embarks on some alterations or improvements to his land it can render a descriptive guide useless. For example 'after passing through the stile, walk up the track and take the third gate on the right-hand side' is apparently clear and unambiguous, but what if the farmer decides on an alteration to his fields and either removes one of the gates and fills the gap with fencing, or substitutes a stile for which the walker is not looking? With a good illustrative guide, the changes would not be so confusing because the walker would have a very clear idea of how far he had to walk before reaching the gate and there should be other features such as field boundaries to help him identify the route. Nevertheless, good descriptive guides can be perfectly adequate in uncultivated country, where there is little likelihood of significant changes and where the paths and tracks are clearly defined, and are preferred by those who lack confidence in map-reading.

Writing a Footpath Guide

There is a great demand for footpath guides. The market for them in popular walking areas is considerable (countless thousands of Mr Wainwright's guides have been sold) and there is a great demand from local people in areas which have no special scenic qualities and which are unlikely to be visited by many walkers from outside the area. The publication of a footpath guide is a sure recipe for getting local paths walked and if done by a rambling club can provide a useful addition to club funds. It can also become a fascinating hobby.

Careful consideration should be given to the kind of guide required and the principles on which it should be compiled. Experience shows that circular walks of about ten kilometres are the most popular with the general public. If, from each starting point, two walks are always given, this will cater for those who like to walk a longer distance.

Much thought must be given to the information to be included in the guide. In lowland areas, the most important features are field boundaries, roads and streams. It is helpful to indicate the kind of field boundary, whether it be hedge, post and rail fence or barbed wire, and any other permanent features such as barns, pylons and telegraph poles. Unless your calligraphy is superb it will be found easier to indicate stiles, gates, footpath and bridleway signs by single letters rather than writing them out in full. Once these decisions have been made, it is sensible to compile the key to the finished map to ensure consistency throughout. Most good reference libraries have a number of footpath guides in their collection and the would-be cartographer can pick up some useful ideas by examining them. Anyone devising a new long-distance path should consult the Long-Distance Path Advisory Service (see p301).

Surveying

Every path must be surveyed and this will involve you in a great deal of work and walking. A book containing twenty circular ten kilometre walks adds up to a minimum of two hundred kilometres. In addition, it will be necessary to note any difficulties such as missing footbridges and stiles, locked gates, obstructions etc., and take them up with the landowner or responsible local authority, which will result in further visits to check that the work has been done.

The following items are required for surveying:
  clipboard
  2H pencil attached to the clipboard by nylon cord
  pencil sharpener
  eraser
  relevant map

The clipboard can be improved by gluing some 5 mm plastic angle moulding, obtainable from a hardware shop, to the edges to form a frame. A piece of thick flexible transparent plastic will protect the map on the clipboard from sweaty hands and a large transparent plastic bag will protect the clipboard from the rain. The map used should be the 1:25000, preferably the Outline Edition which omits contours. Mark in rights of way using the Definitive Map, where available, checking with the appropriate authority that there are no diversions or extinguishments. Next, walk the chosen route marking the map as you go with all the features you intend to include, not forgetting to amend the map where development has now rendered it inaccurate. It will not be possible for you to locate the additional features you require with complete accuracy. Nevertheless, with a little experience you will find how easy it is to line up telegraph poles and pylons with other physical features and then to estimate the distance they lie from one of these features. It is a great help to know the exact number of normal walking paces you take to cover one hundred metres. Use a surveyor's tape to measure the distance and then walk it ten times counting your paces. It is likely that the number of paces will vary each time so take the average figure. Once this information is known, you will find it easy to judge distances by counting your steps and measuring short distances on the map with the help of a romer scale.

Drawing the Map

Once the survey is completed, the final map can be drawn. The following items will be necessary:

> drawing board
> T-square
> 4 drawing-board clips
> Rotring micronorm pen with 0.25-mm. nib
> Rotring black drawing ink
> Rotring pen cleaner
> studio gum
> correcting fluid
> best-quality tracing paper
> graph paper
> Letraset

Mount the map on the drawing board using studio gum if necessary, and hold the tracing paper on the drawing board with the four clips. In pencil mark out the size of the page and then, within this border, make a tracing of the map and the features to be included. If the guide is to be a club venture, it may be possible to find a draughtsman or someone with similar skills to draw and letter the map. Most people, with a little patience and practice, can learn to letter acceptably, for neatness and a personal style is more important than perfect proportions. Books on lettering and calligraphy can be obtained from the public library. When lettering, it is helpful to mount the tracing paper on graph paper as this will help to get the lettering straight and properly proportioned. The plates for printing can be made direct from the traced maps but for ease of handling it is better to mount them with studio gum on best-quality bond typing paper. The wording on the cover and the heading on each map can be done with Letraset and a small line drawing on the cover will help to make it attractive and eyecatching.

The development of desk-top publishing (known in the trade as DTP) using personal computers (PCs) has revolutionised the production of booklets such as footpath guides. It is now possible for the amateur to design a publication of letterpress quality entirely on a sophisticated home computer. The design can be reproduced on a laser printer and the printing house can then be given the camera-ready copy, thus saving the cost of design and conventional typesetting.

Costings

Bookshops normally sell books at the cover price because under the terms of the Net Book Agreement, which has the approval of the Restrictive Practices Court, publishers have the right to set the price at which their books may be sold. This makes costing for the amateur publisher relatively easy.

Production costs include artwork, copyright fees for photos and maps, setting the manuscript in type, printing and binding. Get firm estimates from several printers for the setting, printing and binding, then to obtain your retail price, add a sum to cover your expenses in selling the book plus a profit margin then divide it by the number of copies you are printing.

Of course there are economies of scale i.e. the more books you print the cheaper each one is, but remember that even 1000 books is a lot to sell. Try to be realistic about the numbers you print – friends and family rarely account for more than 50 sales and if you are doing a guide to a local path you should consider how many outlets there are to stock your book and if possible talk to the owners of the shops before you print to see how many they think they will be able to sell in a year. This little bit of market research could save you hundreds of pounds in wrongly estimating the number of books you should print. In 1990, a typical estimate for a 40 page, A5 saddle-stitched (stapled) guide printed in one colour and with a stiff cover was £750 per thousand copies plus £550 per thousand run-on (i.e. printed at the same time). Note that these figures are based on camera-ready copy produced on a personal computer. The cost would be considerably higher if the printer was required to typeset from a manuscript.

Legal Requirements

Before printing the guide, there are certain legal requirements to be met. Application must be made to the Copyright Division of the Ordnance Survey (see p306) for permission to reproduce the map based on Ordnance Survey maps that are still subject to copyright. A form will have to be completed and the copyright fee paid before publication. The Ordnance Survey find it helpful if photocopies of the maps are enclosed with the copyright forms. The words 'Crown copyright reserved' must appear on every map in copyright and an acknowledgement appear in the book: 'The maps in this guide are based upon the Ordnance Survey maps with the sanction of the Controller of HM Stationery Office. Crown copyright reserved.'

The copyright fees charged by the Ordnance Survey for redrawn maps, and especially for reproduction of maps, can amount to a significant percentage of the total production costs of a footpath guide. Under Section 39 of the Copyright Act, 1956 copyright subsists in all Ordnance Survey maps for a period of fifty years from the end of the year in which each map is made. Once this period has expired then reproduction may be made without reference to the Ordnance Survey. This means that it is possible to reproduce any edition or series of Ordnance Survey maps fifty years *after* the first publication of the series that *replaced* them. For example, the Fifth Edition of the One Inch (1:63360) maps was introduced in 1931–2 so the Fourth Edition, which was published between the years 1918–1932 is now out of copyright. All 1:25000 maps are still in copyright but the County Edition of the Six Inch (1:10560) series (on which the 1:25000 was originally based) is now out of copyright and is important because it shows field boundaries.

Naturally, many alterations will have taken place, especially in lowland areas, but the only major changes likely to be noticed in upland regions are reservoirs, forests and new roads. When up-dating old maps, no attempt should be made to copy features from modern maps as this could constitute infringement of copyright, and the Ordnance Survey is very jealous of its rights. All up-dating should be done by means of personal survey which can be done quite easily by anyone proficient in the use of map and compass.

The best source for locating old maps is the local history department of the public library in the area covered by the map. The address can be obtained from *The Municipal Yearbook* which can be consulted in any reference library, but if in doubt your local librarian will be able to advise. Once the maps have been located it will be possible to photocopy the required sections. Ordnance Survey Information Leaflet 23 *Copyright – Publishing* lists copyright and publishing information and gives the scale of charges for reproducing Ordnance Survey maps in copyright. It may be obtained from the Ordnance Survey (see p306).

Although not a legal requirement, application should be made to the International Standard Book Numbering Agency, 12 Dyott Street, London WC1A 1DF to be assigned an International Standard Book Number which is used in the book trade for identifying books. Also request, from the same address, a Whitaker Information Form which will ensure that the book is listed in *The Bookseller* and *Whitaker's Books in Print*. *The Bookseller* is a weekly trade publication that lists all books published during the previous week and is used extensively by booksellers and librarians. *Whitaker's Books in Print* is published regularly on microfiche and lists all books published and distributed in the United Kingdom that are currently in print. No charge is made for these listings.

By law a copy of the guide must be sent to the British Library Bibliographical Services Division, Store Street, London WC1E 7DG. This copy will be added to the stock of the British Library (formerly the British Museum Library) and will appear under author, title and subject in the *British National Bibliography,* a title used extensively by librarians for tracing books and information. It will also appear in the catalogue of the British Library. The Crown Agent has the right to demand, free of charge, an additional four copies of the guide, one each for the university libraries of Oxford and Cambridge, the National Library of Scotland and the Library of Trinity College, Dublin.

Printing

Photographic offset lithography is the most suitable process for printing a footpath guide because mistakes in the copy can be painted over with correcting fluid and redrawn without having to start the whole map afresh. All imperfections will disappear in the photographic process and the copy can be enlarged or reduced to fit the page. Printing in colour will add significantly to the cost of the guide but even monochrome guides can be made attractive by the use of coloured ink and tinted paper.

Marketing and Distribution

When the guide is published, a press release describing its purpose and main features should be sent with a copy of the book to the local radio station and to the editors of all local newspapers and county magazines as well as to the periodicals listed in Appendix One. Visit all local booksellers and sell copies to them at normal trade terms, usually 33% but some shops expect 40%. The local public library will probably want to buy copies but may prefer to deal with one of the local bookshops.

If the guide covers a much-used area, it is worth offering the manuscript to one of the companies specialising in footpath guides. Footpath Publications specialises in publishing guides to little-walked localities such as the south midlands and East Anglia, that most conventional publishers would not even consider. Among the best-known publishers of footpath guides are:

John Bartholomew and Son, 12 Duncan Street, Edinburgh EH9 1TA.

Cicerone Press, 2 Police Square, Milnthorpe, Cumbria LA7 7PY.

Constable and Co., 3 The Lanchesters, 162 Fulham Palace Road, London W6 9ER.

Countryside Books, 6 Pound Street, Newbury, Berks RG14 6AB.

Dalesman Publishing Company Ltd., Clapham, Lancaster LA2 8EB.

Footpath Publications, 86 Burford Gardens, London N13 4LP.
Shire Publications, Cromwell House, Church Street, Princes Risborough, Aylesbury, Bucks HP17 9AJ.
Stile Publications, Mercury House, Otley, West Yorkshire LS21 3HE.
Thornhill Press, 24 Moorend Road, Cheltenham, Glos GL53 0EU
Frederick Warne, 27 Wright's Lane, London W8 5TZ.
Westmorland Gazette, 22 Stricklandgate, Kendal, Cumbria LA9 4NE.

Bibliography

Finch, Peter, *How to Publish Yourself,* Allison and Busby, 1987.

Mulholland, Henry, *Guide to Self-publishing, A–Z Guide to getting Yourself into Print,* Mulholland-Wirral, 1984.

Wilkinson, Jack, *A Step in the Right Direction, the Marketing of Circular Walks,* Sports Council in association with the Countryside Commission, 1985.

Zeitlyn, Jonathon, *Print – How You Can do it Yourself,* Interchange Books. 1986.

Westacott, Hugh, *Writing and Publishing a Footpath Guide: Do-it-yourself Information for Authors and Rambling Clubs,* Footpath Publications, 86 Burford Gardens, London N13 4LP, 1988.

SECTION 3: WHERE TO WALK

13 National Parks

The world's first national park was the Yellowstone Park in the USA, which was established in 1872 by an Act of Congress. In 1889, there was a farsighted leader in the *Manchester Guardian* which suggested that the Lake District should be nationalised or, failing that, some kind of conservation should be adopted to prevent spoliation of the area by commercial interests. During the next fifty years, a movement developed to gain more public access to mountains, and Bills were introduced in Parliament in 1908, 1924, 1926 and 1927 in an attempt to achieve this end. For various reasons they were not successful and in 1932 a mass trespass took place on Kinder Scout. Fighting took place between gamekeepers and walkers, the police stepped in and a number of arrests were made. The local magistrates handed out some savage prison sentences, but the plight of those who suffered for their obvious love of the mountains caught the public imagination.

During the war a number of committees sat and reports were commissioned that resulted in significant social changes in the post-war years. Some, like the Beveridge Report, have radically changed our lives; others are not so well known to the public but have nevertheless improved the quality of our lives. Into the latter category falls a report by a committee presided over by Lord Justice Scott which stated in 1942 that 'the establishment of national parks in Britain is long overdue'. In 1943 the new Ministry of Town and Country Planning was formed and one of the Minister's first acts was to ask an architect, John Dower, to write a report on the problems involved in setting up national parks. John Dower defined a national park as 'an extensive area of beautiful and relatively wild country in which, for the nation's benefit and by appropriate national decision and action, (a) the characteristic landscape beauty is strictly preserved; (b) access and facilities for public open air enjoyment are amply provided; (c) wildlife and buildings and places of architectural and historic interest are suitably protected, while (d) established farming areas are effectively maintained'.

The minister set up a new Committee in 1945 under Sir Arthur Hobhouse to consider the Dower proposals and recommended that national parks should be set up in the following areas:

Brecon Beacons
Dartmoor
Exmoor
Lake District
North York Moors
Northumberland
Peak District
Pembrokeshire Coast
Snowdonia
Yorkshire Dales
South Downs
Norfolk Broads

All these areas are now national parks except the South Downs (the Broads now has national park status). The Hobhouse Committee drew up a list of regions of outstanding landscape value deserving of being conservation areas which have formed the basis of the programme for Areas of Outstanding Natural Beauty.

The Ramsey Committee was set up to examine the feasibility of establishing national parks in Scotland but its proposals were never implemented.

It should be noted that in British national parks there is normally no change in the ownership of the land. The nation does not own its national parks, as some countries do, so the right of access for walkers, riders and others using them for recreation is no greater than in other parts of the country unless local arrangements have been negotiated.

Every national park is administered by an executive committee made up of representatives from interested organisations such as County Councils, and has its own national park officer who is responsible to the executive committee. Most of the funds for national parks come from central government and are used for providing such things as car parks, toilets, picnic areas, camp sites, footpaths, bridleways and nature trails, information centres, publicity and ranger services. The executive committee is also the planning authority and keeps a very tight control on all development to ensure that it fits in with the traditional style of building of the area. Any industrial development has to be properly screened and made as unobtrusive as possible.

One of the criteria for selecting areas for national parks is that they should contain a high proportion of open country, which is defined in the National Parks and Access to the Countryside Act, 1949 as 'mountain, moor, heath, down, cliff or foreshore' and excludes agricultural land except rough grazing for sheep and cattle. Thus national parks are particularly suitable for walking holidays. Much of the terrain is rugged and must be treated by the novice with great caution. Many national parks organize walks led by experienced walkers with the aim of introducing people to the pleasures of upland walking. For those who do not wish to venture into the moors and mountains, there are numerous delightful walks to be taken in the valleys of the national parks.

Note that the bibliographies listed under each national park are selective and include only the best footpath guides.

Bibliography

Redhead, Brian, *The National Parks of England and Wales*, Oxford Illustrated Press, 1988.

Smith, Roland, *Visitor's Guide to the National Parks: 'Wildest Britain'*, Blandford Press, New Ed., 1986.

Brecon Beacons

The Brecon Beacons National Park was established in 1957 and covers an area of 1344 square kilometres bordered by the towns of Hay-on-Wye. Abergavenny, Brynamman, Llandeilo, Llandovery and Brecon. The most characteristic feature is the flat-topped mountains which rise to a height of 886 metres, and it is possible to walk for considerable distances without descending below 600 metres. By way of contrast, the 50 kilometres of towpath of the Monmouthshire and Brecon Canal can be walked by those who fancy less strenuous exercise. There are numerous sites of archaeological interest, three National Nature Reserves, and at Agen Allwed, the most extensive cave system yet discovered in the United Kingdom.

National Park Headquarters: 7 Glamorgan Street, Brecon, Powys LD3 7DP (Tel. 0874-4437).

Information Centres: Abergavenny—Monk Street (Tel. 0873-3254); Brecon—Watton Mount (Tel. 0874-4437); Libanus—Mountain Centre

(Tel. 0874-3366); Llandovery—Broad Street (Tel. 0550-20693).

Official Guidebook: Thomas, Roger, *Brecon Beacons,* Webb & Bower/ Michael Joseph, 1987.

Maps: 1:50000 Landranger sheets 159, 160, 161; 1:25000 Outdoor Leisure Maps 11 (Brecon Beacons—Central), 12 (Brecon Beacons— Western), 13 (Brecon Beacons—Eastern).

Footpath Guides: Barber, Chris, *Exploring the Brecon Beacons, Black Mountains and Waterfall Country; a Walkers Guide,* Regional Publications, 2nd. Rev. Ed., 1985; Poucher, W. A., *The Welsh Peaks,* Constable, 9th Rev. Ed., 1987. Thomas, Roger, *Great Walks; Brecon Beacons and Pembroke-shire Coast,* Ward Lock, 1989; Walker, Kevin, *Mountain Walking in the Crickhowell Area,* Heritage Guides, 1986; Walker, Kevin, *Mountain Walking in the Brecon Beacons,* Heritage Guides, 1986; Walker, Kevin, *Family Walking in the Crickhowell Area,* Heritage Guides, 1986; Walker, Kevin, *The Ascent of Table Mountain,* Heritage Guides, 1986.

The Broads

A 280-square-kilometre region of watery landscape in Norfolk and Suffolk lying to the east of Norwich that contains 200 kilometres of lock-free navigation. A broad is a lake-like expanse of water formed by the flooding of medieval peat workings. The rivers Bure, Waveney and Yare, and their tributaries the Ant, Chet and Thurne link the forty or so broads, making it a paradise for inland sailors.

The status of the Broads is unique. It was not designated a National Park by the National Parks and Access to the Countryside Act, 1949, and in 1978 the local councils in the Broads area, with encouragement from the Countryside Commission, set up the Broads Authority to manage the Broads and to reduce pollution and other environmental damage. As a result of pressure from the Countryside Commission, the Council for National Parks, local councils, and the original Broads Authority, Parliament enacted the Broads Act in 1988 which established a new Broads Authority with responsibility for managing the area, and granting it national park status in everything except name.

The Broads contain a network of rights of way but the area is unlikely to appeal to walkers and backpackers as much as the other British national parks which are all situated in upland areas.

Broads Authority Headquarters: Thomas Harvey House, 18 Colegate, Norwich NR3 1BQ (Tel. 0603-610734).

Information Centres: Beccles – The Quay, Fen Lane (Tel. 0502-713196); Hoveton/Wroxham – Station Road, Hoveton (Tel. 0603-782281); Ludham – Toad Hole Cottage Museum, How Hill (Tel. 069262-763); Ranworth – The Staithe (Tel. 060549-453).

Maps: 1:50000 Landranger sheet 134; 1:25000 Pathfinder sheets P862 (TG 22/32, P863 (TG 42), P883 (TG 21/31), P884 (TG 41/51), P903 (TG 20/30), P904 (TG 40/50), P924 (TM 29/39), P925 (TM 49/59).

Footpath guide: Le Surf, Jeanne, *Explore the Broads,* Bartholomew, 1987.

Dartmoor

Dartmoor National Park covers an area of 945 square kilometres in central and south Devonshire between Exeter and Plymouth. It was established in 1951 and is the only piece of really wild country left in southern England. Much of Dartmoor lies 300 metres above sea level with High Willhays reaching 621 metres. Its many outcrops of granite have been eroded by the wind into strange shapes and in some places the huge granite blocks have been shattered into 'clitters' by the action of snow and ice.

On a warm summer's day with the roads jammed by the cars of holidaymakers it is difficult to imagine the very real dangers of Dartmoor, but the paths and tracks over the moors are not always clearly defined and there are large areas of treacherous bog. Moreover, mists can form very quickly and catch the unwary which can be a very frightening experience. Unfortunately, the army uses a large part of the northern part of the moor for training exercises and artillery practice. Red flags are flown when firing is taking place and information about dates and times of firing can be obtained from National Park information centres and local post offices.

National Park Headquarters: 'Parke', Haytor Road, Bovey Tracey, Devon TQ13 9JQ (Tel. 0626-832093).

Information Centres: Bovey Tracey—'Parke', Haytor Road (Tel. 0626-832093); New Bridge—on the road between Ashburton and Dartmeet (Tel. 03643-303); Dunsford—Steps Bridge on B3212 (Tel. 0647-52018); Okehampton—Courtyard of White Hart Hotel (Tel. 0837-53020); Postbridge—car park on B3212 (Tel. 0822-88272); Princetown—Duchy Hotel (Tel. 082 289-414); Tavistock—Town Hall, Bedford Square (Tel. 0822-612938).

National Park Newspaper: Dartmoor Visitor.

Official Guidebook: Weir, John, *Editor, Dartmoor,* Webb & Bower/ Michael Joseph, 1987.

Maps: 1:63360 Tourist Map of Dartmoor; 1:50000 Landranger sheets 191, 201, 202; 1:25000 Outdoor Leisure Map 28 Dartmoor.

Footpath Guides: Walks booklets compiled and published by the Dartmoor National Park: *No 1: Moretonhampstead/Manaton/Lustleigh, No 2: Southwest Dartmoor, No 3: The Dart Valley, No 4: Haytor and Area;* Earle, John, *Walking on Dartmoor,* Cicerone Press, 1987; Starkey, F. H.,

Exploring Dartmoor, published by the author at High Orchard, Haytor Vale, Newton Abbot, Devon TQ13 9EP, 1981; Starkey, F. H., *Exploring Dartmoor Again,* published by the author at High Orchard, Haytor Vale, Newton Abbot, Devon TQ13 9EP, 2nd. Rev. ed., 1988.

Exmoor

Exmoor National Park is the second smallest in Britain, covers 686 square kilometres and was established in 1954. It stretches along the coast from Combe Martin in Devon to Minehead in Somerset and goes inland as far as Dulverton. The scenery is mostly moorland intersected by deep wooded valleys known as combes, and there are magnificent cliffs along the coast. Much of Exmoor lies above 300 metres and the highest point is Dunkery Beacon (559 metres). Exmoor probably offers some of the easiest walking in any of the national parks.

National Park Headquarters: Exmoor House, Dulverton, Somerset TA22 9HL (Tel. 0398-23665).

Information Centres: Combe Martin—'Seacot', Cross Street (Tel. 027 188-3319); County Gate, Countisbury on A39 (Tel. 059 87-321); Dulverton—Exmoor House (Tel. 0398-23665); Dunster—Dunster Steep car park (Tel. 0643-821835); Lynmouth—The Esplanade (Tel. 0598-52509).

Official Guidebook: Court, Glyn, *Exmoor,* Webb & Bower/Michael Joseph, 1987.

National Park Newspaper; The Exmoor Visitor.

Maps: 1:63360 Tourist Map of Exmoor; 1:50000 Landranger sheets 180, 181; 1:25000 Pathfinder sheets P1213 (SS44/54), P1214 (SS64/74), P1215 (SS84/94), P1216 (ST04/14), P1234 (SS63/73), P1235 (SS83/93), P1236 (ST03/13), P1256 (SS82/92).

Footpath Guides: Butler, David, *Exmoor Walks for Motorists,* Warne, 1979; Walks guides compiled and published by the Exmoor National Park: *Suggested Walks and Bridleways: North Devon* (Combe Martin, Woody Bay, Lynton, Lynmouth, Malmsmead and Brendon Common); *Walks from County Gate; Waymarked Walks 1:* (Dunster, Minehead, Brendon Hill, Luxborough, Roadwater), *Waymarked Walks 2:* (Porlock, Oare, Dunkery, Malmsmead, Exford, Simonsbath), *Waymarked Walks 3:* (Dulverton, Winsford Hill, Tarr Steps, Anstey Common, Haddeo Valley).

Lake District

The Lake District National Park is the largest in Britain, covers an area of 2292 square kilometres and contains the highest mountains in England. It is roughly lozenge shaped and is bordered by the towns of Penrith, Cockermouth, Millom and Kendal. The Lake District's unique beauty lies in the combination of numerous lakes nestling among steep-sided mountains. As the region is so near the sea, the mountains appear higher than they actually are because they rise dramatically from low ground. The beauty of the Lake District is enhanced by its beautiful, if humble, stone buildings. The larger towns—Keswick, Ambleside and Windermere—can be horribly crowded in high summer, but there are some quiet hamlets and villages, and providing the more popular walks are avoided, it is still possible to be alone in the mountains.

National Park Headquarters: National Park Visitor Centre, Brockhole, Windermere, Cumbria LA23 1LJ (Tel. 09662-6601).

Information Centres: Bowness Bay—The Glebe (Tel. 09662-5602 or 2895); Coniston—1 Yewdale Road (Tel. 05394-41533); Gosforth—Information Caravan, main car park (Tel. 09467-25285); Grasmere—Redbank Road (Tel. 09665-245); Hawkshead—main car park (Tel. 09666-525); Keswick—Moot Hall, Market Place (Tel. 07687-72803); Pooley Bridge—Finkle Street (Tel. 07684-86530); Seatoller—Dalehead Base (Tel. 07687-77294); Ullswater—Beckside car park (Tel. 07684-82414); Waterhead—car park (Tel. 05394-32729).

Official Guidebook: Wyatt, John, *Lake District,* Webb & Bower/Michael Joseph, 1987.

National Park Newspaper: The Lake District Guardian.

Maps: 1:63360 Tourist Map of the Lake District; 1:50000 Landranger sheets 85, 89, 90, 96, 97; 1:25000 Outdoor Leisure Maps The English Lakes 4 (NW area), 5 (NE area), 6 (SW area), 7 (SE area).

Footpath Guides: Duerden, Frank, *Best Walks in the Lake District,* Constable, 1986. Parker, J., *Walk the Lakes: 40 Easy Walks,* Bartholomew, 1983. Parker, J., *Walk the Lakes Again: 38 Easy Walks,* Bartholomew, 1983. Poucher, W.A., *The Lakeland Peaks,* Constable, 1984. Wainwright, Alfred, *A Pictorial Guide to the Lakeland Fells,* Westmorland Gazette, 7 vols. 1955—1966. (NB this is the classic guide to walking in the Lake District but it is now very out of date and must be used with caution.)

North York Moors

The North York Moors National Park covers an area of 1432 square kilometres bordered by the towns of Saltburn, Scarborough, Helmsley and Northallerton. It contains the largest heather moor in England and makes a marvellous picture when in flower in August. Another feature of this national park is the magnificent cliff scenery which includes Robin Hood's Bay and the beautiful fishing village of Staithes. The moors are littered with reminders of prehistoric man and there are a number of medieval crosses. By contrast, the huge, weird concrete domes of the early-warning radar system are situated on Fylingdales Moor.

National Park Headquarters: The Old Vicarage, Bondgate, Helmsley,

York YO6 5BP (Tel. 0439-70657).

Information Centres: Danby—The Moors Centre (Tel. 0287-660654); Hutton-le-Hole—Rydale Folk Museum (Tel. 075 15-367); Pickering—The Station (Tel. 0751-73791); Ravenscar—National Trust Centre (Tel. 0723-870138); Sutton Bank on A170 (Tel. 0845-597426).

Official Guidebook: Carstairs, Ian, *North York Moors,* Webb & Bower/Michael Joseph, 1987.

National Park Newspaper: North York Moors Visitor.

Maps: 1:63360 Tourist Map of the North York Moors; 1:50000 Landranger sheets 93, 94, 99, 100, 101; 1:25000 Outdoor Leisure Maps North York Moors 26 (Western area), 27 (Eastern area).

Footpath Guides: Collins, Martin, *North York Moors; Walks in the National Park,* Cicerone Press, 1987. Hannon, Paul, *Walks on the North York Moors, 3 Vols,* Hillside Publications; *Book One—Western Moors; The Cleveland and Hambleton Hills, 1988; Book Two—Southern Moors; Rosedale, Farndale and the Tabular Hills, 1988; Book Three—Northern Moors; Eskdale and the Coast;* Ramblers' Association, *Walking on the North York Moors,* Dalesman, 1987; Spencer, Brian, *Walk the North York Moors; 40 Family Walks,* Bartholomew, 1986.

Northumberland

The Northumberland National Park is long and narrow stretching from just west of Hexham to the Scottish border. In its 1031 square kilometres the park includes the Cheviot, rising to a height of 816 metres, and the best preserved section of Hadrian's Wall. A visit to the Wall is a remarkable experience which demonstrates the might, power and orderliness of the Romans. Walkers exploring the park have numerous routes from which to choose, and traditionally, access to open country has always been permitted providing game and livestock are not disturbed.

National Park Headquarters: Eastburn, South Park, Hexham, Northumberland NE46 1BS (Tel. 0434-605555).

Information Centres: Cawfields—Hadrian's Wall (seasonal information van); Harbottle, Upper Coquetdale (weekends and Bank Holidays only); Housesteads—Hadrian's Wall, Military Road, Bardon Mill (Tel. 0434-344525); Ingram—(Tel. 066 578-248); Once Brewed—Military Road, Bardon Mill (Tel. 0434 344396); Rothbury—Church House, Church Street (Tel. 0669-20887); Tower Knowe—Kielder (Tel. 0434-240398).

Official Guidebook: Hopkins, Tony, *Northumberland,* Webb & Bower/ Michael Joseph, 1987.

Maps: 1:50000 Landranger sheets 74, 75, 80, 81, 87; 1:25000 Pathfinder sheets P463 (NT83/93), P475 (NT82/92), P476 (NU02/12), P486 (NT61/ 71), P487 (NT81/91), P488 (NU01/11), P498 (NT60/70), P499 (NT80/90),

P500 (NU00/10), P509 (NY69/79), P510 (NY89/99), P511 (NZ09/19), P521 (NY68/78), P522 (NU88/98), P533 (NY67/77), P534 (NY87/97), P546 (NY66/76), P547 (NY86/96).

Footpath Guides: Bleay, Janet, *Walks in the Hadrians' Wall Area,* Northumberland National Park, 1985; Williams, J., *Walks in the Cheviot Hills,* Northumberland National Park, 1981.

Peak

The Peak National Park was the first national park to be designated in Britain, and covers an area of 1304 square kilometres bordered by the towns of Huddersfield, Sheffield, Ashbourne and Stockport. The southern part of the park is largely limestone and known as the White Peak, whereas the northern section is millstone grit and referred to as the Dark Peak. The former is gentler, greener and more cultivated than the latter which is mountainous and contains a wilderness of groughs, the local name for peat bogs, which stretch for miles. The Kinder plateau (637 metres) is the highest point and is a stern test for walkers and there are numerous caverns in the Castleton area which can be visited. Some villages still keep up the old custom of well-dressing, when the wells are decorated with flowers to illustrate a bible story. Access agreements have been negotiated with some landowners, although sections of these moors may be closed during the grouse-shooting season. Notices giving details of closures are posted.

National Park Headquarters: Aldern House, Baslow Road, Bakewell, Derbyshire DE4 1AE (Tel. 062 981-4321).

Information Centres: Bakewell—Old Market Hall (Tel. 062 981 3227); Castleton—Castle Street (Tel. 0433-20679); Edale—Fieldhead (Tel. 0433-70207); Fairholmes in the Upper Derwent valley near the Derwent dam; Torside in the Longdendale valley on the B6105 near the dam (weekends and Bank Holidays only); Hartington—Old Railway Station on the B5064 2km east of the village (weekends and Bank Holidays only).

Official Guidebook: Smith, Roland, *The Peak,* Webb & Bower/Michael Joseph, 1987.

National Park Newspaper: The Peakland Post.

Maps: 1:63360 Tourist Map of the Peak District; 1:50000 sheets 109, 110, 118, 119; 1:25000 Outdoor Leisure Maps of the Peak District 1 (Dark Peak), 24 (White Peak),

Footpath Guides: Duerden, Frank, *Best Walks in the Peak District,* Constable, 1988; Hyde, George, *Circular Walks around Bakewell,* Dalesman, 1984; Sanders, Norman, *A Walker's Guide to the Upper Derwent,* Peak District National Park, 1984; Richards, Mark, *High Peak Walks,* Cicerone Press, 1982; Richards, Mark, *White Peak Walks:* Vol 1:

Northern Dales, Cicerone Press, 1985, Vol 2: *Southern Dales*, Cicerone Press, 1988; *Walks Around* series compiled and published by the Peak District National Park: *Six Walks around Tideswell Dale*, 1984; *Six Walks around Bakewell*, 1986; *Eight Walks around Edale*, 1987, *Walks around Longdendale*, 1977; *Six Walks around Hartington*, 1987; *Walks around Dovedale*, 1987.

Pembrokeshire Coast

The Pembrokeshire Coast Park is the smallest in Britain covering an area of only 583 square kilometres in South Wales. It is quite different in character from the other parks in that it has only one small tract of moorland in the Prescelly Hills. Its chief glory and attraction is its large area of magnificent, unspoiled coastal scenery. There are many prehistoric remains in the park and a surprisingly large number of medieval castles.

National Park Headquarters: County Offices, Haverfordwest, Dyfed SA61 1QZ (Tel. 0437-764591).

Information Centres: Broad Haven—National Park car park (Tel. 0437-781412); Kilgetty—Kingsmoor Common (Tel. 0834-812175); Newport—Bank Cottages, Long Street (Tel. 0239-820912); Pembroke—Drill Hall, Main Street (Tel. 0646-682148); St David's—City Hall (Tel. 0437-720392); Saundersfoot—Harbour car park (0834-811411); Tenby—The Croft (Tel. 0834-2402).

Official Guidebook: Williams, Herbert, *Pembrokeshire Coast*, Webb & Bower/Michael Joseph, 1988.

National Park Newspaper: Coast to Coast.

Maps: 1:50000 Landranger sheets 145, 157, 158; 1:25000 Pathfinder sheets P1010 (SN04/14), P1032 (SM83/93), P1033 (SN03/13), P1055 (SM62/72), P1057 (SN02/12), P1079 (SM81/91), P1080 (SN01/11), P1102 (SM70), P1103 (SM80/90), P1104 (SN00/10), P1124 (SR89/99), P1125 (SS09/19).

Footpath Guides: Walks leaflets compiled and published by the National Park: *Carew Jubilee Walk, Deer Park and Marloes, Ffos y Mynach, Goodwick-Carreg Wasted, Gwaun Valley Woodland Walk, St David's to Caerfai, Stackpole Lakes, Upton Castle Grounds, Walk around Carew, Walk around St David's Head.*

Thomas, Roger, *Great Walks; Brecon Beacons and Pembrokeshire Coast*, Ward Lock, 1989.

Snowdonia

The Snowdonia National Park is the second largest among British parks covering an area of 2171 square kilometres. It covers the coastline from Aberdovey to just north of Harlech and is then bounded by the towns of Conway, Bala and Machynlleth. Snowdon (1085 metres) is the highest mountain in Britain outside Scotland, and the Snowdon range contains some of the wildest country in Britain, with numerous lakes to enhance the beauty of the mountains. Over the years, much slate has been quarried and this park in under constant threat from industry thirsting to create more reservoirs and hungry to exploit its minerals.

National Park Headquarters: Penrhyndeudraeth, Gwynedd LL48 6LS (Tel. 0766-770274).

Information Centres: Aberdyfi (Tel. 065 472-321); Bala (Tel. 0678-520367); Betws-y-Coed (Tel. 0690-710426 and 710665); Blaenau Ffestiniog (Tel. 0766-830360); Dolgellau (Tel. 0341-422888); Harlech (Tel. 0766-78-0658); Llanberis (Tel. 0286-870636).

Official Guidebook: Styles, Showell, *Snowdonia,* Webb & Bower/Michael Joseph, 1987.

National Park Newspaper: The Snowdonia Star.

Maps: 1:126720 ($^1/2$ in. to the mile) Tourist Map of Snowdonia; 1:50000 Landranger sheets 115, 116, 124, 125, 135; 1:25000 Outdoor Leisure Maps of Snowdonia 16 (Conwy Valley area), 17 (Snowdon area), 18 (Harlech and Bala areas), 23 (Cadair Idris area).

Footpath Guides: Walks leaflets and maps compiled and published by Snowdonia National Park: Footpaths on Cader Idris: *Minffordd Path, Pony Path from Ty Nant, Pony Path from Llanfihangel y Pennant.*
Footpaths on Snowdon: *Llanberis Path, Miner's Track, Rhyd Ddu Path, Snowdon Ranger, Watkin Path, Branwen's Walk (Harlech), Bridges and Rivers (Betws-y-Coed), Cwmorthin, Glyn Aran (Dolgellau), Precipice Walk (Dolgellau), Torrent Walk (Dolgellau), Walks around Maentwrog.*

Contour Maps: *Llanberis Path, Miners' Track and Pyg Path, Snowdon Ranger and Rhyd Ddu, Watkin Path.*

Other guides: Ashton, Steve, *Hill Walking in Snowdonia,* Cicerone Press, 1989; Maddern, Ralph, *Walk in the Beautiful Conwy Valley,* Focus Publications, 5th Rev. Ed., 1986; Maddern, Ralph, *Walk in Magnificent Snowdonia,* Focus Publications, 3rd Rev. Ed., 1986; Maddern, Ralph, *Walk in the Vale of Ffestiniog,* Focus Publications, 1986; Poucher, W.A., *The Welsh Peaks,* Constable, 9th Rev. Ed.; 1987, Rowland, E. G., *The Ascent of Snowdon,* Cicerone Press 5th Rev. Ed., 1975; Rowland, E.G. *Hill Walking in Snowdonia,* Cicerone Press, 4th Rev. Ed., 1975; Sale, Richard, *Best Walks in North Wales,* Constable, 1989.

Yorkshire Dales

The Yorkshire Dales National Park is Britain's third largest park and covers an area of 1760 square kilometres bounded by the towns of Skipton, Settle, Sedbergh and Richmond. The dales themselves, with their enchanting villages, are long, narrow valleys which cut into the Pennines. This is wonderful country for the walker, and except for one or two places such as Malham and Kettlewell, relatively uncrowded. One of the features of the dales is the scars where the rocks have slipped, because of a geological fault, leaving the limestone as a huge cliff, as at Malham Cove and Gordale Scar.

National Park Headquarters: Colvend, Hebden Road, Grassington, Skipton, North Yorkshire BD23 5LB (Tel. 0756-752748).

Information Centres: Aysgarth Falls (Tel. 0969-66324); Clapham (Tel. 04685-419); Grassington (Tel. 0756-752748); Hawes (Tel. 0969-667450); Malham (Tel. 07293-363); Sedbergh (Tel. 0587-20125).

Official Guidebook: Waltham, Tony, *Yorkshire Dales,* Webb & Bower/ Michael Joseph, 1987.

National Park Newspaper: The Visitor.

Maps: 1:50000 Landranger sheets 91, 92, 97, 98, 99, 103, 104; 1:25000 Outdoor Leisure Maps Yorkshire Dales 2 (Western area), 10 (Southern area), 30 (Northern and Central).

Footpath Guides: Gemmell, Arthur, *Aysgarth Area Footpath Map,* Stile Publications, 5th Rev. Ed., 1987; Gemmell, Arthur, *Bolton Abbey Footpath Map,* Stile Publications, 4th Rev. Ed., 1987; Gemmell, Arthur, *Grassington and Area Footpath and Town Maps and Walking Guide,* Stile Publications, 3rd. Rev. Ed., 1987; Gemmell, Arthur, *Malhamdale Footpath Map,* Stile Publications, 7th Rev. Ed., 1988; Gemmell, Arthur, *Upper Swaledale Footpath Maps and Guide,* Stile Publications, 2nd. Rev. Ed., 1987; Gemmell, Arthur, *Wayfarer Walks in Upper Wharfedale,* Stile Publications, 2nd Rev. Ed., 1988; Hannon, Paul, *Dales Walks; a Comprehensive Walking Guide to the Yorkshire Dales,* Cordee, 1988; Sellers, Gladys, *The Yorkshire Dales; a Walker's Guide to the National Park,* Cicerone Press, 1984.

14 Areas of Outstanding Natural Beauty in England and Wales, the Channel Islands and the Isle of Man

Areas of Outstanding Natural Beauty (known as AONBs) are areas of England and Wales where the landscape is of such quality that the Countryside Commission and the local authorities have decided to submit to the Secretary of State for the Environment a request that the region be declared an Area of Outstanding Natural Beauty.

Once an AONB has been designated the local authority pays particular attention to planning development so that the unique character of the area can be preserved. The local authority remains responsible for AONBs, but they often set up advisory bodies containing representatives of amenity groups that can make recommendations on all matters concerning the Area. Not all AONBs make special facilities available for walkers and it does not necessarily follow that paths will be particularly well looked after. Nevertheless, their scenic quality alone make AONBs attractive to walkers and they offer much easier walking than the more difficult parts of the national parks.

On 1st January 1990 a total of thirty-eight AONBs had been designated covering approximately 19,265 square kilometres or 13% of England and Wales. Unfortunately the boundaries of Areas of Outstanding Natural Beauty are not shown on Ordnance Survey maps (except as insets on the 1:250000 Routemaster Maps) but they are clearly marked on the RAC series of three miles to the inch Regional Maps. Under the name of each Area of Outstanding Natural Beauty is given the sheet numbers of the relevant Ordnance Survey maps and the names of the English Regional Tourist Boards in which the AONB lies (sometimes they extend over more than one) are given. Many of the Regional Tourist Boards publish walks leaflets and accommodation lists that they will supply on request. The address of every Regional Tourist Board is given on pages 298-9. The Wales Tourist Board has no regional offices and enquiries should be made to their Cardiff office. In some cases local authorities publish information about walks and it is worth writing to the Planning Officers of the County Council and the District Council whose addresses can be found in *The Municipal Yearbook* which may be consulted in most public libraries. Wherever possible, a list of footpath guides is given. The lists are not exhaustive and preference has been given to guides covering a wide area and those issued by recognised publishers.

Anglesey

An area of 215 square kilometres covering nearly all this island off the coast of North Wales, forming part of the county of Gwynedd. The scenery may be described as a low plateau with a few isolated hills rising to just over 200 metres and containing a number of shallow valleys. The coastline is particularly attractive with a series of crescent-shaped bays and rocky headlands. There are fine views across to the mountains of Snowdonia. The island has numerous prehistoric remains.

Maps: 1:50000 Landranger sheet 114; 1:25000 Pathfinder sheets P733 (SH29/39/49), P734 (SH28/38), P735 (SH48/58), P750 (SH27/37), P751 (SH47/57), P752 (SH67), P768 (SH36/46), P769 (SH56).

Footpath Guide: Sale, Richard, *Best Walks in North Wales,* Constable 1988.

Wales Tourist Board, Brunel House, 2 Fitzalan Road, Cardiff CF2 1UY (Tel. 0222-499909).

Arnside and Silverdale

This AONB is situated on the north-east shore of Morecambe Bay on the southern tip of the Lake District National Park in the counties of Cumbria and Lancashire. This is limestone country with hills up to 150 metres high giving splendid views over Morecambe Bay and to the mountains of the Lake District. The particular charm of this 75-square kilometre AONB lies in its miniature landscape.

Maps: 1:50000 Landranger sheet 97; 1:25000 Pathfinder sheets P627 (SD48/58), P636 (SD37/47), P637 (SD57).

Footpath Guide: Evans, R. Brian, *Walks in the Silverdale/Arnside AONB,* Cicerone Press 1986.

Cumbria Regional Tourist Board, Ashleigh, Holly Road, Windermere, Cumbria LA23 2AS (Tel. 09662-4444), North West Regional Tourist Board, The Last Drop Village, Bromley Cross, Bolton, Lancs BL7 9PZ. (Tel 0204-591511).

Cannock Chase

An area of 68 square kilometres near Stafford which is one of the traditional lungs of the Black Country. The landscape is made up of bracken-clad heathland and woods broken up by attractive valleys. There are access agreements for the wilder parts of the Chase and some of it is free from vehicular traffic and specially reserved for walkers and riders.

Maps: 1:50000 Landranger sheets 127, 128; 1:25000 Pathfinder sheets P850 (SJ82/92), P851 (SK02/12), P871 (SJ81/91), P872 (SK01/11).

Footpath Guide: Merrill, John N., *Short Walks in the Staffordshire Moorlands,* JNM Publications, 1986.

Heart of England Regional Tourist Board, Woodside, Larkhill, Worcester WR5 2EQ. (Tel. 0905-763436).

Chichester Harbour

75 square kilometres of harbour and estuary around Chichester and Emsworth in West Sussex and Hampshire. This is pre-eminently a sailing centre, and although the salt marshes are very attractive, it is not primarily a walking area.

Maps: 1:50000 Landranger sheet 197; 1:25000 Pathfinder sheets P1304 (SU60/70), P1305 (SU80/90), P1323 (SZ89).

South East Regional Tourist Board, The Old Brewhouse, Warwick Park, Tunbridge Wells, Kent TN2 5TU. (Tel. 0892-540766).

The Chilterns

An 800-square-kilometre area of chalk hills stretching in a broad band from Goring-on-Thames, where it links with the North Wessex Downs AONB, to Luton in the counties of Oxfordshire, Buckinghamshire, Hertfordshire and Bedfordshire. This is very popular with Londoners as it is so easy to reach by public transport. It contains some excellent walking country with well-defined paths and is famous for its attractive and stately beech woods and lovely villages.

Maps: 1:50000 Landranger sheets 165, 166, 176, 176; 1:25000 Pathfinder sheets P1048 (TL03/13), P1072 (TL02/12), P1094 (SP81/91), P1095 (TL01/11), P1117 (SP60/70), P1118 (SP80/90), P1119 (TL00/10), P1138 (SU89/99), P1139 (TQ09/19), P1155 (SU48/58), P1156 (SU68/78), P1157 (SU88/98), P1172 (SU67/77), P1173 (SU87/97), P1187 (SU46/56), P1188 (SU66/76).

Footpath Guides: Basham, Vaughan, *Local Walks; South Bedfordshire and North Chilterns,* The Book Castle, 1988; Chiltern Society, *1:25000 Footpath Maps,* Shire Publications, 1986: *1. High Wycombe and Marlow, 2. Henley and Nettlebed, 3. Wendover and Princes Risborough, 4. Henley and Caversham, 5. Sarratt and Chipperfield, 6. Amersham and the Penn Country,*

7. *West Wycombe and Princes Risborough, 8. Chartridge and Cholesbury, 9. The Oxfordshire Escarpment, 10. Ewelme and District, 11. The Hambledon Valley, 12. The Hughenden Valley and Great Missenden, 13. Beaconsfield and District, 14. Stokenchurch and Chinnor, 15. Crowmarsh Gifford, 16. Goring and Mapledurham, 17. Chesham and Berkhamsted, 18. Tring and Wendover.*

Moon, Nicholas, *Walks in the Hertfordshire Chilterns,* Shire Publications, 1986; Pilgram, Ron, *Discovering Walks in the Chilterns,* Shire Publications, Rev. Ed., 1989.

Thames and Chiltern Regional Tourist Board, The Mount House, Church Green, Witney, Oxon OX8 5DZ. (Tel. 0993-778800).

Clwydian Hills

A long narrow AONB of 156 square kilometres stretching south from Prestatyn, Clwyd to the A525. The Clwydian Hills rise to 500 metres and the final part of Offa's Dyke Path passes through them. This is lovely, unspoiled countryside.

Maps: 1:50000 Landranger sheets 116, 117; 1:25000 Pathfinder sheets P737 (SJ08/18), P755 (SJ07/17), P772 (SJ06/16), P773 (SJ26/36), P788 (SJ05/15), P789 (SJ25/35), P805 (SJ04/14).

Footpath Guide: Sale, Richard, *Best Walks in North Wales,* Constable, 1988.

Wales Tourist Board, Brunel House, 2 Fitzalan Road, Cardiff CF2 1UY, (Tel. 0222-499909).

Cornwall

Cornwall is a county of contrasts. It contains some of the finest coastal scenery in England, and some of the interior is very attractive, especially Bodmin Moor. Unfortunately, much of the county outside the designated area of 2122 square kilometres is dull and spoiled by ribbon development, mining and china clay workings.

Maps: 1:50000 Landranger sheets 190, 200, 201, 203, 204; 1:25000 Pathfinder sheets P1310 (SX19), P1311 (SX29/39), P1325 (SX08/18), P1326 (SX28/38), P1337 (SW87/97), P1338 (SX07/17), P1339 (SX27/37), P1346 (SW86/96), P1347 (SX06/16), P1348 (SX26/36), P1352 (SW75), P1354 (SX05/15), P1355 (SX25/35), P1356 (SX45/55), P1359 (SW54/64), P1360 (SW74/84), P1361 (SW94/SX04), P1364 (SW33/43), P1366 (SW83), P1368 (SW32/42), P1369 (SW52/62), P1370 (SW72), P1372 (SW61/71).

Footpath Guides: Smith, Eleanor, *Cornish Coastal Walks for Motorists; 30 Circular Walks,* Warne, 1983; Vage, Donald, *Walking Cornwall,* Devon Books, 1987; Ward, Ken, *Land's End and the Lizard,* Jarrold, 1986.

West Country Regional Tourist Board, Trinity Court, 37 Southernhay East, Exeter EX1 1QS. (Tel. 0392-76351).

The Cotswolds

Bounded by the towns of Bath, Cheltenham and Cirencester, the 1507 square kilometres of this AONB contain hills of limestone and sandstone from which the buildings of the exceptionally beautiful villages have been constructed. Excellent walking country in the counties of Gloucestershire, Hereford and Worcester, Oxfordshire, Avon and Wiltshire.

Maps: 1:63360 Cotswold Tourist Map; 1:50000 Landranger sheets 150, 151, 163, 164, 172, 173; 1:25000 Pathfinder sheets P1019 (SO84/94), P1020 (SP04/14), P1042 (SO83/93), P1043 (SP03/13), P1044 (SP23/33), P1066 (SO82/92), P1067 (SP02/12), P1068 (SP22/32), P1089 (SO81/91), P1090 (SP01/11), P1091 (SP21/31), P1110 (SP20/30), P1113 (SO80/90), P1114 (SP00/10), P1117 (SO60/70), P1132 (ST69/79), P1133 (ST89/99), P1151 (ST68/78), P1152 (ST88/98), P1167 (ST67/77), P1168 (ST87/97), P1183 (ST66/76).

Footpath Guides: Airey, John, *Cotswolds Walks with a Point,* Foulsham, 1986; Hargreaves, Harry, *Cotswold Rambles,* Thornhill Press, 1983; Hargreaves, Harry, *Second Book of Cotwold Rambles,* Thornhill Press, 1985; Kershaw, R., and Robson, B., *Discovering Walks in the Cotswolds,* Shire Publications, 3rd Rev. Ed., 1983.

Heart of England Regional Tourist Board, Woodside, Larkhill, Worcester WR5 2EQ. (Tel. 0905-763436), West Country Regional Tourist Board, Trinity Court, 37 Southernhay East, Exeter EX1 1QS. (Tel. 0392-76351), Thames and Chilterns Tourist Board, The Mount House, Church Green, Witney, Oxon OX8 5DZ. (Tel. 0993-778800).

Cranborne Chase and West Wiltshire Downs

An area of 960 square kilometres, mostly in Wiltshire but including parts of Dorset, Hampshire and Somerset, bounded by Frome, Salisbury, Wimborne Minster and Shaftesbury. The western edge joins the Dorset AONB. This is a delightful mixture of downland and rolling wooded hills with charming villages and small towns.

Maps: 1:50000 Landranger sheets 183, 184, 194, 195; 1:25000 Pathfinder sheets P1219 (ST64/74), P1220 (ST84/94), P1221 (SU04/14), P1239 (ST63/73), P1240 (ST83/93), P1241 (SU03/13), P1261 (ST82/92), P1262 (SU02/12), P1281 (ST81/91), P1282 (SU10/11), P1300 (ST80/90), P1301 (SU00/10).

Footpath Guides: Jones, Roger, *Wiltshire Rambles,* Countryside Books, 1987; Legg, Rodney, *Blackmore Vale and Cranborne Chase Walks,* Dorset Publishing Co., 1987.

West Country Regional Tourist Board, Trinity Court, 37 Southernhay East, Exeter EX1 1QS. (Tel. 0392-76351).

Dedham Vale

72 square kilometres of the Constable country between Manningtree in Essex and Wayland in Suffolk. It is full of picturesque villages and is a 'typically English' pastoral landscape.

Maps: 1:50000 Landranger sheets 155, 168, 169; 1:25000 Pathfinder sheets P1030 (TM04/14), P1031 (TM24/34), P1052 (TL83/93), P1053 (TM03/13), P1054 (TM23/33).

Footpath Guide: Pratt, Jean and Geoff, *Suffolk Rambles,* Countryside Books, 1987.

East Anglia Regional Tourist Board, Toppesfield Hall, Hadleigh, Suffolk IP7 5DN (Tel. 0473-822922).

Dorset

Over one-third of Dorset, including nearly the whole of the coastline amounting to 1036 square kilometres, was designated in 1957. Apart from the splendid coastal and downland scenery, the area contains extensive prehistoric remains including Maiden Castle. The north-eastern edge joins the Cranborne Chase and West Wiltshire Downs AONB and the western edge abuts the East Devon AONB.

Maps: 1:50000 Landranger sheets 193, 194, 195; 1:25000 Pathfinder sheets P1281 (ST81/91), P1297 (ST20/30), P1298 (ST40/50), P1299 (ST60/70), P1300 (ST80/90), P1316 (SY29/39), P1317 (SY49/59), P1318 (SY69/79), P1319 (SY89/99), P1331 (SY58), P1332 (SY68/78), P1334 (SZ08), P1343 (SY67/77), plus Outdoor Leisure Map 15 Purbeck.

Footpath Guides: Edwards, Anne Marie, *Discovering Hardy's Wessex.* 2nd Ed. 1982; Legg, Rodney, *Hardy Country Walks; 22 Walks of Moderate Length through the Heart of Thomas Hardy's Dorset,* Dorset Publishing Co., 1984; Legg, Rodney, *Purbeck Walks; 21 Country Walks on Public Paths on the Isle of Purbeck,* Dorset Publishing Co., 1983; Legg, Rodney, *Walks in Dorset's Hardy Country,* Dorset Publishing Co., 1987; Legg, Rodney, *Walks in West Dorset; 20 Walks of Moderate Length along Public Paths through Superb Scenery,* Dorset Publishing Co., 1986; Shurlock, Barry, *Dorset Rambles; 10 Country Walks around Dorset,* Countryside Books, 1987.

West Country Regional Tourist Board, Trinity Court, 37 Southernhay East, Exeter EX1 1QS. (Tel. 0392-76351).

East Devon

Bordering on the western edge of the Dorset AONB, the East Devon

AONB covers 267 square kilometres. It runs westward as far as Exmouth and inland as far as Honiton although small areas around Seaton, Beer and Sidmouth are excluded. The area contains some fine coastal scenery including some of the magnificent red cliffs so typical of Devon. Inland are found charming villages and lovely rolling farmland.

Maps: 1:50000 Landranger sheets 192, 193; 1:25000 Pathfinder sheets P1296 (ST00/10), P1297 (ST20/30), P1315 (SY09/19), P1316 (SY29/39), P1330 (SY08/18).

Footpath Guides: Clarke, Nigel J., *West Dorset and East Devon Walks and Local Attractions,* published by the author at 3 Russell House, Lyme Close, Lyme Regis, Dorset, DT7 3DE, 1982; Stoker, Hugh, *East Devon Walks,* Mill House Publications, 1984.

West Country Regional Tourist Board, Trinity Court, 37 Southernhay East, Exeter EX1 1QS. (Tel. 0392-76351).

East Hampshire

A triangular area of 391 square kilometres of rolling farmland on the Hampshire/Sussex borders, between Winchester and Petersfield, where it links with both the Sussex Downs and Surrey Hills AONBs. Apart from the fine downland scenery, there is in the area, the birthplace of cricket and Butser Hill Farm – an iron-age farm that is run just as it was when the original farmers tilled the ground.

Maps: 1:50000 Landranger sheets 185. 186, 196, 197; 1:25000 Pathfinder sheets P1244 (SU63/73), P1264 (SU42/52), P1265 (SU62/72), P1285 (SU61/71).

Footpath Guide: Parker, Brenda, *Walks in East Hampshire,* Paul Cave Publications, Rev. Ed., 1981.

Southern Regional Tourist Board, 40 Chamberlayne Road, Eastleigh, Hampshire SO5 5JH. (Tel. 0703-620006).

Forest of Bowland

Covers an area of 803 square kilometres of mostly open moorland between Carnforth, Settle and Clitheroe in the counties of North Yorkshire and Lancashire. This AONB links with the Yorkshire Dales National Park and is really part of the Pennines but is separated from them by the Lune Valley. Pendle Hill is famous because George Fox, the Quaker, climbed it in 1652 and described the event in his *Journal.* It is even better known for its association with the Pendle witches who were tried and executed in 1612.

Maps: 1:50000 Landranger sheets 102, 103; 1:25000 Pathfinder sheets P649 (SD56), P650 (SD66/76), P651 (SD86/96), P659 (SD45/55), P660 (SD65/75), P668 (SD44/54), P669 (SD64/74), P670 (SD84/94), P679 (SD43/53), P680 (SD63/73).

Footpath Guide: Lord, A.A., *Wandering in Bowland; a Walker's Guide to the Footpaths and Byways of Bowland,* Westmorland Gazette, New Ed., 1983.

North West Regional Tourist Board, The Last Drop Village, Bromley Cross, Bolton, Lancs BL7 9PZ. (Tel. 0204-591511).

The Gower

The very first AONB designated in 1956, the Gower is an area of 189 square kilometres on a peninsula to the west of Swansea in the county of West Glamorgan. It contains fine beaches, coves and sand dunes and has no towns of any size.

Maps: 1:50000 Landranger sheet 159; 1:25000 Pathfinder sheets P1126 (SS49/59), P1127 (SS69/79), P1145 (SS48/58/68).

Footpath Guide: Jones, Roger, *Thirty Walks in Gower,* published by the author at 45 Greyhound Lane, Stourbridge, West Midlands DY8 3AD, 1982.

Wales Tourist Board, Brunel House, 2 Fitzalan Road, Cardiff CF2 1UY (Tel. 0222-499909).

High Weald

An area of 1450 square kilometres in the counties of Kent, East Sussex and West Sussex bounded by the towns of Tenterden, Hastings, Haywards Heath, Horsham, Crawley and Tonbridge. It includes some downland but it is mostly well-wooded, gently rolling low hills and it includes many attractive towns and villages.

Maps: 1:50000 Landranger sheets 187, 188, 198, 199;
1:25000 Pathfinder sheets P1228 TQ44/54), P1229 (TQ64/74), P1247 (TQ23/33), P1248 (TQ43/53), P1249 (TQ63/73), P1250 (TQ83/93), P1268 (TQ22/32), P1269 (TQ42/52), P1270 (TQ62/72), P1271 (TQ82/92), P1289 (TQ41/51), P1290 (TQ61/71), P1291 (TQ81/91).

Footpath Guides: On Foot in East Sussex; 24 Rambles based on Brighton, Lewes, Eastbourne, Seaford, Hastings, Battle, Rye, Winchelsea, Wadhurst and Uckfield Areas, Society of Sussex Downsmen, 254, Victoria Drive, Eastbourne, East Sussex, BN20 8QT, 1986; *Twenty Short Circular Walks around East Grinstead,* compiled and published by the Ashdown Rambling Club, 98 Holtye Road, East Grinstead, West Sussex, RH19 3EA.

South East Regional Tourist Board, The Old Brewhouse, Warwick Park, Tunbridge Wells, Kent TN2 5TU. (Tel. 0892-540766).

Howardian Hills

The Howardian Hills AONB is an area of 205 square kilometres which runs north-north-west from Malton, North Yorkshire to join the North York

Moors. It contains delightful, unspoiled villages and there are beautiful views from the hilltops.

Maps: 1:50000 Landranger sheet 100; 1:25000 Pathfinder sheets P642 (SE47/57), P643 (SE67/77), P665 (SE66/76) plus Outdoor Leisure Map 26 North York Moors (Western area).

Footpath Guide: White, Geoffrey, and Green, Geoffrey, *Walks North of York,* Dalesman, 1983.

Yorkshire and Humberside Regional Tourist Board, 312 Tadcaster Road, York YO2 2HF. (Tel 0904-707961).

Isle of Wight

189 square kilometres – approaching two-thirds of the island – have been designated including some of the finest beaches. The scenery of the hinterland is rolling downland with charming villages nestling in the valleys. This is excellent walking country with many waymarked routes vigorously promoted by the county council.

Maps: 1:50000 Landranger sheet 196; 1:25000 Outdoor Leisure Map 29 Isle of Wight.

Footpath Guides: McInnes, R. G., *Isle of Wight Walks for Motorists,* Warne, 1982; Spibey, Patricia, *Walking in the Isle of Wight,* Hale, 1988; *West Wight Ways,* compiled and published by West Wight Hotel and Catering Association, Sandford Lodge, Totland Bay, IoW PO39 DN, 1984.

Southern Regional Tourist Board, 40 Chamberlayne Road, Eastleigh, Hampshire SO5 5JH. (Tel. 0703-620006).

Isles of Scilly

A group of islands covering 16 square kilometres situated 45 kilometres south-west of Land's End. They are exceptionally beautiful and are climatically so mild that sub-tropical plants grow in profusion. Motor vehicles are banned except on St. Mary's.

Maps: 1:50000 Landranger sheet 203; 1:25000 Outdoor Leisure Map 12 Isles of Scilly.

West Country Regional Tourist Board, Trinity Court, 37 Southernhay East, Exeter EX1 1QS. (Tel. 0392-76351).

Kent Downs

Covering an area of 845 square kilometres and running from Orpington, where it joins the Surrey hills AONB, to Dover, the Kent Downs AONB includes classic chalk downland scenery which makes for excellent walking country which is very popular with Londoners.

Maps: 1:50000 Landranger sheets 178, 179, 187, 188; 1:25000 Pathfinder sheets P1192 (TQ46/56), P1193 (TQ66/76), P1194 (TQ86/96), P1208

(TQ45/55), P1209 (TQ65/75), P1210 (TQ85/95), P1211 (TR05/15), P1212 (TR25/35), P1228 (TQ44/54), P1230 (TQ84/94), P1231 (TR04/14), P1232 (TR24/34), P1251 (TR03), P1252 (TR13/23).

Footpath Guides: Plascott, Roy, *Kent Rambles; 10 Country Walks in Kent,* Countryside Books, 1987; Reynolds, Kev, *Walking in Kent,* Cicerone Press, 1988; Spayne, Janet, and Krynsl.i, *Walks in the Hills of Kent,* Spurbooks, 1981; Tidy, Brian, *Kentish Times Ramblers' Book,* Kentish Times, 1987.

South East Regional Tourist Board, The Old Brewhouse, Warwick Park, Tunbridge Wells, Kent TN2 5TU. (Tel. 0892-540766).

Lincolnshire Wolds

The Lincolnshire Wolds are a series of chalk hills rising to some 170 metres which run from the north-east corner of the country, parallel to the sea, but about 20 kilometres inland. Because much of the surrounding country is flat, they offer extensive views over coast and fen. Very good walking country and well worth exploring.

Maps: 1:50000 Landranger sheets 113, 121, 123; 1:25000 Pathfinder sheets P719 (TA00/10), P720 (TA20/30), P730 (TF09/19), P731 (TF29/39), P747 (TF08/18), P748 (TF28/38), P766 (TF27/37), P767 (TF47/57), P783 (TF26/36), P784 (TF46/56).

Footpath Guides: Tennyson Trails; Walks in the Lincolnshire Wolds, compiled and published by the Boston Group of the Ramblers' Association, 79 Sydney Street, Boston, Lincs PE21 8NZ, 1985; *Walks in South Humberside and Lincs,* compiled and published by the Wanderlust Rambling Club, 5 Pelham Crescent, Keelby, Grimsby DN37 8EW, 1985.

East Midlands Tourist Board, Exchequergate, Lincoln LN2 1PZ. (Tel. 0522-531521).

Lleyn

Lleyn is a peninsula in Gwynedd running westwards into the Irish Sea and containing the towns of Pwllheli, Abersoch, Aberdaron and Nevin. Most of the beautiful coastline is included in the 155 square kilometres of the designated area. This is an exceptionally beautiful and remote part of the country with narrow lanes running through gorse, bracken and rough pasture. There are white cottages and hills that give extensive views across the rocky headlands, tiny harbours and bays of the coast.

Maps: 1:50000 Landranger sheet 123; 1:25000 Pathfinder sheets P785 (SH45/55), P801 (SH34/44), P821 (SH13/23), P822 (SH33/43), P843 (SH12/22/32).

Wales Tourist Board, Brunel House, 2 Fitzalan Road, Cardiff CF2 1UY (Tel. 0222-499909).

Malvern Hills

Lying between Great Malvern and Ledbury, the Malvern Hills AONB covers 104 square kilometres in the counties of Gloucestershire, Hereford and Worcester. There are a number of summits over 300 metres with magnificent views over the surrounding countryside. There are many excellent footpaths and this is fine walking country.

Maps: 1:50000 Landranger sheet 150; 1:25000 Pathfinder sheets P995 (SO65/75), P1018 (SO64/74), P1041 (SO63/73).

Footpath Guides: Country Walks: East Malvern, compiled and published by Malvern Hills District Footpath Society, 8 Kingshill Close, Malvern, Worcs WR14 2BP, 1985; *Country Walks; West Malvern,* compiled and published by Malvern Hills District Footpath Society, 8 Kingshill Close, Malvern, Worcs WR14 2BP, 1987.

Heart of England Regional Tourist Board, Woodside, Larkhill, Worcester WR5 2EQ. (Tel. 0905-763436).

Mendip Hills

Stretching for 202 square kilometres from Weston-Super-Mare to the cathedral city of Wells in the counties of Avon and Somerset, the Mendip has short turf, limestone walls and typical limestone scenery. There are a number of hills over 300 metres giving views over the Bristol Channel. Wookey Hole and Cheddar Gorge form part of a large cave system for which the area is famous. There are numerous drove roads suitable for walking.

Maps: 1:50000 Landranger sheet 183; 1:25000 Pathfinder sheets P1182 (ST46/56), P1197 (ST25/35), P1198 (ST45/55), P1199 (ST65/75), P1218 (ST44/54).

Footpath Guide: Wright, Peter, *Mendip Rambles,* Ex Libris, 1985.

West Country Regional Tourist Board, Trinity Court, 37 Southernhay East, Exeter EX1 1QS. (Tel. 0392-76351).

Norfolk Coast

This AONB runs round the Norfolk coast from King's Lynn to Mundesley and covers 450 square kilometres of beaches, mud flats and salt marsh. Not particularly good walking country but it appeals greatly to those who love the peculiar atmosphere of flat coastal scenery.

Maps: 1:50000 Landranger sheets 132, 133; 1:25000 Pathfinder sheets P818 (TF64/74), P819 (TF84/94), P820 (TG04/14), P838 (TF43/53), P839 (TF63/73), P840 (TF83/93), P841 (TG03/13), P842 (TG23/33). P858 (TF42/52), P859 (TF62/72).

Footpath Guide: Kennett, David, *Discovering Walks in Norfolk,* Shire Publications, 1985.

East Anglia Regional Tourist Board, Toppesfield Hall, Hadleigh, Suffolk IP7 7DN. (Tel. 0473-822922).

North Devon

The whole of the north Devon coast from the boundary with Cornwall to the Exmoor National Park is included in this 171 square kilometres of rugged coastline, high cliffs and beautiful seascapes. It contains much beautiful scenery and charming old villages with thatched cottages.

Maps: 1:50000 Landranger sheets 180, 190; 1:25000 Pathfinder sheets P1253 (SS22/32), P1273 (SS21/31), P1292 (SS20/30).

Footpath Guides: Coastal Rambles, compiled and published annually by North Devon Print, 5 Oxford Grove, Ilfracombe, Devon EX34 8HG.

West Country Regional Tourist Board, Trinity Court, 37 Southernhay East, Exeter EX1 1QS. (Tel. 0392-76351).

North Pennines

A large AONB located in North Yorkshire, County Durham, Cumbria and Northumberland, that was designated in 1989. It stretches from the northern tip of the Yorkshire Dales National Park to the northern edge of the Tyne valley almost connecting with the Northumberland National Park. This AONB contains superb walking country and includes Crossfell (893 metres), the highest summit in England outside the Lake District National Park.

Maps: 1:50000 Landranger sheeets 86, 87, 91, 92; 1:25000 Pathfinder sheets P546 (NY 66/76), P547 (NY 86/96), P558 (NY 45/55), P559 (NY 65/75), P560 (NY 85/95), P568 (NY 44/54), P569 (NY 64/74), P570 (NY 84/94), P571 (NZ 04/14), P578 (NY 63/73), P580 (NZ 05/15), P597 (NY 61/71), P598 (NY 81/91), P607 (NY 60/70), P608 (NY 80/90) plus Outdoor Leisure Map 31 *Teesdale.*

Footpath Guides: Watson, Keith, *Walking in Teesdale,* Dalesman, 1978; *Walking in the Northern Dales* compiled by the North Yorkshire & South Durham Area of the Ramblers' Association, Dalesman, 1981. Cumbria Tourist Board, Adhleigh, Holly Road, Windermere, Cumbria LA23 2AS (Tel. 09662-4444), Northumbria Tourist Board, Aykley Heads, Durham DH1 5UX (Tel. 091386-2160), Yorkshire and Humberside Tourist Board, 312 Tadcaster Road, York Y02 2HF (Tel. 0904-707961).

Northumberland Coast

The Northumberland Coast AONB contains some marvellous scenery in its 129 square kilometres stretching from Berwick-on-Tweed southwards to Amble. The cold exposed beaches discourage conventional holidaymakers so it is quite unspoiled. There are magnificent castles, charming fishing villages, Holy Island and the Farne Islands to explore.

Maps: 1:50000 Landranger sheets 75, 81; 1:25000 Pathfinder sheets P452 (NU04/14), P465 (NU13/23), P477 (NU22), P489 (NU21/22), P501 (NU20).

Footpath Guide: Hopkins, Tony, *Walks on the Northumberland Coast,* Northumberland County Council, 1983.

Northumbria Regional Tourist Board, Aykley Heads, Durham DH1 5UX. (Tel. 091386-6905).

North Wessex Downs

This large AONB covers 1738 square kilometres in Hampshire, Wiltshire, Oxfordshire and Berkshire, bordered by the towns of Reading, Newbury, Andover, Devizes and Swindon. This area contains the largest and least-spoiled tract of chalk downland in southern England and the north-east corner joins the Chilterns AONB. There are several hills over 250 metres high and the area includes some of the most important prehistoric sites in the country. Very good walking country.

Maps: 1:50000 Landranger sheets 164, 173, 174; 1:25000 Pathfinder sheets P1136 (SU49/59), P1153 (SU08/18), P1154 (SU28/38), P1155 (SU48/58), P1169 (SU07/17), P1170 (SU27/37), P1171 (SU47/57), P1172 (SU67/77), P1184 (ST86/96), P1185 (SU06/16), P1186 (SU26/36), P1187 (SU46/56), P1201 (SU05/15), P1202 (SU25/35), P1203 (SU45/55), P1223 (SU44/54).

Footpath Guides: Channer, Nick, *North Hampshire Walks; 10 Country Rambles Near Winchester, Alton, Andover and Basingstoke,* Countryside Books, 1981; Parker, Brenda, *Walks in North Hampshire,* Paul Cave Publications, 1984.

Southern Regional Tourist Board, 40 Chamberlayne Road, Eastleigh, Hampshire SO5 5JH. (Tel. 0703-620006). West Country Regional Tourist Board, Trinity Court, 37 Southernhay East, Exeter EX1 1QS. (Tel. 0392-76351). Thames and Chilterns Regional Tourist Board, The Mount House, Church Green, Witney, Oxon OX8 5DZ. (Tel. 0993-778800).

Quantock Hills

The Quantocks are a range of hills in Somerset which run from just north of Taunton to Watchet on the coast. 99 square kilometres have now been designated and the area includes wooded combes, bracken-clad hills and picturesque villages.

Maps: 1:50000 Landranger sheets 181, 182; 1:25000 Pathfinder sheets

P1216 (ST04/14), P1236 (ST03/13), P1237 (ST23/33), P1257 (ST02/12), P1258 (ST22/32).

Footpath Guides: Rivers, Lyn, *Walk Exmoor and the Quantocks,* Bartholomew, 1990; *Walks on the Quantocks,* compiled by the Friends of the Quantocks, Merlin Press, 1987.

West Country Regional Tourist Board, Trinity Court, 37 Southernhay East, Exeter EX1 1QS. (Tel. 0392-76351).

Shropshire Hills

An irregularly shaped AONB to the south of Shrewsbury including the towns of Wellington, Church Stretton and Craven Arms. In the 777 square kilometres of the designated area will be found fine walking in the hills, that rise in places to over 500 metres, giving some splendid views.

Maps: 1:50000 Landranger sheets 126, 137; 1:25000 Pathfinder sheets P870 (SJ61/71), P888 (SJ20/30), P889 (SJ40/50), P890 (SJ60/70), P909 (SO29/39), P910 (SO49/59), P911 (SO69/79), P929 (SO08/18), P930 (SO28/38), P931 (SO48/58), P932 (SO68/78), P949 (SO07/17), P950 (SO27/37), P951 (SO47/57), P952 (SO67/77).

Footpath Guides: Smart, Robert, *Church Stretton and South Shropshire Rambles,* published by the author at 'Brackendale', Longhills Road, Church Stretton, Salop SY6 6DS, 1985.

Heart of England Regional Tourist Board, Woodside, Larkhill, Worcester WR5 2EQ. (Tel. 0905-763436).

Solway Coast

The Solway Coast AONB stretches from the Scottish border to Maryport in Cumbria and covers an area of 107 square kilometres overlooking the Solway Firth to Scotland. Although the area is flat, containing fine sandy beaches, the views across to the hills of Scotland are magnificent.

Maps: 1:50000 Landranger sheets 85, 89; 1:25000 Pathfinder sheets P543 (NY06/16), P544 (NY26/36), P556 (NY05/15), P557 (NY25/35), P566 (04/14), P575 (03/13).

Cumbria Regional Tourist Board, Ashleigh, Holly Road, Windermere, Cumbria LA23 2AS. (Tel. 09662-4444).

South Devon

One of the most popular holiday areas in the country, the South Devon AONB runs from Torbay to Plymouth, including most of the South Hams, and covers 332 square kilometres. This region is famous for its fine beaches, cliff scenery and the beautiful estuaries and inlets that stretch for miles inland.

Maps: 1:50000 Landranger sheets 201, 202; 1:25000 Pathfinder sheets P1356 (SX45/55), P1357 (SX65/75), P1362 (SX54/64) plus Outdoor Leisure Map 20 South Devon.

Footpath Guides: 15 Walks in the Kingsbridge Area, compiled and published by the South Hams Group of the Ramblers' Association, 'St Malo', Stentiford, Fore Street, Kingsbridge, Devon TQ7 1AX, 1986; *16 Walks around Salcombe,* compiled and published by the South Hams Group of the Ramblers' Association, 'St Malo', Stentiford, Fore Street, Kingsbridge, Devon TQ7 1AX, 1986.

West Country Regional Tourist Board, Trinity Court, 37 Southernhay East, Exeter EX1 1QS. (Tel. 0392-76351).

South Hampshire Coast

This, like Chichester Harbour AONB, is a famous sailing centre and covers 78 square kilometres from just east of Beaulieu to west of Lymington with the northern edge bordered by the New Forest.

Maps: 1:50000 Landranger sheet 196; 1:25000 Outdoor Leisure Map 22 New Forest.

Southern Regional Tourist Board, 40 Chamberlayne Road, Eastleigh, Hampshire SO5 5JH. (Tel. 0703-620006).

Suffolk Coast and Heaths

This area contains 391 square kilometres of coast from Ipswich and the Orwell estuary almost to Lowestoft. The region is very flat and contains some beautifully wooded estuaries and many creeks that are the haunt of wild fowl.

Maps: 1:50000 Landranger sheets 134, 156; 1:250000 Pathfinder sheets P946 (TM48/58). P966 (TM47/57), P987 (TM46), P1008 (TM25/35), P1009 (TM44/45), P1031 (TM24/34), P1054 (TM23/33).

Footpath guides: Barrett, Elizabeth, *Exploring Bridleways,* published by the author at Pip's Peace, Kenton, Stowmarket, Suffolk IP14 6JS: *3. Suffolk Coast between the Deben and the Alde, 1983, 4. Suffolk Coast between the Alde and the Blyth, 1984; Country Walks,* compiled and published by Suffolk Coastal District Council, Council Offices, Melton Hill, Woodbridge, Suffolk IP12 1AU, 1983.

East Anglia Regional Tourist Board, Toppesfield Hall, Hadleigh, Suffolk IP7 7BN. (Tel. 0473-822922).

Surrey Hills

Another popular walking area for Londoners, the Surrey Hills AONB contains 414 square kilometres of chalk downland and greensand that stretches from Farnham and Haslemere eastwards to the Kent boundary and links with both the Sussex Downs and Kent Downs AONBs. The Greensand Hills, which include Leith Hill, at 294 metres the highest point in south-east England, run to the south of the chalk downs and offer contrasting vegetation of bracken and silver birches and splendid views across the Weald to the South Downs, and even to the sea from one or two places.

Maps: 1:50000 Landranger sheets 186, 187; 1:25000 Pathfinder sheets P1206 (TQ05/15), P1207 (TQ25/35), P1208 (TQ45/55), P1225 (SU84/94), P1226 (TQ04/14), P1227 (TQ24/34), P1228 (TQ44/54), P1245 (SU83/93).

Footpath Guides: Adams, A. L., *Walk the Charming Footpaths of South West Surrey*, published by the author at 2 Dryden Court, Lower Edgeborough Road, Guildford, Surrey, GU1 2EX, 1983; Adams, A. L., *Walk in the Charming Country around Dorking*, published by the author at 2 Dryden Court, Lower Edgeborough Road, Guildford, Surrey, GU1 2EX, 1984; Bagley, William A., *Surrey Walks for Motorists; 30 Circular Walks*, Warne Gerrard, 2nd. Ed., 1982; Haine, Angela, and Owen, Susan, *Discovering Walks in Surrey*, Shire Publications, 1981; Hyde, George, *Five-Mile Walks in South-West Surrey* and *More Five-Mile Walks in South-West Surrey*, Footpath Publications, 69 South Park, Godalming, Surrey GU7 1SU, 1988; Palmer, Derek, *Surrey Rambles; 10 Country Walks around Surrey*, Countryside Books, 1987.

South East Regional Tourist Board, The Old Brewhouse, Warwick Park, Tunbridge Wells, Kent TN2 5TU. (Tel. 0892-540766).

The Sussex Downs

A series of whaleback chalk hills that run from Petersfield in West Sussex, where they link with both the East Hampshire and Surrey Hills AONBs to Eastbourne in East Sussex and cover 981 square kilometres. This is fine walking country with extensive views northwards across the Weald and southwards to the coast. Near Eastbourne the Downs reach the sea and form cliffs over 150 metres high.

Maps: 1:50000 Landranger sheets 197, 198, 199; 1:25000 Pathfinder sheets P1245 (SU83/93), P1265 (SU62/72), P1266 (SU82/92), P1267 (TQ02/12), P1285 (SU61/71), P1286 (SU81/91), P1287 (TQ01/11), P1288 (TQ21/31), P1289 (TQ41/51), P1304 (SU60/70), P1305 (SU 80/90), P1306 (TQ00/10), P1307 (TQ20/30), P1308 (TQ40/50), P1324 (TV49/59/69).

Footpath Guides: Perkins, Ben, *South Downs Walks for Motorists*, Warne, 1986; *On Foot in East Sussex; 24 Rambles based on Brighton, Lewes, Eastbourne, Seaford, Hastings, Battle, Rye, Winchelsea, Wadhurst and Uckfield Areas*, Society of Sussex Downsmen, 254, Victoria Drive, Eastbourne, East Sussex, BN20 8QT, 1986; Ulph, Colin, *Southdown Walks;*

32 Downland Rambles from Brighton, Worthing and Surrounding District, published by the author at 281 Upper Shoreham Road, Shoreham-by-Sea, West Sussex BN4 6BB, 2nd Rev. Ed., 1986.

South East Regional Tourist Board, The Old Brewhouse, Warwick Park, Tunbridge Wells, Kent TN2 5TU. (Tel. 0892-540766).

The Wye Valley

The 325 square kilometres of the Wye Valley from Chepstow northwards almost to Hereford contain some superb river scenery including, in the lower half, cliffs and gorges. Above Ross, the river is narrower and runs more quickly. This AONB lies in the counties of Gwent, Hereford and Worcester, and Gloucestershire.

Maps: 1:50000 Landranger sheets 149, 162; 1:25000 Outdoor Leisure Map 14 Wye Valley and the Forest of Dean.

Footpath Guides: Hurley, Heather, *Wyedean Walks*, Forest Bookshop, 8 St John Street, Coleford, Glos GL16 8AR, 1986; Hurley, Heather, *and* John, *Paths and Pubs of the Wye Valley,* Thornhill Press, 1986; Jones, Roger, *Exploring the Wye Valley and Forest of Dean*, published by the author at 45 Greyhound Lane, Stourbridge, West Midlands DY8 3AD.

Heart of England Regional Tourist Board, Woodside, Larkhill, Worcester WR5 2EQ. (Tel. 0905-763436).

Channel Islands

This group of beautiful islands situated nearer France than England contains much attractive countryside. The Channel Islands are responsible for their own mapping although the (British) Ordnance Survey has published a 1:25000 map of Jersey.

Footpath Guides: Barber, Alan, *Explore Sark, Three Guided Walks*, Bailiwick Publications, 1985; Barber, Alan, *Walks with a Car in Guernsey*, Bailiwick Publications, 1984; Barber, Alan, *Walks with a Meal in Guernsey*, Bailiwick Publications, 1986; Bois, F. de L., *Jersey Walks for Motorists*, Warne, 1979.

Useful Addresses: States of Guernsey Tourist Board, PO Box 23, White Rock, Guernsey, CI. (Tel 0481-26611); States of Jersey Tourism Department, Weighbridge, Jersey, CI. (Tel. 0534–78000).

Isle of Man

The Isle of Man covers an area of 227 square miles in the Irish Sea midway between England and Ireland. It has much attractive scenery including rough moorland, cliffbound coasts and wooded glens.

Maps: 1:50000 Landranger sheet 95 (NB the Ordnance Survey 1:25000 Pathfinder series does not include the Isle of Man)

Footpath guides: Manx Hill Walks, compiled and published by the Manx Conservation Council (Footpath Group).
Useful Address: Department of Tourism and Transport, 13 Victoria Street, Douglas, IOM. (Tel. 0624-74323).

15 Long-distance Paths of the United Kingdom

Long-distance paths may be defined as routes over which it is possible for the walker to make a journey that will take two days or more to complete.

There are two kinds of long-distance path; those 'official' paths designated and cared for by a central government agency, and the 'unofficial' routes created by an individual, organisation or local authority devising an interesting route along existing rights of way, giving it a suitable name and publishing a guide to the walk. The Countryside Commission is responsible for the official routes in England and Wales, in Scotland it is the Countryside Commission for Scotland, and in Northern Ireland it is the Sports Council for Northern Ireland. In 1988 the official long-distance paths of England and Wales were re-named National Trails.

During the past fifteen years there has been an enormous growth in the number of unofficial long-distance paths in England and Wales (the Scottish walking tradition is different and frowns upon such routes) which now number in the region of three hundred and fifty and it is now possible to walk from Land's End to the Scottish border using long-distance paths. Some parts of the country, notably the North York Moors, have too many long-distance routes which has resulted in damage to the environment.

The official long-distance paths were established first after the Hobhouse Committee on Footpaths and Access to the Countryside recommended that continuous rights of way over some of the country's finest mountain, moorland, downland and coastal scenery be created. The National Parks and Access to the Countryside Act, 1949 provided the necessary legislation for creating such long-distance footpaths in England and Wales. In Scotland, the Countryside (Scotland) Act, 1967, is the legal basis. These paths were always intended to be based on some strong physical or historic feature so they are not merely routes for getting from one place to another.

The procedure for establishing long-distance paths is as follows. In England and Wales the Countryside Commission makes recommendations to the Secretary of State for the Environment, in Scotland the Countryside Commission submits proposals to the Secretary of State for Scotland, and in Northern Ireland the Sports Council for Northern Ireland deals with the Secretary of State for Northern Ireland. Once the minister has approved the recommendations then the body which submitted the proposals assists local authorities in establishing the exact line of the path and negotiating with landowners and other interested parties.

Considerable sections of long-distance paths were already rights of way, but some stretches had to be created by negotiating with the landowners and paying compensation. One of the most difficult tasks was establishing who owned the land, but only rarely has it been necessary to establish a right of way by statute, and obviously it is better to create paths by negotiation rather than applying the law, to avoid antagonising landowners unnecessarily.

The symbol used by the Countryside Commission for Scotland is a thistle. National Trails are waymarked using the Countryside Commission symbol of an acorn. These are non-directional signs and should be used merely to confirm that the walker has not strayed from the path. Ordnance Survey maps, or a good footpath guide, are necessary to walk these paths accurately. The 1:25000 map should be used for all of them except, perhaps, for the Pennine Way the Cleveland Way, and those in Scotland and Northern Ireland where the smaller-scale map may suffice, especially if supplemented with one of the guides to these routes.

Walking one of the long-distance paths is something of an adventure. The walker sees the countryside in a way that no other traveller does and will be surprised at how empty our densely populated country is once the main roads are forsaken. Much pleasure can be had in planning a long-distance walk. Nights spent poring over maps, bus and railway timetables and accommodation directories will give many anticipatory thrills.

The biggest problem is likely to be accommodation. Camping would seem to offer the greatest flexibility, but not all the long-distance paths are suitable for camping because they often lack convenient sites and water. It is advisable to book accommodation well in advance especially during the busier seasons of the year.

Members of the Youth Hostels Association can take advantage of the package booking scheme provided by the Association for some of the more popular long-distance paths.

Blazing sunshine is not essential to enjoy a walking holiday; indeed walking in great heat is usually uncomfortable, so it is worth considering an out-of-season holiday. The countryside is very beautiful in spring and autumn and can be enjoyable in the winter months when the bare beauty of the trees is so attractive. But neither the Pennine Way nor the Cleveland Way should be attempted between November and April except by the hardiest and most experienced walkers.

It is not necessary to complete a long-distance path in consecutive days, although this method is probably the most enjoyable, and gives the greatest sense of achievement. With careful planning, it is often possible to walk a path in a series of weekends or even odd days.

Long-distance paths are for pleasure and recreation, not record breaking. There is no merit in walking the Pennine Way in fourteen days rather than fifteen. Some people like to walk a considerable distance each day with only a few stops; others like to dawdle, pausing frequently to observe what is going on around them. The style of walking, whether it be purposeful or leisurely, does not matter, except that any companion must be of a similar temperament. Before attempting any of the long-distance paths, walkers should have a clear idea of their walking abilities and know how much ground they can cover each day. If carrying a heavy pack, it is advisable to do some practice walking with a full rucksack to become accustomed to it.

Official Long-Distance Paths

The Cleveland Way
The Cleveland Way starts at Helmsley on the edge of the North York Moors National Park and runs for 161 kilometres around three sides of the park to finish at Filey on the coast. The scenery varies between moorland and magnificent cliffs along the coast.

The path leaves Helmsley skirting Duncombe Park before crossing the River Rye about half a mile from the ruins of Rievaulx Abbey. It follows wooded valleys to Cold Kirby to reach the steep cliff at Sutton Bank with fine views across the Vale of York to the Pennines. There follows a cliff edge walk above Gormire Lake, along Boltby Scar to Sneck Yat, until the old drove road is picked up at High Paradise. After climbing to some 450 metres the path leaves the drove road in Oakdale and reaches Osmotherley.

Just north of Osmotherley, the path joins the line of the Lyke Wake Walk for 32 kilometres and then crosses Carlton Bank, Cringle Moor, Cold Moor and Hasty Bank. Next comes Urra Moor and Botton Head, which at

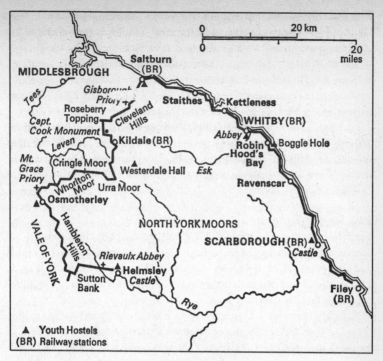

Fig. 43 The Cleveland Way

460 metres is the highest point of the North York Moors. At Blaworth Crossing, the path turns north-north-west to the top of Greenhow Bank, Battesby Bank and on to Kildale.

From Kildale the path climbs Easby Moor to the monument to Captain Cook and then over Great Ayton Moor and on to Highcliff, Guisborough and Skelton and so to the sea at Saltburn.

The rest of the walk is a coastal path over Boulby Cliff, the highest cliff on the English coast, to the charming fishing village of Staithes and on to Runswick, Lythe Bank and Whitby. Past Whitby, the path goes on to the North Cheek of Robin Hood's Bay to finish just short of Filey. The energetic can then start the Wolds Way at Filey and finish at North Ferriby (see p213).

This part of England is blessed with a dry climate, but it can be bleak and cold. It is not a difficult walk but considerably harder than the Ridgeway and the North and South Downs Ways, and it is advisable to dress as for fell-walking.

Accommodation is plentiful in parts, especially along the coast, but there is practically nothing in the 40 kilometres between Osmotherley and Guisborough. Camping seems to be the ideal solution as the hinterland has plenty of water and there are numerous organised sites along the coast.

Youth Hostels: Helmsley, Osmotherley, Westerdale Hall, Saltburn, Whitby, Boggle Hole and Scarborough.

Maps: 1:50000 Landranger sheets 93, 94, 99, 100, 101; 1:25000 Outdoor Leisure Maps North York Moors 26 (Western area), 27 (Eastern area).

Footpath Guides: Boyes, Malcolm, *Walking the Cleveland Way and the Missing Link*, Cicerone Press, 1989; Hannon, Paul, *Cleveland Way Companion*, Hillside Publications, 1986; Sampson, Ian, *Cleveland Way*, Aurum Press in association with the Countryside Commission and the Ordnance Survey, 1989.

The North Downs Way

The North Downs Way runs for 227 kilometres over the chalk downs from Farnham in Surrey to Dover in Kent. There is a popular misconception that this National Trail follows the line of the ancient Pilgrim's Way. It does in one or two places, but the route was chosen for its scenic qualities not for its historical associations.

The path starts very conveniently at Farnham railway station on the Waterloo line, follows the River Wey for a short distance, then climbs to the north of Crooksbury Hill, passes the village of Seale, keeping just south of the summit of the Hog's Back, and continues to Puttenham. It then passes under the A3, the Guildford Bypass, to the River Wey navigation on the southern side of Guildford, where it joins the historic Pilgrim's Way to climb St Martha's Hill with its tiny chapel and over Newlands Corner and Albury Downs to Netley Heath, White Down and Ranmore Common to the A24 at Box Hill.

Box Hill is one of those curious places where vast numbers of people congregate on fine weekends. One edge of the hill is a cliff formed by the River Mole, where it cuts through the chalk, but there are many higher hills and better viewpoints on the North Downs. The reason for its popularity probably lies in its proximity to a railway station and main road rather than its scenic qualities and associations with George Meredith, Keats and Lord Nelson.

The River Mole is crossed by stepping stones and there is then a very steep climb up Box Hill and over the escarpment above the Betchworth chalk quarries to Colley Hill and Reigate Hill, where the A217 is crossed by a footbridge, and on past Gatton Park to Merstham on the A23, the Brighton Road. From the Brighton Road, the path goes over White Hill to Gravelly Hill on the A22, the Eastbourne Road, and on to Tatsfield in Kent. It crosses Chevening Park and on through Dunton Green to Otford.

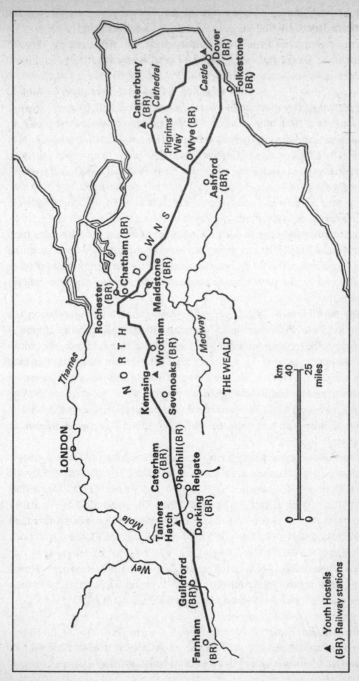

Fig. 44 The North Downs Way

187

The path climbs up to the scarp of the Downs to Wrotham and the Hastings Road, the A20.

The escarpment is climbed again and the path passes through Whitehorse Wood and over Holly Hill until it reaches the Medway near Rochester. A footbridge alongside the M2 crosses the river. The path now turns south via Bluebell Hill to Detling and on past Thurnham Castle and Cat Mount to Hollingbourne, where it rejoins the ancient Pilgrim's Way to Charing and Boughton Aluph. At this point, an alternative route to Canterbury branches off past Soakham Down, Godmersham and Chilham Park to Chilham and Canterbury. The path then goes through Patrixbourne and over Barham Downs to Waldershare Park to Dover.

The main path leaves Boughton Aluph and goes through Wye and over the Downs to Stowting and Cherry Garden Hill, Castle Hill and Sugarloaf Hill to the main A620 road, just north of Folkestone, and on to Creteway Downs and the Valiant Sailor public house. From the pub there is a path over the cliffs to Dover but it may be necessary to make a detour along the coast road when the firing ranges at Lyddon Spout are being used. The official end of the path is at Shakespeare Cliff, overlooking the English Channel.

The North Downs Way is very easy walking and a strong walker could do it comfortably in one week. Accommodation tends to be sparse but it should not be too difficult to find bed and breakfast establishments or inns in some of the towns along the route. Many of the main roads that cross the Way have bus services to nearby towns. It is not really practicable to camp as there are few suitable sites and no potable water on the Downs. This walk is very easy to do in occasional day-trips from London as there are so many railway stations along the route. No special kit or equipment is required.

Youth Hostels: Tanner's Hatch, Kemsing, Canterbury, Dover.

Maps: 1:50000 Landranger sheets 177, 178, 179, 186, 187, 188, 189; 1:25000 Pathfinder sheets P1193 (TQ66/76), P1206 (TQ05/15), P1207 (TQ25/35), P1208 (TQ45/55), P1209 (TQ65/75), P1210 (TQ85/95), P1211 (TR05/15), P1212 (TR25/35), P1225 (SU84/94), P1226 (TQ04/14), P1230 (TQ84/94), P1231 (TR04/14), P1232 (TR24/34), P1252 (TR13/23).

Footpath Guides: Allen, David J., and Imrie, Patrick, *Discovering the North Downs Way*, Shire Publications, 2nd Ed., 1987; Herbstein, Denis, *The North Downs Way*, HMSO, 1982; Wright, C. J., *A Guide to the Pilgrims' Way and the North Downs Way*, Constable, 1982.

Offa's Dyke Path

Offa's Dyke Path runs for 270 kilometres from near the Severn Bridge to Prestatyn in North Wales. For most of its route, it follows Offa's Dyke, an earthwork constructed by the King of Mercia in the eighth century to mark the boundary between his lands and those of the Welsh.

From the Severn Bridge, the path goes to Chepstow and then climbs Tutshill to Wintour's Leap—a cliff with a magnificent view. It follows the Wye and the Dyke to Shorn Cliff and the Devil's Pulpit, with fine views of Tintern Abbey, and so on to Monmouth, where the rivers Wye and Monnow are crossed. The path follows a route through pleasant countryside past White Castle before, at Pandy, commencing the long climb up the Black Mountains. A long ridge, rising to 600 metres is crossed before dropping down to Hay-on-Wye.

From Hay, the path goes to Gladestry and Kington, where the Dyke can be clearly seen on Rushock Hill and Herrock Hill. From Knighton, the path follows the Teme and up Panpunton Hill, Llanvair Hill, Spoad Hill and Clun Forest before descending near Montgomery. After crossing the plain actually on the Dyke, the path climbs Long Mountain and Beacon Ring and then reaches the Severn at Buttington. The river is followed for some way but then the path strikes out through Llanymynech to Baker's Hill, past Chirk Castle and crosses the valley of the Dee by the Pontcysyllte aqueduct 37 metres above the valley.

The Vale of Llangollen is now followed to Eglwyseg Mountain, the End of the World and then over the moors to Llandegla where the River Alun is crossed a number of times before reaching the Clwydian Hills, a high ridge walk rising to about 600 metres. The path continues through Bodfari and on at last to Prestatyn.

On the whole, this is an easy walk, but the two high sections over the Black Mountains and the Clwydian Hills must be treated with respect, especially in bad weather.

Path Association: Offa's Dyke Association (see p306).

Youth Hostels: Chepstow, St Briavel's, Monmouth, Capel-y-ffin, Knighton, Clun Mill, Llangollen and Maeshafn.

Maps: 1:50000 Landranger sheets 116, 117, 126, 137, 148, 161, 162, 172; 1:25000 Pathfinder sheets P737 (SJ08/18), P755 (SJ07/17), P772 (SJ06/16), P788 (SJ05/15), P789 (SJ25/35), P806 (SJ24/34), P827 (SJ23/33), P847 (SJ22/32), P868 (SJ21/31), P888 (SJ20/30), P909 (SO29/39), P930 (SO28/38), P950 (SO27/37), P971 (SO 26/36), P993 (SO25/35), P1016 (SO24/34), P1039 (SO23/33), P1086 (SO21/31), P1087 (SO41/51), P1111 (SO40/50), P1131 (ST49/59), plus Outdoor Leisure Maps, 13 Brecon Beacons (Eastern), 14 Wye Valley and Forest of Dean.

Footpath Guides: Kay, Ernie and Kathy and Richards, Mark, *Offa's Dyke Path*, Aurum Press in association with the Countryside Commission and the Ordnance Survey, 1989; Kay, Kathy and Ernie, *Path Guide Notes, North – South* and *Path Guide Notes: South – North*, both titles published

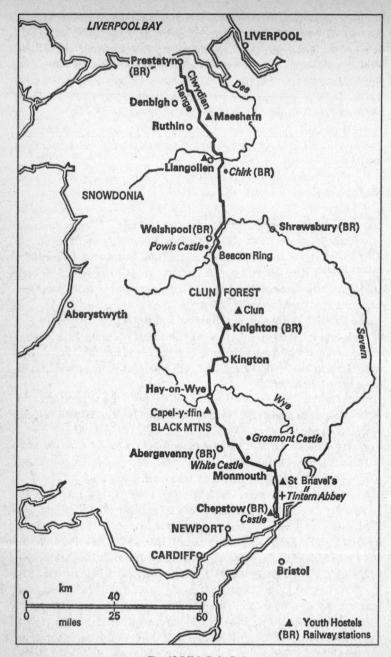

Fig. 45 Offa's Dyke Path

by the Offa's Dyke Association, 1985; Noble, Frank, *The Offa's Dyke Association Book of Offa's Dyke Path*, Offa's Dyke Association, 1981; *Offa's Dyke Path Backpackers' Camping List* published annually by Offa's Dyke Association; *Offa's Dyke Path Accommodation and Transport List* published annually by Offa's Dyke Association; Richards, Mark, *Through Welsh Border Country Following Offa's Dyke*, Thornhill Press, 1985; Wright, C. J., *A Guide to Offa's Dyke Path*, Constable, 1987.

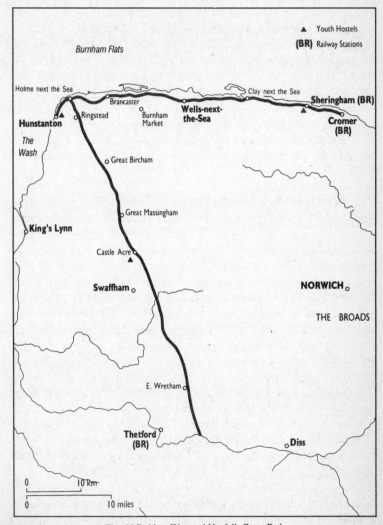

Fig. 46 Peddars Way and Norfolk Coast Path

The Peddars Way and Norfolk Coast Path

This runs for 138 kilometres from Knettishall, near Thetford through Norfolk to Holme-next-the-Sea and then east along the coast to Cromer (there is also a south-west spur that leads to Hunstanton). The terrain is very flat, making for fast, easy walking through pleasant, atmospheric countryside following, for the first half of the route, a Roman road. This route makes an ideal introduction to the pleasures of long-distance walking.

Path Association: The Peddars Way Association (see p307).

Youth Hostels: Castle Acre, Hunstanton and Sheringham.

Maps: 1:50000 Landranger sheets 132, 133, 134; 1:25000 Pathfinder sheets P818 (TF64/74), P819 (TF84/94), P820 (TG04/14), P839 (TF63/73), P842 (TG23/33), P859 (TF62/72), P880 (TF61/71), P881 (TF81/91), P901 (TF80/90), P922 (TL89/99), P943 (TL88/98).

Footpath Guides: Kenneth, David, *A Guide to the Norfolk Way*, Constable, 1983; Robinson, Bruce, *The Peddars Way and Norfolk Coast Path*, HMSO, 1986; *Walking the Peddars Way/Norfolk Coast Path and the Weaver's Way* compiled and published by the Peddars Way Association, 1987.

The Pembrokeshire Coast Path

The Pembrokeshire Coast Path runs for 270 kilometres from the county border at Poppit Sands about 2 kilometres north of St Dogmaels along cliffs, beaches and dunes to the Teifi estuary. As the path follows the extreme edge of the coast, except for one or two places where it has to go inland, it is unnecessary to give the route in detail. The scenery is very beautiful and largely unspoiled and it is very easy walking. Accommodation is plentiful but likely to be full at peak holiday times so booking is essential. There are plenty of camp sites and there should be no difficulty in obtaining water. During the summer, there is a special Coast Path bus service which links all the coastal car parks from Dale to Newgale. Walkers should beware of sunburn!

Youth Hostels: Poppit Sands, Pwll Deri, Trevine, St. David's. Broad Haven, Marloes Sands, Manorbier, Pentlepoir.

Maps: 1:50000 Landranger sheets 145, 157, 158; 1:25000 Pathfinder sheets P1010 (SN04/14), P1032 (SM83/93), P1033 (SN03/13), P1055 (SM62/72), P1056 (SM82/92), P1079 (SM81/91), P1102 (SM70), P1103 (SM80/90), P1104 (SN00/10), P1124 (SR89/99), P1125 (SS09/19).

Footpath Guides: John, Brian, *Pembrokeshire Coast Path*, Aurum Press in association with the Countryside Commission and the Ordnance Survey (publication scheduled for autumn 1989); Wright, Christopher John, *A Guide to the Pembrokeshire Coast Path*, Constable, 1986; Accommodation

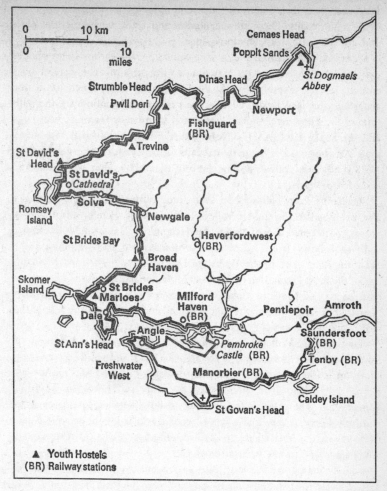

Fig. 47 The Pembrokeshire Coast Path

List available from the Pembrokeshire Coast National Park Office, County Offices, Haverfordwest, Dyfed SA61 1QZ.

The Pennine Way

Unquestionably the most famous of the long-distance footpaths, it is also the roughest and toughest and suitable only for experienced fell-walkers. It runs for 400 kilometres from Edale in Derbyshire to Kirk Yetholm just over the border in Scotland, through some of the wildest scenery in England along the top of the Pennines. One of the fascinations of the

Pennine Way is the numerous evidence of old mine workings, drove roads and Roman roads. There are magnificent waterfalls, huge limestone cliffs and, for the naturalist, sub-alpine flora.

From Edale, the path makes a steep climb up Grindsbrook to the Kinder plateau, which is 600 metres high and a wilderness of quaking peat bogs entirely lacking in proper paths. At Kinder Downfall, which has a fine waterfall after heavy rain (which means in normal conditions!), the path follows the Edge for a short distance and then heads for more peat bogs and the Snake Pass (A57). Beyond the A57 is Bleaklow Hill with many more peat bogs before the path descends to the Crowden reservoir and the A628 road. Now follows a long climb to Black Hill, after which the A62 and M62 are crossed.

Blackstone Edge follows and then some rather dull walking along a reservoir road to the Calder Valley. This is Brontë country and the Way passes the reputed site of Wuthering Heights on Haworth Moor. Easier walking follows from Lothersdale onwards, especially alongside the beautiful River Aire in the Yorkshire Dales National Park. At Malham, one of the most fascinating parts of the route, the path climbs the limestone cliff known as Malham Cove. This was once a waterfall larger than Niagara but now the river goes underground and emerges at the base of the cliff.

After passing Malham Tarn, there is a long slog to the summit of Fountains Fell followed by a descent to the road and another very steep climb up to the marvellous viewpoint of Pen-y-Ghent. From Horton-in-Ribblesdale, there is a fine packhorse trail to Hawes in beautiful Wensleydale. The valley is followed for a short distance passing close to Hardraw Force, a very fine waterfall behind which it is possible to walk. Now begins the long climb up to Great Shunner Fell (713 metres) and down again to Thwaite in Swaledale.

From Thwaite there is a long, but easy, ascent over Stonesdale Moor to Tan Hill and the highest pub in England (528 metres). The route now divides—one arm going to Bowes and the A66 and the other, the more direct route, to Blackton reservoir, where the Bowes alternative rejoins the main route before descending to Middleton-in-Teesdale. An easy and beautiful section follows along the River Tees past the famous waterfall of High Force and on to a less well-known, but much more spectacular, waterfall of Cauldron Snout below the Cow Green reservoir. Beyond the reservoir the path follows the Maize Beck until reaching the natural amphitheatre of High Cup Nick and then descends to Dufton and the Vale of Eden.

After Dufton, the Way climbs up to Knock Fell, Great Dun Fell, Little Dun Fell to Cross Fell, the highest point on the Way (893 metres). It is also

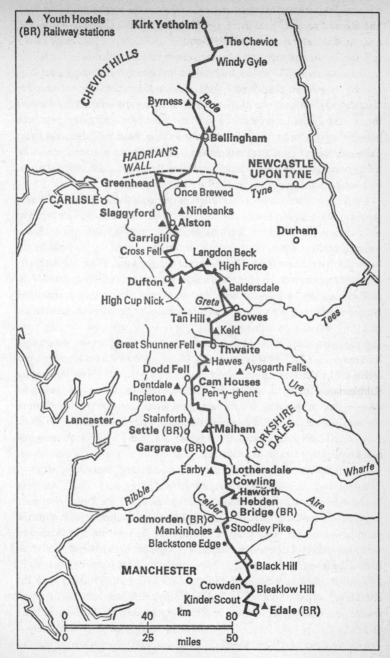

Fig. 48 The Pennine Way

195

a magnificent view point, with extensive views to the mountains of the Lake District and to the Scottish border. A steep descent is made to the Old Corpse Road which is followed to Garrigill. The valley of the South Tyne is followed to Alston, Slaggyford and Greenhead.

The Way now follows Hadrian's Wall for several miles, including some of the best-preserved and most spectacular sections, almost to Housesteads, which is one of the most interesting forts on the Wall. Beyond the Wall is a large expanse of forest which makes for dull walking through the quiet and eerie fir trees; then there is a steep climb to Shitlington Crags before dropping down to Bellingham on the River North Tyne. Now follows an easy section along Hareshaw Burn and over Lord's Shaw, Brownrigg Head and through the forest of Redesdale to Byrness.

The last section is one of the toughest of them all. It starts with a very steep climb out of Redesdale to Coquetdale and the Cheviots. For much of the route the border fence helps to define the path through the extensive bogs. There is a short alternative route which goes to the summit of the Cheviot (816 metres) for anyone who can summon up sufficient energy. At long last, the path starts to descend until it reaches Kirk Yetholm.

There is a fair amount of bed and breakfast accommodation along the Pennine Way but also some long stretches with no towns or villages. Probably the most satisfactory method is to camp, because there is never any shortage of drinking water, and there are many suitable camp sites on the fells.

Trans Pennine Transport, 3/25 Cathcart Hill, London N19 5QN run a daily summer minibus service for Pennine wayfarers and will transport people and collect and deliver unaccompanied luggage between youth hostels, bed and breakfast accommodation, and camp sites.*

Anyone attempting to walk the Pennine Way must be properly equipped and know how to use a map and compass. The weather in the Pennines is notorious for its heavy rainfall, high winds and mists, even in summer.

Path Association: Pennine Way Council (see p307).

Youth Hostels: Edale, Crowden, Mankinholes, Haworth, Earby, Malham, Stainforth, Dentdale, Hawes, Keld, Baldersdale, Langdon Beck, Dufton, Alston, Greenhead, Once Brewed, Bellingham, Byrness and Kirk Yetholm.

Maps: 1:50000 Landranger sheets 74, 75, 80, 86, 87, 91, 92, 98, 103, 109, 110; 1:25000 Pathfinder sheets P486 (NT61/71), P487 (NT81/91), P475 (NT82/92), P498 (NT60/70), P509 (NY69/79), P510 (NY89/99), P522 (NY88/98), P533 (NY67/77), P534 (NY87/97), P546 (NY66/76), P559 (NY65/75), P569 (NY64/74), P661 (SD85/95), P670 (SD84/94), P701 (SD81/91), P702 (SE01/11), P714 (SE00/10) plus Outdoor Leisure Maps 1 The Peak District (Dark Peak), 2 Yorkshire Dales (Western area), 10

* *Now ceased trading.*

196

Yorkshire Dales (Southern area), 30 Yorkshire Dales (Northern & Central), 31 Teesdale.

Footpath Guides: Hardy, Graeme, North to South along the Pennine Way, Warne Gerrard, 1983; Hopkins, Tony, Pennine Way North, Aurum Press in association with the Countryside Commission and the Ordnance Survey, 1989; Hopkins, Tony, Pennine Way South, Aurum Press in association with the Countryside Commission (publication scheduled for autumn 1989); The Pennine Way: Map and Guide, 2 vols, Footprint, 1988: Vol. 1: Edale to Teesdale, Vol. 2: Teesdale to Kirk Yetholm; Wainwright, A., The Pennine Way Companion, Westmorland Gazette, 1968. (NB: this is the classic guide to the route but it is now very out of date and must be used with caution); Westacott, Hugh, A Practical Guide to Walking the Pennine Way, Footpath Publications, 1989*; Wright, C. J., A Guide to the Pennine Way, Constable, 1983.

The Ridgeway

The Ridgeway path runs from Ivinghoe in Buckinghamshire to Overton Hill near Avebury in Wiltshire, a distance of some 137 kilometres. Its name causes some confusion, as the Great Ridgeway is a prehistoric route which ran from The Wash to Axmouth in Devon. The line of the long-distance path coincides with the Great Ridgeway between Streatley on the Thames and Overton Hill. The first 66 kilometres uses ancient routes only occasionally. The latter half is all bridleway and thus of interest to riders and cyclists.

The path starts near the village of Ivinghoe at Ivinghoe Beacon, a 244-metre high summit with extensive views, and then continues, either on the summit or along the scarp, until it descends to cross the Tring gap. It then climbs the escarpment again and takes a high-level route, passing through some glorious beechwoods to descend again at Wendover. From Wendover, Coombe Hill is climbed and there are more beechwoods before the Chequers Estate is crossed. There is more beechwood and downland before the path drops down to Princes Risborough.

There is now a short section on metalled roads before the path takes to the fields and then climbs Lodge Hill before joining the Upper Icknield Way, which at this point is a broad track. This track follows the foot of the scarp for several miles and makes for dull if fast walking passing underneath the M40.

Now follows a short stretch of road and then the path heads across Swyncombe Down and through Ewelme Park before turning due west at Nuffield following Grim's Ditch, the ancient boundary, to Mongwell and North Stoke and the River Thames. The path follows the river to Goring and from there takes the road to Streatley.

* Not available.

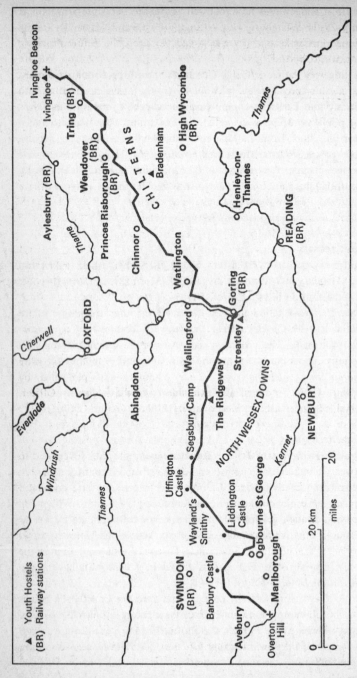

Fig. 49 The Ridgeway Path

The Great Ridgeway is now followed across the Berkshire Downs past Segsbury Castle, Whitehorse Hill, Uffington Castle and Wayland's Smithy to Liddington Castle, Barbury Castle and Hackpen Hill before dropping down to West Overton.

The Ridgeway Path is probably the easiest of the long-distance footpaths and requires no special kit except stout shoes. The western end of the path in Wiltshire and Berkshire cannot easily be walked in separate day trips because public transport is so limited, but Londoners can walk the eastern half starting either from Luton or Aylesbury, and catching the bus to Ivinghoe Beacon. There are railway stations at Tring, Wendover and Princes Risborough. Accommodation, too, is limited as this is not really bed and breakfast country, but small inns can be found in some towns. Camping is not recommended as there is no water.

Path Association: Friends of the Ridgeway (see p 300-1).

Youth Hostels: The Ridgeway, Streatley, Bradenham, Ivinghoe.

Maps: 1:50000 Landranger sheets 164, 165, 173, 174, 175; 1:25000 Pathfinder sheets P1094 (SP81/91), P1117 (SP60/70), P1118 (SP80/90), P1137 (SU69/79), P1154 (SU28/38), P1155 (SU48/58), P1156 (SU68/78), P1169 (SU07/17), P1170 (SU27/37), P1185 (SU06/16).

Footpath Guides: Burden, Vera, *Discovering the Ridgeway,* Shire Publications, 1985; Charles, Alan. *Exploring the Ridgeway,* Countryside Books, 1988; Curtis, Neil, *The Ridgeway,* Aurum Press in association with the Countryside Commission and the Ordnance Survey, 1989; *Ridgeway Information and Accommodation Guide* compiled and published by Oxfordshire County Council and available from the Ridgeway Officer, Countryside Section, Library Headquarters, Holton, Oxford OX9 1QQ.

The South Downs Way

The South Downs Way is the only long-distance bridle path yet created so it may be used by riders and cyclists as well as walkers. It runs for some 129 kilometres from Eastbourne in Sussex to near Petersfield in Hampshire.

The path leaves the outskirts of Eastbourne and then climbs Willingdon Hill, passes through Jevington and crosses Windover Hill to Alfriston. There is an alternative route, for walkers only, starting from Beachy Head and following the cliffs to the Seven Sisters where it turns north to meet the bridleway near Alfriston. From Alfriston, the path climbs the Downs and crosses Firle Beacon to Southease.

The path now turns inland to avoid Brighton, crosses the A27, passes just south of Plumpton and climbs Ditchling Beacon to the A23, south of Pyecombe. There is now another climb to the Devil's Dyke, Edburton Hill and Truleigh Hill before dropping into the Alder Valley near Botolphs. Chanctonbury Ring is the next notable landmark, followed by Highden

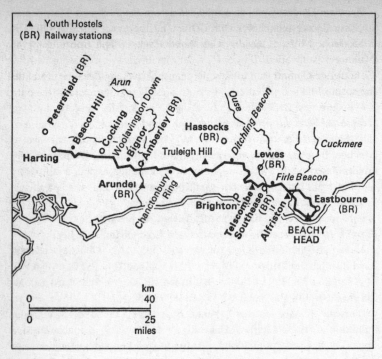

Fig. 50 The South Downs Way

Hill, Kithurst Hill and Rackham Hill to Amberley station. Next comes Bury Hill, Bignor Hill, Burton Down, Woolavington Down, Graffham Down and so to the A286 south of Cocking. The path now crosses Linch Down, Philliswood Down and Beacon Hill to the B2141 and B2146 near South Harting.

This is easy walking on downland turf. Although there are some stiff climbs, no special kit or equipment is required. There is an excellent rail network which crosses the path at several points and the Southdown bus services are very good. It is quite practicable, with some planning, to walk this path in a series of separate day outings from London. Camping is not recommended because of the lack of water, but there is plenty of accommodation en route.

Youth Hostels: Beachy Head, Alfriston, Telscombe, Truleigh Hill and Arundel.

Maps: 1:50000 Landranger sheets 197, 198, 199; 1:25000 Pathfinder sheets P1285 (SU61/71), P1286 (SU81/91), P1287 (TQ01/11), P1288 (TQ21/31), P1306 (TQ00/10), P1307 (TQ20/30), P1308 (TQ40/50), P1324 (TV49/59/69).

Footpath Guides: Comber, Harry, *Along the South Downs Way,* Society of Sussex Downsmen, 254 Victoria Drive, Eastbourne, Sussex, BN20 8QR, 1985; Jebb, Miles, *A Guide to the South Downs Way,* Constable, 1984; Millmore, Paul, *South Downs Way,* Aurum Press in association with the Countryside Commission and the Ordnance Survey (publication scheduled for spring 1990).

The Southern Upland Way

The Southern Upland Way runs for 340 kilometres through southern Scotland from the fishing village of Portpatrick, eight kilometres southwest of Stranraer on the west coast, to Cockburnspath, thirteen kilometres southeast of Dunbar on the Berwickshire coast.

From the farmlands of The Rhins, the route embarks on an undulating wasteland of bog and forestry from Glenluce, via Knowe, to reach Glen Trool. It then weaves through the wild Galloway Hills, beneath the Awful Hand and Rhinns of Kells, via the Black Water of Dee and Clatteringshaws Loch, to St John's Town of Dalry.

A serious 43 kilometre hill traverse ensues via Glen Ken to the watershed before descending to Sanquhar. An easy short leg by the old lead-mining settlement of Wanlockhead followed by another strenuous section over roads and tracks following the Ettrick Valley to St. Mary's Loch. The River Tweed is reached from Yarrow by following an old drove road across Minch Moor via the Three Brethren.

The route then passes through Galashiels and the charming little town of Melrose and heads north to Lauder to follow a Roman road and traverse the Lammamuir Hills. From Longformacuson the route wends through the attractive White Adder valley to reach the sea at Cockburnspath.

The Southern Upland Way is probably the most strenuous and demanding of the official long-distance paths, even though it often avoids the tops, and should be undertaken by very experienced fell-walkers. Accommodation in parts is very sparse and there are considerable stretches where none is available so backpacking is to be preferred.

Youth Hostels: Minnigaff, Kendoon, Wanlockhead Broadmeadows, Melrose, Coldingham.

Maps: 1:50000 Landranger sheets 67, 71, 74, 76, 77, 78, 79, 82; 1:25000 Pathfinder sheets P409 (NT67/77), P422 (NT 66/76), P435 (NT45/55), P436 (NT65/75), P449 (NT44/54), P460 (NT23/33), P472 (NT22/32), P481 (NS61/71), P482 (NS81/91), P483 (NT01/11), P484 (NT21/31), P493 (NS60/70), P494 (NS80/90), P495 (NT00/10), P461 (NT43/53), P504 (NX69/79), P515 (NX48/58), P516 (NX68/78), P526 (NX27/37), P527 (NX47/47), P537 (NW95/96/97), P538 (NX06/16), P539 (NX26/36), P551 (NX05/15).

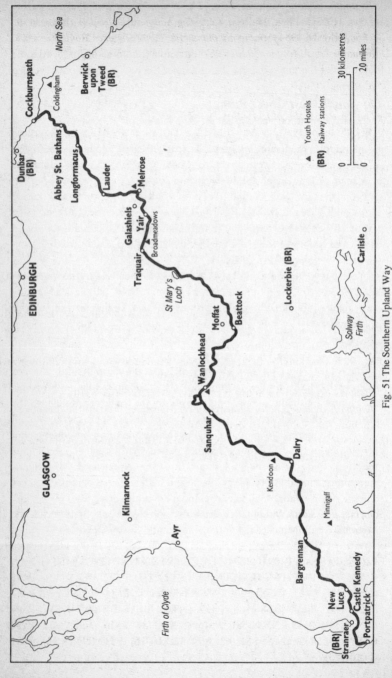

Fig. 51 The Southern Upland Way

Footpath guides: Andrew, Ken, *The Southern Upland Way; Eastern Section,* HMSO, 1984; Andrew, Ken, *The Southern Upland Way; Western Section,* HMSO, 1984; *Southern Upland Way Long Distance Route, General Information and Accommodation,* Countryside Commission for Scotland, 1988.

The South-West Coast Path

There is a continuous path of some 920 kilometres following, as far as possible, the very edge of the coast from Minehead in Somerset to Poole in Dorset through some of the finest coastal scenery in England. A description of the route is not necessary as it follows the coast all the way. The path is divided into sections:

1. The Somerset and North Dorset Coast Path (132 kilometres)
2. The Cornwall Coast Path (431 kilometres)
3. The South Devon Coast Path (235 kilometres)
4. The Dorset Coast Path (122 kilometres)

There is plenty of accommodation and numerous camp sites on the route of the path but advance booking is advisable during the holiday season.

No special kit or equipment is necessary. The weather in the south-west is often warm and sunny which, combined with the salt spray and reflection from the sea, makes for a high sunburn risk.

Path Association: The South West Way Association (see p310).

Footpath Guides: There are no guides currently in print to the complete path but *The South West Way: the Complete Guide to Great Britain's Longest Footpath,* Devon Books, gives invaluable information about ferries, tides, accommodation and the state of the path although it is not a step-by-step guide.

Somerset and North Devon Coast Path

Youth Hostels: Minehead, Lynton, Ilfracombe, Instow, Hartland.

Maps: 1:5000 Landranger sheets 180, 181, 190; 1:25000 Pathfinder sheets P1213 (SS44/54), P1214 (SS64/74), P1215 (SS84/94), P1233 (SS43/53), P1253 (SS22/32), P1254 (SS42/52), P1273 (SS21/31).

Footpath Guides: Collings, A. G., *Along the South West Way: Part 1 Minehead to Bude,* Tabb House, 1985; Tarr, Roland, *South West Coast Path: Minehead to Padstow,* Aurum Press in association with the Countryside Commission and the Ordnance Survey (publication scheduled for spring 1989).

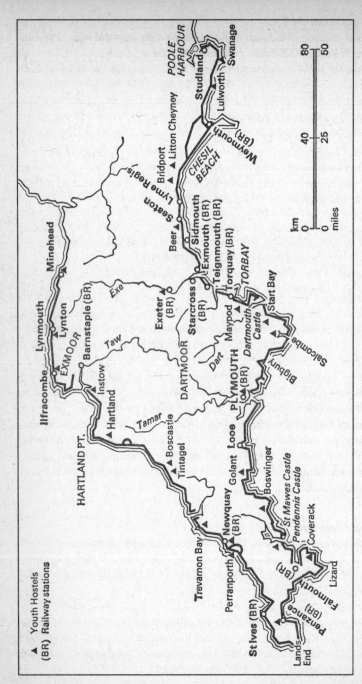

Fig. 52 The South-West Coast Path

204

Cornwall Coast Path

Youth Hostels: Boscastle, Tintagel, Treyarnon Bay, Newquay, Perran-porth, Penzance, Coverack, Pendennis, Boswinger, Golant.

Maps: 1:50000 Landranger sheets 190, 200, 201, 203, 204; 1:2500 Pathfinder sheets P1273 (SS21/31), P1292 (SS20/30), P1310 (SX19), P1325 (SX08/18), P1337 (SW87/97), P1346 (SW86/96), P1352 (SW75), P1354 (SX05/15), P1355 (SX25/35), P1356 (SX45/55), P1359 (SW54/64), P1361 (SW94/SX04), P1364 (SW33/43/53), P1365 (SW63/53/73), P1366 (SW83/73/93), P1368 (SW32/42), P1369 (SW52/62/72), P1370 (SW72/82), P1372 (SW61/71).

Footpath Guides: Tarr, Roland, *South West Coast Path: Minehead to Padstow,* Aurum Press in association with the Countryside Commission and the Ordnance Survey (publication scheduled for spring 1989); Macadam, John, *South West Coast Path: Padstow to Falmouth,* Aurum Press in association with the Countryside Commission and the Ordnance Survey (publication scheduled for spring 1990).

South Devon Coast Path

Youth Hostels: Plymouth, Salcombe, Start Bay, Maypool, Exeter, Beer.

Maps: 1:50000 Landranger sheets 192, 193, 201, 202; 1:25000 Pathfinder sheets P1316 (SY29/39), P1330 (SY08/18), P1342 (SX87/97), P1351 (SX86/96), P1356 (SX45/55), P1362 (SX54/64), P1367 (SX73/63/83) plus Outdoor Leisure Map 20 South Devon.

Footpath Guides: Gant, Roland, *A Guide to the South Devon and Dorset Coast Path,* Constable, 1982; Le Messurier, Brian, *South West Coast Path: Falmouth to Exmouth,* Aurum Press in association with the Countryside Commission and the Ordnance Survey (publication scheduled for spring 1990); Tarr, Roland, *South West Coast Path: Exmouth to Poole,* Aurum Press in association with the Countryside Commission and the Ordnance Survey, 1989.

Dorset Coast Path

Youth Hostels: Bridport, Litton Cheney, Lulworth, Swanage.

Maps: 1:50000 Landranger sheets 193, 194, 195; 1:25000 Pathfinder sheets P1316 (SY29/39), P1317 (SY49/59), P1331 (SY58), P1332 (SY68/78), P1343 (SY67/77), P1344 (SY87/97/SZ07) plus Outdoor Leisure Map 15 Purbeck.

Footpath Guides: Gant Roland, *A Guide to the South Devon and Dorset Coast Path,* Constable, 1982; Tarr, Roland, *South West Coast Path: Exmouth to Poole,* Aurum Press in association with the Countryside Commission and the Ordnance Survey, 1989.

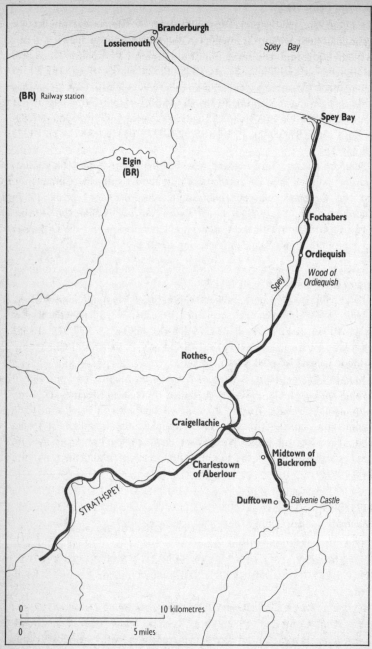

Fig 53 Speyside Way

The Speyside Way

When complete, the Speyside Way will run for 97 kilometres from Tugnet on the coast at Spey Bay, Grampians to Ballindalloch. From here it will run via Nethybridge and Abernethy Forest to Glenmore Lodge near Aviemore. At the time of writing only the first 48 kilometres from Tugnet to Ballindalloch is open. This section is an easy, very beautiful walk following, for much of the way, a disused railway. Although not part of the official route the District Council in co-operation with local landowners have opened a route from Ballindalloch to Tomimtoul.

Youth Hostel: Tomintoul, Aviemore.

Maps: Landranger sheet 28, 1:25000 Pathfinder sheets P147 (NJ36/46), P163 (NJ25/35), P179 (NJ04/14), P180 (NJ24/34), P195 (NJ03/13).

Footpath Guides: A set of leaflets available from Moray District Council, District Headquarters, High Street, Elgin, Morayshire IV30 1BX.

The Thames Path

A lovely route along the banks of the Thames that will almost certainly be designated a national trail. When complete, it will run for 290 kilometres from Thames Head near Kemble, Gloucestershire, to the Thames Barrier, Woolwich, in east London. It has not yet been officially opened, but in practice is walkable along the towpath from Putney Bridge westwards, although a few diversions along roads are necessary here and there. It is a very easy route that passes through many picturesque towns and villages set in beautiful countryside.

Youth Hostels: London, Windsor, Henley-on-Thames, Streatley, Oxford, and Inglesham.

Maps: 1:50000 Landranger sheets 163, 164, 174, 175, 176. 1:25000 Pathfinder sheets P1115 (SP 20/30), P1116 (SP 40/50), P1133 (ST 89/99), P1134 (SU 09/19), P1135 (SU 29/39), P1136 (SU 49/59), P1137 (SU 69/79), P1151 (ST 68/78), P1152 (ST 88/98), P1155 (SU 48/58), P1156 (SU 68/78), P1157 (SU 88/98), P1159 (TQ 28/38), P1171 (SU 47/57), P1172 (SU 67/77), P1173 (SU 87/97), P1174 (TQ 07/17), P1175 (TQ 27/37), P1190 (TQ 06/16).

Footpath Guides: Jebb, Miles, *A Guide to the Thames Path,* Constable, 1988; Perrott, David, Editor, *The Ordnance Survey Guide to the River Thames and River Wey,* Robert Nicholson Publications, 2nd Ed., 1989 (covers the navigable part of the river as far as Cricklade which is 20 kilometres from the source at Thames Head); Sharp, David, *The Thames Walk,* Ramblers' Association, 2nd Ed., 1990.

The Ulster Way

Northern Ireland's longest footpath encircles the Province passing through

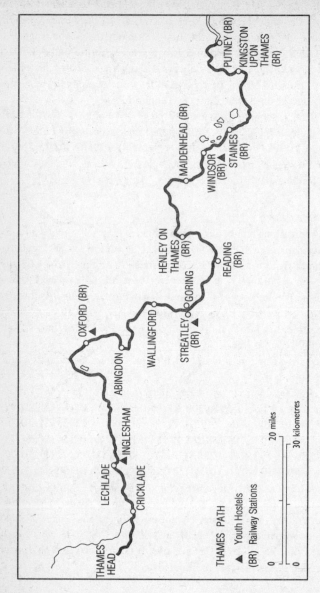

Fig. 54 Thames Path

THAMES HEAD
LECHLADE
CRICKLADE
INGLESHAM
ABINGDON
OXFORD (BR)
WALLINGFORD
STREATLEY (BR)
GORING
HENLEY ON THAMES (BR)
READING (BR)
MAIDENHEAD (BR)
WINDSOR (BR)
STAINES (BR)
PUTNEY (BR)
KINGSTON UPON THAMES (BR)

THAMES PATH
▲ Youth Hostels
(BR) Railway Stations

20 miles
30 kilometres

0

0

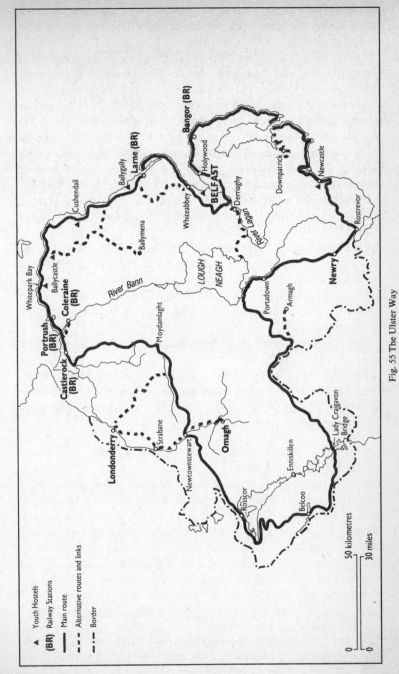

Fig. 55 The Ulster Way

Youth Hostels
(BR) Railway Stations
Main route
Alternative routes and links
Border

50 kilometres
30 miles

Whitepark Bay
Whiteparkstown
Portrush (BR)
Castlerock (BR)
Coleraine (BR)
Ballycastle
Cushendall
Ballygally
Larne (BR)
Bangor (BR)
Holywood
Whiteabbey
BELFAST
Dernaghy
River Lagan
Ballymena
Downpatrick
Newcastle
Rostrevor
Newry
River Bann
LOUGH NEAGH
Portadown
Armagh
Moydamlaght
Londonderry
Strabane
Newtownstewart
Omagh
Enniskillen
Rosscor
Belcoo
Lady Craigavon Bridge

209

some of its finest scenery. Not all of the Way is officially open but nearly 500 kilometres of it have been waymarked and in practice it is walkable throughout its length of 725 kilometres.

It starts at Belfast and heads north for the glens, moors and coast of County Antrim and runs past the Giant's Causeway to Portrush, Portstewart, and Coleraine to the hills and forests of north Londonderry. At Castlerock the path turns south to reach Moydamlaght Forest and the Sperrins, the most extensive range of mountains in Northern Ireland. The Way then passes through Gortin Glen Country Park to Baronscourt Forest and the lakeland country of County Fermanagh. It crosses Upper Lough Erne by the Lady Craigavon Bridge and continues to the Mourne Mountains passing through Rostrevor and Newcastle. The Ulster Way now follows the coast of County Down and then passes through Downpatrick and along the western shores of Strangford Lough to reach Belfast.

A number of major link paths are being created which will lead to the Way from large centres of population. There are also a number of alternative paths that allow the walker to make a series of day excursions along the Ulster Way.

Youth Hostels: Belfast, Ballygally, Cushendall, Ballycastle, Whitepark Bay, Newscastle.

Maps: Ordnance Survey of Northern Ireland 1:50000 sheets 4, 5, 7, 12, 15, 17, 18, 19, 21, 26, 27, 28.

Footpath Guides: The Ulster Way, compiled and published by the Sports Council of Northern Ireland, 1988: *South East Section, North West Section, South West Section;* Warner, Alan, *On Foot in Ulster: a Journal of the Ulster Way,* Appletree Press, 1983.

The West Highland Way

The West Highland Way runs for 153 kilometres from Milngavie, 10 kilometres north of Glasgow, to Fort William. The route follows the banks of Loch Lomond, climbs Glen Falloch to Crianlarich, takes a low-level route to Tyndrum and Bridge of Orchy before climbing over Rannoch Moor and the Devil's Staircase to Kinlochleven. Then it follows an old military road to Glen Nevis and Fort William. In general, it is well waymarked and the only strenuous sections are over Rannoch Moor and a short stretch near Glen Nevis.

Youth Hostels: Glasgow, Rowardennan, Crianlarich and Glen Nevis.

Maps: 1:50000 Landranger Sheets 41, 50, 56, 57, 64; 1:25000 Pathfinder sheets P277 (NN07/17), P290 (NN06/16), P291 (NN26/36), P306 (NN25/35), P320 (NN24/34), P333 (NN23/33), P346 (NN22/32), P357 (NN21/31),

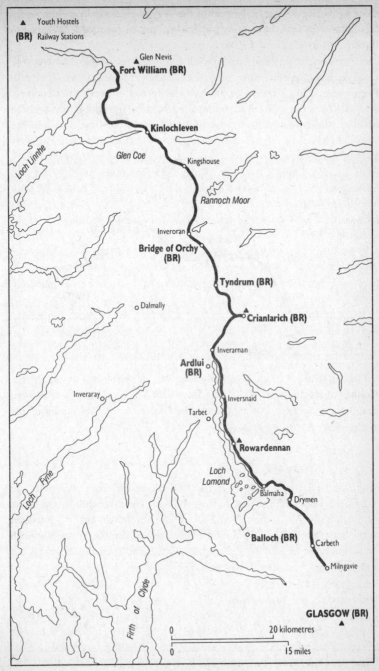

Fig. 56 The West Highland Way

211

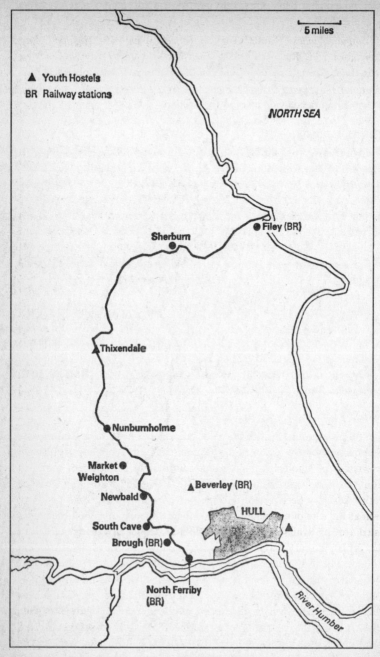

Fig. 57 The Wolds Way

P368 (NN20/30), P380 (NS29/39), P381 (NS49/59), P391 (NS48/58), P403 (NS47/57).

Footpath Guides: Hunter, Tom, *A Guide to the West Highland Way,* Constable, 2nd, Rev. Ed., 1984; *The West Highland Way: a Complete Map-Guide Giving Lots of Information for Walkers,* Footprint, 1988; *West Highland Way Long Distance Route; General Information and Accommodation,* Countryside Commission for Scotland, 1988.

The Wolds Way

The Wolds Way runs for 127 kilometres from Filey on the Yorkshire coast where it links with the Cleveland Way, via Sherburn, Thixendale, Nunburnholme, Newbald, South Cave and Brough to North Ferriby on Humberside. By crossing the Humber Bridge it is possible to join the Viking Way and continue as far as Oakham in Leicestershire.

The route follows the northern and eastern edges of the Wolds, a range of chalk hills giving commanding views over the surrounding countryside. This is a very easy walk through cultivated farmland and many charming villages.

Youth Hostels: Thixendale, Beverley.

Maps: 1:50000 Landranger sheets 100, 101, 106; 1:25000 Pathfinder sheets P624 (TA08/09/18), P644 (SE87/97), P645 (TA07/17), P656 (SE86/96), P666 (SE85/95), P675 (SE84/94), P686 (SE83/93), P695 (SE82/92), P696 (TA02/12).

Footpath Guides: Ratcliffe, Roger, *The Wolds Way,* HMSO, 1982; Rubenstein, David, *The Wolds Way,* Dalesman, 1979.

Other Long-Distance Paths

The following routes, which have not been sanctioned by the Countryside Commission or the Countryside Commission for Scotland, are usually referred to as 'unofficial' long-distance paths. This list has been compiled from various sources, including the register compiled by the Long Distance Paths Advisory Service (see p. 301), but does not claim to be complete even at the date of compilation, nor is there any guarantee that the guides listed are still available. The bibliographical details have been checked in the British Library Catalogue (formerly known as the British Museum Catalogue) and *Whitaker's Books in Print* but in many cases it is clear that the guides were neither deposited at the British Library as the law requires nor were *Whitaker Information Forms* completed. This is a pity as it means that in time there will be no record of their existence. Where a guide appears under the imprint of an established publisher, no address is given because the book can be obtained by ordering it from a bookshop. The easiest way to obtain a guide where an address is given is to write requesting it and enclosing a signed cheque crossed 'not to exceed £5-00'. Leave the details of payee and the amount payable blank for the recipient to complete. Be sure to put your address on the top left-hand corner of the envelope so that the Post Office can return it if the addressee has moved.

National grid numbers are given for the start and finish of each route.

Abbott's Hike 127 kilometres through the Yorkshire Dales National Park and Pennines from Ilkley (SE 117476), North Yorkshire, to Pooley Bridge (NY 470247), Cumbria.

Footpath Guide: Abbott, Peter, *Abbott's Hike,* published by the author at 6 Hillstone Close, Greenmount, Bury, Lancashire BL8 4EZ.

Allerdale Ramble 80 kilometres through the Lake District National Park from Seathwaite (NY 235119) to Grune Point (NY 145571).

Footpath Guide: Appleyard, Harry, *The Allerdale Ramble,* 2nd Ed., The Tourism Officer, Allerdale District Council, Holmewood, Cockermouth, Cumbria CA13 0DW, 1985.

Angles Way A 124-kilometre waymarked route from Great Yarmouth (TG 522081), Norfolk, to Knettishall Heath (TM 944807), Suffolk.

Footpath Guide: The Angles Way, compiled and published by the Norfolk & Suffolk Areas of the Ramblers' Association, 150 Armes Street, Norwich NR2 4EG, 1989.

Anglesey Coast Path A 202-kilometre circular route around the island from the Menai Bridge (SH 556716) following paths and roads.

Footpath Guide: Rowlands, E., *Anglesey Guide to Walks,* Ynys Môn group of the Ramblers' Association, 6 Fayars Bay, Llanfaes, Beaumaris, Anglesey, Gwynedd LL58 8RE.

Around Norfolk Walk A 357-kilometre waymarked circular route from Knettishall Heath (TM 944807), Suffolk, comprising the Peddar's Way and North Norfolk Coast Path, the Weavers Way, and the Angles Way.

Leaflet available from Norfolk County Council, County Hall, Martineau Lane, Norwich NR1 2DH.

Avon Walkway A 50-kilometre waymarked route from Pill (ST 525759), near Bristol, to the Dundas Aqueduct (ST 785626), near Bath, following rivers and canals.

Footpath Guide: The Avon Walkway, 1984. A map of the route compiled and published by the Avon County Council, Planning Department, PO Box 46, Avon House North, St James Barton, Bristol BS99 7NF.

Aylesbury Ring A 50-kilometre circular route encircling Aylesbury, Buckinghamshire.

Footpath Guide: Gulland, Peter and Diana, *The Vale of Aylesbury Walker,* published by the authors at 12 Wykeham Way, Haddenham, Aylesbury, Bucks, HP18 8BL, 1989.

Bakewell Circular Walk A 160-kilometre circular route through the best of the Peak National Park from Bakewell (SK 217685), Derbyshire.

Footpath Guide: Hyde, George, *Circular Walks around Bakewell; 100 miles in the Peak District,* Dalesman, 1984.

Beacon Way A 30-kilometre path through Beacon Country Park, Walsall, that leads from the heart of the West Midlands to the Staffordshire border. This delightful 'green' route runs past lakes, through nature reserves and woods, and along the banks of canals.

Leaflet available from the Department of Leisure Services, Civic Centre, Darwall Street, Walsall WS1 1TZ.

Bilsdale Circuit A 50-kilometre circular waymarked challenge walk through the North York Moors National Park from Newgate Bank Top (SE 564890), near Helmsley, North Yorkshire.

Footpath Guide: Teanby, Michael, *The Bilsdale Circuit: a 30-mile Challenge Walk across the North York Moors,* Dalesman, 1981.

Bob Graham Round A 116-kilometre circular route through the Lake District National Park from Keswick Moot Hall (NY 266234) which includes 42 major peaks and involves approximately 7200 metres of ascent. It was devised as a challenge for super-fit fell-runners, but it also makes a grand walk.

Footpath Guide: Smith, Roger, *42 Peaks; the Story of the Bob Graham Round,* Bob Graham 24 Hour Club, 1982.

Bolton Boundary Walk An 80-kilometre circular challenge walk around Bolton starting at Affetside Cross (SD 753158), Greater Manchester.

Footpath Guide: Cresswell, Michael, *The Bolton Boundary Walk,* 2nd Ed., Bolton Metropolitan Borough Council, Public Relations and Information Officer, Town Hall, Bolton, BL1 1RU.

Bounds of Ainsty A 70-kilometre circular route from Tadcaster (SE 488434), North Yorkshire, following the rivers Wharfe, Nidd and Ouse.

Footpath Guide: Townson, Simon, *The Ainsty Bounds Walk; a 44-mile Circular Walk of the Vale of York,* Dalesman, 1984.

Bournemouth Coast Path 32 kilometres from the end of the South West Coast Path at Sandbanks (SZ 037871), Dorset, along cliffs and promenades to Milford-on-Sea (SZ 292918), Hampshire.

Footpath Guide: Hatts, Leigh, *The Bournemouth Coast Path: Swanage, Bournemouth, Christchurch and Lymington,* Countryside Books, 1985.

Bradford Ring A 51-kilometre circular route around the city of Bradford starting at Cottingley Bridge (SE 112380).

Footpath Guide: Sheldon, Paul and Gemmell, Arthur, *Bradford Ringwalks,* Stile Publications, 1982.

Bradley 20 A 32-kilometre (20-mile) circular route through the Lincolnshire Wolds starting at Bradley Woods (TA 242059), south of Grimsby.

Footpath Guide: The Bradley 20 and Walks on the Eastern Lincolnshire

Wolds, compiled and published by Humberside County Council, Technical Services Department, County Hall, Beverley, North Humberside HU17 9XA.

Brindley Trail 97 kilometres from Buxton (SK 218686) to Stoke-on-Trent (SJ 872479) following a route associated with James Brindley, the canal engineer.

Footpath Guide: Speakman, Lydia, *The Brindley Trail,* Scenesetters, Bircher Cottage, Little Stretton, Shropshire SY6 6RE, 1989.

Bristol Countryway 130 kilometres from the Slimbridge Wildfowl Trust nature reserve (SO 722048) in Gloucestershire to Weston-super-Mare (ST 317614), Avon.

Footpath Guide: Main, Laurence, *A Bristol Countryway,* Thornhill Press, 1980.

Bristol to London Long Distance Path 277 kilometres from the Clifton Suspension Bridge (ST 565731), Avon, to Westminster Bridge (TQ 305797), London, mainly following rivers and canals.

Footpath Guide: Critchley, Edward, *Face the Dawn; the Bristol to London Walk,* The Ramblers' Association, 1/5 Wandsworth Road, London SW8 2XX, 1984.

Brontë Round A 37-kilometre circular challenge walk through the Brontë country from Hebden Bridge (SD 992272), West Yorkshire.

Leaflet available from Derek Magnall, 217 Booth Street, Tottington, Bury, Lancashire BL8 3JD.

Calderdale Way An 81-kilometre circular waymarked walk around the Calder valley starting at Greetland (SE 097214), West Yorkshire.

Footpath Guide: The Calderdale Way, 2nd Ed., written and published by the Calderdale Way Association and the West Yorkshire Metropolitan Council, Department of Recreation and Arts, 1983. Available from the Tourist Information Centre, Piece Hall, Halifax HX1 IRS.

Cal-Der-Went Walk A 48-kilometre challenge walk linking the rivers Calder and Derwent from Horbury Bridge (SE 280179) near Wakefield, West Yorkshire, to the Ladybower reservoir (SK 205865) in the Peak National Park.

Footpath Guide: Carr, Geoffrey, *The Cal-Der-Went Walk,* Dalesman, 1979.

Cambrian Way 427 kilometres from Cardiff (ST 180765) to Conwy (SH 783775), Gwynedd, following a high-level route over some of the wildest and toughest country in Britain.

Footpath Guides: Drake, A. J., *The Cambrian Way; the Mountain Connoisseur's Walk,* Cordee, 2nd Ed., 1985; Sale, Richard, *A Cambrian Way; a Personal Guide to an Unofficial Route,* Constable, 1983.

The Camuplodunum A 40-kilometre circuit around Colchester (the

Roman Camulodunum—hence the appalling pun) which starts at Colchester Hythe station (TM 016248) and finishes at the Rising Sun public house (TM 015248).

Footpath Guide: Keeble, Derek, *The Camuplodunum; a Pedestrian Route around Britain's Oldest Recorded Town—Colchester,* Roy Tover Venture Routes, 9 Shelley Road, Colchester CO3 4JN, 2nd Ed., 1982.

The Castles Alternative 50 kilometres from Monmouth (SO 505129), Gwent, to Hay-on-Wye (SO 229425), Powys, devised as an unofficial alternative to part of Offa's Dyke Path.

Footpath Guide: Kay, Kathy and Kay, Ernie, *The Castles Alternative,* Offa's Dyke Association, The Old Primary School, West Street, Knighton, Powys LD7 1EW, Rev. Ed., 1987.

Cestrian Link Walk 180 kilometres from Edale (SK 125858) in the Peak National Park across the Cheshire plain to Prestatyn (SJ 081838) on the north Wales coast.

Footpath Guide: Davenport, John N., *A Cestrian Link Walk; a Route Linking the Pennine Way to Offa's Dyke Path,* Westmorland Gazette 1983.

Cheshire Ring Canal Walk A 156-kilometre circular waymarked route along towpaths starting at Marple (SJ 961887), Greater Manchester.

Footpath Guides: The Cheshire Ring, 11 booklets compiled and published by Cheshire County Council, Countryside and Recreation Department, Goldsmith House, Hamilton Place, Chester CH1 1SE; Merrill, John, *Canal Walks Vol 4; the Cheshire Ring,* JNM Publications, 1989.

Clarendon Way A 39-kilometre waymarked route from Salisbury (SU 143297), Wiltshire, to Winchester (SU 483293), Hampshire.

Footpath Guide: Shurlock, Barry, *The Test Way and the Clarendon Way,* Hampshire County Council, Recreation Department, North Hill Close, Andover Road, Winchester, Hants SO22 6AQ.

Coast to Coast Trek 193 kilometres from Arnside (SD 456788), Cumbria, to Saltburn (NZ 668216), Cleveland. (NB Despite the similar name this route is entirely different from the *Coast to Coast Walk* below.)

Footpath Guide: French, Richard, *A One Week Coast to Coast Trek,* published by the author at Expedition North, Wilkinstile, Dowbiggin, Sedbergh, Cumbria LA10 5LS.

Coast to Coast Walk 306 kilometres from St Bees Head (NX 959119), Cumbria, to Robin Hood's Bay (NZ 953048), North Yorkshire.

Footpath Guide: Wainwright, A., *A Coast to Coast Walk,* Westmorland Gazette, 1973.

Accommodation list available from Mrs Doreen Whitehead, East Stonesgate Farm, Keld, Richmond, North Yorkshire DL11 6LJ.

Coed Morgannwg Way A 50-kilometre waymarked route across Forestry Commission land from Cwmdare (SN 985025), Mid Glamorgan, to Margam

(SS 814852), South Glamorgan.

Footpath Guide: The Coed Morgannwg Way, written and published by the Forestry Commission, London Road, Neath, West Glamorgan SA1 3SG.

Cotswold Way A 161-kilometre waymarked route from Bath (ST 751647) along the Cotswold escarpment to Chipping Campden (SP 153392), Gloucestershire.

Footpath Guides: Reynolds, Kev, *The Cotswold Way,* Cicerone Press, 1990; Richards, Mark, *The Cotswold Way; the Complete Walker's Guide,* Penguin Books, 1984 (NB this is the classic guide to the route); Sale, Richard, *A Guide to the Cotswold Way,* Constable, 1980. *The Cotswold Way Handbook,* compiled and published by the Gloucestershire Area of the Ramblers' Association, 1/5 Wandsworth Road, London SW8 2XX. (NB this is revised biennially and gives essential information about accommodation, public transport etc.)

Cumberland Way 131 kilometres across the Lake District National Park from Ravenglass (SD 084963) to Appleby (NY 683204).

Footpath Guide: Hannon, Paul, *The Cumberland Way,* Hillside Publications, 1988.

Cumbria Way 113 kilometres across the Lake District National Park from Ulverston (SD 284785) to Carlisle (NY 400554).

Footpath Guide: Trevelyan, John, *The Cumbria Way,* 3rd Ed., Dalesman, 1987.

d'Arcy Dalton Way A 104-kilometre waymarked route from Wormleighton Reservoir (SP 448518), Warwickshire, to Wayland's Smithy (SU 281853), Oxfordshire, on the Ridgeway Path.

Footpath Guide: The d'Arcy Dalton Way, compiled and published by the Oxford Fieldpaths Society, High Bank, Wootton, Woodstock, Oxford OX7 1EH, 1987.

Dales Traverse A 40-kilometre circular challenge walk in the Yorkshire Dales National Park commencing at Kilnsey (SD 974679), North Yorkshire.

Footpath Guide: Townson, Simon, *The Dales Traverse: a 25-mile Circular Challenge Walk in Upper Wharfedale,* Dalesman, 1984.

Dales Way A 130-kilometre waymarked route from Ilkley (SE 117476), West Yorkshire, to Bowness-on-Windermere (SD 402968), Cumbria, that links the Yorkshire Dales National Park with the Lake District National Park.

Footpath Guide: Gemmell, Arthur and Speakman, Colin, *The Dales Way Route Guide: with Associated Walks: Specially Drawn Maps of Associated Footpaths,* Stile Publications, 1983. *The Dales Way Handbook,* compiled and published by the West Riding Area of the Ramblers'

Association, 9 Church Avenue, Bilton, Harrogate HG1 4HE. (NB this is revised annually and gives details of accommodation, public transport etc.)

Delamere Way A 35-kilometre waymarked route from Stockton Heath (SJ 615858) near Warrington, Cheshire, through Delamere Forest to Frodsham (SJ 519781), Cheshire.

Footpath Guide: Waymarked walks in Central Cheshire, compiled and published by the Mid-Cheshire Footpath Society, 72 Osborne Grove, Chavington, Crewe CW2 5BX.

Derbyshire Gritstone Way 90 kilometres from Derby (SK 353365) to Edale (SK 125858) in the Peak National Park where it links with the Pennine Way.

Footpath Guide: Burton, Steve and others, *The Derbyshire Gritstone Way,* Thornhill Press, 1980.

Derwent Way 145 kilometres from Barmby-on-the-Marsh (SE 690285), Humberside, following the river Derwent to its source at Lilla Howe (SE 889987) in the North York Moors National Park.

Footpath Guide: Kenchington, Richard C., *The Derwent Way; an 80-mile Walk from North Humberside to the North York Moors via Malton,* Dalesman, 1978.

Diocesan Way 64 kilometres from Newchurch to Montgomery designed as an unofficial alternative to part of Offa's Dyke Path.

Footpath Guide: Kay, Kathy and Kay, Ernie, *Diocesan Way,* Offa's Dyke Association, The Old Primary School, West Street, Knighton, Powys LD7 1EW, 1982.

Dorset Downs Walk 76 kilometres from Blandford Forum (ST 888067) to Bridport (SY 466929).

Footpath Guide: Proctor, Alan, *A Dorset Downs Walk,* Thornhill Press, 1982.

Dorset Walk 161 kilometres from Sherborne (ST 376164) to South Haven Point (SZ 036866) where it links with the South West Coast Path.

Footpath Guide: Dacombe, Ron, and others, *The Dorset Walk; a Hundred Mile Walk, Staggered into Stages, across the Dorset Downs and Coast from Sherborne to Shell Bay,* Dorset Publishing Co., Knock-Ne-Cre, Milborne Port, Sherborne, Dorset DT9 5HJ, 1984.

Downs Link A 48-kilometre waymarked bridleway that runs from St Martha's Hill (TQ 032483) near Guildford, Surrey, to St Botolph's Church (TQ 193094) south of Bramber, West Sussex, and links the North Downs Way to the South Downs Way.

Footpath Guides: The Downs Link, compiled and published by Waverley District Council, The Burys, Godalming, Surrey GU7 1HR; Reynolds, Kev, *The South Downs Way and the Downs Link,* Cicerone Press, 1989.

Ebor Way A 112-kilometre waymarked route through North Yorkshire from Helmsley (SE 611839) in the North York Moors National Park to Ilkley (SE 117476), West Yorkshire.

Footpath Guide: Piggin, J. K. E., *The Ebor Way; a 70-Mile Walk from Helmsley to Ilkley Passing the Ancient City of York,* Dalesman, 1978.

Eden Trail A 55-kilometre challenge walk through the Vale of Eden from Brougham (NY 575288) near Penrith, Cumbria.

Footpath Guide: Explore Eden, compiled and published by the Westmorland Visitor Centre, Brough School, Brough, Penrith, Cumbria CA10 2AE.

Eden Way A route following the course of the river Eden from its source in Mallerstang (SD 776970), Cumbria, to Carlisle (NY 400566).

Footpath Guide: Emett, Charlie, *The Eden Way,* Cicerone Press, 1989.

Esk Valley Walk 50 kilometres through the North York Moors National Park from Blakey (SE 683989) to Whitby (NZ 900117).

Footpath Guide: The Esk Valley Walk, compiled and published by the North York Moors National Park, The Old Vicarage, Bondgate, Helmsley, York YO6 5BP, 1982.

Eskdale Way A 132-kilometre circular route from Whitby (NZ 900117) through the North York Moors National Park.

Footpath Guide: Dale, Louis S., *The Eskdale Way; an 82-Mile Circular Walk in the North York Moors National Park,* Dalesman, 1983. (An accommodation list is available from the author at 10 Mulgrave View, Stainsacre, Whitby, North Yorkshire YO22 4NX.)

Essex Clayway A 120-kilometre waymarked route from Burnham-on-Crouch (TQ 948965) to Witham (TL 820151).

Footpath Guide: Dowding, J., and others, *The Essex Clayway,* Matthews/Bitten Publications, 'Glen View', London Road, Abridge, Romford RM4 1UX.

Essex Way A 130-kilometre waymarked route from Epping (TL 465012) to Harwich (TM 259329).

Footpath Guide: Matthews, Fred and Bitten, Harry, *The Essex Way,* Matthews/Bitten Publications, 'Glen View', London Road, Abridge, Romford RM4 1UX, 1984.

Falklands Way A 72-kilometre circular walk from Kirkby Stephen (NY 775085), Cumbria.

Footpath Guide: The Falklands Way and the Mallerstang Horseshoe and Nine Standards Yomp, P. N. Denby Ltd, Kirkby Stephen, Cumbria.

Fells Way A 394-kilometre route from Leek (SJ 989565), Staffordshire, to Haltwhistle (NY 707638), Northumberland.

Footpath Guide: St John, Ian, *The Fells Way,* Footpath Guides, PO Box 369, Addlestone, Surrey KT15 1LT, 1990.

Ffordd y Bryniau (sometimes known as the Ridgeway Walk) A 32-kilometre waymarked route through Mid Glamorgan from Heol-y-Cyw (SS 969862) near Pencoed to Caerphilly (ST 155852).

Leaflet, published in 1980, available from Taff-Ely Borough Council, Planning Department, County Buildings, Mill Street, Pontypridd, Mid Glamorgan CF37 2TU.

Fife Coastal Walk A 152-kilometre partly waymarked route that runs from the Forth Road Bridge (NT 1279) just north of Edinburgh around the coast to Newburgh (NO 2318) on the Tay estuary.

A set of leaflets is available from Wemyss Environmental Centre, East Wemyss Primary School, School Wynd, East Wemyss, Fife KY1 4RN.

Footpath Touring; the Cotswolds A 134-kilometre waymarked route from Stratford-upon-Avon (SP 203549) to Cheltenham (SO 950225).

Footpath Guide: Ward, Ken, *Footpath Touring; the Cotswolds,* Jarrold, 1988.

Forest Way A 32-kilometre route that links Epping Forest (TQ 420995) with Hatfield Forest (TL 530187).

Footpath Guide: The Forest Way, compiled and published by Essex County Council, County Planning Department, Globe House, New Street, Chelmsford, CM1 1LF.

Foss Walk A 45-kilometre route from York (SE 603522) along the banks of the river Foss to Easingwold (SE 528698).

Footpath Guide: The Foss Walk, compiled and published by the River Foss Amenity Society, Millfield Lane, Nether Poppleton, York YO2 6NA.

Fountains Walk 60 kilometres from Malham (SD 901628), North Yorkshire, through the Yorkshire Dales National Park to Fountains Abbey (SE 271683), near Ripon, North Yorkshire.

Footpath Guide: The Fountains Walk, compiled and published by the Yorkshire Dales Society, c/o the National Trust, Fountains Abbey, Fountains, Ripon, North Yorkshire HG4 3DZ.

Furness Boundary Walk A 177-kilometre circular route around the Furness peninsula in Cumbria starting at Barrow-in-Furness (SD 190688).

Footpath Guide: Dillon, Paddy, *The Furness Boundary Walk,* published by the author at 82 Arthur Street, Barrow-in-Furness, Cumbria LA14 1BH.

Furness Way 120 kilometres through the Lake District National Park from Arnside (SD 456788) to Ravenglass (SD 084963).

Footpath Guide: Hannon, Paul, *The Furness Way,* Hillside Publications, 1982.

Glyndwr's Way A 193-kilometre waymarked route through central Wales from Knighton (SO 283724) to Welshpool (SJ 229071) linking with Offa's Dyke Path at each end.

Footpath Guide: Sale, Richard, *Owain Glyndwr's Way,* Hutchinson, 1985.

Grafton Way A 20-kilometre waymarked route from Wolverton (SP 821415), Buckinghamshire, to Green's Norton (SP 671490), Northamptonshire, that links with the North Bucks Way and the Knightley Way to form an 87-kilometre waymarked route.

Footpath Guide: The Grafton Way, compiled and published by Northamptonshire County Council, Leisure and Libraries Dept., 27 Guildhall, Northampton NN1 1EF, 1984.

Grassington Circuit Walk A 36-kilometre near-circular route in the Yorkshire Dales National Park from Grassington (SD 999639) to Threshfield (SD 993639) 2 kilometres from Grassington.

Footpath Guide: Belk, Les, and Hills, John, *The Grassington Circuit Walk,* published by the authors at 82 Northcote Crescent, Leeds LS11 6NN.

Greensand Ridge Walk A 40-kilometre route through Bedfordshire from Leighton Buzzard (SP 9225) to Sandy (TL 1649). It passes through the grounds of Woburn Abbey and some of Bedfordshire's finest countryside.

Leaflet available from the Department of Leisure Services, County Hall, Bedford MK42 9AP.

Greensand Way An 89-kilometre waymarked route across Surrey from Haslemere (SU 898329) to Limpsfield (TQ 436522). There are plans for an extension through Kent.

Footpath Guides: Adams, A. J., *Walk the North Downs Way and the Greensand Way,* published by the author at 2 Dryden Court, Lower Edgeborough Road, Guildford GU1 2EX; McLennan, Jim, *The Greensand Way,* Gemplan Services Ltd, PO Box 185, Harrow, HA2 8UB; *The Greensand Way in Surrey,* compiled and published by Surrey County Council, County Engineer's Dept., Rights of Way Section, 21 Chessington Road, West Ewell, Epsom, Surrey KT17 1TT, 1989.

Gritstone Trail A 29-kilometre waymarked route in Cheshire from Lyme Park (SJ 962823), southeast of Stockport, to Rushton Spencer (SJ 935625), Staffordshire, where it joins the Staffordshire Way.

Footpath Guide: The Gritstone Trail Walker's Guide, compiled and published by Cheshire County Council, Countryside and Recreation Department, Goldsmith House, Hamilton Place, Chester CH1 1SE, 1986.

Guildford Boundary Walk A 32-kilometre circular challenge walk around Guildford, Surrey, starting at St Catherine's Chapel (SU 993483) on the North Downs Way.

Footpath Guide: Blatchford, Alan and Barbara, *The Guildford Boundary Way and Other Walks,* Greenway Publications, 11 Thornbank, Guildford GU2 5PL, 1979.

Hadrian's Wall Walk 118 kilometres along Hadrian's Wall from Wallsend (NZ 304660), Tyne & Wear, to Bowness-on-Solway (NY 225628), Cumbria.

Footpath Guide: Mizon, Graham, *Guide to Walking Hadrian's Wall,* Hendon Publishing Co., 1977.

Harcamlow Way A 225-kilometre figure-of-eight walk commencing at Harlow (TL 445113), Essex, and crossing Hertfordshire and Cambridgeshire.

Footpath Guide: Matthews, Fred, and Bitten, Harry, *The Harcamlow Way,* Matthews/Bitten Publications, 1980.

Harrogate Ringway A 34-kilometre circular route around Harrogate, North Yorkshire, commencing at Pannal (SE 307514).

Footpath Guide: Further Walks around Harrogate, compiled and published by the Harrogate Group of the Ramblers' Association, 20 Pannal Ash Grove, Harrogate HG2 0HZ, 1984.

Haslemere Hundred A 160-kilometre figure-of-eight route through Surrey and West Sussex commencing at Haslemere station (SU 898329).

Footpath Guide: Hyde, George, *The Haslemere Hundred: Walking the Best of Surrey and Sussex; Two 50-mile Circular Routes Arranged in a Series of Easy Walks,* Footpath Publications, 69 South Hill, Godalming Surrey GU7 1 JU, 1988.

Headland Walk A 34-kilometre waymarked route around Flamborough Head from Bridlington (TA 176680), Humberside, to Filey Brigg (TA 126817), North Yorkshire.

Leaflet available from Humberside County Council, Technical Services Department, County Hall, Beverley, North Humberside HU17 9XA.

Heart of England Way A 131-kilometre route from Cannock Chase (SJ 990166), Staffordshire, to Chipping Campden (SP 153392), Gloucestershire.

Footpath Guides: Watts, J. T., Ed, *The Heart of England Way Walker's Guide,* compiled by the Heart of England Way Steering Committee, Thornhill Press, 1982; Roberts, J. S. *Heart of England Way,* WALKWAYS, 4 Gilldown Place, Birmingham B15 2LR, 2nd Ed., 1989.

Hereward Way A 164-kilometre waymarked route from Oakham, (SK 861088), Leicestershire, to Harling Road station (TL 978879) near Thetford, Norfolk.

Footpath Guide: Noyes, Trevor, *The Hereward Way,* published by the author at 8 Welmore Road, Glinton, Peterborough PE6 7LU.

Heritage Way A 113-kilometre waymarked circular route around Newcastle-upon-Tyne and Gateshead, focusing on industrial archaeology, that starts at Wylam (NZ 119647), Northumberland, west of Newcastle.

Footpath Guide: The Heritage Way, 4 leaflets compiled and published by Tyne & Wear County Council, Planning Department, Sandyford House, Newcastle-upon-Tyne NE2 1ED, 1985.

Herriot Way An 89-kilometre circular route from Aysgarth (SE 012885),

North Yorkshire, through the Yorkshire Dales National Park.

Footpath Guide: Scholes, Norman F., *The Herriot Way,* published by the author at YHA, 96 Main Street, Bingley, West Yorkshire BD16 2JH.

High Hunsley Circular A 39-kilometre circular challenge walk in the Yorkshire Wolds which starts at Walkington (SE 999368), Humberside, near Beverley.

Footpath Guide: The High Hunsley Circular, compiled and published by Humberside County Council, Technical Services, County Hall, Beverley, North Humberside HU17 9XA.

Holderness Way A 34-kilometre route through Humberside from Kingston-upon-Hull (TA 097288) to Hornsea (TA 208479).

Footpath Guide: Dresser, Roy, *The Holderness Way,* published by the author at 128 Kirklands Road, Kingston-upon-Hull HU5 5AT.

Howden 20 A 32-kilometre (20-mile) circular route starting at Howden (SE 748283), north of Goole, Humberside.

Footpath Guide: The Howden 20, compiled and published by Humberside County Council, Technical Services, County Hall, Beverley, North Humberside HU17 9XA.

Hull Countryway An 83-kilometre waymarked semi-circular route through Humberside from Kingston-upon-Hull (TA 097288) to Hedon (TA 188287).

Footpath Guide: Killick, Alan, *The Hull Countryway,* Lockington Publishing Co. Ltd.

Humber Bridge Link Walk A 55-kilometre circular walk from Hessle (TA 035256), Kingston-upon-Hull, with circuits on both sides of the Humber that are linked by the Humber Bridge.

Footpath Guide: The Humber Bridge Link Walk, compiled and published by Humberside County Council, Technical Services, County Hall, Beverley, North Humberside HU17 9XA.

Icknield Way 168 kilometres from Ivinghoe Beacon (SP 960168), near Tring, Hertfordshire, to Knettishall Heath (TM 944807), near Thetford, Norfolk.

Footpath Guide: The Icknield Way; a Walker's Guide, compiled and published by the Icknield Way Association, 19 Boundary Road, Bishops Stortford, Herts CM23 5LF, 1988.

Inkpen Way 100 kilometres from Monk Sherborne (SU 609561), near Basingstoke, Hampshire, to Salisbury (SU 143297).

Footpath Guide: Ward, Ian, *The Inkpen Way,* Thornhill Press, 1979.

Isle of Man Coastal Footpath A 145-kilometre circular route around the coast of the Isle of Man starting at Douglas (SC 379754). It is also known as Raad Ny Foillan (the Gull's Road).

Footpath Guide: Evans, Aileen, *Isle of Man Coastal Path; 'Raad ny*

Foillan'—The Way of the Gull; includes also the Millenium Way and the 'Bayr ny Skeddan'—The Herring Way, Cicerone Press, 1988.

Isle of Wight Coastal Path A 105-kilometre waymarked route encircling the island starting at Rye (SZ 596919).

Footpath Guides: Charles, Alan, *The Isle of Wight Coast Path,* Thornhill Press, 1986; Merrill, John, *Isle of Wight Coastal Path,* JNM Publications, 1988.

Kettlewell Three Walk A strenuous 53-kilometre circular challenge walk in the Yorkshire Dales National Park from Kettlewell (SD 968723).

Footpath Guide: Belk, Les, and Hills, John, *The Kettlewell Three Walk,* published by the authors at 82 Northcote Crescent, Leeds LS11 6NN.

King Alfred's Way 174 kilometres from Portsmouth (SU 628006) to Oxford (SP 516060).

Footpath Guide: Main, Laurence, *King Alfred's Way,* Thornhill Press, 1980.

Knightley Way A 19-kilometre waymarked route in Northamptonshire from Greens Norton (SP 671490) to Badby (SP 560587). It links with the Grafton Way, which in turn joins the North Bucks Way, to form an 87-kilometre route.

Footpath Guide: The Knightley Way, compiled and published by North-ants County Council, Leisure and Libraries Dept., 27 Guildhall, Northampton NN1 1EF, 1983.

Lakes Link A 196-kilometre circular route through the Lake District National Park from Ambleside (NY 376045).

Footpath Guide: Dixon, Michael, *The Lakes Link; a 128-mile Circular Route from Ambleside Connecting all the Major Lakes,* Dalesman, 1984.

Lancashire Trail 113 kilometres from St Helens (SJ 512956), Merseyside, to Thornton-in-Craven (SD 906484), North Yorkshire, west of Skipton.

Footpath Guide: The Lancashire Trail; a Series of Short Walks which Link Together to form a long-distance Route Connecting St Helens, Wigan, Bolton, Blackburn and Burnley with the Pennines, 2nd Ed., compiled and published by the St Helens District CHA and Holiday Fellowship Rambling Club, 40 St Mary's Avenue, Birchley, Billinge, Wigan WN5 7QL, 1982.

Langbaurgh Loop A 61-kilometre waymarked circular route from Saltburn-by-the-Sea (NZ 668216), Cleveland.

Leaflet available from Langbaurgh Business Association, Jordans Guest House, 15 Pearl Street, Saltburn-by-the-Sea, Cleveland TS12 1DU.

Leeds Country Way A 97-kilometre waymarked circular route around Leeds starting at Golden Acre Park (SE 267417).

Leaflet available from Leeds Metropolitan Borough Council, Civic Hall LS1 1UR, 1981.

Leeds Dalesway A 32-kilometre walk through West Yorkshire from Leeds (SE 293351) to Ilkley (SE 117476).

Footpath Guide: Gemmell, Arthur and Speakman, Colin, *The Dales Way Route Guide: with Associated Walks: Specially Drawn Maps of Associated Footpaths,* Stile Publications, 1983.

Leeds to the Sea 145 kilometres from Roundhay (SE 336372), Leeds, to Saltburn-by-the-Sea (NZ 668216), Cleveland. The guide mentioned below covers 71 kilometres of the route from Roundhay to the Kilburn White Horse (SE 514813) in the North York Moors National Park where it joins the Cleveland Way. From then on it is necessary to use a Guide to this long-distance path.

Footpath Guide: A Walk from Leeds to the Sea, compiled and published by the West Riding Area of the Ramblers' Association, 9 Church Avenue, Bilton, Harrogate HG1 4HE, 1983.

Leicestershire Round A 161-kilometre circular waymarked route through the county from Burrough Hill Country Park (SK 766115), near Melton Mowbray.

Footpath Guide: The Leicestershire Round, written and published in three sections by the Leicestershire Footpath Association and available from the Tourist Information Bureau, 12 Bishop Street, Leicester LE1 6AA.

Limestone Way A 42-kilometre waymarked route through the Peak National Park from Matlock (SK 298603) to Castleton (SK 150829).

Leaflet available from West Derbyshire District Council, Town Hall, Bank Road, Matlock, Derbyshire DE4 3NN.

Limey Way 64 kilometres from Castleton (SK 150829) through the Peak National Park to Thorpe (SK 157054), north of Ashbourne.

Footpath Guide: Merrill, John, *The Limey Way,* JNM Publications, 1989.

Lindsey Loop A 161-kilometre figure-of-eight route from Market Rasen (TF 111897), Lincolnshire.

Footpath Guide: Collier, Brett, *The Lindsey Loop,* Lincolnshire and South Humberside Group of the Ramblers' Association, Chloris House, 208 Nettleham Road, Lincoln LN2 4DH, 1986.

Lipchis Way 42 kilometres from Liphook (SU 842309), Hampshire, to Chichester (SU 858043), West Sussex (hence the name).

Footpath Guide: Clark, David, and Clark, Margaret, *The Lipchis Way,* published by the authors at 21 Chestnut Close, Liphook, Hants GU30 7JA, 1985.

Llwybr Bro Gwy A 58-kilometre waymarked route through Powys from Hay-on-Wye (SO 229425) to Rhayader (SN 968679).

Leaflet available from Powys County Council, Shire Hall, Llandrindod Wells LD1 5LG.

London Countryway A 330-kilometre circular route around London from Box Hill (TQ 173513), near Dorking, Surrey.

Footpath Guide: Chesterton, Keith, *A London Countryway*, 2nd Ed., Constable, 1981.

Lyke Wake Walk A 64-kilometre challenge walk across the North York Moors National Park from Beacon Hill (SE 459997), near Osmotherley, to Ravenscar (NZ 980018) on the coast.

Footpath Guide: Cowley, William, *The Lyke Wake Walk and the Lyke Wake Way: Forty Miles across the North York Moors in 24 hours or 50 Miles in a Day as Long as You Like!: with, in Addition, the Shepherd's Round, the Monk's Trod and the Rail Trail Thrown in for Good Measure*, Dalesman, 1988.

Maidstone Circular Walk A 32-kilometre circular route around Maidstone, Kent starting at Sandling (TQ 755581).

Footpath Guide: The Maidstone Circular Walk, compiled and published by the Maidstone Group of the Ramblers' Association, 18 Firs Close, Aylesford, Maidstone ME20 7LH.

Mallerstang Horseshoe and Nine Standards Yomp A 37-kilometre circular challenge walk from Kirkby Stephen (NY 775087), Cumbria.

Footpath Guide: The Falklands Way and the Mallerstang Horseshoe and Nine Standards Yomp, P. N. Denby Ltd, Kirkby Stephen, Cumbria.

Millenium Way A 45-kilometre waymarked route across the Isle of Man from Sky Hill (SC 432945), Ramsey, to Castletown (SC 265675).

Footpath Guides: Evans, Aileen, *Isle of Man Coastal Path; 'Raad ny Foillan'—The Way of the Gull; includes also the Millenium Way and the 'Bayr ny Skeddan'—The Herring Way*, Cicerone Press, 1988; *Millenium Way*, compiled and published by the Isle of Man Tourist Board, 13 Victoria Street, Douglas, I.O.M.

Minster Way An 81-kilometre waymarked route from Beverley (TA 038393), Humberside, to York (SE 603522).

Footpath Guide: Wallis, Ray, *The Minster Way*, Lockington Publishing Co. 1979.

Navigation Way 161 kilometres along canal towpaths from Birmingham (SP 064864) to Chasewater (SK 041073), near Brownhills, West Midlands.

Footpath Guide: Groves, Peter, *The Navigation Way; a Hundred Mile Towpath Walk around Birmingham and the West Midlands*, Tetradon Publications, 40 Hadzor Road, Oldbury, Warley, West Midlands B68 9LA for the University of Aston in Birmingham, 1978.

Nidderdale Way An 85-kilometre waymarked circular route from Hampsthwaite (SE 259587), near Harrogate, North Yorkshire.

Footpath Guide: Piggin, J. K. E., *The Nidderdale Way; a 53-Mile Walk around the Valley of the River Nidd*, Dalesman, 1983.

North Bowland Traverse A 52-kilometre route from Slaidburn (SD 712524), Lancashire, to Stainforth (SD 822673), North Yorkshire.

Footpath Guide: Johnson, David, *The North Bowland Traverse,* Hillside Publications, 1987.

North Buckinghamshire Way 50 kilometres from Chequers Knap (SP 830053), near Wendover to Wolverton (SP 821415), Milton Keynes.

Footpath Guide: The North Buckinghamshire Way, compiled and published by the Buckinghamshire and West Middlesex Area of the Ramblers' Association and available from the Ramblers' Association, Southern Area, 1/5 Wandsworth Road, London SW8 2XX, 3rd Ed.

North Wolds Walk A 32-kilometre circular walk from Millington Road End (SE 836567), 24 kilometres east of York.

Footpath Guide: Watson, R. N., *The North Wolds Walk,* published by the author and available from him at the Library and Information Service, Reckitt & Colman Pharmaceutical Division, Kingston-upon-Hull HU8 7DS.

North Worcestershire Path A 34-kilometre waymarked route through Hereford and Worcester from Forhill picnic site (SP 055755), south of Birmingham, to Kingsford Country Park, north of Kidderminster.

Leaflet: *The North Worcestershire Path (Countryside Recreation Service Information Sheet no. 7),* compiled and published by Hereford and Worcester County Council, County Planning Department, Spetchley Road, Worcester WR5 2NP.

North York Moors Challenge Walk A 40-kilometre circular challenge walk in the North York Moors National Park commencing at Goathland (NZ 838014).

Footpath Guide: Merrill, John, *John Merrill's North York Moors Challenge Walk,* JNM Publications, 1986.

Northumberland Coast Walk A 40-kilometre waymarked route from Alnmouth (NU 248108) to Budle (NU 155350).

Footpath Guide: Hopkins, Tony, *Walks on the Northumberland Coast,* Northumberland County Council, 1983.

Offa's Wye Frontier 96 kilometres from Monmouth (SO 505129), Gwent, to Kington (SO 298566), Hereford and Worcester, designed as an unofficial alternative to part of Offa's Dyke Path.

Footpath Guide: Kay, Kathy and Kay, Ernie, *Offa's Wye Frontier,* Offa's Dyke Association, The Old Primary School, West Street, Knighton, Powys LD7 1EW, 1987. Richards, Mark, *Through Welsh Border Country following Offa's Dyke Path,* Thornhill Press, 1985.

Oxfordshire Trek A 103-kilometre circular route from Sir Winston Churchill's tomb at Bladon (SP 449149), near Woodstock.

Footpath Guide: Main, Laurence, *Guide to the Oxfordshire Trek,* Kittiwake Press, 1989.

Oxfordshire Way A 105-kilometre waymarked route from Bourton-on-the-Water (SP 170209), Gloucestershire to Henley-on-Thames (SU 757833), Oxfordshire.

Footpath Guide: The Oxfordshire Way, compiled and published by Oxford County Council, Speedwell House, Speedwell Street, Oxford OX1 1SD.

Painters' Way 39 kilometres from Sudbury (TL 877410), Suffolk, to Manningtree (TM 094322), Essex, through countryside associated with Turner and Gainsborough.

Footpath Guide: Turner, Hugh R. P., *The Painters' Way,* Peddar Publications, Croft End Cottage, Bures, Suffolk CO8 5JN, 1982.

Peak District Challenge Walk A 40-kilometre circular challenge walk through the Peak National Park from Bakewell (SK 217685).

Footpath Guide: Merrill, John, *John Merrill's Peak District Challenge Walk,* JNM Publications, 1986.

Peak District High Level Route A 145-kilometre circular challenge walk around the Peak National Park from Matlock (SK 298603).

Footpath Guide: Merrill, John, *The Peak District High Level Route,* JNM Publications.

Peakland Way A 155-kilometre circular challenge walk through the Peak National Park from Ashbourne (SK 178479).

Footpath Guide: Merrill, John, *The Peakland Way Guide,* JNM Publications, 1989.

Peel Trail A 56-kilometre circular route from Bury (SD 809123), Greater Manchester.

Footpath Guide: Burton, Michael, *The Peel Trail,* published by the author at 6 Carrwood Hey, Ramsbottom, Lancashire BL0 9QT.

Pendle Way A 72-kilometre waymarked circular route from Barrowford (SD 863398), Lancashire.

Leaflet available from Pendle Borough Council, Bank House, Albert Road, Colne, Lancashire BB8 0AQ.

Pilgrims' Way A 210-kilometre waymarked route from Winchester (SU 483293), Hampshire, to Canterbury (TR 150579), Kent, following a prehistoric trackway. Considerable sections run parallel to or concurrent with the North Downs Way which is now a national trail.

Footpath Guide: Wright, Christopher John, *Guide to the Pilgrims' Way and the North Downs Way,* Constable, 1982.

Plogsland Round A 72-kilometre circular route around Lincoln starting at Fiskerton (TF 058715).

Footpath Guide: Collier, Brett, *The Plogsland Round,* published by the author at Chloris House, 208 Nettleham Road, Lincoln LN2 4DH, 1982.

Ramblers' Way 61 kilometres through the Peak National Park from Castleton (SK 150829) to Hathersage (SK 232815).

Footpath Guide: Newton, Andrew, and Summers, Paul, *The Ramblers' Way,* published by the authors and available from Mountain Peaks Climbing Club, 17 Humberston Road, Wollaton, Nottingham NG8 2SU.

Red Kite Trail A 119-kilometre circular route from Llanwrtyd Wells (SN 879467), Powys LD5 4RB.

Leaflet available from Gordon Green, Neuadd Arms Hotel, Llanwrtyd Wells, Powys.

Ribble Way A 116-kilometre waymarked route from Longton (SD 458255), near Preston, Lancashire, to near Horton-in-Ribblesdale (SD 813827), North Yorkshire, following the river Ribble from its estuary to its source.

Footpath Guide: Sellers, Gladys, *The Ribble Way,* Cicerone Press, 1985.

Ridge Walk A 32-kilometre circuit around upper Nidderdale, North Yorkshire, starting at Middlesmoor (SE 091741).

Footpath Guide: Belk, Leslie, and Hills, John, *The Ridge Walk,* published by the authors at 82 Northcote Crescent, Leeds LS11 6NN.

Rivers Way A 64-kilometre challenge walk across the Peak National Park, mainly following rivers, from Edale (SK 125858) to Ilam (SK 135508).

Footpath Guide: Merrill, John, *The Rivers Way,* JNM Publications, 1987.

Robin Hood Way A 142-kilometre waymarked route through Nottinghamshire from Nottingham Castle (SK 569392) to Edwinstowe Church (SK 626669) where Maid Marian is reputed to have married Robin Hood.

Footpath Guide: The Robin Hood Way, compiled and published by the Nottingham Wayfarers Rambling Club, 22 The Hollows, Silverdale, Wilford, Nottingham NG11 7FJ, 1985.

Rossendale Way A 72-kilometre circular route through Lancashire from Sharneyford (SD 889246) near Bacup.

Footpath Guide: Goldthorpe, Ian, *The Rossendale Rambles including the Rossendale Way and Selected Town and Village Trails,* 2nd Ed., Rossendale Groundwork Trust and the Rossendale Borough Council, Planning Department, 6 St James Square, Bacup, Lancashire OL13 9AA, 1985.

St Peter's Way 73 kilometres through Essex from Chipping Ongar (TL 551036) to Bradwell-on-Sea (TM 032082).

Footpath Guide: Matthews, Fred, and Bitten, Harry, *The St Peter's Way; a Long-distance Route from Chipping Ongar to the Ancient Chapel of St Peter-on-the-Wall at Bradwell-on-Sea, Essex,* Matthews/Bitten Publications, 1978.

Saints Way A 42-kilometre route across Cornwall from Padstow (SW 920754) on the north coast to Fowey (SX 127522) on the south coast.

Footpath Guide: Gill, M., and Colwill, S., *The Saints Way,* Co-operative Retail Society, 29 Dantzic Street, Manchester M4 4BA, 1986.

Sandstone Trail A 51-kilometre waymarked route through Cheshire from Frodsham (SJ 519781) to Grindley Brook (SJ 522433), Shropshire.

Footpath Guide: The Sandstone Trail, compiled and published by Cheshire County Council, Countryside and Recreation Department, Goldsmith House, Hamilton Place, Chester CH1 1SE, 1986.

Saxon Shore Way A 225-kilometre waymarked route along the Kent coast from Gravesend (TQ 647744) to Rye (TQ 918205) in East Sussex.

Footpath Guides: Guides are being prepared (and some sections have already been published) by the Kent Area of the Ramblers' Association, 11 Thirlmere Drive, Barnehurst, Kent DA7 6PL.

Severn to Solent Walk 193 kilometres from Burham-on-Sea (ST 302480), Somerset, to the Hampshire coast near Lymington (SZ 364953).

Footpath Guide: Proctor, Alan, *A Severn to Solent Walk,* Thornhill Press, 1981.

Severn Way An 80-kilometre route along the east bank of the river Severn from Tewkesbury (SO 8932), through Gloucestershire to Berkeley Power Station (ST 6699).

Footpath Guide: Gidman, Stanley, *Guide to the Severn Way,* Arts & Museum Service, Gloucestershire County Council, Quayside Wing, Shire Hall, Gloucester GL1 2HY, 1989.

Sheffield Country Walk An 85-kilometre waymarked circular route around Sheffield starting at Eckington (SK 434798), Derbyshire.

Footpath Guide: The Sheffield Country Walk, compiled and published by the South Yorkshire County Council, Recreation Culture and Health Department, 70 Vernon Road, Worsborough Bridge, Barnsley S70 5LH.

Shepherd's Round A 65-kilometre waymarked challenge walk across the North York Moors National Park commencing at Scarth Nick (SE 471994), near Osmotherley.

Footpath Guide: Cowley, William, *The Lyke Wake Walk and the Lyke Wake Way; Forty Miles across the North York Moors in 24 hours or 50 Miles in a Day as Long as You Like!: with, in Addition, the Shepherd's Round, the Monk's Trod and the Rail Trail Thrown in for Good Measure,* Dalesman, 1988.

Sheriff's Way 44 kilometres through North Yorkshire from York (SE 603522) to Malton (SE 786704).

Footpath Guide: The Sheriff's Way, compiled and published by the Moor and Fell Club (Hon. Sec. Mrs B. Batty), Nestlé, The Cocoa Works, York YO1 1XY.

Shropshire Way A 201-kilometre waymarked circular route from Wem (SJ 517289).

Footpath Guide: Kirk, Robert, *The Shropshire Way; a Walker's Guide to the Route and Matters of Local Interest,* Thornhill Press, 1983.

Six Dales Hike A 67-kilometre challenge walk through North Yorkshire from Settle (SD 820636) to Skipton (SD 990518).

Footpath Guide: Burland, J. D., *The Six Dales Hike,* Dalesman, 1983.

Snowdonia Panoramic Walk A 48-kilometre challenge walk through Snowdonia National Park from Aber (SH 662720), near Llanfairfechan, Gwynedd, to Pant-glas (SH 473483), north of Criccieth, Gwynedd.

Leaflet available from E. Dalton, 'Mountain View', Fachell, Hermon, Bodorgan, Gwynedd LL62 5LL.

Solent Way A 97-kilometre waymarked route through Hampshire from Milford-on-Sea (SZ 292918) to Emsworth (SU 753055).

Footpath Guide: Shurlock, Barry, *The Solent Way; a Guide to the Hampshire Coast,* Hampshire County Council, Recreation Department, North Hill Close, Andover Road, Winchester, Hants SO22 6AQ, 1984.

Somerset Way 174 kilometres from Minehead (SS 972467) to Bath (ST 751647).

Footpath Guide: Main, Laurence, *A Somerset Way,* Thornhill Press 1980.

South Cheshire Way A 50-kilometre waymarked route from Grindley Brook (SJ 522433) to Mow Cop (SJ 856573).

Footpath Guide: The South Cheshire Way, compiled and published by the Mid-Cheshire Footpath Society, 72 Osborne Grove, Chavington, Crewe CW2 5BX.

South Coast Way 130 kilometres from Dover Castle (TR 324419), Kent, to Eastbourne Pier (TV 618989), East Sussex.

Footpath Guide: Main, Laurence, *A South Coast Way,* Thornhill Press, 1980.

South Wessex Way 188 kilometres from Petersfield (SU 746233), Hampshire, to Sandbanks (SZ 037871), Poole Harbour, Dorset, that links the South Downs Way with the South West Coast Path.

Footpath Guide: Main, Laurence, *A South Wessex Way,* Thornhill Press, 1980.

Staffordshire Way A 148-kilometre waymarked route from Mow Cop (SJ 856573) to Kinver Edge (SO 829822).

Footpath Guide: The Staffordshire Way, compiled and published by Staffordshire County Council, Planning and Development Department, Martin Street, Stafford ST16 2LE.

Stockport Circular Walk A 43-kilometre circular walk around Stockport (SJ 893903), Greater Manchester.

Footpath Guide: Brammal, Geoffrey, *The Stockport Circular Walk,* The Old Vicarage Publications, Reades Lane, Congleton, Cheshire CW12 3LL, 1986.

Suffolk Coast Path An 80-kilometre waymarked route from Felixstowe (TM 324364) to Lowestoft (TM 548926).

Footpath Guide: The Suffolk Coast Path, compiled and published by Suffolk County Council, Planning Department, St Peter's House, Cutler Street, Ipswich IP1 1UR.

Sussex Border Path 242 kilometres from Emsworth (SU 753055), Hampshire, to Rye (TQ 918205), East Sussex.

Footpath Guide: Perkins, Ben, and Mackintosh, Aeneas, *The Sussex Border Path,* published by the authors at 11 Old London Road, Brighton BN1 8XR.

Swan Way A 105-kilometre waymarked route from Goring and Streatley railway station (SU 602806), Berkshire, to Salcey Forest (SP 802513), Northamptonshire, between Milton Keynes and Northampton.

Leaflet available from the County Engineer, County Hall, Aylesbury, Buckinghamshire HP20 1BR.

Ten Reservoirs Walk A 35-kilometre circular challenge walk from Binn Green (SE 018044), Greater Manchester.

Footpath Guide: Tait, Bob, *Walks around Saddleworth,* published by the author at 6 Leefields Close, Uppermill, Oldham OL3 6LA, 1979.

Test Way A 71-kilometre waymarked route along the Test valley from Totton (SU 360140), near Southampton, to SU 369621 near Walbury Hill (popularly known as Inkpen Beacon), 7 kilometres southeast of Hungerford, Berkshire.

Footpath Guide: Shurlock, Barry, *The Test Way and the Clarendon Way,* Hampshire County Council, Recreation Department, North Hill Close, Andover Road, Winchester, Hants SO22 6AQ, 1986.

Thames Valley Heritage Walk 172 kilometres from Whitehall (TQ 300801), central London, to Woodstock (SP 447166), Oxfordshire.

Footpath Guide: Jebb, Miles, *The Thames Valley Heritage Way,* Constable, 1980.

Thetford Forest Walk A 37-kilometre waymarked route from High Ash Forest (TL 813967), Norfolk, to West Stow (TL 815715), Suffolk.

Footpath Guide: The Thetford Forest Guide Map, compiled and published by the Forestry Commission, District Office, Santon Downham, Brandon, Suffolk IP27 0TJ.

Three Forests Way A 97-kilometre waymarked circular route from Harlow (TL 445113), Essex.

Footpath Guide: Matthews, Fred, and Bitten, Harry, *The Three Forests Way; a Long-distance Circular Walk Linking the Three Essex Forests of Epping, Hatfield and Hainault,* Matthews/Bitten Publications, 'Glen View', London Road, Abridge, Romford RM4 1UX, 1977.

Three Reservoirs Challenge A 40-kilometre circular challenge walk in the Peak National Park commencing at the Ladybower Reservoir (SK 205865).

Footpath Guide: Newton, Andrew, and Summers, Paul, *The Three Reservoirs Challenge,* published by the authors at Mountain Peaks Climbing Club, 17 Humberstone Road, Wollaton, Nottingham NG8 2SU.

Three Towers Circuit A 56-kilometre challenge walk commencing at Tottington (SD 776129), Lancashire.

Leaflet available from Derek Magnall, 217 Booth Street, Tottington, Bury, Lancashire BL8 3JD.

Trans-Pennine Walk 87 kilometres from Adlington (SD 610130), near Bolton, Lancashire, to Haworth (SE 030372), near Keighley, West Yorkshire.

Footpath Guide: Mackrory, Richard, *The Trans-Pennine Walk,* Dalesman, 1983.

Two Crosses Circuit A 40-kilometre challenge walk commencing at Tottington (SD 776129), Greater Manchester.

Leaflet available from Derek Magnall, 217 Booth Street, Tottington, Bury, Lancashire BL8 3JD.

Two Moors Way A 166-kilometre partly waymarked route from Ivybridge (SX 636563), near Plymouth, south Devon, to Lynmouth (SS 724494), north Devon, linking the Dartmoor National Park with the Exmoor National Park.

Footpath Guide: Rowett, Helen, *The Two Moors Way,* Devon Area of the Ramblers' Association and available from the Ramblers' Association, 1/5 Wandsworth Road, London SW8 2XX.

Two Seasons Way 48 kilometres from Watton-at-Stone (TL 297193), near Stevenage, Hertfordshire, to Good Easter (TL 629121), northwest of Chelmsford, Essex.

Footpath Guide: Matthews, Fred, and Bitten, Harry, *The Two Seasons Way,* Matthews/Bitten Publications, 'Glen View', London Road, Abridge, Romford RM4 1UX, 1990.

Upper Lea Valley Through Walk A 46-kilometre waymarked route from Luton (TL 061249), Bedfordshire, to Ware (TL 359142), Hertfordshire.

Footpath Guide: The Upper Lea Valley Through Walk, compiled and published by the Community Council for Hertfordshire, 2 Townsend Avenue, St Albans AL1 3SG.

Upper Nidderdale Way A 37-kilometre route in North Yorkshire from Pateley Bridge (SE 157658) to Kettlewell (SD 968723) in the Yorkshire Dales National Park.

Footpath Guide: Belk, Leslie, and Hills, John, *The Upper Nidderdale Way,* published by the authors at 82 Northcote Crescent, Leeds LS11 6NN.

Usk Valley Walk A 40-kilometre waymarked route through Gwent from Caerleon (ST 342902) to Abergavenny (SO 292139).

Footpath Guide: The Usk Valley Walk, compiled and published by

Gwent County Council, Planning Department, County Hall, Cwmbran, Gwent NP44 2XH, 1983.

Vanguard Way 101 kilometres from Croydon (TQ 328657) to Seaford (TV 482992), East Sussex.

Footpath Guides: The Vanguard Way, compiled and published by the Vanguard Rambling Club, 10 Selsdon Park Road, Croydon CR2 8JJ, 2nd Ed, 1986. Reynolds, Kev, *The Wealdway and the Vanguard Way,* Cicerone Press, 1987.

Vermuyden Way A 32-kilometre circular route around the Isle of Axholme in south Humberside commencing at Haxey (SE 770000).

Footpath Guide: Walks South of the Humber, compiled and published by the Humberside County Council, Technical Services Department, County Hall, Beverley, North Humberside HU17 9XA.

Viking Way A 225-kilometre waymarked route from the Humber Bridge (TA 028234) to Oakham (SK 861088), Leicestershire. The Countryside Commission has issued a consultation paper proposing that this route should become a national trail.

Footpath Guides: Stead, John, *The Viking Way,* Cicerone Press, 1990; *The Viking Way,* compiled and published by Lincolnshire County Council, Recreational Services Department, County Offices, Newlands, Lincoln LN1 1YL, 1984.

A Viking Way accommodation leaflet is available from Major Brett Collier, Chloris House, 208 Nettleham Road, Lincoln LN2 4DH.

WALKWAYS; Birmingham to Aberystwyth A 220-kilometre route from Birmingham (SP 064864) to Aberystwyth (SN 580813), Dyfed.

Footpath Guides: Roberts, John S., *WALKWAYS Series 2; Birmingham to Ludlow.* Roberts, John S., *WALKWAYS Series 2; Ludlow to Aberystwyth.* (Both titles published by WALKWAYS, 15 Gilldown Road, Birmingham B15 6JR.)

WALKWAYS; Llangollen to Snowdon A 98-kilometre route from Llangollen (SJ 215420), Clwyd to Snowdon (SH 607546) in the Snowdonia National Park.

Footpath Guides: Roberts, John S., *WALKWAYS Series 1; Llangollen to Bala.* Roberts, John S., *WALKWAYS Series 1; Bala to Snowdon.* (Both titles published by WALKWAYS, 15 Gilldown Road, Birmingham B15 6JR.)

Wayfarer's Walk A 113-kilometre waymarked route across Hampshire from Emsworth, Hampshire, to SU 369621 near Walbury Hill (popularly known as Inkpen Beacon), 7 kilometres southeast of Hungerford, Berkshire.

Footpath Guide: Herbst, Linda, *The Wayfarer's Walk,* Hampshire County Council, Recreation Department, North Hill Close, Andover Road, Winchester, Hants SO22 6AQ, 2nd Ed, 1989.

Wealdway   A 131-kilometre waymarked route across Kent and Sussex from Gravesend (TQ 647744) to Eastbourne (TV 588991).

Footpath Guides: The Wealdway, compiled and published by the Wealdway Steering Group, 11 Old London Road, Brighton BN1 8XR, 1981; *The Wealdway Accommodation and Transport Guide,* available from the above address; Mason, John H. N., *A Guide to the Wealdway,* Constable, 1984; Reynolds, Kev, *The Wealdway and the Vanguard Way,* Cicerone Press, 1987.

Wear Valley Way A 74-kilometre route across County Durham and Tyne & Wear from Waskerley Reservoir (NZ 027430), to Willington (NZ 194354) between Wallsend and Tynemouth.

Footpath Guide: Earnshaw, Alan, *The Wear Valley Way,* Discovery Guides, 1 Market Place, Middleton-in-Teesdale, Co. Durham DL12 0QG, 1983.

Weardale Way 126 kilometres from Monkwearmouth (NZ 408587), Tyne & Wear, to the source of the river Wear near Cowshill (NY 855405), Cumbria.

Footpath Guide: Piggin, J. K. E., *The Weardale Way; a 78-mile Walk Following the River Wear from Monkwearmouth to Cowshill,* Dalesman, 1984.

Weaver Valley Way A 32-kilometre route through Cheshire from Bottom Flash (SD 657655), near Winsford to Weaver Lock (SD 508798), Runcorn.

Leaflet available from Cheshire County Council, Countryside and Recreation Department, Goldsmith House, Hamilton Place, Chester CH1 1SE.

Weavers' Way A 90-kilometre waymarked route through Norfolk from Cromer (TG 215420) to Great Yarmouth (TG 522081).

Footpath Guides: Walking the Peddars Way/Norfolk Coast Path and the Weaver's Way, compiled and published by the Peddars Way Association, 150 Armes Street, Norwich NR2 4EG, 1987; *The Weavers' Way,* compiled and published by Norfolk County Council, Planning Department, County Hall, Martineau Lane, Norwich NR1 2DH.

Wessex Way 166 kilometres from Overton Hill (SU 118681), west of Marlborough, Wiltshire, to Swanage (SZ 034804), Dorset.

Footpath Guide: Proctor, Alan, *The Wessex Way,* Thornhill Press, 1980.

West Mendip Way A 48-kilometre waymarked route through Somerset from Wells (ST 549461) to Weston-super-Mare (ST 315585).

Footpath Guide: Eddy, Andrew, *The West Mendip Way,* published by the Rotary Club of Weston-super-Mare and available from the Weston-super-Mare Civic Society, 3–6 Wadham Street, Weston-super-Mare, Avon BS23 1JY.

West Midland Way A 261-kilometre circular route around Birmingham from Meriden (SP 238823), near Coventry.

Footpath Guide: Leek, Ronald, and Jones, Eric, *A Guide to the West Midland Way,* Constable, 1979.

Westmorland Boundary Way A 274-kilometre circular route around the Lake District National Park commencing at Kendal (SD 520931), Cumbria.

Footpath Guide: Emett, Charlie, *In Search of the Westmorland Way,* Cicerone Press, 1985.

Westmorland Heritage Walk An anti-clockwise near-circular route from Arnside (SD 456788) roughly based on the boundaries of the old county of Westmorland but making diversions to include the best walking country. The high level route is 320 kilometres and the alternative low level route is 290 kilometres.

Footpath Guide: Richards, Mark and Wright, Christopher, *The Westmorland Heritage Walk,* Cicerone Press, 1988.

Westmorland Way 158 kilometres through the Lake District National Park from Appleby-in-Westmorland (NY 683204), Cumbria, to Arnside (SD 456788), Cumbria.

Footpath Guide: Hannon, Paul, *The Westmorland Way,* Hillside Publications, 1983.

Wey-South Path 58 kilometres from Guildford (SU 994493), Surrey, to Amberley (TQ 026118), near Arundel, West Sussex.

Footpath Guide: Mackintosh, Aeneas, *The Wey-South Path; from Guildford to the South Downs,* Wey and Arun Canal Trust, 24 Griffiths Avenue, Lancing, West Sussex BN15 0HW, 1987.

White Peak Way A 129-kilometre circular route through the Peak National Park commencing at Bakewell (SK 217685).

Footpath Guide: Haslam, Robert, *The White Peak Way; an 80 Mile Circular Walk within the Peak National Park,* 2nd Ed, Cicerone Press, 1990.

White Rose Walk A 174-kilometre challenge walk across the North York Moors National Park from Newton under Roseberry (NZ 571128), Cleveland, to the Kilburn White Horse (SE 514813), North Yorkshire.

Footpath Guide: White, Geoffrey, *The White Rose Walk,* 2nd Ed, Dalesman, 1976.

Wight Heritage Trail A 121-kilometre circular waymarked route commencing at Ryde (SZ 596919), Isle of Wight.

Footpath Guide: The Wight Heritage Trail, compiled and published by the Isle of Wight County Council, County Surveyor, County Hall, Newport, Isle of Wight PO30 1UD.

Wiltshire Way A 261-kilometre circular route from Salisbury (SU 143297).

Footpath Guide: Main, Laurence, *A Wiltshire Way; a Walker's Guide,* Thornhill Press, 1980.

Witches Way 48 kilometres through Lancashire from Rawtenstall (SD 812232) to Slaidburn (SD 712524).

Footpath Guide: Johnson, David and Ashton, James, *The Witches' Way; a 30-mile Walk through Upland Lancashire,* Dalesman, 1984.

Worcestershire Way A 58-kilometre waymarked route through the county of Hereford and Worcester from Kingsford (SO 836821) to North Malvern (SO 766477).

Leaflet available from Hereford and Worcester County Council, County Hall, Spetchley Road, Worcester WR5 2NP.

Wychavon Way A 64-kilometre waymarked route from Winchcombe, Gloucestershire (SP 025283), near Cheltenham to Holt Fleet (SO 824633), near Worcester.

Footpath Guide: Richards, Mark, *The Wychavon Way,* Wychavon District Council, 37 High Street, Pershore, Worcester WR10 1AH, 1982.

Wye Valley Walk A 132-kilometre waymarked route from Chepstow (ST 529924), Gwent, to Hereford (SO 509395).

Leaflet available from Wye Valley AONB Joint Advisory Committee, County Planning Department, Gwent County Council, Cwmbran, Gwent NP44 2XF.

Yoredale Way 161 kilometres from York (SE 603522) to Kirkby Stephen (NY 775087), Cumbria, following the river Ure to its source.

Footpath Guide: Piggin, J. K. E., *The Yoredale Way,* Dalesman, 1980.

Yorkshire Dales Centurion Walk A 161-kilometre circular challenge walk through the Yorkshire Dales National Park from Horton-in-Ribblesdale (SD 809725).

Footpath Guide: Ginesi, Jonathan, *The Official Guidebook to the Yorkshire Dales Centurion Walk,* John Siddall Ltd, Horncastle Street, Cleckheaton, West Yorkshire BD19 3HJ.

Yorkshire Dales Challenge Walk A 40-kilometre circular challenge walk through the Yorkshire Dales National Park commencing at Kettlewell (SD 968723).

Footpath Guide: Merrill, John, *John Merrill's Yorkshire Dales Challenge Walk,* JNM Publications, 1986.

Yorkshire Pioneer Walk A 106-kilometre circular route through the Yorkshire Dales National Park commencing at the former Dacre Banks Youth Hostel (SE 198618), northwest of Harrogate.

Footpath Guide: Scholes, Norman F. *The Yorkshire Pioneer Walk,* published by the author and available from the YHA, 96 Main Street, Bingley, West Yorkshire BD16 2JH.

Bibliography

Blachford, Barbara, *The Long Distance Walker's Handbook,* A. and C. Black, 2nd Ed, 1990.

16 Walking in Scotland

Scotland contains far more wild and unspoilt countryside than exists in England and Wales put together. Unfortunately, in recent years some of the country's most beautiful areas have been put at risk by the development of skiing, bulldozed tracks and roads and above all, the widespread and insensitive conifer afforestation. There are also a number of hydroelectric power stations, but on the whole their effect on the landscape has not been disastrous. Scotland must have a chapter to itself, not only because of its very special qualities as a walker's paradise, but also because walking tends to be a much more serious undertaking and because there are special problems and difficulties.

There are no national parks in Scotland because the Ramsey Committee's proposals were never implemented by legislation. This is surprising considering that the country contains some of the most remote and beautiful countryside in Great Britain. Whereas in England, and to a lesser extent Wales, a hill-walking expedition almost invariably means visiting a national park, with all the risk of overcrowding that this involves, this is not the case in Scotland. Walking in Scotland requires considerably more skill and experience than an expedition to mountainous areas of England and Wales, not just because the terrain is more rugged but also because of the remoteness and emptiness of much of Scotland and the likely weather conditions. Route-finding is not only more difficult, but much more critical, and a certain amount of scrambling is necessary on some paths. Scrambling is really the most elementary form of rock-climbing, where roping is not necessary to keep one's balance. If a walker were taken secretly to any mountainous area of England and left with a compass but no map, one day's supply of food and proper clothing and boots he could, by noting the direction that the mountains and valleys ran, use his compass to enable him to walk in a straight line and before many hours had passed he would reach a road, farm or settlement. This is not the case in Scotland. The walker's supply of food could easily run out long before he reached a road, let alone a croft or village.

The weather conditions, too, are likely to be much worse even in summer. Wind, mist and heavy rain must be expected, especially in the western parts of Scotland. In winter the conditions can be truly arctic, with temperatures well below zero and winds at times so strong that it is impossible to walk against them. Even in summer the walker can experience blizzards, and snow is likely to lie in some of the corries until June.

It is absolutely essential for every walker to be an expert with map and compass, to leave word with someone responsible and to report safe arrival, never to go alone unless very experienced, to take proper account of weather forecasts and to be ready to turn back if the weather suddenly deteriorates. One of the marks of an experienced walker is that he is prepared to retrace his steps when conditions worsen. The problems of fatigue and hypothermia are immeasurably greater on the Scottish hills than in the rest of Great Britain and when tired and cold it is terrifyingly easy to get into very great danger.

May, June and September are usually the driest months and June also has the advantage of exceptionally long days. In the north of the country it does not really get dark at all during this month. Eastern Scotland is markedly drier than the west coast. Some towns, including Inverness, average less than 76cm of rain per year compared with Loch Quoich in the Western Highlands which has 287cm per year.

There are many mountains which will provide the walker with considerable route-finding difficulties. Because the weather is so uncertain the likelihood of walking in thick mist is far greater and frequently survival will depend on the accuracy of one's route-finding. On the way up it is very easy to be tempted on to more and more difficult ground until the way forward demands the skills of a rock-climber and the way back has become dangerous. Sometimes very skilled people have been killed or injured on what are really ordinary, but very narrow paths. Two examples of such paths are those along the summit of Liathach (1037 metres) in Glen Torridon and the path from Achnambeithach to the corrie below Stob Coire nan Lochan (1097 metres) in Glencoe. Both demand care, judgement and a head for heights. But apart from the frequent difficulty of finding the way onto a large and complex mountain or ridge, there is the added need to be sure of finding the right way down. Circular routes are always the most satisfying, but the descent can, and often does, demand more of the walker than the ascent. Glencoe and Glen Etive both provide good examples of the problem. In Glencoe one of the most rewarding and magnificent mountains to traverse, by a number of different routes, is Bidean nam Bian (1130m). Part of the traverse takes the walker above a lovely corrie called Coire nam Beith, encircled by magnificent rock walls. On a clear day it is obvious that a descent from the ridge by way of this corrie is out of the question for walkers, but in a mist the story is different. From the ridge there are a number of grassy rakes which lead to relatively easy gullies which, in turn, develop into rock walls without warning. Many people who have been tired and cold have tried to descend some of these, sometimes with fatal results.

The Ben Starav (1062m) group in Glen Etive provides another example of the trouble a walker can meet. Here the descent from the considerable horseshoe, of which Ben Starav is the first peak, is safely made from one fairly sizeable point on Glas Bheinn Mhor (977m), where the correct route takes the walker to the head waters of Allt Mheuran. But a small error in compass reading will lead the unwary onto a face of steeply sloping boiler-plate slabs. These are difficult to negotiate when dry, but when, as they normally are, they are wet and greasy, they become a death-trap.

In Eastern Scotland, particularly in the Cairngorm range, problems of another kind are encountered. Here much of the walking in this magnificent country is over what is very like high moorland. Some of the hills are over 1200 metres high and are marked by great cliffs, huge gullies and deep glens. The peaks are in general not so well-defined as they are in the west, hence route-finding in bad weather presents obvious difficulties. Far more important than this is the violence of the weather, particularly in the spring and autumn. Blizzards are common, but the combination of rain at an otherwise reasonable temperature with a high wind is an even more serious threat. For the cooling effect of such conditions rapidly leads to hypothermia in the ill-equipped and is one of the commonest causes of mountain deaths in the region.

In describing these dangers it is clear that the line between walking and mountaineering is difficult to draw and that walking in Scotland frequently calls for the all-round skills of the mountaineer. But Scotland can lay some claim to possessing the finest, most beautiful and most exciting terrain that a walker could ever hope to meet.

Sporting Interests

Although the most beautiful parts of Scotland are thinly populated and will support only sheep farming and forestry, it must not be supposed that the land has no other uses. Many of the wilder parts of Scotland belong to large estates, where shooting, fishing and deer-stalking interests are very important. The walker must be aware that huge sums of money are invested in Scottish sporting interests and they play an important part in the tourist industry and thus in the economy of the country.

Walkers have good reason to bless the sportsman because many of the estates have constructed access roads and tracks which have opened up areas of the country which were poorly served by paths. Such tracks and access roads are frequently not rights of way, but walkers are usually permitted to use them, though they may be closed at certain times during the season. In return for the use of these privileges it is not unreasonable to expect walkers to be meticulous in respecting sporting rights. Walkers can unwittingly ruin other people's recreation if they cross land on which stalking or shooting is taking place. During the main deer-stalking season, which lasts from the beginning of August until the middle of October (the culling of hinds continues until 15 February and grouse-shooting until 10 December), walkers should select routes which will not interfere with sporting interests. Information about where shooting and stalking is taking place on particular dates should be obtained locally from the factor's (estate manager's) office, post office, police station, public house, hotel or Youth Hostel, or from a local person. The names, addresses and telephone numbers of landowners, factors and keepers can be found in *Heading for the Scottish Hills* compiled by the Mountaineering Council for Scotland and the Scottish Landowners' Federation, Scottish Mountaineering Club, 1988.

Transport

Scotland is very well served by public transport. There is a rail network which covers most of the country except the extreme north-west and a remarkably widespread system of bus and post-bus routes which seem to link practically every village and town. Some of these services are operated by local carriers with no published timetable, so inquiries should be made locally. Ferries operate to most of the inhabited islands and there are also air services.

Accommodation

One of the curiosities of Scotland is the number of large hotels often found far from any centre of population. At the opposite end of the scale, there are camping and caravan sites and bed and breakfast accommodation available at some of the crofts. Many of the latter do not advertise and inquiries should be made locally.

The Scottish Tourist Board has in the last few years introduced the 'Book a bed ahead' scheme. Tourist Information centres have been established in numerous towns through the country, each displaying the 'bed' symbol.

Any of these centres will arrange accommodation, ranging from large hotels to humble crofts, for visitors on payment of a small fee and a deposit. When settling the account at the accommodation booked, the deposit is deducted from the bill. This is an invaluable service for travellers and can save many frustrating hours searching for suitable accommodation. There is a good network of Youth Hostels.

It should be noted that in the more modest establishments high tea rather than dinner is more likely to be served. High tea is a splendid Scottish institution consisting of something cooked such as bacon and eggs, sausage or fish followed by bread and butter and jam, scones, cakes and a pot of tea. In terms of both quality and quantity the difference between high tea and dinner to a hungry walker is largely academic.

Rights of Way
As there are no Definitive Maps of Scotland, the Ordnance Survey maps do not distinguish between private and public paths and tracks, although the 1:25000 Outdoor Leisure maps show some routes which have been walked regularly. As has been stated earlier, some paths and tracks have been created for shooting and deer-stalking purposes but as a general rule it will be found that walkers use nearly all paths and tracks marked on Ordnance Survey maps, although during the shooting and stalking season inquiries should be made locally. The Scottish Mountaineering Club have issued a series of splendid District Guides covering the whole of the country which give a large number of suggested routes. They are not given in detail but provide sufficient information for the walker to mark the route on his Ordnance Survey map. Climbing guides, too, can be useful to the hill-walker as they give details of the route to be followed to reach the climbing area, which is often stituated a long way from the nearest road or centre. Such guides are listed under the various Scottish regions below.

Regional footpath guides are listed under each area, but the following guides that cover larger regions will also be found to be useful: Bennet, Donald, *The Munros*, Scottish Mountaineering Club, 1985; Inglis, Harry, *Hill Path Contours of the Chief Mountain Passes in Scotland*, Gall and Inglis, 1976; Innes, Athol, *Let's Walk There!; Southern Scotland*, Javelin, 1987; McNeish, Cameron, *Let's Walk There!; Northern Scotland*, Javelin, 1987; Moir, D.G., *Scottish Hill Tracks, 2 Vols*, Bartholomew, 1975. Vol. 1 *Southern Scotland*, Vol. 2 *Northern Scotland*; Murray, W. H., *Scotland's Mountains; Scottish Mountaineering Club Guide*, Scottish Mountaineering Trust, 1987; Poucher, W. A., *Scottish Peaks: a Pictorial Guide to Walking in this Region and the Safe Ascent of its Most Spectacular Mountains*, Constable, 6th, Rev. Ed., 1982; *Scotland: Hill Walking*, Scottish Tourist Board, Rev. Ed., 1988; Storer, Ralph, *100 Best Routes on Scottish*

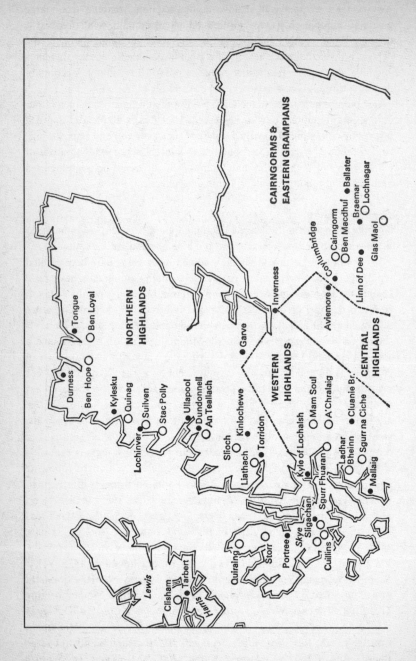

CAIRNGORMS &
EASTERN GRAMPIANS

Cairngorm
Ben Macdhui
Ballater
Braemar
Lochnagar
Columbridge
Linn of Dee
Glas Maol

Inverness

Aviemore

NORTHERN
HIGHLANDS

Tongue
Ben Loyal

Durness
Ben Hope

Garve

CENTRAL
HIGHLANDS

WESTERN
HIGHLANDS

Kyleku
Quinag
Suilven
Stac Polly

Lochinver

Ullapool
Dundonnell
An Teallach

Kinlochewe

Mam Soul
A'Chralaig
Cluanie Br.
Sgurr na Ciche

Slioch
Liathach
Torridon

Kyle of Lochalsh

Sgurr Fhuaran

Ladhar
Bheinn

Mallaig

Skye
Sligachan

Quiraing
Storr
Portree
Cuillins

Lewis

Clisham
Tarbert
Harris

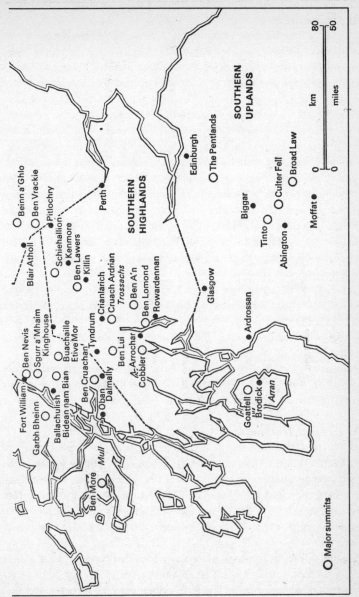

Fig. 58 Scotland

SOUTHERN UPLANDS

SOUTHERN HIGHLANDS

Moffat
Broad Law
Culter Fell
Abington
Tinto
Biggar
Ardrossan
The Pentlands
Edinburgh
Glasgow
Perth
Pitlochry
Ben Vrackie
Beinn a'Ghlo
Blair Atholl
Schiehallion
Kenmore
Ben Lawers
Killin
Crianlarich
Cruach Ardrian
Trossachs
Ben A'n
Ben Lomond
Rowardennan
Tyndrum
Ben Lui
Arrochar
Cobbler
Dalmally
Oban
Ben Cruachan
Bidean nam Bian
Ballachulish
Garbh Bheinn
Fort William
Ben Nevis
Sgurr a'Mhaim
Kinghouse
Buachaille Etive Mor
Ben More
Mull
Goatfell
Brodick
Arran

km   80
miles 50
0   0

O Major summits

245

Mountains, David and Charles, 1987; *Walks and Trails in Scotland*, Scottish Tourist Board, 1988.

The Cairngorms

Although containing some of the highest land in the United Kingdom, the Cairngorms, which lie on the eastern side of Scotland between the rivers Dee and Spey, are not so dramatic as other parts of Scotland. This is because they are plateaux that have been eroded into mountains often giving an unexciting slope on one side with magnificent corries and walls of cliff on the other side. There is splendid hill-walking in the area, especially on Cairn Toul (1272 metres), Braeriach (1264 metres), Ben Macdui (1289 metres) and the Lairig Ghru, an ancient pass, rising to over 800 metres makes an interesting route for anyone who wishes to avoid the high tops.

The Cairngorms have a significantly lower rainfall than other mountainous regions of Scotland and even on the highest mountains it does not exceed 150 centimetres per year. Extremes of temperature are more likely in this region, and the Cairngorms are often warmer in summer than other parts of Scotland and significantly colder in winter, with a great deal of snow and high winds are prevalent. Skill with map and compass, and good equipment is essential.

Maps: 1:50000 Landranger sheets 278, 28, 29, 36, 37, 43, 44; 1:63360 Tourist map of the Cairngorms; 1:25000 Outdoor Leisure map 3 Aviemore and the Cairngorms.

Guidebook: Watson, Adam, *The Cairngorms*, Scottish Mountaineering Trust, Rev. Ed., 1975.

Footpath Guides: Cairngorm Passes Path Map, Scottish Rights of Way Society Ltd., 1980; MacInnes, Hamish, *Highland Walks Vol. 4: Cairngorms and Royal Deeside*, Hodder & Stoughton, 1988.

The Central Highlands

The Central Highlands are situated largely in Inverness-shire and Argyll between the Western Highlands and the Cairngorms. The boundary of the region is formed in the south by Bridge of Orchy, Dalmally and Connel; on the western side by Loch Linnhe and the Great Glen; on the north from Whitebridge to Aviemore; and on the east from Aviemore southwards to Dalnacardoch, Kinloch Rannoch and along the railway line to Bridge of Orchy.

The whole area is mountainous and includes Ben Nevis, at 1321 metres the highest peak in the United Kingdom, as well as several other peaks more than 1200 metres high. There is a good network of paths and it is possible to walk for miles without crossing a road. There are a number of superb ridge walks, one of the most famous being Ben Cruachan.

Ben Nevis itself is a superb viewpoint and in summer can be climbed easily from Fort William or Glen Nevis. In winter, however, it can be very hazardous. Until the beginning of the century there was an hotel and observatory on the summit. Walkers must be prepared for plenty of rain in the Central Highlands. Records from the observatory show that on Ben Nevis in 1898 no less than 610 centimetres of rain fell, and 122 centimetres was recorded in December 1900.

Maps: 1:50000 Landranger sheets 41, 42, 49, 50, 51; 1:66360 Tourist map of Ben Nevis and Glen Coe.

Guidebook: Hodgkiss, Peter, *The Central Highlands*, Scottish Mountaineering Club, 1984.

Footpath Guides: MacInnes, Hamish, *Highland Walks Vol 1: Ben Lui to the Falls of Glomach*, Hodder and Stoughton, 1984; *Principal Rights of Way in the West Central Highlands: Path Map*, Scottish Rights of Way Society Ltd, 1983; Williams, Noel, *Walks in Lochaber*, Cicerone Press, 1989.

The Northern Highlands

The Northern Highlands include Sutherland, the northern half of Ross-shire and the southwest corner of Caithness.

The area is defined by Dingwall, Garve, and Strath Ban to Achnasheen and westwards to Glen Carron and the western seaboard. There is some spectacular mountain scenery with a wild and largely uninhabited hinterland crossed by a number of old drove roads that give excellent walking.

Maps: 1:50000 Landranger sheets 9, 10, 15, 16, 17, 19, 20, 21, 24, 25, 26; 1:25000 Outdoor Leisure map 8 of Cuillin and Torridon Hills covers part of the region.

Guidebook: Strang, Tom, *The Northern Highlands*, Scottish Mountaineering Trust, 2nd Rev. Ed., 1982.

Footpath Guides: MacInnes, Hamish, *Highland Walks Vol 2: Skye to Cape Wrath*, Hodder and Stoughton, 1984.

Skye

Skye is a large mountainous island about 80 kilometres long off the west coast of Scotland. For the really tough fell-walker Skye probably offers the finest walking in the whole of the United Kingdom. No part of the island is more than 8 kilometres from the sea and the coastline is heavily indented by sea lochs. These are twelve peaks over 900 metres offering wonderful vistas of mountains and seascape. Some of the peaks are only accessible to rock-climbers and all walkers must expect some scrambling. The Black Cuillin, probably the finest ridge in Scotland, cannot be walked at all without some rock-climbing.

Skye has other problems apart from its exceptionally rugged terrain. The weather is fickle and can change in a short time from marvellous to appalling. From July onwards there is a plague of pernicious midges that can prove very annoying, especially to campers.

Maps: 1:50000 Landranger sheets 23, 24, 32, 33; 1:25000 Outdoor Leisure Map 8 of the Cuillin and Torridon Hills covers part of the island.

Guidebook: Fabian, D., and others, *The Islands of Scotland including Skye*, Scottish Mountaineering Club, 1990.

Footpath Guides: MacInnes, Hamish, *Highland Walks Vol 2: Skye to Cape Wrath*, Hodder and Stoughton, 1984; Parker, J. Wilson, *Scrambles in Skye, Guide to Walks and Scrambles in the Black Cuillin*, Cicerone Press, 1983.

The Southern Highlands

The Southern Highlands are bounded in the north by the rivers Orchy and Tummel which form the boundary with the Central Highlands and run down almost to the Glasgow–Edinburgh axis. They are truly mountainous in character and include Loch Lomond and the Trossachs. As this area lies so close to Scotland's industrial belt it is the country's most popular walking area and its most famous mountains include Ben Lomond, The Cobbler and Ben Lawers.

Maps: 1:50000 Landranger sheets 49–52 inclusive and 55–58 inclusive; 1:63360 Tourist Map of the Trossachs.

Guidebook: Bennet, D. J., *The Southern Highlands*, Scottish Mountaineering Trust, 2nd, Rev. Ed., 1985.

Footpath Guides: MacInnes, Hamish, *Highland Walks Vol 1: Ben Lui to the Falls of Glomach*, Hodder and Stoughton, 1984.

The Southern Uplands

Also known as the Lowlands this area comprises that section of the country lying south of the Glasgow – Edinburgh axis and runs down to the border. Although the term 'Lowlands' is something of a misnomer as they contain mountains almost as high as any in England, this region lacks the rugged quality normally associated with Scottish scenery. The A74 road divides the region into two. On the eastern side lies the Border country formed by the river Tweed and its tributaries, where the hills are smooth in outline and covered in grass. On the western side the hills tend to be more rugged and generally have a more mountainous appearance. This is fine walking country more akin to the Lake District and the Pennines than the more truly mountainous regions of Scotland.

Maps: 1:50000 Landranger sheets 63–67 inclusive and 70–87 inclusive.

Guidebooks: Andrew, K. M., and Thrippleton, A. A., *The Southern

Uplands, Scottish Mountaineering Trust, 1972.

Footpath Guides: Moir, D. G., *Scottish Hill Tracks: Old Highways and Drove Roads, Southern Scotland*, Bartholomew, 1975; Walton, Robert D., *Dumfries and Galloway Highways and Byways: Guide to 200 Walks and Climbs*, T. C. Farries, 1985; Walton, Robert D., *Seventy Walks in Arran*, published by the author at 27 Castle Douglas Road, Dumfries DG2 7PA, 1987.

The Western Highlands

The Western Highlands include part of the western seaboard and run north from Loch Linnhe and the Great Glen to a line drawn from the Cromarty Firth along the valleys of the rivers Conon, Bran and Carron to Loch Carron. The area measures approximately 140 kilometres from north to south and about 50 kilometres from west to east. It includes Ardnamurchan, the most westerly point on the mainland of Great Britain.

The whole area, which includes Glen Affric, Glen Cannich and Glen Strathfarrar, which are generally acknowledged to be the three most beautiful glens in Scotland, is mountainous and there are a number of ranges that attain a height of nearly 1200 metres.

The Western Highlands have few roads and these follow the coast and glens. For the experienced hill-walker there is a splendid network of paths that reach into every part of the area.

Unfortunately, this region is one of the wettest areas of Scotland and the walker must expect many days when it will be quite impossible to venture into the mountains.

Maps: 1:50000 Landranger sheets 24, 25, 26, 33, 34, 40, 47, 49.

Guidebook: Bennet, D. J., *The Western Highlands*, Scottish Mountaineering Trust, 1983.

Footpath Guides: Brown, Hamish, *The Island of Rhum; a Guide for Walkers*, Cicerone Press, 1988; MacInnes, Hamish, *Highland Walks Vol 1: Ben Lui to the Falls of Glomach*, Hodder and Stoughton, 1984; MacInnes, Hamish, *Highland Walks Vol 2: Skye to Cape Wrath*, Hodder and Stoughton, 1984.

Regional Parks

In addition to the main walking areas listed above, Regional Parks have been established at Loch Lomond, the Pentland Hills and Fife which offer much easier walking than the wilder parts of the country. They have proved very popular as they are readily accessible from some of the larger centres of population.

Long-Distance Paths

Long-distance paths have been established with encouragement from the

Countryside Commission for Scotland against considerable opposition from those Scottish walkers who regard them as alien to the Scottish walking tradition. The Southern Upland Way, the Speyside Way and the West Highland Way are described in Chapter 15. The possibility of a route through the Great Glen from Fort William to Inverness is being considered, but even if the scheme comes to fruition it is unlikely to open officially before 1995 (in practice it has always been possible to walk from Fort William to Inverness following the Caledonian Canal and minor roads).

17 Walking in Ireland

Just across a short stretch of water from the mainland of Great Britain lies an island famed for the beauty of its scenery and the friendliness and hospitality of its people. The influence of Ireland on history has been out of all proportion to the size of her population. Irish monks kept the flame of Christian civilisation burning during the Dark Ages and Ireland has produced great saints, writers, politicians and generals. The Irish have populated vast areas of the United States and have had a profound influence on the history of that country, providing it with one of its greatest political dynasties.

Despite centuries of close political links, most inhabitants of Great Britain are woefully ignorant of their Irish neighbours. A sense of guilt is probably partly responsible, for the English in particular have always treated the Irish badly—and when the whole of Ireland was subject to the British crown, the record of misgovernment, callousness and indifference makes shameful reading.

Too few people cross the Irish Sea to walk in a country with a mild climate, beautiful and varied scenery, and where it is so easy to leave the crowds far behind.

Northern Ireland

Most parts of the Province of Ulster are worth exploring on foot. The Access to the Countryside (Northern Ireland) Order, 1983 places responsibility on district councils to map and keep open rights of way and create new ones where necessary. It also gives district councils the power to close rights of way where they are no longer needed. Under common law certain individuals, families and those engaged in a particular pursuit such as the extraction of timber or turf may have the right of passage in particular circumstances, but such considerations do not normally apply to the walker.

The walker (if he keeps away from the vicinity of large towns where, over the years, friction may have developed between 'townies', and farmers) is unlikely to encounter any difficulties using paths and tracks shown on Ordnance Survey maps, especially if he keeps a civil tongue in his head and is prepared to ask permission to cross private land. Walkers are more likely to be invited to share a cup of tea than be turned back! There is a dense network of lanes and minor roads on which motor traffic is sparse, but comparatively few field or mountain paths, except in the Mourne Mountains. There are also more than fifty state forests and several country parks where walking is encouraged. An important long-distance path, the Ulster Way, is described in the chapter dealing with long-distance paths of the United Kingdom. Despite the 'troubles', it is not dangerous to walk in Ulster and the chances of being involved in an incident are remote.

Maps: The Ordnance Survey of Northern Ireland (see p306) is the government agency responsible for surveying and mapping Ulster and it has no connection with the British Ordnance Survey at Maybush, Southampton. The best map for walkers is the new 1:50000 series which covers Northern Ireland in eighteen sheets (although these maps show fewer tracks than the series they replace). Some of the third series 1:63360 maps are still available but when stocks are exhausted they will not be reprinted. Ordnance Survey maps of Northern Ireland may be obtained from Edward Stanford Ltd., 12 Long Acre, London WC2E 9LP (Tel. 071-836-1321) or in case of difficulty by post from the Belfast office.

Walking Areas

The best walking is to be found in the Areas of Outstanding Natural Beauty designated by the Department of the Environment for Northern Ireland plus the Lakeland Country of County Fermanagh.

Antrim Coast and Glens An AONB that stretches from Larne to Ballycastle. It has a long coastline of black and white cliffs with a hinterland of high rough moorland, broken by beautiful glens, that provide excellent walking on heather and short grass. The northern tip joins the Causeway Coast AONB.

Maps: 1:50000 sheets 5, 8, 9.

Footpath Guides: Hamill, James, *North Ulster Walks Guide,* Appletree Press, 1988; Rogers, R., *Irish Walks Guides North East; Down and Antrim,* Gill and Macmillan, 1980.

Causeway Coast An AONB in Northern Ireland that stretches from

Ballycastle, where it joins the Antrim Coast and Glens AONB, to just east of Portrush. It includes the Giant's Causeway and Rathlin Island.

Maps: 1:50000 sheets 4, 5.

Footpath Guides: Hamill, James, *North Ulster Walks Guide,* Appletree Press, 1988; Rogers, R., *Irish Walks Guides North East; Down and Antrim,* Gill and Macmillan, 1980.

Lagan Valley This AONB lies in the green belt of the Belfast–Lisburn conurbation. It is much used by walkers from Belfast and was created to relieve the pressure for development.

Maps: 1:50000 sheets 15, 20.

Lakeland Country of County Fermanagh An attractive region that lies in the extreme south-west of the Province, centred on Enniskillen, that offers some excellent walking. It contains a number of beautiful lakes dotted with islands, extensive state forests, and some nature reserves.

Maps: 1:50000 sheets 17, 18, 26, 27.

Footpath Guide: Simms, P., and Foley, G., *Irish Walks Guides North West; Donegal, Sligo, Armagh, Derry, Tyrone and Fermanagh,* Gill and Macmillan, 1979.

Lecale Coast An AONB that lies in County Down between the Mourne and Strangford Lough AONBs. It is a region of extensive low dunes and sands that is much used by the military.

Maps: 1:50000 sheet 21.

Mourne This AONB is situated in County Down on the south-east coast. It is one of the most beautiful areas in the Province, and offers excellent hill-walking. The highest peak is Slieve Donard (849 metres), and there are numerous other peaks over 600 metres high. The region has the best network of mountain paths in Northern Ireland, and on the lower slopes there are beautiful forests containing many waymarked trails and nature trails.

Maps: 1:50000 sheets 20, 21, 29.

Footpath Guide: Rogers, R., *Irish Walks Guides North East; Down and Antrim,* Gill and Macmillan, 1980.

North Derry This AONB includes the Foyle estuary, and contains some of Ireland's finest beaches including Magilligan Strand onto which are washed innumerable shells of all sizes and varieties. It is one of the best walking areas in the Province.

Map: 1:50000 Ordnance Survey of Northern Ireland sheet 4.

Footpath Guides: Hamill, James, *North Ulster Walks Guide,* Appletree Press, 1988; Simms, P., and Foley, G., *Irish Walks Guides North West; Donegal, Sligo, Armagh, Derry, Tyrone and Fermanagh,* Gill and Macmillan, 1979.

South Armagh An AONB centred on Slieve Gullion Mountain to the east of Newry, which is rich in archaeological remains. It joins the Mourne AONB, which in turn links with the Lecale Coast and Strangford Lough AONBs.

Maps: 1:50000 sheets 28, 29.

Footpath Guide: Simms, P., and Foley, G., *Irish Walks Guides North West; Donegal, Sligo, Armagh, Derry, Tyrone and Fermanagh,* Gill and Macmillan, 1979.

Sperrin This AONB includes Ulster's most extensive mountain range. It contains the highest peaks outside the Mourne AONB, including Sawel Mountain (683 metres), and is one of the Province's most attractive walking areas. Sperrin contains a large number of prehistoric archaeological sites.

Maps: 1:50000 sheets 7, 8, 13, 18, 19.

Footpath Guides: Hamill, James, *North Ulster Walks Guide,* Appletree Press, 1988; Simms, P., and Foley, G., *Irish Walks Guides North West; Donegal, Sligo, Armagh, Derry, Tyrone and Fermanagh,* Gill and Macmillan, 1979.

Strangford Lough An AONB that is located between Bangor and Downpatrick. It links with the Mourne and the Lecale Coast AONBs. This is a low-lying area of drumlins that have been flooded by the rising sea level leaving the tips as islands.

Map: 1:50000 sheet 21.

Footpath Guide: Rogers, R., *Irish Walks Guides North East; Down and Antrim,* Gill and Macmillan, 1980.

Useful Organisations

The following organisations are concerned with walking and rights of way (their addresses are given in Appendix Two): Forest Service, National Trust, Ordnance Survey of Northern Ireland, Sports Council for Northern Ireland, Ulster Federation of Rambling Clubs, Ulster Society for the Protection of the Countryside, Youth Hostels Association of Northern Ireland.

Eire

Walking conditions in Eire are very similar to those obtaining in Northern Ireland. The country is thinly populated with comparatively few field paths or mountain tracks, but there is a maze of country lanes which carry very little traffic. Much of the countryside near the coast is mountainous with some peaks exceeding 900 metres. Although there are not many paths in the mountains, anyone proficient in the use of map and compass can virtually roam at will in glorious, uncultivated countryside.

A number of long-distance paths have been established (and more are planned) which will ultimately result in a continuous walking route all around Ireland. These long-distance paths are waymarked and utilise field paths, mountain, farm and forest tracks, boreens (narrow lanes), drove roads, butter roads and coffin roads.

The Irish Tourist Board (see below) publishes *Walking Ireland—Only the Best* an informative leaflet containing a folding map, useful addresses and much helpful advice.

Maps: The Irish Ordnance Survey has mapped the country completely on a scale of 1:126720 ($^1/2$ inch to the mile) based on a survey made in the late 1970s and early 1980s. Most of the country, except the border areas, is covered by the 1:63360 Black Outline series based on the 1899–1900 survey, and there are four coloured 1:63360 District Maps covering Dublin, Killarney and Wicklow. There are plans for a 1:50000 series but the only one currently available is for Macgillacuddy's Reeks. Some paths and tracks are shown on all Ordnance Survey maps mentioned above but they are not necessarily rights of way. Edward Stanford Ltd, 12 Long Acre, London WC2E 9LP (Tel. 071-836-1321) stock Irish Ordnance Survey maps.

Walking Areas

The best walking areas are generally reckoned to be the following:

The Comeraghs The Comeraghs are situated in the south-east of the country in County Waterford. Their main features are the splendid corries and the flat, plateau-like summits. They extend westward to meet the Knockmealdowns which are much less rugged and offer somewhat easier walking. The highest peak is Fauscoum (779 metres).

Maps: Irish Ordnance Survey 1:63360 sheets 167, 177, 178. 1:126720 sheet 22.

Footpath Guides: Martindale, Frank, *Irish Walks Guides South East: Tipperary and Waterford,* Gill and Macmillan, 1979.

The Connemara Mountains These comprise several groups of mountains in the far west in County Galway and include the Twelve Bens and the Maumturks.

Maps: Irish Ordnance Survey 1:63360 sheets 83, 84, 93, 94. 1:126720 sheets 10, 11.

Footpath Guides: Lynam, Joss and Robinson, Tim, *The Mountains of Connemara: Guidebook and Map,* Folding Landscapes, 1988. (Distributed in UK by Cordee); Robinson, Tim, *Connemara: Map and Guide,* Folding Landscapes, 1988. (Distributed in UK by Cordee); Whilde, T., *Irish Walks Guide West: Clare, Galway and Mayo,* Gill and Macmillan, 1979.

Donegal Situated in the far north of the country, practically the whole of the area is mountainous and is one of the favourite regions for walking and mountaineering.

Maps: Irish Ordnance Survey 1:63360 sheets 1, 2, 3, 4, 5, 6, 9, 10, 11, 15, 16, 17, 22, 23, 24, 32. 1:126720 sheets 1, 3.

Footpath Guides: Simms, P., and Foley, G., *Irish Walks Guides North West; Donegal, Sligo, Armagh, Derry, Tyrone and Fermanagh.* Gill and Macmillan, 1979.

Galty Mountains Situated in south west County Tipperary, this range offers a good ridge walk from north of Mitchelstown to Galtymore and has some fine rocky crags. The highest peak is Galtymore (905 metres).

Maps: Irish Ordnance Survey 1:63360 sheets 154, 155, 165, 166. 1:126720 sheets 18, 22.

Footpath Guides: Martindale, Frank, *Irish Walks Guides South East: Tipperary and Waterford,* Gill and Macmillan, 1979.

Kerry and West Cork This is probably the finest walking and scrambling country in the whole of Ireland with some superb views. The area includes Macgillycuddy's Reeks, and the peninsulas of Invereagh, Beare and Dingle. Killarney with its beautiful lakes is the largest town and makes a good centre.

Maps: Irish Ordnance Survey 1:63360 District Map of Killarney. 1:126720 sheets 20, 21, 24.

Footpath Guides: Mersey, Richard, *The Hills of Cork and Kerry,* Sutton, 1987; O'Suilleabhain, Sean and Lynam, Joss, *Irish Walks Guides South West: Kerry and West Cork,* Gill and Macmillan, 1979.

The Nephins and North Mayo Highlands An isolated group of mountains in the far northwest of County Mayo. There are few roads and it is necessary to walk quite long distances to enjoy them properly. The highest peak is Nephin (806 metres).

Maps: Irish Ordnance Survey 1:63360 sheets 63, 64. 1:126720 sheet 6.

Footpath Guide: Whilde, T., *Irish Walks Guides West: Clare, Galway and Mayo,* Gill and Macmillan, 1979.

Sligo and Leitrim This is a high plateau of limestone with vertical cliffs that have fractured into sheer rock spires. W.B. Yeats often wrote about the many legends associated with the area, and he is buried at the foot of Ben Bulben.

Maps: Irish Ordnance Survey 1:63360 sheets 43, 44, 55, 56. 1:126720 sheet 7.

Footpath Guide: Simms, P., and Foley, G., *Irish Walks Guides North West: Donegal, Sligo, Armagh, Derry, Tyrone and Fermanagh,* Gill and Macmillan, 1979.

The Wicklow Mountains The Wicklow Mountains cover an extensive area southwards from Dublin. They lack ridges and their most notable features are the characteristic rounded domes and deep glens. They tend to be boggy underfoot and the highest peak is Lugnaquillia (912 metres).

Maps: Irish Ordnance Survey 1:63360 District Map of Wicklow. 1:126720 sheet 16.

Footpath Guides: Herman, David, *Hill Walker's Wicklow,* Shanksmare Publications (distributed in the UK by Cordee, 1989); Herman, David, *Irish Walks Guides East: Dublin and Wicklow,* Gill and Macmillan, 1979; Moriarty, Christopher, *On Foot in Dublin and Wicklow,* Wolfhound Press, 1989.

Footpath Guides to Other Areas: Robinson, Tim, *The Aran Isles, County Galway,* Cordee, 1986; Robinson, Tim, *The Burren: a Map of the Uplands of North West County Clare,* Cordee, 1977.

Long-Distance Paths

The Kerry Way A magnificent route that runs for 60 kilometres from Killarney National Park to Glenbeigh which will ultimately be extended to provide a circuit of the Iveragh peninsula. The Kerry Way passes through the beautiful mountains and lakes of Killarney and rises to a maximum elevation of 366 metres.

Maps: Irish Ordnance Survey 1:126720 sheet 20 and 1:63360 District Map of Killarney.

Leaflet: Irish Tourist Board Information Sheet 26c *The Kerry Way.*

The Kildare Way A 37-kilometre route along canal towpaths from Kildare to Edenderry with a link to Rathangan. The Kildare Way links with a number of other designated routes so that it is possible to plan a longer itinerary that is suitable for casual walkers.

Maps: Irish Ordnance Survey 1:126720 sheet 16.

Footpath Guide: The Kildare Sports Advisory Committee, VEC, Naas, Co Kildare publish *A Walker's Guide to Towpath Trails in Kildare* as well as leaflets and maps about the route.

The Munster Way An 81-kilometre walk through County Waterford from The Vee to Carrick-on-Suir where it links with the South Leinster Way which in turn joins the Wicklow Way giving the wayfarer a total of 307 kilometres of waymarked path that will take him all the way to Dublin. Ultimately the Munster Way will extend westward to link with the Kerry Way at Killarney. The route is strenuous in places and rises to over 300 metres.

Maps: Irish Ordnance Survey 1:126720 sheet 22.

Leaflet: Irish Tourist Board Information Sheet 26J *The Munster Way (Stage One).*

Sli Chorcha Dhuibhne (Dingle Way) This route traverses almost the entire length of the Dingle peninsula, County Kerry, from Tralee to Dingle giving delightful views of the sea and the mountains of the Iveragh. It is an easy itinerary running for 50 kilometres along boreens, country roads and mountain tracks that are suitable for casual walkers.

Maps: Irish Ordnance Survey 1:126720 sheet 20.

Leaflet: Irish Tourist Board Information Sheet 26G *Sli Chorcha Dhuibhne.*

The Slieve Bloom Way A circular walking route of 50 kilometres through the Slieve Bloom mountains in the counties of Offaly and Laoise. The itinerary includes forest roads, firebreaks, mountain tracks and riverside paths.

Maps: Irish Ordnance Survey 1:126720 sheet 15.

Leaflet: Irish Tourist Board information Sheet 26F *The Slieve Bloom Way.*

The South Leinster Way The South Leinster Way runs for 94 kilometres from the end of the Munster Way at Carrick-on-Suir, County Kilkenny to the beginning of the Wicklow Way at Kildavin, County Carlow making a total route of 307 kilometres. The scenery is an interesting combination of forest tracks, mountain trails rising to 450 metres, and riverside paths.

Maps: Irish Ordnance Survey 1:126620 sheets 19, 22 & 23.

Leaflet: Irish Tourist Board Information Sheet 26D *The South Leinster Way.*

The Wicklow Way This route runs for 132 kilometres from its junction with the South Leinster Way at Clonegal, County Carlow to Dublin forming the final section of a 307 kilometre path from Clogheen, County Waterford. The scenery ranges from quiet field paths to glens and rugged mountain scenery. The maximum elevation reached is 661 metres.

Maps: Irish Ordnance Survey 1:126720 sheets 16 & 19.

Leaflet: Irish Tourist Board Information Sheet 26B *The Wicklow Way.*

Footpath Guides: Fewer, Michael, *The Wicklow Way: from Marley to Glenmalure,* Gill and Macmillan, 1988; Malone, J.B., *The Complete Wicklow Way,* The O'Brien Press, 1988.

Castlebar International Four-Day Walks

This event is held annually at Castlebar, County Mayo in June. A wide range of walks is offered varying in length and difficulty. It is a non-competitive event but certificates of fitness are awarded to all who complete the walks. There is a very pleasant atmosphere of international friendship. For details write to the Secretary, Castlebar International Four-Day Walks, Castlebar, Co. Mayo.

Useful Organisations

Irish Tourist Board, 150 New Bond Street, London W1Y 0AQ. Tel. 071-493-3201; Forest and Wildlife Service, Leeson Lane, Dublin 2. Will provide information and leaflets on forest walks; Irish Ramblers' Club, Dolores Featherston, Trinity College School of Pharmacy, 18 Shrewsbury Road, Dublin 4; Irish Youth Hostel Association (An Oige), 39 Mountjoy Square, Dublin 1; Ordnance Survey Office, Phoenix Park, Dublin.

18 Walking Abroad

Before embarking on an overseas walking holiday, the wayfarer should have some experience of walking in Britain and have a clear idea of his walking capabilities. British weather is as fickle as any in the world but we do not experience extremes of heat and cold. In many countries the weather is more settled and reliable but in summer it is likely to be hotter than in Britain and this can have an adverse effect on the walker until he becomes acclimatised.

There is no reason why walkers should not plan their own walking holidays in western Europe, the United States, Canada, South Africa, Australia and New Zealand but most walkers will find it more satisfactory to join a tour when visiting eastern Europe and Third World countries. A number of travellers *do* explore under-developed countries and have interesting and rewarding experiences, but such holidays need careful planning and it may be necessary to take medicines and antibiotics. It is important to have some understanding of the culture and customs of the country and to respect them at all times.

All travellers should have adequate insurance to cover medical expenses and loss of personal belongings. Insurance can be arranged through most travel agents for conventional holiday trips but if going to an out-of-the way destination consult West Mercia Insurance Brokers, High Street, Wombourne, Wolverhampton WV5 9DN.

The two best directories that list packaged walking tours and expeditions are: Ninehan, Gillian, Editor, *Adventure Holidays,* published annually by Vacation Work; Shales, M.,Editor, *The Traveller's Handbook,* Heineman in association with Wexas, 5th Rev. Ed., 1987.

Advertisements for walking tours appear in the outdoor magazines listed in Appendix One and in the quality Sunday newspapers.

Maps and Footpath Guides

Under each of the countries described in this chapter are listed details of the national map survey and information about maps and footpath guides that are likely to be of interest to walkers. Those who require further information should consult the following books: Parry, R. B., and Perkins, C.R., *World Mapping Today*, Butterworths. 1987. This remarkable book describes in some detail the maps published by each country. It not only lists the names and addresses of the mapping agencies but also includes graphic indexes which are invaluable when trying to trace a map covering a particular area. The information was compiled in 1984-86, is kept on a database and the *Introduction* hints that new editions are planned.

Geo Katalog, Geo Center Internationales Landkartenhaus. Stuttgart, Postfach 80 08 30, 7000 Stuttgart 80. This German publication, written in English and French as well as German, is a trade catalogue of maps from all over the world stocked by the Geo Center and lists innumerable maps giving brief details of title and scale. This useful catalogue is constantly referred to by map retailers.

The best retailers of foreign maps and footpath guides in this country are:

MacCarta Ltd., 122 King's Cross Road, London WC1X 9DS (Tel. 071-278-8276) who are the official British agents for the French and Spanish national map surveys. The company carries a wide range of walking maps and footpath guides to many parts of the world and will obtain items not in stock to order. They specialise in covering material on walking, climbing and travelling off the beaten track. They publish a series of catalogues of material stocked, classified by country or region, offer a mail-order service and the staff are knowledgeable and helpful. An associated company publishes English translations of some of the more popular Topoguides to French long-distance paths.

Edward Stanford Ltd, 12 Long Acre, London WC2E 9LP (Tel. 071-836-1321) stocks a wide selection of foreign maps and guides.

YHA Services Ltd, 14 Southampton Street, London WC2E 7HY (Tel. 071-836-8541) imports guides to some of the more unusual destinations.

English-language footpath guides to the more popular walking areas of the world are now beginning to appear. Except for the guides to individual long-distance paths they tend to be fairly general in scope and describe in detail selected walks in a large geographical area (eg *100 Hikes in the Alps*.). McCarta Ltd and Edward Stanford Ltd (see above) are the best sources for obtaining footpath guides. Many walkers will wish to visit a national park in the country of their choice and a useful publication, now out of print but available through public libraries, is Harroy, Jean-Paul, *National Parks of the World,* Orbis Books, 1974.

Also useful are publishers' catalogues such as the following.

Bradt Publications, 41 Nortoft Road, Chalfont St Peter. Bucks SL9 0LA (Tel. 02407-3478) specialise in publishing and distributing general and walking guides to Africa, north, central and south America and other exotic destinations. They have a mail-order department.

Cicerone Press Ltd, 2 Police Square, Milnthorpe, Cumbria LA7 7PY (Tel. 04482-2069) specialise in publishing walking and mountaineering guides to various parts of the world. They have a mail-order service.

Cordee, 3a De Montford Street, Leicester LE1 7HD (Tel. 0533-543579) publish, import and distribute footpath guides and English-language books on outdoor recreation. They also publish a stocklist and sell their titles by mail order.

Roger Lascelles, 47 York Road, Brentford, Middlesex TW8 0QP (Tel. 081-847-0935) specialises in travel guides and maps of Africa, Asia and central and south America. He is the distributor in Britain for the excellent Australian publisher Lonely Planet which has a series of books about walking and travelling in unusual places.

Foreign maps may be consulted in the following libraries:

The British Map Library, Great Russell Street, London WC1B 3DG. This is a section of the British Library (formerly the British Museum Library) and application has to be made for a reader's ticket.

The Library of the Royal Geographical Society, Kensington Gore, London SW7 2AR. Members of the public are permitted limited access to the library.

Europe

Most European countries have tourist offices in London and many of them are able to supply information on walking. When compiling the information on which this chapter is based, I formed the impression that, despite *glasnost,* some eastern European countries are still reluctant to allow walkers to roam their countryside unescorted. Intourist, the state travel agency of the USSR, did not bother to reply to my enquiries, and the information supplied by some other members of the Warsaw Pact was either too generalised to be of any use or they referred me to other offices which either did not reply or directed me to somebody else; I began to understand how Kafka felt. The exception was Poland where a helpful gentleman from the State Tourist Office in Warsaw took the trouble to write a very informative letter enclosing a 1:50000 map covering part of the Tatra Mountains.

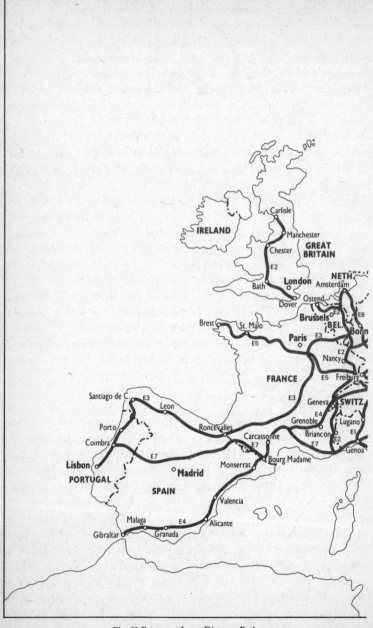

Fig. 59 European Long-Distance Paths.

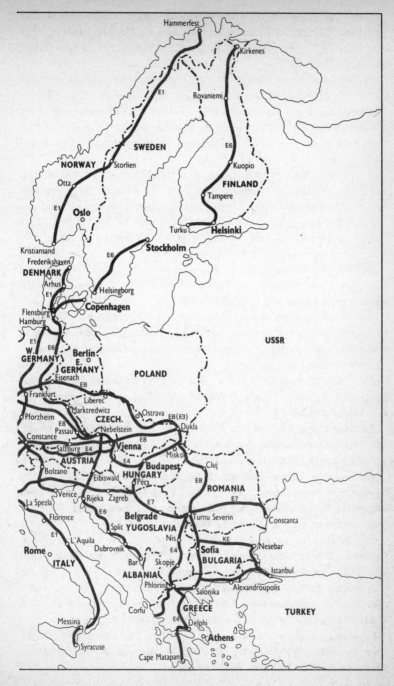

A good general introduction to walking in Europe is: Howcroft, Arthur, and Sale, Richard. *A Walker's Guide to Europe*, Wildwood House, 1983. Also useful is: Unsworth, Walt, Editor, *Classic Walks in Europe*, Oxford Illustrated Press, 1985.

International Long-Distance Paths: Eight international long-distance paths (see Fig. 58), known as E Routes, have been established by the European Ramblers' Association (Europäische Wandervereinigung e. V.), Reichsstrasse 4, D-6600 Saarbrücken, West Germany. Many of them have been formed by providing links between existing national long-distance paths.

E1: North Sea – Mediterranean from Flensburg via Hamburg, Frankfurt, Constance, Lugano, Genoa to Florence. 2800 kilometres. Extensions to Hammerfest, Norway and Syracuse, Sicily are planned.

E2: North Sea–Mediterranean from Ostend or the Hook of Holland via Liège, Echternach, Grand Ballon, Nyon, Chamonix to Nice. 2600 kilometres. An extension to Carlisle is planned.

E3: Atlantic Ocean–Forest of Bohemia from Roncevalles via Le Puy, Paris, Bouillon, Echternach, Fulda, Coburg, to Marktredwitz, 2600 kilometres. An extension to Lisbon is planned.

E4: Pyrenees–Balaton from Montserrat via Carcassonne, Grenoble, Chasseral, Constance, Bregenz, Sonthofen, Salzburg, Vienna, Koszeg to Budapest. 3500 kilometres. An extension to Mount Olympus in Greece is planned.

E5: Lake Constance–Adriatic Sea from Constance via Bregenz, Sonthofen, Bolzano, Verona to Venice. 600 kilometres. An extension to Brittany is planned.

E6: Baltic Sea–Adriatic Sea from Copenhagen via Lubeck, Coburg, Marktredwitz, Nebelstein, Mariazell, Eibiswald to Riga. 2800 kilometres. An extension to Greece is planned.

E7: Atlantic Ocean–Slovenia from Lisbon via Madrid, Lourdes, Carcassonne, Nice, Genoa, Lake Garda, Skopje Loka, to Kumrovec. 3500 kilometres. NB this route is still in the planning stage but already there are long-term plans to extend it to the Black Sea.

E8: North Sea–Carpathians from Amsterdam via Aachen, Bonn, Coblenz, Worms, Rothenburg, Passau, Vienna to Hainburg. 2200 kilometres. An extension to Tokay is planned.

A leaflet *Europäische Fernwanderwege* giving details of the routes together with addresses from where further information may be found is available from the European Ramblers' Association (see above).

German-language guides to route E1 to E6 inclusive may be purchased from Deutscher Wanderverlag, Dr Mair & Schnabel & Co., Zeppelin-strasse 44/1, 7302 Osfildern, West Germany.

National Parks Most European countries have established national parks and they include some of the best walking areas in each country. Usually they are located in mountainous areas, but some protect unusual habitats. A useful guide is: Waycott, Angus, *National Parks of Western Europe,* Inklon Publications, 1983.

Austria Most of Austria is mountainous and therefore offers exceptionally fine opportunities for walking. Routes are well-waymarked and there is a choice of grades to suit every kind of walker from the ambler to the alpinist.

Useful Addresses: Austrian National Tourist Office, 30 St George Street, London W1R 9FA. Tel. 071-629-0461. *Ramblers' Organisation:* The Austrian Alpine Club, 13 Longcroft House, Fretherne Road, Welwyn Garden City, Herts AL8 6PQ. (Tel. Welwyn Garden (0707) 324835 or 331133 ext 27). NB this is the UK branch of Osterreichischer Alpenverein. *National Map Survey:* Bundesamt für Eich-und Vermessungswesen (BEV), Landesaufnahme, Krotenhallergrasse 3, A-1080, Vienna. *Official Survey Maps:* Osterreichischer Karte 1:50000 in four editions of which the standard edition shows footpaths. *Other Maps:* Kompass Wanderkarte 1:50000 show footpaths graded according to degree of difficulty, and mountain refuges. Alpenverein Walking Maps cover the mountainous areas on a scale of 1:25000 and show footpaths.

Guide to Walking: Evans, Craig, *On Foot through Europe; a Trail Guide to Austria, Switzerland and Leichtenstein,* Quill, 1982.

Footpath guides: Caselli, G., *and* Sugden, K., *Ancient Pathways in the Alps,* George Philip, 1988; Davies, Cecil, *Mountain Walking in Austria,* Cicerone Press, 1986; Hurdle, Jonathan, *Walking Austria's Alps: Hut to Hut,* Cordee, 1988; Proctor, Alan, *The Kalkalpen Traverse; a Long Distance Walk in the Limestone Alps of Austria,* Cicerone Press, 1986; Speakman, Fleur and Colin, *Walking the Salzkammergut,* Cicerone Press, 1990; Spencer, Brian, *Walking in the Alps,* Moorland Publishing, 1983; Spencer, Brian, *Walking in Austria,* Moorland Publishing, 1988; Spring, Ira, and Edwards, Harvey, *100 Hikes in the Alps,* Cordee, 1979.

Belgium Belgium is a small country containing a great variety of scenery including extensive forests and charming towns and villages. The best area for walking is in the south-east of the country, in the Ardennes, where the highest land rises to 683 metres.

Useful Addresses: Belgian National Tourist Office, 38 Dover Street, London W1X 3RB. Tel. 071-499-5379. *Ramblers' Organisation:* Comité National Belge des Sentiers de Grande Randonnée. Boite Postale 10, Liege 4000. *National Map Survey:* Institut Geographique Militaire, Abbaye de la Cambre 13, Bruxelles 1050. *Official Survey Maps:* Carte Topographique de Base de Belgique 1:50000. Carte Topographique de Belgique 1:25000. Footpaths are marked on both series.

Guide to Walking: Evans, Craig, *On Foot through Europe: a Trail Guide to France and the Benelux Countries,* Quill, 1982.

Denmark Denmark, the smallest of the Scandinavian countries, consists of some five hundred islands, of which about one hundred are inhabited. The scenery is a pleasant combination of rolling hills, forests and lakes.

All local tourist offices in Denmark have a large selection of leaflets giving details of walks in their areas and the Dansk Skovforening (Danish Forestry Commission – see below) publishes numerous walks leaflets.

In common with other European countries the Danes have a tradition of massed start long-distance walks or marches which are organised by Dansk Marchforbund (Danish March Association – see below). Another organisation that arranges walks throughout the year and publishes an annual calendar is the Dansk Gangforbund (see below).

Useful Addresses: The Danish Tourist Board, Sceptre House, 169/173 Regent Street, London W1R 8PY. Tel. 071-734-2637. *Ramblers' Organisations:* Dansk Vandrelaug, Kultorvet 7, DK 1175, Copenhagen K; Dansk Gangforbund, Indraettans Hus, 2605 Brondby Strand; Dansk Marchforbund, Solsikkevej 105, 8700 Horsens. *Forestry Commission:* Dansk Skovforening, Direktoratet for Statsskovbruget, Strandvejen 863, 2930 Klampenborg. *National Map Survey:* Geodaetisk Institut, Riggsdagsgarden 7, DK1218, Copenhagen K. *Official Survey Maps:* Kort over Danmark 1:50000 and 1:25000 (both series show paths).

Walking Guide: Evans, Craig, *On Foot through Europe: a Trail Guide to Scandinavia,* Quill, 1982.

Finland Finland, Suomi in Finnish, is a large, thinly-populated Scandinavian country bordering on Norway, Sweden and the USSR. The total land area of Finland consists of 10% water (there are nearly 200,000 lakes), 65% forest and only 8% cultivated land. Much of the country is tableland between 120 and 200 metres and the highest point in the country is Haltia Mountain in the north west which rises to 1324 metres. Finland has temperate summers and the advantage of very long days.

There are many long-distance paths, details of which can be obtained from the Hiking Department of the Finnish Travel Association (see below). In northern Finland there are huts beside the tracks in which walkers and skiiers may spend the night. The Finnish Tourist Board has published an excellent booklet *Finland: Hiking Routes* which gives much useful information and they can also provide information about guided walking tours.

Useful Addresses: The Finnish Tourist Board, 66 Haymarket, London SW1Y 4RF. Tel. 071-839-4048; *Ramblers' Organisation:* Hiking Department, Finnish Travel Association, Mikonkatu 25, 00100 Helsinki, *National Map Survey:* Map Centre of the National Board of Survey, Opastinsilta

12, B, Box 85, 5F-60521, Helsinki. *Official Survey Maps:* 1:20000, 1:25000 and 1:50000. All these series show footpaths.

Guide to Walking: Evans, Craig, *On Foot through Europe: a Trail Guide to Scandinavia,* Quill, 1982.

France France has a great variety of scenery and regional differences ranging from the placid scenery of Normandy and the Loire Valley to the magnificent high mountain ranges of the Alps and Pyrenees. Walking is extremely popular and very well organised with more than 20,000 kilometres of long-distance paths as well as an extensive local path network. The best source of information about walking in France is McCarta (see p260) which is the official agents in Britain for the Institut Geographique National (IGN). They also have a wide selection of books and walking guides and have translated and published several of the famous Topoguides to French long-distance paths.

Useful Addresses: French Government Tourist Office, 178 Piccadilly, London W1V 0AL. Tel. 071-491-7622. *Ramblers' Organisation:* Fédération Française de la Randonnée Pedestre, 92 Rue de Clignancourt, 75883 Paris Cedex 18. At the same address is located the Comité National des Sentiers de Grande Randonnée which is responsible for long-distance paths. *National Map Survey:* Institut Geographique National, 107 Rue La Boetie, 75008 Paris. (*UK agent:* McCarta, 122 King's Cross Road, London WC1X 9DS. Tel. 071-278-8276). *Official Survey Maps:* Carte de France 1:50000 and 1:25000. Both series show footpaths. *Other maps:* Didier Richard (once a separate imprint but now part of Institut Geographique National) publish a series of excellent 1:50000 and 1:25000 maps to the mountainous regions of France showing footpaths.

Guides to Walking: Evans, Craig, *On Foot through Europe: a Trail Guide to France and the Benelux Countries,* Quill, 1982; Hunter, Rob, and Wickers, David, *Classic Walks in France,* Oxford Illustrated Press, 1985; Hunter, Rob, *Walking in France,* Oxford Illustrated Press, 1982, Nicolson, Adam, *The Elf Book of Long Walks in France,* Weidenfeld & Nicolson, 1983.

Footpath Guides: Battagel, Arthur, *Pyrenees, Andorra, Cerdagne,* Gastons-West Col, 1980; Battagel, Arthur, *Pyrenees East,* Gastons-West Col, 1975; Caselli, G., and Sugden, K., *Ancient Pathways in the Alps,* George Philip, 1988; Bishop, H., *The Way of St James; GR65,* Cicerone Press, 1990; Castle, Alan, *The Corsican High Level Route; Walking the GR20,* Cicerone Press, 1987; Castle, Alan, *The Pyrenean Trail,* Cicerone Press, 1990; Castle, Alan, *The Tour of the Queyras,* Cicerone Press, 1990; *Coastal Walks: Normandy & Brittany; a Guide to 900 Kilometres of Footpaths along the Dramatic Coastline of Brittany and Normandy,* Robertson McCarta in association with the Fédération Française de Randonnée Pédestre, 1989; Collins, Martin, *Walking the French Alps; GR5 Lake*

Geneva to Nice, Cicerone Press, 1984; Collins, Martin, *Chamonix – Mont Blanc; a Walker's Guide,* Cicerone Press, 1989; Collins, Martin, *Walking in Northern France,* Moorland Publishing, 1987; Collomb, Robin, G., *Mercantour Park,* West Col, 1985; Harper, Andrew, *Tour of Mont Blanc,* Cicerone Press, 1982; Harper, Andrew, *Tour of the Oisans; GR54; a Circular Walk round the Dauphiné Alps,* Cicerone Press, 1986; *Normandy and the Seine; a Guide to 799 Kilometres of Footpaths along the Seine from Paris to the Coast and through the Gentle Normandy Countryside,* Robertson McCarta in association with the Fédération Française Randonnée Pédestre, 1989; Parker, Malcolm and Nicola, *Grande Traverse: the GR5,* Diadem, 1986; Reynolds, Kev, *Classic Walks in the Pyrénées,* Oxford Illustrated Press, 1989; Reynolds, Kev, *Walks and Climbs in the Pyrénées,* Cicerone Press, 2nd Ed, 1983; Spencer, Brian, *Walking in the Alps,* Moorland Publishing, 1983; Spring, Ira, and Edwards, Harvey, *100 Hikes in the Alps,* Cordee, 1979; Veron, Georges, *Pyrenees High Level Route,* Gastons-West Col, 1981; *Walking the Pyrénées; a Guide to 7000 kilometres of Footpaths along the Pyrénées, from the Mediterranean to the Atlantic (GR10),* Robertson McCarta in association with the Fédération Française de Randonnée Pédestre, 1989; *Walking through Brittany; a Guide to 1100 Kilometres of Footpaths through the Countryside and Villages of Brittany,* Robertson McCarta in association with the Fédération Française de Randonnée Pédestre, 1989; *Walks in Provence; a Guide to over 300 kilometres of Footpaths through the Hills of Provence and Down to the Sea,* Robertson McCarta in association with the Fédération Française de Randonnée Pédestre, 1989; *Walks in the Auvergne; a Guide to 400 Kilometres of Footpaths through the Spectacular Volcanic Landscape of France's Auvergne,* Robertson McCarta in association with the Fédération Française de Randonnée Pédestre, 1989.

Germany The Germans have always been keen walkers and have developed a large number of well-waymarked long-distance routes as well as a dense local network of paths. Favourite walking areas are the Black Forest and the Bavarian Alps.

Useful Addresses: German National Tourist Office, 61 Conduit Street, London W1R 0EN. Tel. 071-734-2600. *Ramblers' Organisation:* Verband Deutscher Gebirgs und Wandervereine, Reichsstrasee 4, 6600 Saarbrucken 3. *National Map Survey:* There is no national map survey as each state in the Federal Republic is responsible for its own mapping. *Official Survey Maps:* Topographische Karte official state surveys are available in four editions. The Wanderwegausgabe edition with scales of 1:50000 and 1:25000 show footpaths. *Other maps:* Two series of Wanderkarte, published respectively by: Reise-und-Verkehrsverlag, GmbH, Neumarkter Str 8, 8000 Munich 80, and: Gleumes, D-5000, Cologne, 1 Hohenstaufenring 47-51. These cover, in various scales, the more popular walking areas and show footpaths. Kompas Wanderkarten 1:50000 cover selected areas and show footpaths.

Walking Guide: Evans, Craig, *On Foot through Europe: A Trail Guide to West Germany,* Quill, 1982.

Footpath Guides: Caselli, G., and Sugden, K., *Ancient Pathways in the Alps,* George Philip, 1988; Proctor, Alan, *The Kalkalpen Traverse; a Long Distance Walk in the Limestone Alps of Austria,* Cicerone Press, 1986; Speakman, Fleur and Colin, *King Ludwig Way; a 120 Kilometre Long Distance Footpath through Bavaria from Lake Starnberg to Castle Neuschwanstein,* Cicerone Press, 1987; Speakman, Fleur and Colin, *Walking in the Black Forest,* Cicerone Press, 1990. Spring, Ira, and Edwards, Harvey, *100 Hikes in the Alps,* Cordee, 1979.

Greece Greece is the cradle of western civilisation and is blessed with a wonderful cultural heritage, a magnificent coastline as well as superb mountains rising to a height of 2917 metres. The country is made up of mainland Greece and numerous islands some of which are uninhabited. In recent years tourists have flocked to Greece to sun themselves on the beaches but walkers will leave the crowds behind when they explore the lovely countryside.

Large scale official Greek survey maps are difficult to obtain because they are published by the military and contain sensitive information. McCarta Ltd (see p260) stock reproductions of the 1:50000 official survey maps, with sensitive material removed, published by a Greek mountaineering magazine covering the Pindos Mountains and some other areas.

Useful Addresses: National Tourist Organisation of Greece, 195-197 Regent Street, London W1R 8DL. Tel. 071-734-5997. *Ramblers' Organisation:* Hellenic Federation of Mountaineering Clubs, 7 Karageorgi Servias str., 105 63 Athens. (This organisation looks after the interests of walkers and mountaineers and has offices throughout the country).

Guides to Walking: Evans, Craig, *On Foot through Europe: a Trail Guide to Central Southern and Eastern Europe,* Quill, 1979.

Footpath Guides: Dubin, Marc S., *Backpacker's Greece,* Bradt Enterprises, 1982; Dubin, Marc S., *Greece on Foot; Mountain Treks, Island Trails,* Cordee, 1986; Salmon, Tim, *The Mountains of Greece; a Walker's Guide,* Cicerone Press, 1986; Sfikas, George, *The Mountains of Greece,* Efstathiadis, 1982.

Holland Holland is a very small country which appears comparatively flat to British eyes. Its charm lies in the neatness of its landscape, its flowers, and its beautiful towns. The Dutch have a tradition of marching festivals, which are long-distance events, often along roads, for which teams come from abroad to compete.

There are a number of long-distance paths and most tourist offices, known universally as VVVs, are able to provide maps and walking routes. Some VVVs organise walking tours where, for a fixed fee, a map, footpath guide, rucksack and accommodation are all provided. Address your enquiry to VVV followed by the name of the town.

Useful Addresses: Netherlands Board of Tourism, 25-28 Buckingham Gate, London SW1E 6LD. Tel. 071-630-0451. *Ramblers' Organisation:* Nederlandse Wandelsport Bond, Pieterskerhof 22, 3512 JS, Utrecht. *National Map Survey:* Topographische Dienst, Bendienplein 5, Postbus 115, 7800 AC Emmen, Delft. *Official Survey Maps:* Topographische Kaart 1:50000 and 1:25000 (footpaths are shown on both scales). *Guide to Walking:* Evans, Craig, On foot through Europe, a Trail Guide to France and the Benelux Counties, Quill, 1982.

Iceland Iceland is the second largest island in Europe lying just south of the arctic circle. It is a land of mountains, glaciers, volcanoes and geysers and is a wonderful country in which to walk and backpack in rugged conditions. Despite its northerly latitude Iceland has a remarkably temperate climate and the short summers can be quite pleasant. Iceland is the most thinly populated European country with only a quarter of a million inhabitants of which ninety thousand live in the capital Reykjavik. It is ideally suited to those who love remote places. The best British source for walking tours, books, maps etc is Dick Phillips Specialist Icelandic Travel Service (see below).

Useful Addresses: Icelandair/Iceland Tourist Information Bureau, 3rd Floor, 172 Tottenham Court Road, London W1P 9LG. Tel. 071-388-5599. Dick Phillips Specialist Icelandic Travel Service, Whitehall House, Nenthead, Alston, Cumbria CA9 3PS. Tel. 0498-81440. Utivist (Outdoor Life Tours), Grofinni 1, Reykjavik. *Ramblers' Organisation:* Feroafelag Islands, 3 Oldugata, Reykjavik. *National Map Survey:* Landmailingar Islands, PO Box 5536 Laugavegur 178, 105 Reykjavik. *Official Survey Maps:* Atlas Blondin 1:100000, Fjordungsblondin 1:50000 (in progress). Both series show tracks, cairned paths and indistinct paths.

Guides to Walking: Escritt, Tony, *Iceland: a Handbook for Expeditions,* Iceland Information Centre, 2nd. Rev. Ed., 1986. Evans, Craig, *On Foot through Europe: a Trail Guide to Scandinavia,* Quill, 1982.

Italy Italy is a predominantly mountainous country with two significant mountain regions. The Alps in the north include the distinctive peaks of the Dolomites as well as the beautiful lakes of Como, Maggiore and Lugano. The Apennines run for 1200 kilometres down the leg of Italy and are, in places, 200 kilometres wide. In the south there are several active volcanoes and the country is renowned for its beautiful coastline. Add to this the innumerable beautiful cities, towns and villages and the incomparable architecture and it is easy to see that Italy has a great deal to offer the discerning walker.

Useful Addresses: Italian State Tourist Office, 1 Princes Street, London W1R 8AY. Tel. 071-408-1254. *Ramblers' Organisation:* Federazione Italiana Escursionismo Consiglio Nazionale, 1-10143 Turin, Via Cibrario 33. *National Map Survey:* Instituto Geografico Militare, Via Cesare Battisti 10, Florence 1-50100. *Official Survey Maps:* Carta Topografica d'Italia 1:50000 (in progress) and 1:25000. Both series show footpaths. *Other maps:* Carta delle Zone Turistiche 1:50000 published by the Touring Club Italiano, Milan, cover such areas as the Alps and the Bay of Naples and show footpaths. Kompass Wanderkarten 1:50000 maps cover selected areas and show footpaths.

Guides to Walking: Evans, Craig, *On Foot through Europe: a Trail Guide to Central Southern and Eastern Europe,* Quill, 1982.

Footpath Guides: Ardito, Stefano, *Backpacking and Walking in Italy; Long and Short Walks from the Alps to Sicily,* Bradt Publications, 1987; Caselli, G., *and* Sugden, K., *Ancient Pathways in the Alps,* George Philip, 1988; Collins, Martin, *Alta Via; High Level Walks in the Dolomites,* Cicerone Press, 1986; Fras, Höffler, Werner, *Via Ferrata; Scrambles in the Dolomites,* Cicerone Press, 1990; Harper, Andrew, *Tour of Mont Blanc,* Cicerone Press, 1982; Sedge, Michael, *Walking Adventure Guide to Italy,* Moorland Publishing, 1988; Spencer, Brian, *Walking in the Alps,* Moorland Publishing, 1983; Spring, Ira, and Edwards, Harvey, *100 Hikes in the Alps,* Cordee, 1979.

Luxembourg The Grand Duchy of Luxembourg is a tiny country of 2587 square kilometres lying at the southern tip of Belgium. Geographically it is divided into two; in the north lies the upland area of the Ardennes while in the south there is rolling farmland and woods bordered on the east by the beautiful Moselle valley. Luxembourg has a splendid network of well-maintained waymarked public paths. There are a number of long-distance paths based on the network of youth hostels as well as more than 140 circular one-day walks from village centres. Footpath guides and maps are available from local bookshops.

Useful Addresses: Luxembourg National Tourist and Trade Office, 36/37 Piccadilly, London WIV 9PA. Tel. 071-434-2800. *Ramblers' Organisation:* Luxembourg Youth Hostel Association, 18 Place d'Armes, L-2013, Luxembourg. (This organisation looks after the interests of walkers and can provide information about routes). *National Map Survey:* Administration du Cadastre et Topographie, Service de la Topographie, Cartographie, 54 Ave Gaston Diderich, L-1420, Luxembourg. *Official Survey Maps:* 1:20000 and 1:25000 all show footpaths.

Norway Norway is an exceptionally beautiful country consisting largely of mountains and having a long, deeply indented coastline. It is a paradise for walkers, with numerous long-distance paths and a large number of tourist huts within a day's march of each other. The Open Air Act, passed in 1957, grants the right to walk and camp anywhere except on enclosed land – which gives the walker the freedom of 96 per cent of the countryside.

A most helpful booklet, *Mountain Touring Holidays in Norway,* available from the Norwegian Tourist Board (see below), gives an account of the mountain ranges and offers much practical advice.

Useful Addresses: Norwegian Tourist Board, 20 Pall Mall, London SW1Y 5NE. Tel. 071-839-6255, *Ramblers' Organisation:* Den Norske Turistforening, PO Box 1963 Vika, N-0125 Oslo 1. *National Map Survey:* Statens Kartverk, Monserudveien N-3500 Honefoss. *Official Survey Maps:* Topografiske Kart 1:50000 (shows paths and tourist shelters). Turistkart – various scales from 1:50000 to 1:200000 of main tourist areas (show footpaths).

Guide to Walking: Evans, Craig, *On Foot through Europe: a Trail Guide to Scandinavia,* Quill, 1982.

Poland Walking is very popular in Poland, especially among young people, and there are 36000 kilometres of public paths. Main routes are waymarked in red and connecting routes in black and there are notices at the beginning of each route describing the degree of difficulty. 524 kilometres of the 2717 kilometre International Friendship Route which runs from Eisenbach, East Germany to Budapest, Hungary passes through Poland. The best walking areas are the Tatra Mountains in the south and the Carpathian Mountains.

Useful Addresses: Polorbis Travel Ltd, 82 Mortimer Street, Regent Street, London W1N 7DE. Tel. 071-636-2217. *Ramblers' Organisation:* PTTK (Polish Tourist and Country-lovers' Association), Senatorska str., Warszawa 11. (NB this organisation deals with tourism in general, including walking, and maintains mountain refuges and hostels). The section dealing with visitors from overseas and which also organises walking tours is PTTK (Foreign Tourist Office). Swietokrzyska 36, 00-116 Warszawa. *National Map Survey:* PPWK (State Office of Cartography) Ulica Solic 18-20, PL-00 410, Warsaw publishes maps showing footpaths on scales varying from 1:37500 to 1:75000. These are readily available in local bookshops and have the key printed in Polish, Russian, German and English.

Portugal Although part of the Iberian peninsula, Portugal is quite distinct both culturally and scenically from its larger neighbour, Spain. The backbone of the country is formed by the Beira Alta which form the divide between the two major valleys of the Douro and the Tagus. The landscape is well-wooded with lush green valleys.

Useful Addresses: Portuguese Tourist Office, New Bond Street House, 1 New Bond Street, London W1Y 0NP. Tel. 071-493-3873. *Ramblers' Organisation:* Federacao Portuguesa de Campismo e Caravanismo, Avenue 5 de Outubri, 15-3°, P-1000 Lisbon. *National Map Survey:* Instito Geografico e Cadastral, Praca da Estrela, 1200, Lisbon. *Official Survey Maps:* Carta Corografica de Portugal 1:5000 (covers the whole country and shows footpaths). *Guide to Walking:* Evans, Craig, *On Foot Through Europe; a Trail Guide to Spain and Portugal,* Quill, 1982.

Spain Spain is a predominantly mountainous country. The Meseta is a 600-metre high plateau in the centre of the country which is surrounded by a series of mountain ranges with the highest peak in the country being Mulhacen (3478 metres) in the Sierra Nevada. The evocative landscape combined with the Moorish influence and its own particular form of Catholicism makes it a fascinating country.

Useful Addresses: Spanish National Tourist Office, 57-58 St James's Street, London SW1A 1LD. Tel. 071-499-0901. *Ramblers' Organisation:* Federacion Espanola de Montanismo, Alberto Aguilera 3, Madrid 15. *Official Survey Maps:* Servicio Geografico del Ejercito 1:50000 (shows footpaths). *National Map Survey:* Servicio Geografico del Ejercito, Deportamento de Distribuciónde Cartografia, C/Dario Gazapo No. 8 (Ctel Alfonso X), 28024 Madrid. *Other Maps:* Editorial Alpina maps with scales of 1:80000, 1:40000 and 1:25000 cover some of the best walking areas and show footpaths and mountain refuges.

Guide to Walking: Evans, Craig, *On Foot through Europe; a Trail Guide to Spain and Portugal,* Quill, 1982.

Footpath Guides: Collomb, Robin G., *Gredos Mountains and Sierra Nevada,* West Col, 1987; Martinez Bermejo, Angel, *Backpacking and Walking in Spain,* Bradt Publications, publication due 1990; Parker, June, *Walking in Mallorca,* Cicerone Press, 1986; Reynolds, Kev, *Walks and Climbs in the Pyrenees,* Cicerone Press, 2nd. Ed., 1983.

Sweden Sweden is a large country with numerous mountains, lakes and long-distance paths. The north of the country, which includes part of Lapland, has been described as the last wilderness in Europe. Sweden caters well for walkers and has a law, Allemansratten (Everyman's Right), that allows the walker to wander at will and camp anywhere for one night without permission, except in private gardens.

Useful Addresses: Swedish National Tourist Office, 3 Cork Street, London W1X 1HA. Tel. 071-437-5816. *Ramblers' Organisation:* Sevenska Turistforeningen, Box 25. S 101 20, Stockholm. Personal callers: Vasagartan 48, Stockholm. *National Map Survey:* National Land Survey of Sweden, 801 12 Gavle. *Official Survey Maps:* Topografiska Kartan 1:50000 and 1:25000 (both scales show footpaths). *Other Maps:* Fjallkartan, with scales of 1:100000 and 1:50000, are based on the official survey and cover some of the best mountain areas. They show footpaths and mountain huts.

Guide to Walking: Evans, Craig, *On Foot through Europe: a Trail Guide to Scandinavia,* Quill, 1982.

Switzerland Switzerland is famous for its beautiful mountain scenery and dense and splendidly waymarked network of paths. All kinds of walkers can explore and enjoy Switzerland as the paths are graded according to difficulty and there are many lowland paths that pass through meadows allowing the walker to enjoy distant prospects of the mountains. The Swiss National Tourist Office (see below) can usually supply booklets giving information about suggested walking tours.

Useful Addresses: Swiss National Tourist Office, Swiss Centre, New Coventry Street, London W1V 8EE. Tel 071-734-1921. *Ramblers' Organisation:* Schweizerische Arbeitsgemeinschaft fuer Wanderwege (SAW), Im Hirshalm 49, CH 4125 Riehen. *National Map Survey:* Eidgenoessische Landestopographie, Seftigenstrasse 264, 2084 Wabern. *Official Survey Maps:* Maps which cover the whole country and which show footpaths are available in scales of 1:100000, 1:50000 and 1:25000. *Other Maps:* Kummerley and Frey, Hallerstrasse 6-10, CH-3001 Berne publish maps in scale from 1:150000 to 1:20000 which show footpaths, and walker's guides (in French and German only). Kompass Wanderkarten 1:50000 cover selected areas and show footpaths.

Guide to Walking: Evans, Craig, *On Foot through Europe: a Trail Guide to Austria, Switzerland and Leichtenstein,* Quill, 1982.

Footpath Guides: Caselli, G., and Sugden, K., *Ancient Pathways in the Alps,* George Philip, 1988; Harper, Andrew, *Tour of Mont Blanc,* Cicerone Press, 1982; Hurdle, Jonathan, *The Alpine Pass Route,* Dark Peak, 1983; Lieberman, Marcia, *Walking Switzerland the Swiss Way,* Cordee, 1987; Reynolds, Kev, *Walks in the Engadine Switzerland,* Cicerone Press, 1988. Reynolds, Kev, *Walks in the Valais, Switzerland,* Cicerone Press, 1989; Spencer, Brian, *Walking in the Alps,* Moorland Press, 1983; Spencer, Brian, *Walking in Switzerland,* Moorland Press, 1986; Spring, Ira, and Edwards, Harvey, *100 Hikes in the Alps,* Cordee, 1979.

Walking Guides to other European Countries Dublin, Marc, and Lucas, Enver, *Trekking in Turkey,* Lonely Planet, 1989. (Distributed in the UK by Roger Lascelles); Hayman, Simon, *Guide to Czechoslovakia,* Bradt Publications, 1987; Letcher, Piers, *Yugoslavia, a Walking and Cultural Guide,* Bradt Publications, 1989;

Walking in other Continents

The information listed below under the name of each continent and in some countries, should help the enthusiast to plan a walking tour. Reliable guides are listed and the information kept to a minimum to avoid repetition.

Africa

The best general guides to walking in the continent of Africa are: Bradt, Hilary, *Backpacker's Africa; East and Southern Africa,* Bradt Publications, 3rd Rev. Ed. 1988; Bradt, George and Hilary, *Backpacker's Africa: Seventeen Walks off the Cape-to-Cairo Route,* Bradt Publications, 2nd Rev. Ed. 1982; Else, D., *Backpacker's Africa: West and Central,* Bradt Publications, 1988; Else, David, *Kenya Camping Guide,* Bradt Publications, 1989.

Also useful are: Gordon, Rene, *National Parks of Southern Africa,* Struik, Rev. Ed., 1987 (Distributed in the UK by New Holland Publishers); Williams, John, and Arlott, Norman, *National Parks of East Africa,* Collins, 2nd Rev. Ed., 1982.

South Africa South Africa, being the most prosperous country in southern Africa and with a sizeable European population, offers better walking and backpacking opportunities than any other in the continent and most visitors are captivated by its beautiful scenery. All hiking facilities are integrated.

The National Hiking Way Board is in the process of developing a long-distance path that will run for hundreds of miles in a huge horseshoe through the most mountainous areas of the country from the Soutpans range in the north to the Cedarberg Wilderness Area in Cape Province. Parts of this trail are now waymarked and open and there are huts and refuges along the route. Permits are required to walk the trail and a small charge is made. A brochure, *Follow the Footprints* is available from the South African Tourism Board. More information and guides are available from the National Hiking Way Board.

The following are some of the major hiking trails in the country:

Soutpansberg Hiking Trail: between Louis Trichardt and Levuba in Northern Transvaal. Distance 90 kilometres, four huts, five days' duration. Address for information and reservations: Northern Transvaal Forest Region, Private Bag X2413, Louis Trichardt 0920.

Fanie Botha Hiking Trail: Fanie Botha Hiking Trail between Sabie and God's Window in the Eastern Transvaal. Distance 79 kilometres, four huts, five days' duration. Address for information and reservations: The Regional Director. Eastern Transvaal Forest Region, Private Bag X503, Sabie 1260.

The Blyderiviierspoort Hiking Trail: between God's Window and the Blyderpoort Dam in the eastern Transvaal. Distance 64 kilometres, four huts, five days' duration. Address for information and reservations: The

Regional Director, Eastern Transvaal Forest Region, Private Bag X503, Sabie 1260.

Prospector's Hiking Trail: starting from Pilgrim's Rest in the Eastern Transvaal. Distance 69 kilometres, four huts, five days' duration. Address for information and reservations: The Regional Director, Eastern Transvaal Forest Region, Private Bag X503, Sabie 1260.

Drakensberg: Giant's Cup section: from Sani Pass to Bushman's Neck. Distance 63 kilometres, four huts, five days' duration. Address for information and reservations: The Regional Director, Natal Forest Region, Private Bag X9029, Pietermaritzburg 3200.

Otter Hiking Trail: between Stormsriver mouth and Nature's Valley. Distance 45 kilometres, four huts, five days' duration. Address for information and reservations: The Reservations Officer, National Parks Board, PO Box 787, Pretoria 0001.

Outeniqua Hiking Trail: between George and Knysna. Distance 137 kilometres, seven huts, eight days' duration. Address for information and reservations: The Regional Director, Southern Cape Forest Region, Private Bag X12, Knysna 6570.

Boland Hiking Trail: Hottentotsholland section between Sir Lowry's Pass and Franschhoek Pass. Distance 53 kilometres, two huts, three days' duration. Address for information and reservations: The Regional Director, Western Cape Forest Region, Private Bag X9005, Cape Town 8000.

Rhebok Hiking Trial: is a circular route from Glen Reenen Rest Camp in the Golden Gate Highland National Park, Orange Free State. Distance 31 kilometres, one hut, two days' duration. Address for information and reservations: The Reservations Officer, National Parks Board, PO Box 787, Pretoria 0001.

Useful Addresses: South African Tourism Board, Regency House, 1/4 Warwick Street, London W1R 5WB. Tel. 071-439-9661. *Ramblers' Organisation:* Federation of Hiking and Rambling Clubs. (No permanent address as each rambling club in turn takes on the duties for a year. The National Hiking Way Board can supply the current address.) National Hiking Way Board, Private Bag X447, Pretoria 0001 is the government department responsible for long-distance paths. *National Map Survey:* Directorate of Surveys and Mapping, Private Bag Mowbray 7705. *Official Survey Maps:* the whole country is covered by 1:50000 maps on which footpaths are marked.

Footpath guides are published by the National Hiking Way Board (see above), the Department of Forestry, Private Bag X313, Pretoria 0001 and the National Parks Board, PO Box 787, Pretoria 0001.

Walking Guide. The most detailed guide to walking in South Africa is

Levy, Jaynee, *Complete Guide to Walks and Trails in Southern Africa*, Struik, 1988. (Distributed in the UK by New Holland Publishers).

Asia

Asia, the largest continent is so varied that it is impossible to describe it in a book of this kind. The mecca for many walkers is Nepal and the Himalayas and a number of tour operators arrange trekking tours to these places.

Maps: A series of 1:50000 and 1:25000 maps to the more popular walking routes in the Himalayas is available from Roger Lascelles (see p261).

Footpath Guides: Armington, Stan, *Trekking in the Nepal Himalayas*, Lonely Planet, 1985. (Distributed in the UK by Roger Lascelles); Bezruchka, Stephen, *Trekking in Nepal*, Cordee, 5th Rev. Ed., 1985; Chabloz, Philippe, *Hiking in Zanskar and Ladakh*, Editions Olizane, 1986. (Distributed in the UK by Cordee); Hayes, John L., *Trekking North of Pokhara, Jomson, The Thak Cola Canyon and the Annarpurna Sanctuary*, Roger Lascelles, 1985; Martin, Stephen, *Katmandu and the Everest Trek*, Roger Lascelles, 1987; Weare, Garry, *Trekking in the Indian Himalayas*, Lonely Planet, 1986. (Distributed in the UK by Roger Lascelles).

Australasia

Walking in Australia and New Zealand is very well organised and there are many opportunities for exciting and rewarding holidays.

Australia Backpacking is known in Australia as bushwalking and requires skills unknown to the British backpacker, including the ability to read signs that denote the presence of underground water. The scenery and climate of Australia is very varied but it includes large areas of arid country and several mountain ranges. The emptiness of Australia (sixteen million people in a country almost as large as the United States) could hardly provide a greater contrast to our over-crowded island.

There is no national organisation of bushwalkers but a number operate at state level and these have been listed below together with the state addresses of the National Parks and Wildlife Service.

Publishers of footpath guides include the Hill of Content Publishing Company Pty Ltd, 86 Bourke Street, Melbourne, Victoria 3000, and the Kangaroo Press, PO Box 75, Kenthurst, NSW 2156.

Useful Addresses: Australian Tourist Commission, Heathcote House, 20 Savile Row, London WIX 1AP. Tel. 071-434-4371. Australian High Commission, Australia House, The Strand, London WC2B 4LA. Tel. 071-379-4334. The reference library is open to the public and contains a collection of books and materials about Australia, including the Australian

National Bibliography, which is an invaluable source of information about footpath guides. *National Map Survey:* Division of National Mapping, PO Box 31, Belconnen, ACT 2616. *National Survey Maps:* 1:50000 (in progress).

Maps and guides are available from the following state addresses: *New South Wales:* National Parks and Wildlife Service, Bridge Street, Hurstville, NSW 2220; New South Wales Federation of Bushwalking Clubs, GPO Box 2090, Sydney, NSW 2001. *Queensland:* National Parks and Wildlife Service, MLC Centre, 239 George Street, Brisbane, Qld 4000; Queensland Federation of Bushwalking Clubs, GPO Box 1573, Brisbane, Qld 4001. *South Australia:* National Parks and Wildlife Service, 55 Grenfell Street, Adelaide, SA 5000; Adelaide Bushwalkers Inc. PO Box 178, Unley, SA 5061. *Tasmania:* National Parks and Wildlife Service, 134 Manquarie, Hobart, Tas 7000; Hobart Walking Club, GPO Box 753 H, Hobart, Tas 70001. *Victoria:* National Parks and Wildlife Service, 240 Victoria Parade, East Melbourne, Vic 3002; Federation of Victorian Walking Clubs, GPO Box 815F, Melbourne, Vic 3001. *Western Australia:* National Parks and Wildlife Service, 50 Hayman Road, Como WA 6152.

Guide to Walking: Chapman, J and M., *Bushwalking in Australia,* Lonely Planet (distributed in the UK by Roger Lascelles).

Footpath Guides: Dewhurst, Janice and White Margaret, *Sydney Walkabout 1,* Kangaroo Press. Groom, Tony and Gynther, Trevor, *100 Walks in South Queensland,* Hill of Content, 1980. Gunter, John, *Sydney by Ferry and Foot,* Kangaroo Press. McDougall, Garry and Shearer-Heriot, Leigh. *The Great North Walk; Sydney to Newcastle,* Kangaroo Press. Morgan, Kim, *Canberra Walks,* Kangaroo Press, 1989. Paton, Neil, *Sydney Bushwalks,* Kangaroo Press. Paton, Neil, *Walks in the Blue Mountains National Park,* Kangaroo Press. Paton, Neil, *Walks in the Sydney Harbour National Park,* Kangaroo Press. Thomas Tyrone, *20 Best Walks in Australia,* Hill of Content, 1988. Thomas, Tyrone, *120 Walks in Victoria,* Hill of Content, 5th Ed., 1989. Thomas, Tyrone, *100 Walks in New South Wales,* Hill of Content, 3rd Ed., 1988. Thomas, Tyrone, *100 Walks in Tasmania,* Hill of Content, 2nd Ed., 1978. Thomas, Tyrone, *50 Walks in the Grampians,* Hill of Content, 3rd Ed., 1986.

New Zealand New Zealand is an extremely beautiful, mountainous country with a well-developed network of national and forest parks. Walking, often referred to as tramping, is a popular pastime and there are many long-distance routes. There is no local footpath network such as we have in Britain but the government has established the New Zealand Walkway Commission which is responsible for the creation of a network of walkways throughout the country. On some of the long-distance routes a permit is required which can be obtained in advance from the New Zealand

High Commission (see below) which can also provide information about travel companies specialising in walking tours.

A leaflet, *New Zealand National Parks Publications,* available from the Department of Conservation (see below), gives the addresses of national parks together with information about footpath guides.

Publishers of footpath guides include: Government Printing Office, Mulgrave Street, Wellington; Methuen (New Zealand), PO Box 4439, Auckland; A.H. and A.W. Reed Ltd, Private Bag, Wellington; Whitcoullis Ltd, Private Bag, Wellington.

Useful Addresses: New Zealand Travel Commissioner/New Zealand Government Tourist Bureau/New Zealand High Commission, New Zealand House, Haymarket, London SW1Y 4TQ. Tel. 071-930-8422. The reference library, which is open to the public, contains a useful collection of books about the country as well as the New Zealand National Bibliography on microfiche from which details of up to date footpath guides can be found under the heading 'Trails'. *Ramblers' Organisation:* New Zealand Walkway Commission, c/o Department of Conservation, PO Box 10420, Wellington. *National Map Survey:* Department of Survey and Land Information, Private Bag, Charles Ferguson Building, Bowen St, Wellington. *Official Survey Maps:* 1:63360 cover the whole country and show footpaths and a 1:50000 series is in progress.

Guides to Walking: Burton, R., *A Tramper's Guide to New Zealand's National Parks,* Read Methuen, 1987; Cobb, John, *The Walking Tracks of New Zealand's National Parks,* Endeavour Press, 1985.

Footpath Guides: AA guide to Walkways, Landsdowne Press, 1987. 2 Vols: North Island, South Island; Dufresne, Jim, *Tramping in New Zealand,* Lonely Planet, 1982. (Distributed in the UK by Roger Lascelles); Pickering, Mark, *101 Great Tramps in New Zealand,* Read Methuen, Revised and Enlarged Edition, 1988.

Central and South America

There are many possibilities for exploring parts of Central and South America on foot. Although political upheaval seems endemic in some countries, and the continent is notorious for the sheer nastiness of some of its dictators, this in no way reflects on the warmth of the people. It is a vast continent containing many countries with great varieties of scenery including jungles, forests, swamps and mountains higher than any in Europe.

An invaluable general guide, revised annually, is: Brooks, John, *The South American Handbook,* Trade and Travel Publications. The best walking guides to the region are published by Bradt Publications (see p261).

Footpath Guides: Bradt, Hilary, *Backpacking in Chile and Argentina,* Bradt Publications, 1990; Bradt, Hilary, *Backpacking and Trekking in Peru and Bolivia,* Bradt Publications, 4th Rev. Ed., 1987; Bradt, Hilary, *The No Frills Guide to Backpacking in Venezuela,* Bradt Publications, 1989; Bradt, Hilary, *and* Rachowiecki, Rob, *Backpacking in Mexico and Central America; a Guide for Walkers and Naturalists,* Bradt Publications, 3rd Rev. Ed., 1989. (Includes Guatemala, El Salvador, Honduras, Costa Rica, Panama and the Darien Gap); Brod, Charles, *Apus and Incas: a Cultural Walking and Trekking Guide to Cuzco,* Published by the author, 1987. (Distributed in the UK by Bradt Publications); Rachowiecki, Rob, *Climbing and Hiking in Ecuador,* Bradt Publications, Rev. Ed., 1987.

North America

Both the United States and Canada offer wonderful opportunities for backpacking and walking (which on the other side of the Atlantic is always referred to as hiking). There are numerous long-distance paths and national parks that allow the adventurous to explore the most beautiful parts of the New World.

There is no local footpath network such as we have in Britain but there are many specially constructed hiking trails. Maps of these trails can be purchased from local backpacking shops and the offices of state and national parks.

The best general guide for Britons intending to walk in the United States and Canada is: Bradt, George and Hilary, *Backpacking in North America; the Great Outdoors,* Bradt Enterprises, 1979. Even though it was published some time ago and some of the addresses will be out of date, it is still very useful. The section dealing with the United States can be supplemented by Hargrove, Penny and Liebrenz, Noelle, *Backpackers' Sourcebook; a Book of Lists,* Wilderness Press, 3rd. Ed., 1987. (Distributed in the UK by Cordee).

North Americans take backpacking very seriously and have developed philosophical theories about which visitors should have at least some knowledge.

United States The United States is a very large country (Texas alone is two and a half times the size of the United Kingdom) with enormous variations in climate and landscape. Britons will find the western states of California, Arizona, Colorado, Utah, Nevada, Wyoming, Montana, Idaho, Oregon, Washington and Alaska, the most scenic, but good walking can also be found in the Appalachian Mountains in the states of Vermont, Maine, New Hampshire, New York, Virginia, Kentucky, Tennessee and the Carolinas, as well as in New Mexico. There is little to attract the British walker in the rolling prairies of the midwestern states.

Walking in the United States usually involves visiting one of the national parks which are quite different in character from British national parks. The federal government actually owns the national parks and in many cases makes a small admission charge. Many parks, especially in the west, are closed to visitors except during the summer months. Visitors are hedged about by rules and regulations and a permit, obtainable from the park office, is usually required for 'back country' (off-trail) backpacking.

Descriptions of America's national parks can be found in the following books distributed in the United Kingdom: *Guide to the National Park Areas*, Choke Pequot Press, *Eastern States*, 1988, *Western States*, 1988; Frome. M., Editor, *National Park Guide*, Rand McNally, 1988.

Further information can be obtained from the Regional Offices of the National Park Service listed below.

There are a number of long-distance paths. Among the most famous are the Appalachian Trail that runs for over 3200 kilometres from Maine to Georgia, the Pacific Crest Trail that runs for 4122 kilometres from the Mexican border through California, Oregon and Washington to the Canadian border, and the 5000-kilometre Continental Divide Trail from near the Mexican border in New Mexico along the watershed of the Continental Divide to the Canadian border in Glacier National Park. Guidebooks to national parks can be found under the heading 'National Parks' and to long-distance paths under 'Trails' in *The Subject Guide to American Books in Print* which may be consulted in most British reference libraries.

Generally speaking, topographical maps are not readily available in the United States although some outdoor shops and map specialists stock them for their own area.

Useful Addresses: The United States does not have a tourist office in Britain and assistance can only be obtained from travel agents specialising in American tourism. The American Embassy, Grosvenor Square, London W1A 1AE (Tel. 071-499-9000) has an excellent reference library which may be consulted by appointment and at the discretion of the librarian. The library staff will answer enquiries by post and telephone. *Ramblers' Organisations:* American Hiking Society, 1015 31st Street NW, Washington DC 20007. *Sierra Club,* 730 Polk Street, San Francisco, CA 94109 (a powerful environmental lobby that campaigns on behalf of all who seek to enjoy the great outdoors). There are chapters in every state and branches in most large cities (check the telephone directory or call the public library) and they arrange walks and outings and welcome visitors. The Sierra Club organises expensive walking holidays in the United States and throughout the world. *National Map Survey:* United States Geological Survey, 507 National Center, Reston VA 22092 (the office to which enquiries for information should be made) and the Distribution Branch, Geological Survey, Federal Center, Building 41, Box 25286, Denver, CO 80225 (the office from which maps may be purchased). *Official Survey Maps:* 1:250000, 1:125000 (certain areas only), 1:62500 (certain areas only), 1:24000 (certain areas only).

Regional Offices of the National Park Service: Alaska: 2525 Gambell Street, Anchorage, AK 99593. *Mid Atlantic:* 143 South Third Street, Philadelphia, PA 19106 (for the states of Delaware, Maryland, Pennsylvania, Virginia, West Virginia). *Mid West:* 1709 Jackson Street, Omaha, NB 68102 (for the states of Illinois, Indiana, Iowa, Kansas, Michigan, Minnesota, Missouri, Nebraska, Ohio, Wisconsin). *North Atlantic:* 15 State Street, Boston, MA 02109 (for the states of Connecticut, Maine, New Hampshire, Massachusetts, New Jersey, New York, Rhode Island, Vermont). *Pacific North West:* 83 S King Street, Suite 212, Seattle, WA 98104 (for the states of Idaho, Oregon, Washington) *Rocky Mountains:* PO Box 25287, Denver CO 80225 (for the states of Colorado, Montana, North Dakota, South Dakota, Utah, Wyoming). *South East:* Federal Building, 75 Spring Street SW, Atlanta, GA 30303 (for the states of Alabama, Florida, Georgia, Kentucky, Mississippi, North Carolina, Puerto Rico, South Carolina, Tennessee, Virgin Islands). *South West:* Old Sante Fe Trail, Box 728, Sante Fe, NM 87504 (for the states of Arkansas, Louisiana, New Mexico, Oklahoma, Texas). *Western:* Box 36063, 450 Golden Gate Avenue, San Francisco, CA 94102 (for the states of Arizona, California, Guam, Hawaii, Nevada, Northern Mariana Islands).

Canada Canada is an enormous country, the second largest in the world, with a population of only twenty-three million people. It contains vast areas of wilderness and the Canadian Rockies is one of the most beautiful mountain ranges in the world.

Useful Addresses: Canadian Government Office of Tourism, Canada House, Trafalgar Square, London SW1Y 5BJ. Tel. 071-629-9492. The Government Office of Tourism maintains a reference library which may be used by the public by appointment. Two useful bibliographies that may be consulted are *The Subject Guide to Canadian Books in Print* and *Canadiana: the Canadian National Bibliography*. *National Map Survey:* Department of Energy, Mines and Resources, Surveys, Mapping and Cartographic Information, 615 Booth Street, Ottawa, Ontario K1A 0E9. *Official Survey Maps:* The only series that covers the whole country is the 1:250000, but certain areas are mapped on the following scales: 1:125000, 1:50000, 1:25000.

Guide to Walking: Katz, Elliott, *The Complete Guide to Backpacking in Canada,* Doubleday, 1985.

Footpath Guides: Ambrosi, Joey, *Hiking Alberta's Southwest,* Douglas &

McIntyre, 1984; Cousins, Jean and Robinson, Heather, *Easy Hiking around Vancouver,* Douglas & McIntyre, 1980; Daffern, Gillean, *Kanaski's Country Trail Guide,* Rocky Mountain Books, 1985; Fairley, Bruce and Culbert, Dick, *A Guide to Hiking and Climbing in Southwestern British Columbia,* Soules, 1986; Harris, Bob, *The Best of B.C.'s Hiking Trails; Twenty Great Hikes,* Special Interest, 1986; Macaree, David and Mary, *109 Walks in British Columbia's Lower Mainland,* Douglas & McIntyre, 1983; Macaree, David and Mary, *103 Hikes in Southwestern British Columbia,* Douglas & McIntyre, 1980; Patton, Brian, and Robinson, Bart, *Canadian Rockies Trail Guide,* Summer Thought, New Ed., 1989. (Distributed in UK by Bradt Publications); Roberge, Claude, *Hiking Garibaldi Park and Whistler,* Douglas & McIntyre, 1983; Robertson, Doug, *The Best Hiking in Ontario,* Hurtig, 1984; Russell, Elizabeth and others, *Waterton and Northern Glacier Trails for Hikers and Riders,* Waterton, 1984; Stewart, Colin, Editor, *Hiking Trails of Nova Scotia,* Canadian Hostelling, 5th ed., 1984; Wadell, Jane, Editor, *Hiking Trails I: Victoria and Vicinity,* Outdoor Club of Victoria, Rev. Ed., 1987; Waddell, Jane, Editor, *Hiking Trails II: Vancouver Island, Area from Kokilah River Park to Mount Arrowsmith,* Outdoor Club of Victoria, 5th Ed., 1982; Waddell, Jane, Editor, *Hiking Trails III: Central and Northern Vancouver Island Including Hiking Routes of Strathcona Park* Outdoor Club of Victoria, 5th Ed., 1982.

19 Challenge Walks

Those who occasionally like an element of competition in their walking and who like to test their strength and endurance will probably enjoy entering challenge walks. The Long Distance Walkers' Association (see p301-2) is the governing body of the sport but every event has its own rules. Competitions and challenges are publicised in the LDWA's journal *The Strider* and are listed in *The Long-distance Walker's Handbook* (see bibliography below).

The general pattern of an event is for each competitor to be given a route card on which a number of checkpoints are listed. The walker has to visit each one to have his card stamped and has to finish within a given time in order to qualify. Some events have prizes for the first man and the first woman home.

Some challenge walks, like the Chiltern Marathon, are comparatively easy and any reasonably fit walker should have no difficulty in completing them within the qualifying time. Others are very tough events over wild country involving long distances and demand a very high standard of fitness.

Peak Bagging

A specialised form of challenge walking is collecting or 'bagging' summits. A summit is defined in various ways according to the classification used. Peak bagging started long before the Ordnance Survey went metric, and for the sake of convenience and standardisation, heights are still expressed in feet. The major challenges are listed below.

The 4000s There are eight peaks and thirteen additional tops over 4000 feet (1219.5 metres) in height. They are all in Scotland, four in the Cairngorms and four in Lochaber. All have been climbed in one expedition that involves 98 miles (158 kilometres) of walking and more than 13000 feet (4000 metres of ascent). The peaks are;

Ben Nevis (4406 feet or 1344 metres), Ben Macdui (4296 feet or 1309 metres), Braeriach (4248 feet or 1296 metres), Cairn Toul (4241 feet or 1293 metres), Cairn Gorm (4084 feet or 1245 metres), Aonach Beag (4060 feet or 1234 metres), Carn Mor Dearg (4012 feet or 1223 metres) and Aonach Mor (4005 feet or 1221 metres).

The Munros In 1891, Sir Hugh Munro published a list of Scottish mountains more than 3000 feet high. This has been subsequently revised and his definitions refined. A summit is a Munro if it is more than 3000 feet (914 metres) high and is separated from another summit by a drop on all sides of at least 500 feet (152 metres), by a considerable distance, or by a natural obstacle. A Munro top must be over 3000 feet high and must have a separate identity of its own.

There are 276 Munros and a further 516 tops and more than 300 walkers are known to have climbed them all. The first person to climb them all in one expedition was Hamish Brown who walked 1639 miles (2639 kilometres) and ascended 449,000 feet (136,890 metres). Since then several people have emulated him and there have been winter expeditions.

The Welsh 3000s There are fourteen summits in Wales that exceed 3000 feet and an unrecorded number of walkers have completed the 30 miles (48 kilometres) and 12000 feet (3700 metres) of climbing involved. The favoured route is to start at Pen-y-Pass and finish at Aber, and to climb them in the following order:

Crib Goch (3023 feet or 922 metres), Crib-y-ddysig (3493 feet or 1065 metres), Snowdon (3560 feet or 1085 metres), Elidir Fawr (3029 feet or 923 metres), Y Garn (3104 feet or 946 metres), Glyder Fawr (3279 feet or 1000 metres), Glyder Fach (3262 feet or 955 metres), Tryfan (3010 feet or 918 metres), Pen-yr-ole-wen (3210 feet or 979 metres), Carnedd Dafydd (3426 feet or 1045 metres), Carnedd Llewelyn (3484 feet or 1062 metres), Yr Elen (3152 feet or 961 metres), Foel Grach (3195 feet or 974 metres), Foel Fras (3091 feet or 942 metres).

The English 3000s There are four summits in England over 3000 feet high and these, too, have been walked in a single expedition:

Scafell (3162 feet or 964 metres), Scafell Pike (3210 feet or 979 metres), Helvellyn (3118 feet or 951 metres), Skiddaw (3053 feet or 931 metres).

The highest summits of Scotland (Ben Nevis, 4406 feet or 1344 metres), Wales (Snowdon 3560 feet or 1085 metres) and England (Scafell Pike, 3210 feet or 979 metres) have all been climbed in one expedition within twenty-four hours using a car for transport between mountains.

Other Summits A Corbett, named after J. Rooke Corbett who first compiled the list, is a Scottish mountain of 2500 feet (762 metres) and under 3000 feet (914 metres) in height with re-ascent of 500 feet (152 metres) on all sides. There are 223 Corbetts.

A Donald, named after Percy Donald who compiled the list, is a summit of at least 2000 feet (610 metres) in the Lowlands of Scotland. There are 87 Hills and 138 Tops.

Both Corbetts and Donalds are included in Munro's *Tables* (see bibliography).

Bibliography

Blatchford, Barbara, *The Long-distance Walker's Handbook*, A. and C. Black, 2nd Ed, 1990, Donaldson, J.C., and Brown, Hamish, *Munro's Tables of the 30000-feet Mountains of Scotland and other Tables of Lesser Height*, Scottish Mountaineering Trust, Rev. Ed., 1984.

Postscript

My task is done; my computer screen is blank and lifeless, and the soporific hum of the hard disk is stilled. The writing of *The Walker's Handbook* has been a labour of love because it combines my twin interests of walking and bibliographical research, and like all researchers, I have been constantly humbled by how little I know.

It is quite remarkable how the wider world of walking has changed and developed in the ten years since I wrote the previous edition of this book. Walking is now by far the most popular outdoor pastime of the British and is no longer the sole province of the woolly hat and vacant grin brigade.

But its very popularity has brought its problems. 'Yet each man kills the thing he loves' wrote Oscar Wilde and something will have to be done to prevent the severe erosion on some of the more popular paths caused by the tramp of innumerable marching feet. The scars on Kinder Scout, the North York Moors and Penyghent are ugly fissures on a beautiful landscape and must be removed by delicate plastic surgery. Paths must be repaired to the standard necessary to prevent further damage which could be done quite easily if the government could be persuaded to divert a minute proportion of the billions of pounds spent on roads to repair some of our paths. There are ancient precedents. Mastiles Lane, the Miners' Track on Snowdon and the Old Corpse Road between Garrigill and Kirkland are able to withstand heavy use by walkers because they were constructed with stone surfaces. Some routes in the Lake District and elsewhere are receiving similar treatment and are beginning to blend into the landscape, and the granite steps constructed on some of the steep hills on the South West Way are an enormous improvement on the ugly and dangerously rutted paths that they replace.

In the forty years since the passing of the National Parks and Access to the Countryside Act I have seen the beauty of our cultivated countryside decline alarmingly. The farming community has constantly assured us that our countryside heritage was safe in their hands. They lied to us and the evidence is around us for all to see. Our countryside has been systematically poisoned, polluted and plundered by farmers using herbicides, pesticides and nitrates, decimating our fauna and almost exterminating our flora. Our woods and fields are skilfully manicured, but like the made-up face of a film star, they lack the depth of character wherein true beauty lies. No longer would Rubert Brooke be able to sing

'Unkempt about those hedges blows
An unofficial English rose.'

To some extent farmers were the willing victims of a lunatic agricultural policy where efficiency is prized above everything and we have to sell our embarassing agricultural surpluses at knock-down prices to the Russians or, madder still, process our butter mountain into cattle feed to produce yet more butter. What *is* inexcusable is the wholesale theft of the paths over which the public have the right to walk. In places like East Anglia and parts of the Midlands, farmers have cynically defied the law by systematically ploughing, obstructing and destroying public rights of way. The only group of people that disregard the law as flagrantly as the farming community are motorists.

My son was born during the writing of this book and I hope that by the time he is old enough to explore the countryside on his own, a sense of balance will have been restored. I hope that the wholesale use of pesticides, herbicides and nitrates will be regarded as bad husbandry. I should like him to be able to walk across farmland on paths that are not obstructed by barbed wire and other obstacles; I want him to drink water uncontaminated by nitrates and other pollutants, and to eat food grown on land free from the risk of chemical poisoning; and I want him to breathe air unpolluted by lead and acid rain. When these conditions are met, our broad-leaved woodlands will recover, wildflowers will reappear in the hedgerows and field-edges, and Britain will again be a green and pleasant land.

APPENDIX ONE
Magazines and Periodicals of Interest to Walkers

Camping & Walking Link House, Dingwall Avenue, Croydon CR9 2TA. Monthly. This magazine incorporates *Camping, Camping & Trailer, Popular Camping and Autocamping* so each issue contains articles about subjects not directly connected with walking. Nevertheless, it is an interesting magazine which occasionally includes outstandingly good articles and is written in a popular style with a strong 'family' flavour. It reviews equipment.

Climber & Hill Walker Outram Magazines, Plaza Tower, The Plaza, East Kilbride, Glasgow G74 1LW. Monthly. Written for experts it concentrates on climbing and to a lesser extent on fell-walking. It contains good, well-illustrated articles, news items, and reviews of guides, books and equipment.

Country Walking EMAP Pursuit Publishing, Bretton Court, Bretton, Peterborough PE3 8DZ. Monthly. A popular magazine containing news items and short, informative articles on walking and the countryside that appeal particularly to families and beginners. Each issue contains general articles, reviews of books and footpath guides and answers to readers' queries as well as pages of suggested walks.

Footpath Worker The Ramblers' Association, 1–5 Wandsworth Road, London SW8 2XX. Published quarterly. A duplicated newsheet of great interest to all those concerned in preserving rights of way. It gives detailed information about court cases, decisions of the Ombudsman and parliamentary business involving public paths.

The Great Outdoors, Outram Magazines, Plaza Tower, The Plaza, East Kilbride, Glasgow G74 1LW. Monthly. A general magazine about walking that covers a wide range of interests and appeals to both family amblers and experienced fell-walkers. It contains news items, tests equipment, and reviews books and footpath guides.

High High Magazine Ltd, Springfield House, 164 Barkby Road, Leicester LE4 7LF (Editorial Office, 336 Abbey Lane, Sheffield S8 0BY Monthly. A magazine devoted to climbing and fell-walking that also includes articles and news about skiing and caving. It contains news items, reviews books and equipment and is at present the official journal of the British Mountaineering Council.

Outdoor Action Hawker Consumer Publications Ltd, 13 Park House, 140 Battersea Park Road, London SW11 4NB. Tel. 071-720-2108. Monthly. A magazine covering many outdoor adventure activities but concentrating on walking and backpacking. It contains articles, news items, brief book reviews and tests equipment.

Rambling Today (formerly *The Rambler*) The Ramblers' Association, 1–5 Wandsworth Road, London SW8 2XX, quarterly. The official journal of the Ramblers' Association. It contains a comprehensive news section covering all matters relating to paths and the countryside together with well-informed comments on the Ordnance Survey and the amenity and conservation scene in general. There are articles about walking and brief notices of books and footpaths guides.

Trail Walker EMAP Pursuit Publishing, Bretton Court, Bretton, Peterborough PE3 8DZ. Monthly. A specialist magazine for those interested in backpacking and walking expeditions. It publishes news and articles on all aspects of the subject, reviews books and tests new equipment.

APPENDIX TWO
Useful Organisations in the United Kingdom

Many of the voluntary organisations listed below do not have a permanent address and have frequent changes of officers. All the addresses and officers were checked in 1989. When writing to an organisation with asterisks before the title be sure to put a return address on your envelope. Should it be returned by the Post Office then place it in a fresh stamped envelope addressed to the organisation you wish to contact, place it in another envelope addressed to either the Ramblers' Association (for organisations marked *) or to the British Mountaineering Council (for organisations marked **) and mail it with a covering letter asking that it be forwarded to the current address.

Adventure and Environmental Awareness Group Hon. Secretary: Geoff Cooper, Low Bank Ground, Coniston, Cumbria LA21 8AA. Tel. 05394-41314.

Aims: To encourage awareness, understanding and concern for the natural environment amongst those involved with education and recreation.

The AEAG pursues its aims by holding workshops and conferences, publishing discussion papers and by developing links with outdoor leaders and environmentalists.

Association for the Protection of Rural Scotland 14a Napier Road, Edinburgh EH10 5AY. Tel. 031-229-1898.

Aims: Founded in 1926 to help keep rural Scotland a desirable place. Encourages appropriate development to keep people there in jobs. Advises on planning matters, restores and records historic bridges, runs environmental improvement and building awards.

Publications: A newsletter and *Rights of Way in Scotland: a Directory of Sources of Information*. The latter publication is a most useful guide to the registers and records kept by local authorities.

Association of Countryside Rangers Hon. Secretary: Mrs Sue Clark, 100 Station Road, Puckeridge, Herts SG11 1TF. Tel. 0920-822600.

The ACR was founded in 1966 and is now one of the most representative bodies of countryside management staff in Britain. It seeks to promote good professional practice in the ranger service and provides a forum for the exchange of ideas and common problems. Membership is open to rangers and wardens employed in national parks, areas of outstanding natural beauty, nature reserves, heritage coasts, country parks, the National Trust, the urban fringe and the wider countryside.

Journal: The Ranger.

**Association of Heads of Outdoor Education Centres (formerly the Association of Wardens of Mountain Centres). Hon Secretary: David Shearman, Aberglaslyn Hall, Beddgelert, Caernarfon, Gwynedd LL55 4YF. Tel. 076686-233.

Aims: 1. To encourage all-round personal development through residential experience and the use of the outdoors.

2. To develop, establish and maintain good safe practice in outdoor activities by all methods available to the Association.

3. To act publicly in the interests of its members.

4. To afford opportunities for its members to meet to discuss items of mutual interest.

5. To liaise with other bodies as appropriate.

**Association of National Park Officers Hon. Secretary: Donald Connolly, Lake District Special Planning Board, Busher Walk, Kendal, Cumbria LA9 4RH. Tel. 0539-724555.

Aims: To promote the study and understanding of national parks in England and Wales, their conservation and effective management.

The Association of Wardens of Outdoor Centres *see* Association of Heads of Outdoor Education Centres.

*Backpackers' Club PO Box 381, 7-10 Friar Street, Reading RG3 4RL. Tel. 04917-739.

Aims: To ensure continual rights of access to meadow, mountain, woodland, moor and shore. To campaign for, and aid provision of, sections of public footpath and rights of access to these. To encourage, by example and instructions, the full use of the established long-distance footpaths, national parks and open areas.

To campaign and aid the establishment of further similar areas in this country and in the European continent.

To encourage and aid the development of lightweight camping, walking and camping equipment.

British Activity Holiday Association Rock Park, Llandrindod Wells, Powys LD1 6AE. Tel. 0597-823902.

BAHA was founded in 1986 after public concern had been expressed about the standard of leadership and supervision among operators in the outdoor leisure holiday industry.

Aims: To maintain standards of safety, instruction and quality of activity and special interest holidays. To provide a network for the exchange of ideas and information on activity and special interest holidays. To manage any matters of common concern to the membership. To focus public attention on the aims and benefits of the Association. To encourage communication and co-operation between related bodies in the field of activity and special interest holidays. To act generally as a professional association for its members.

Publications: a newsletter, *Code of Practice, List of Members.*

**British Association of Mountain Guides c/o British Mountaineering Council, Crawford House, Precinct Centre, Booth Street East, Manchester M13 9RZ. Tel. 061-273-5835.

The ABMG is the professional association of those guides who have passed the exacting standards of the Association and been awarded the British Guide's Carnet and the International Guide's Carnet which is a qualification recognised throughout the mountaineering world. British Mountain Guides will, for a fee, lead and instruct individuals and groups in all mountaineering activities from hill-walking to winter ascents of the major alpine peaks.

British Mountaineering Council Crawford House, Precinct Centre, Booth Street East, Manchester M13 9RZ. Tel. 061-273-5835.

The British Mountaineering Council, founded in 1944, is constituted to foster and promote the interests of British mountaineers and mountaineering in the United Kingdom and overseas. Jointly with the Mountaineering Council of Scotland, it is the representative body of British mountaineers. Full membership is open to mountaineering clubs and organisations whose principal objectives are mountaineering, which have headquarters in the United Kingdom and which are owned and controlled by their members. Associate membership is open to bodies which do not qualify for full membership, and to individuals.

The work of the BMC includes assisting member clubs and, with their co-operation, improving facilities such as guide books, huts, reciprocal rights in club huts, ensuring adequate training for novice mountaineers and medium performers wishing to improve their skills, resisting encroachments on the mountain environment, negotiating access rights for mountain areas, outcrops and sea cliffs and helping expeditions overseas in co-operation with the Mount Everest Foundation and the Alpine Club. The testing of a wide range of equipment is organised. Advice on mountaineering matters is given to a wide variety of organisations. In co-operation with the Mountaineering Council of Scotland, the BMC endorses the Guides' Carnet for experienced mountaineers who wish to perform as mountain guides in Britain and overseas.

Journal: High.

Publications: Guide books, safety handbooks, pamphlets, posters, reports on equipment, general information and advice, videos, filmstrips and slides covering summer and winter mountaineering.

British Textile Technology Group Wira House, West Park Ring Road, Leeds LS16 6QL. Tel. 0532-781381.

Formerly known as the Wira (Wool Industries Research Association) Technology Group, BTTG is an organisation financed by textile companies to provide research, consultancy and testing for the textile industry. Many manufacturers of textiles designed for the outdoor market submit their products for independent testing under laboratory conditions to the Group. There are 254 standard tests available which cover such properties as flammability, abrasion resistance, burst strength, permeability, pilling, seam failure, tear strength, thermal resistance and water repellancy.

British Trust for Conservation Volunteers 36 St Mary's Street, Wallingford, Oxon OX10 0EU. Tel. 0491-39766.

The British Trust for Conservation Volunteers exists to involve people of all ages in practical conservation work including footpath improvement, bridge-building, and the repair of stone walls. The Trust organises residential courses and working holidays in which practical skills can be learned and put to good use.

Journal: The Conserver.

Publications: A series of practical handbooks covering such subjects as dry stone walling, fencing, hedging etc. Of particular interest to walkers is *Footpaths* by Elizabeth Agate published in 1983 and generally accepted as the standard work on footpath management.

*Byways and Bridleway Trust The Granary, Charlcutt, Calne, Wilts SN11 9HL. Tel. 024974-273.

The Trust strives to keep open byways and bridleways for everyone, including trail-riders. It monitors all modification orders pertaining to byways and bridleways and works to ensure that definitive maps are accurate.

Journal: Byway and Bridleway.

Camping and Caravanning Club Greenfields House, Westwood Way, Coventry CV4 8JH. Tel. 0203-694995.

Aims: The promotion of knowledge, love and care of the countryside through camping and kindred activities.

The Club owns or manages 85 full facility camping and caravanning sites and licences a further 2000 minimum facility 'Hideaway' sites. It has special interest groups including some devoted to walking and lightweight camping and it organises walking holidays from some of the Club sites.

Journal: Camping and Caravanning.

Publications: Guides to sites and advice and information on camping and caravanning.

Camping and Outdoor Leisure Association Morritt House, 58 Station Approach, South Ruislip, Middlesex HA4 6SA. Tel. 081-842-1111.

COLA is a trade organisation that looks after the interests of manufacturers, distributors and retailers of outdoor equipment and clothing. It holds an annual trade exhibition at Harrogate that is not open to the public but is widely reported in the outdoor press. In cases of difficulty it will mediate between consumers and retailers.

Journal: COLA News.

Council for National Parks 45 Shelton Street, London WC2H 9HJ. Tel. 071-240-3603.

Aims: To protect and promote the national parks of England and Wales, and the Norfolk and Suffolk Broads.

The Council for National Parks is a charity set up more than fifty years ago that now has 45 member organisations representing over three million supporters of national parks. Individuals can support the Council's work by becoming a Friend of National Parks.

Journal: Tarn and Tor.

Publications: Fifty Years for National Parks, Know Your National Parks and various Reports and Conference Proceedings on matters relating to national parks.

Council for the Protection of Rural England Warwick House, 25 Buckingham Palace Road, London SW1W 0PP. Tel. 071-235-9481.

Aims: Founded in 1926 the Society exists to protect all that is worthwhile in the English countryside. It recognises that changes must take place but where they do they should be for the better. The CPRE concerns itself with new housing and industrial development, power stations, overhead transmission lines, new reservoirs and the extraction of water from rivers and lakes, sand and gravel workings, limestone quarrying and opencast coalmining, the felling and planting of trees, the siting of new roads, especially motorways, and the use of land by government departments.

Whenever necessary, the CPRE co-operates with other amenity bodies and lobbies MPs, briefs counsel for public enquiries, and offers advice to government departments and planning authorities.

There are branches in all counties.

Journal: Countryside Campaigner.

Council for the Protection of Rural Wales (Cymdethas Diogelu Cymru Wiedig) Tŷ Gwyn, 31 High Street, Welshpool, Powys SY21 7JP. Tel. 0938-552525.

The Council for the Protection of Rural Wales is the country's leading independent countryside conservation pressure group. Established in 1928, it plays a vital role in defending the whole of the Welsh coast and countryside. CPRW protects the Welsh landscape from insensitive development and fights for a prosperous and healthy countryside that balances a wide range of needs. It monitors central government and Welsh Office proposals as well as the work of statutory agencies, and acts as an environmental watchdog contributing well researched views on planning issues.

Journal: Rural Wales (Cymry Wledig).

Countryside Commission John Dower House, Crescent Place, Cheltenham, Glos GL50 3RA. Tel. 0242-521381.

The Countryside Commission is a statutory agency which cares for the countryside of England and Wales and helps people to enjoy it. The Commission is an advisory and promotional body, working in partnership with others—local authorities, public agencies, voluntary bodies, farmers, landowners and private individuals—and providing grants and advice for projects which conserve the natural beauty of the countryside and make it more accessible for public enjoyment. To enable people to enjoy the countryside on foot, the Commission establishes national trails, which pass through some of the wildest and finest scenery, and it also supports the development of regional routes, as well as encouraging local authorities to open up rights of way and local paths.

The Commission acts as the Government's adviser on countryside matters and it has special responsibility for designating national parks, areas of outstanding natural beauty and defining heritage coasts.

The Commission was established in 1968 to succeed the National Parks Commission but with wider responsibilities. It has been an independent agency since 1982 with an annual grant from the Department of the Environment.

Journals: Countryside Commission News and National Parks Today.

Countryside Commission for Scotland Battleby, Redgorton, Perth PH1 3EW. Tel. 0738-27921.

The Countryside Commission for Scotland was established under the Countryside (Scotland) Act, 1967 and is an autonomous government agency financed by an annual grant from the Scottish Development Department.

The Commission's duties are:

1. To conserve and enhance the Scottish landscape.

2. To develop and improve public access into the countryside and improve facilities for its enjoyment including the provision of long-distance paths.

3. Have regard for the need for economic and social development in the countryside.

4. Advise the Secretary of State for Scotland, planning authorities, the Foresty Commission and other agencies on development in the countryside.

5. Increase public understanding and awareness and promote the best use of the countryside.

6. Develop and update a factual base from which sound policies can be developed through research and review.

Journal: Scotland's Countryside.

Publications: The Commission publishes a wide range of material on such subjects as the law and tradition of access, countryside conservation for farmers, information sheets and educational leaflets.

English Tourist Board Thames Tower, Black's Road, London W6 9EL. Tel. 071-846-9000.

Aims: To stimulate the development of English tourism by encouraging the British to take holidays in England; and by the provision and improvement of facilities for tourists in England.

To develop and market tourism in close co-operation with Regional and National Tourist Boards, the British Tourist Authority, local authorities and public sector organisations and the private sector.

To advise government and the public bodies on all matters concerning tourism in England.

To maximise tourism's contribution to the economy through the creation of wealth and jobs.

To enhance the image of England as a tourism destination by all appropriate means, including undertaking and encouraging innovative marketing.

To encourage and stimulate the successful development of tourism products of a high standard, which offer good value for money.

To bring greater recognition to tourism as an industry for investment, employment and economic development, by providing information, and where appropriate, advice and financial support.

To produce and disseminate information on tourism to the trade and the consumer.

To research trends in tourism and consumer requirements to show marketing and development needs and opportunities and evaluate past performance, future prospects and the impact of tourism.

To improve the industry's status and performance by encouraging and stimulating the adoption of up-to-date business methods and appropriate technology and the provision of education and training programmes.

To ensure that England's unique character and heritage is recognised and protected through the sensitive management of tourism.

There is a network of Tourist Information Centres throughout the country that can offer assistance and advice. Many of them will make provisional reservations through the Local Bed-Booking and Book-a-Bed Ahead services.

Publications: England Holidays, Where to Stay, Activity and Hobby Holidays, Let's Go! etc. Many of the Regional Tourist Boards (see below) publish guides, pamphlets and lists of accommodation.

Regional Tourist Boards

Cumbria Tourist Board, Ashleigh, Holly Road, Windermere, Cumbria LA23 2AS. (Tel. 09662–4444).

Counties: Cumbria.

AONBs: Arnside and Silverdale, Solway Coast.

East Anglia Tourist Board, Toppesfield Hall, Hadleigh, Suffolk IP7 7DN. (Tel. 0473–822922).

Counties: Cambridgeshire, Essex, Norfolk, Suffolk.

AONBs: Dedham Vale, Norfolk Coast, Suffolk Coast and Heaths.

East Midlands Tourist Board, Exchequergate, Lincoln LN2 1PZ. (Tel. 0522–531521).

Counties: Derbyshire, Leicestershire, Lincolnshire, Northamptonshire, Nottinghamshire.

AONBs: Lincolnshire Wolds.

Heart of England Tourist Board, Woodside, Larkhill, Worcester WR5 2EQ. (Tel. 0905-763436).

Counties: Gloucestershire, Hereford and Worcester, Shropshire, Staffordshire, Warwickshire, West Midlands.

AONBs: Cannock Chase, Cotswolds, Malvern Hills, Shropshire Hills, Wye Valley.

North West Tourist Board, The Last Drop Village, Bromley Cross, Bolton, Lancs BL7 9PZ. (Tel. 0204–591511).

Counties: Cheshire, Greater Manchester, Lancashire, Merseyside.

AONBs: Arnside and Silverdale, Forest of Bowland.

Northumbria Tourist Board, Aykley Heads, Durham DH1 5UX. (Tel. 091386-2160).

Counties: Cleveland, Durham, Northumberland, Tyne and Wear.
AONBs: Northumberland Coast.

South East Tourist Board, The Old Brewhouse, Warwick Park, Tunbridge Wells, Kent TN2 5TU. (Tel. 0892-540766).
Counties: East Sussex, Kent, Surrey, West Sussex.
AONBs: Chichester Harbour, High Weald, Kent, Surrey Hills, Sussex Downs.

Southern Tourist Board, 40 Chamberlayne Road, Eastleigh, Hampshire SO5 5JH. (Tel. 0703-620006).
Counties: Dorset (East), Hampshire, Isle of Wight.
AONBs: Chichester Harbour, Dorset, East Hampshire, Isle of Wight, North Wessex Downs, South Hampshire Coast.

Thames and Chilterns Tourist Board, The Mount House, Church Green, Witney, Oxon OX8 6D2. (Tel. 0993-778800).
Counties: Bedfordshire, Berkshire, Buckinghamshire, Hertfordshire, Oxfordshire.
AONBs: Chilterns, North Wessex Downs.

West Country Tourist Board, Trinity Court, 37 Southernhay East, Exeter EX1 1QS. (Tel. 0392–76351).
Counties: Avon, Cornwall, Dorset (West), The Isles of Scilly, Somerset, Wiltshire, Devon.
AONBs: Cornwall, Cotswolds, Cranborne Chase and West Wiltshire Downs, Dorset, East Devon, Isles of Scilly, Mendip Hills, North Devon, North Wessex Downs, Quantock Hills, South Devon.

Yorkshire and Humberside Tourist Board, 312 Tadcaster Road, York YO2 2HF. (Tel. 0904–707961).
Counties: Humberside, North Yorkshire, South Yorkshire, West Yorkshire.
AONBs: Howardian Hills, Lincolnshire Wolds.

Forest Service for Northern Ireland Dundonald House, Upper Newtownards Road, Belfast BT4 3SB. Tel. 0232-650111.
The Forest Service of the Department of Agriculture is the authority responsible for state forestry in Northern Ireland.
Publications: Numerous guides of general interest about trees and forestry as well as footpath guides and nature trails.

Forestry Commission 231 Corstorphine Road, Edinburgh EH12 7AT. Tel. 031–334–0303.
The Forestry Commission was established by Act of Parliament in 1919 and has the general duty of promoting the interests of forestry, the development of afforestation, the production and supply of timber and the maintenance of reserves of growing trees in Great Britain. It is responsible

for 900,000 hectares of woodland. The Commission operates camping and caravan sites, forest cabins and holiday homes, picnic areas, forest walks and nature trails, visitor centres and arboreta.

Publications: The Commission publishes a *Catalogue of Publications*, available from Publications, Forest Research Station, Alice Holt Lodge, Wrecclesham, Farnham, Surrey GU10 4LH, which lists scientific and technical papers as well as handbooks and guides of interest to the non-specialist.

Friends of the Earth 26–28 Underwood Street, London N1 7JQ. Tel. 071-490-1555.

Friends of the Earth is one of the leading pressure organisations and a major force behind today's growing green movement. It campaigns for energy conservation, wildlife, the countryside, tropical rain forests, public transport, wildlife in general and whales in particular and against pollution and acid rain. It conducts research and publishes reports on environment issues.

There are 250 autonomous local groups which take their lead from the national organisation but also campaign on behalf of purely local interests.

Journal: Friends of the Earth Supporters' Newspaper.

Publications: A wide range of information sheets and reports.

Friends of the Earth (Scotland) Bonnington Mill, 70-72 Newhaven Road, Edinburgh EH6 5QG. Tel. 031-554-9977.

A Scottish organisation that has similar aims to Friends of the Earth (qv).

Journal: Issues.

Publications: A range of leaflets on environmental matters.

*Friends of the Lake District Secretary: J M Houston, No. 3 Yard 77, Highgate, Kendal, Cumbria LA9 4ED. Tel. 0539-720788.

Aims: To promote an energetic and consistent application of unified planning policy for the Lake District as a whole under effective statutory powers created by legislation for national parks; to organise concerted action for protecting the landscape and natural beauty of the Lake District and the county of Cumbria as a whole; to co-operate with other bodies having similar objects or interests.

The Society represents the Council for the Protection of Rural England within the county of Cumbria.

Journal: Conserving Lakeland. The Society also publishes a newsletter.

Friends of National Parks *See* Council for National Parks.

*Friends of the Ridgeway Hon. Secretary: Nigel Forward, 90 South Hill Park, London NW3 2SN. Tel. 071-794-2105.

The Friends of the Ridgeway exist to ensure the preservation and conservation of the Ridgeway national trail for quiet recreational use. It is particularly opposed to its use by motor vehicles and has pressed hard for a Traffic Regulation Order on those parts of the path which vehicles are legally entitled to use.

Publications: a newsletter.

*The Icknield Way Association Hon. Secretary: Ken Payne, 65 London Road, Hitchen, Herts SG4 7NE. Tel. 0462-450089.

The Icknield Way Association has been established in order to promote and publicise the use of the Icknield Way as a route for walkers from the southern end of the Peddars Way to the Ridgeway Path. As a result of this use, it is intended that the association will urge the official adoption and completion of the Way as a national trail. The Association also aims to promote a body of informed opinion that will improve the enjoyment and knowledge of the Way and its amenities.

Publications: The Association publishes a newsletter and a footpath guide *The Icknield Way; a Walker's Guide*, 1988.

**John Muir Trust Director: Dr Terry Isles, Gardenhurst, Newbigging, Broughty Ferry, Dundee DD5 3RH. Tel. 082623-315.

John Muir was born in Scotland and is world-renowned as the leader of the campaign that led to the founding in the United States of the world's first national park system. He was also a leader of the conservation movement and the John Muir Trust aims to become the guardian of some of the wildest and most beautiful areas of Britain.

The Long Distance Paths Advisory Service. Administrator: Gerald Cole, The Barn, Holm Lyon, Burnside, Kendal, Cumbria LA9 6QX. Tel. 0539-727837.

This organisation, funded by a contract with the Countryside Commission, attempts to record all long-distance paths in the United Kingdom. The register, which in 1990 contained at least partial information about over 400 long-distance paths, is kept on a database containing essential documentation including details of footpath guides. The route of every long-distance path in the register is plotted on a master set of 1:50000 Ordnance Survey maps. The LDPAS will advise prospective authors and publishers on the suitability of their proposed route in the light of ecological and other considerations, and the proximity to existing long-distance paths.

*Long Distance Walkers' Association Hon Secretary: Alan Castle, Wayfarers, 9 Tainters Brook, Uckfield, East Sussex TN22 1UQ. Tel. 0825–61803.

Aims: To further the interests of those who enjoy long-distance walking. It is an association of people with the common interests of walking long and ultra long distances especially in rural, mountainous and moorland areas. It promotes organised challenge walks, pioneers new walking routes and receives and publishes information on all aspects of non-competitive walking. It is now recognised as the governing body for the activity of long-distance walking.

The LDWA caters for many kinds of walking including:

1. Challenge walks (such as the annual Association Hundred, Sevenoaks Circular, Ulfkil Stride) which are events in which an objective (usually a set distance) is to be achieved within a time limit.

2. 'Anytime' challenge walks (such as the Welsh 3000's Helm Wind and the Six Shropshire Summits) which are similar in nature but which may be attempted at any time.

3. Walks organised by local groups.

4. Walks along long-distance paths and routes designed by the Association.

5. 'Kanters' (map–reading events) organised by local groups.

Journal: Strider.

*Lyke Wake Club Chief Dirger: Goulton Grange, Swainby, Northallerton, North Yorkshire DL6 3HP.

A club formed to cater for those who have completed the Lyke Wake Walk (see p227) within twenty-four hours.

Publications: A news-sheet and *Lyke Wake Lamentations: the Lyke Wake Walkers' Bogside Book.*

**Mountain Bothies' Association General Secretary: Ted Butcher, 26 Rycroft Avenue, Deeping St James, Peterborough PE6 8NT. Tel. 0778–345062.

The MBA is a voluntary body formed to maintain simple unlocked shelters in mountain country for the use of walkers, climbers and other outdoor enthusiasts in remote places. Agreements are negotiated with the owners of the buildings to permit the Association to keep them in repair. Members are expected to give financial or physical assistance in maintaining the buildings in the care of the Association.

The Bothy Code:

1. Whenever possible seek owner's permission to use a bothy, particularly if proposing to take a group of six or more, or to use it as a base over a period. Note that all use of bothies is at own risk.

2. Do not stray from recognised routes during the stalking and game-shooting seasons (mainly mid-August to mid–October).

3. Leave bothies cleaner, tidier and in better condition as a result of your visit.

4. Burn all rubbish you can; take all tins and glass away with you.

5. Lay in a supply of fuel and kindling for the next user (don't cut live wood).

6. If you leave unused food, date it and leave safe from rodents.

7. Do not burn, deface or damage any part of the structure.

8. Guard against risk of fire and ensure that the fire is safely out before leaving.

9. Secure windows and doors on departure.

10. Safeguard the water supply. Do not use the neighbourhood of the bothy as a toilet.

11. Protect and preserve animal and plant life.

12. Respect the countryside, its occupants and the country way of life.

13. Reports on the state of bothies maintained by the Association will be welcomed by the Maintenance Organiser or the General Secretary.

Publications: an annual journal and a newsletter.

Mountain Walking Leader Training Board Crawford House, Precinct Centre, Booth Street East, Manchester M13 9RZ. Tel. 061–273–5835.

The Mountain Leader Training Board was set up in 1964 to provide a scheme of training for leaders who take groups of young people into the mountains. The Board consists of representatives of the British Mountaineering Council, the Association of Heads of Outdoor Education Centres, the Sports Council and other interested bodies.

Mountain Leader Assessment: This is the basic award which aims at raising the standard of knowledge and competence of leaders in mountainous country. Minimum age: (a) for registration and training, 18 years; (b) for assessment, 20 years.

To obtain the award a candidate must:

1. Complete a training course of at least six days' duration at a training centre approved by the Board; this course is not a beginner's course but an introduction to the scheme. All candidates should be committed hill-walkers or climbers with a substantial recent history of mountainous country activities. *It is not suitable for novices.*

2. Following this, have at least one year's practical experience as an assistant leader or group member of expeditions during week-ends and holidays, details of which must be recorded in a personal log book. This period is designed to allow candidates to prepare for assessment by putting into practice the techniques and theories acquired on the training courses; and to provide the assessor with the evidence needed to carry out a fair assessment.

3. Attend a final week's residential course at an approved centre for assessment.

4. Be conversant with the following books:
    Mountaincraft and Leadership by Eric Langmuir
    Safety on Mountains
    The Mountain Code
    Mountain Rescue and Cave Rescue

303

5.   Produce a current certificate in First Aid of the St John's Ambulance Brigade or of the British Red Cross Society or a First Aid at Work Certificate.

All candidates must be registered with the MWTB and possess a log book.

Exemption: Exemption from training and log book, but not assessment, may be applied for if the candidate is exceptionally experienced and fully conversant with the requirements of the syllabus. Unjustified exemptions can result in failure at assessment.

Mountaineering Instructor's Certificate: This certificate is a progression from the Mountain Walking Leader Training Scheme. Training and certification are designed to meet the needs of anyone instructing in rock or ice-climbing or general mountaineering in the UK, whether on a full or part-time basis.

Mountaineering Council of Scotland National Officer: Ken Howett, 71 King Street, Crieff, Perthshire PH7 3HB. Tel. 0764–4962.

Aims: To promote mountaineering in Scotland. The Mountaineering Council of Scotland is the governing body for the sport in Scotland and represents member clubs in all mountaineering matters at national level and co-operates closely with the British Mountaineering Council.

Publications: A newsletter, a list of Scottish mountaineering clubs' huts. *Heading for the Hills* (see p242).

Mountain Rescue Committee Hon. Secretary: R. J. Davis, 18 Tarnside Fold, Simmondley, Glossop, Derbys SK13 9ND. Tel. 0457–853095.

The Mountain Rescue Committee is a charitable trust and voluntary body comprising organisations formed by official mountain rescue teams and representatives from the Sports Council, the police, the R.A.F. rescue service and other interested bodies. It is an organisation through which the Department of Health and Social Security recognises the affiliated mountain rescue teams and approves the issue of morphia and equipment to them.

Aims

1.   To organise and co-ordinate mountain rescue in England and Wales with the support and recognition of the Department of Health and Social Security, the Home Office and the Welsh Office.

2.   To assist and encourage the formation of mountain rescue teams and posts in England and Wales where the need exists, and to assist the rescue teams in their work.

3.   To promote the exchange of experience and information between teams and others engaged in mountain and cave rescue.

4.   To arrange for the supply of medical first aid equipment and other equipment through the Department of Health and Social Security to

mountain rescue teams and posts.

5. To encourage and arrange investigation and research into methods and apparatus involved in mountain rescue.

6. To make representations on mountain rescue interests to other national, international or government bodies.

Publications: Mountain and Cave Rescue with Lists of Official Rescue Teams and Posts: the Handbook of the Mountain Rescue Committee.

Mountain Rescue Committee for Scotland Hon. Secretary: Malcolm Duckworth, 5 Westfield Terrace, Aberdeen AB2 4RU. Tel. 0224–646995.

The MRCS is the body that co-ordinates the work of mountain rescue organisations in Scotland and is a member of the Mountain Rescue Committee (q.v.).

National Association for Outdoor Education Hon. Secretary: Charlie Care, 50 High View Avenue, Grays, Essex CM17 6RU.

Aims: To promote the use of the outdoors in the social and personal development of young people and adults.

Journal: Adventure Education.

National Trust 36 Queen Anne's Gate, London SW1H 9AS. Tel. 071–222–9251.

The National Trust for Places of Historic Interest or Natural Beauty was founded in 1895 by Miss Octavia Hill, Sir Robert Hunter and Canon H. D. Rawnsley to halt the destruction of the countryside by the uncontrollable growth of industry. The Trust is now the largest private landowner and conservation society in Britain. It has branches throughout the United Kingdom except Scotland which has its own organisation the National Trust for Scotland (qv).

Aims: To educate public opinion and to give people access to the countryside by acting as trustess to the nation by acquiring land and buildings worthy of permanent preservation.

Journal: The National Trust Magazine.

Publications: Numerous guides and handbooks on architecture and the countryside.

National Trust for Scotland 5 Charlotte Square, Edinburgh EH2 4DU. Tel. 031–226–5922.

Aims: To promote the permanent preservation for the benefit of the nation of lands, buildings, places and articles in Scotland of national architectural, artistic, antiquarian or historic interest, or lands of natural beauty, along with, where appropriate, their animal and plant life. Of equal importance is the stated purpose of the Trust to encourage and facilitate the access to and the enjoyment of such places and things by the public.

Journal: Heritage Scotland.

Publications: Numerous guidebooks including footpath guides to Ben Lawers and Torridon.

Nature Conservancy Council Northminster House, Peterborough PE1 1UA. Tel. 0733–340345.

The Nature Conservancy Council is the government body that promotes nature conservation in Great Britain. It gives advice on nature conservation to government and all those whose activities affect our wildlife and wild places. It also selects, establishes and manages a series of National Nature reserves and undertakes or commissions relevant research.

Journal; Earth Science Conservation.

Publication: Newsletters *(Urban Wildlife News, Topical Issues and Batchat)* and numerous handbooks, guides, reports, booklets, information sheets, wallcharts and posters (mail order catalogue available).

Offa's Dyke Association Old Primary School, West Street, Knighton, Powys LD7 1EW. Tel. 0547–528753.

Aims: To promote the conservation, improvement and better knowledge of the Welsh border region along the Offa's Dyke Path.

The Association publishes a newsletter and several guides which are listed in the Offa's Dyke Path bibliography on pages 189-91.

The Open Spaces Society (formerly The Commons, Open Spaces and Footpath Preservation Society). 25a Bell Street, Henley-on-Thames, Oxon RG9 2BA. Tel. 0491–573535.

The Society, founded in 1865, is Britain's oldest conservation body and campaigns for the protection of common land, town and village greens, open spaces and public paths

Journal: Open Space.

The Ordnance Survey Romsey Road, Maybush, Southampton SO9 4DH. Tel. 0703–792000.

The government department responsible for the surveying and mapping England, Wales and Scotland (see p47-59).

Publications: Maps, information leaflets about the services of the Ordnance Survey and numerous books and guides of interest to walkers.

The Ordnance Survey of Northern Ireland Colby House, Stranmillis Court, Belfast BT9 5BJ. Tel. 0232–661244.

The government agency responsible for the surveying and mapping of Northern Ireland.

Publications: 1:63360, 1:50000, 1:25000 (part of Province only), 1:10560 and 1:10000 maps together with various technical works.

Outdoor Writers' Guild Secretary: Hugh Westacott, 86 Burford Gardens, London N13 4LP. Tel. 081-886-1957.

Aims: To promote a high professional standard amongst writers who specialise in outdoor activities.

Journal: a newsletter.

Peddars Way Association Hon. Secretary: George Le Surf, 150 Armes Street, Norwich NR2 4EG. Tel. 0603–623070.

The organisation that seeks to protect and provide information about the Peddars Way and Norfolk Coast Path.

Aims: To promote and publicise the use of the route and its amenities for the benefit of walkers and cyclists.

To promote a body of informed opinion that will improve the enjoyment and knowledge of the Peddars Way.

Publications: A newsletter and *Walking the Peddars Way/Norfolk Coast and the Weaver's Way*.

*Pennine Way Council Hon. Secretary: Chris Sainty, 29 Springfield Park Avenue, Chelmsford CM2 6EL. Tel. 0245–256772.

Aims: To secure the protection of the Pennine Way; to provide information about the Way to the public; to educate users of the Way and its environs in a proper respect for the countryside; to assist in the organisation of voluntary efforts directed at the maintenance of the Way and to provide a forum in which different interests connected with the Way and its use can discuss problems of mutual concern.

Publications: A newsletter and *The Pennine Way Accommodation and Camping Guide*.

Ramblers' Association 1/5 Wandsworth Road, London SW8 2XX. Tel. 071–582–6878.

The RA is the national organisation that protects the interests of walkers.

Aims:

1. To help all persons, especially those of limited means, to a greater love, knowledge and care of the countryside.

2. To work for and assist in

   i)   The provision of and the prevention of obstruction to public rights of way over footpaths and other ways used mainly for footpaths.

   ii) The preservation and enhancement for the benefit of the public of the beauty of the countryside.

   iii) The provision and preservation of public access to open country.

   iv) With the object of improving the conditions of life for the persons for whom the facilities are intended, namely the public at large, and in the interests of social welfare to encourage the provision of facilities for and the organising of healthy open-air recreational activities in the countryside and in particular rambling and mountaineering.

3. To do all such other lawful things as are incidental or conducive to the

attainment of the above objects and which may lawfully be done by a body established for charitable purposes only.

Journals: Rambling Today and *Footpath Worker* (both periodicals are described in Appendix One).

Publications: The Rambler's Yearbook, Making Tracks; a Celebration of fifty years of the Ramblers' Association, Rights of Way; a Guide to Law and Practice, computer print-outs for every county listing footpath guides, and various guides, reports etc.

*Red Rope National Secretary: Jerzy Wieczorek, 3 Barnet Street, Oxford OX4 3AN. Tel. 0865–250180.

Aims: Red Rope is the name of the Socialist Walking and Climbing Club which exists to promote access to the countryside for socialist walkers and climbers. It encompasses all kinds of walking and climbing from gentle strolls to winter mountainering.

Journals: The Bulletin and an information sheet.

Scottish Mountain Leader Training Board Caledonia House, Gyle, Edinburgh EH12 9DQ. Tel. 031–317–7200.

The SMLTB is the body that administers the Scottish Mountain Leader Award (Summer) and the Winter Mountain Leader Scheme which are designed to provide training and assessment in the technical and leading skills required by those who wish to lead groups into the mountains and moorlands of the British Isles.

Scottish Mountain Leader Award (Summer): The purpose of the Scottish Mountain Leader Training Scheme is to encourage the safe enjoyment of the hills by all who go there. It provides training and assessment in the technical and leading skills required by those who wish to lead groups of young people into the mountains and moorlands of the British Isles. It is not a mountaineering or educational qualification. Entrants are strongly advised to attend an approved course and before asssessment must be twenty years old, completed at least forty quality mountain days and obtained a valid first aid certificate. The candidate will submit a log-book of his mountain experience and will be assessed at a centre approved by the Board.

Winter Mountain Leadership Scheme: This scheme provides training and assessment in the special skills and techniques required when leading parties on the hills and mountains of the United Kingdom in winter conditions.

Candidates have to provide evidence of substantial winter experience before they are accepted for registration, training and assessment. They then have to take a rigorous training course at an approved centre and are required to have an approved first aid certificate, complete at least forty quality mountain winter days, including at least ten Grade I winter climbs.

*Scottish Rights of Way Society Ltd Unit 2, John Cotton Business Centre, 10/2 Sunnyside, Edinburgh EH7 5RA. Tel. 031–652–2937.

Aims:

1. The preservation, defence and acquisition of public rights of way in Scotland, and the doing of such acts as may be necessary to preserve or restore such rights of way as may be in danger of being lost.

2. The erection, restoration and repair of bridges, guide-posts, notice or direction boards and plates, fences, stiles, gates and resting places in connection with such rights of way; and also the repairing of the roads and pathways themselves.

3. The defence and prosecution, directly or indirectly, of suits or actions for the preservation or recovery of such rights of way.

4. The doing of such other lawful things as are incident or conducive to the above objects.

Publications: Rights of Way: a Guide to the Law in Scotland.

The Scottish Sports Council Caledonia House, South Gyle, Edinburgh EH12 9DQ. Tel. 031–317–7200.

Aims: To foster the knowledge and practice of sport and physical recreation among the public at large and the provision of facilities therefore in Scotland.

The Scottish Sports Council allocates government grants for sports facilities in Scotland and contributes to the financing of mountain rescue teams and the National Outdoor Training Centre at Glenmore Lodge, Aviemore.,

Scottish Tourist Board 23 Ravelston Terrace, Edinburgh EH4 3EU. Tel. 031–332–2433.

Established under the Development of Tourism Act, 1969, the Board is responsible for promoting Scotland within Britain and administering the hotel incentive scheme. It gives fundamental assistance to other tourist information services, carries out research and works with the British Tourist Authority in publicising Scotland overseas.

Publications: Where to Stay in Scotland, Scotland: Hill Walking and various maps, guides and lists of accommodation.

**Scottish Wild Land Group 1/3 Kilgraston Court, Kilgraston Road, Edinburgh EH9 2ES. Tel. 031–447–0853.

Aims: To promote the conservation wild land and its flora and fauna by increasing public awareness of the problems facing wild land in Scotland. By helping to co-ordinate the efforts of like-minded groups and individuals to create a strong voice through which the case for conservation can be expressed. By pressing for the adoption of planning policies which recognise conservation as a relevant factor in the national economy, compatible with appropriate development, the provision of long-term employment, and the tourist industry, to which the landscape and its particular qualities are vital.

Journal: Wild Land News.

Scottish Youth Hostels Association 7 Glebe Crescent, Stirling FK8 2JA. Tel. 0786–51181.

Aims: To help all, but especially young people of limited means living and working in industrial and other areas to know, use, and appreciate the Scottish countryside and places of historic and cultural interest in Scotland, and to promote their health, recreation and education, particularly by providing simple hostel accommodation for them on their travels.

The SYHA has 81 hostels (there are separate organisations for Northern Ireland and England and Wales – see the Youth Hostels Association of Northern Ireland and the Youth Hostels Association). Most hostels are self-catering (though some provide meals) and there are facilities for members to cook their own meals. Prices are kept low because members have to do a few household chores before departing. Accommodation is in single-sex dormitories although some hostels have family rooms. SYHA organises tours and adventure holidays and a current membership card entitles the holder to use youth hostels throughout the world.

Journal: The Scottish Hosteller.

*The South West Way Association Membership Secretary: Mrs M. MacLeod, 1 Orchard Drive, Kingskerswell, Newton Abbot, Devon TQ12 5DG. Tel. 0803–873061.

Aims: To promote the interests of users of the South West Peninsula Coast Path. The Association brings pressure to bear on the appropriate authorities to improve the path and to provide a coastal route where none exists at present.

Publications: A newsletter, leaflets and maps to various sections of the path. The Association compiles *The South West Way: the Complete Guide to Great Britain's Longest Footpath* published annually by Devon Books which, although no substitute for maps or footpath guides to the route, provides essential information about tides, ferries, changes of route and contains an accommodation list.

Sports Council 16 Upper Woburn Place, London WC1H 0QP. Tel. 071–388–1277.

Aims: To foster the knowledge and practice of sport and physical recreation among the public at large and the provision of facilities.

The Sports Council has given grants to several projects connected with walking.

Sports Council for Northern Ireland House of Sport, Upper Malone Road, Belfast BT9 5LA. Tel. 0232–381222.

Aims: Development of sport in Northern Ireland. The Council has established a committee for the development of the Ulster Way and long-distance footpaths in the Province.

Ulster Federation of Rambling Clubs Hon Secretary: Mary Doyle, 27 Sleivegallion Drive, Belfast BT11 8JN. Tel. 0232–624289.

Aims: To promote walking and the use of footpaths in the Province.

Ulster Society for the Preservation of the Countryside Peskett Centre, 2a Windsor Road, Belfast BT9 7FQ. Tel. 0232–381304.

The Ulster Society for the Preservation of the Countryside was founded in 1937 and is the oldest conservation body in Northern Ireland. It is an independent body of people who recognise the need to cherish and maintain the natural environment and work for the preservation, conservation and improvement of the Northern Ireland countryside. The Society includes within its remit rights of way, protection of trees, afforestation policy, water extraction, mining and quarrying, the siting of motorways and legislation dealing with the preservation of natural amenities.

Journal: Countryside Recorder.

The Volunteer Centre UK 29 Lower King's Road, Berkhamsted, Herts HP4 2AB. Tel 0442–873311.

Aims: To provide information, training and support to people who work with volunteers, including those who work with volunteers in the countryside.

Journal: Involve. The Centre also publishes a newsletter.

Wales Tourist Board Brunel House, 2 Fitzalan Road, Cardiff CF2 1UY. Tel. 0222–499909.

Aims: The Wales Tourist Board gives assistance to tourist projects in Wales, provides tourist information services and generally promotes tourism in Wales.

It is responsible for tourism in the counties of Clwyd, Dyfed, Gwent, Gwynedd, Mid Glamorgan, Powys, West Glamorgan and the AONBs of Anglesey, Clwydian Hills, Gower, Lleyn, Wye Valley.

Publications: Where to Stay in Wales, Wales Walking and other tourist publications.

Youth Hostels Association Trevelyan House, 8 St Stephen's Hill, St Albans, Herts AL1 2DY. Tel. 0727–55215.

Aims: To help all, especially young people of limited means, to a greater knowledge, love and care of the countryside particularly by providing hostels or other simple accommodation for them in their travels, and thus to promote their health, rest and education.

The YHA has 260 hostels in England and Wales (Scotland and Ulster have their own organisations – the Scottish Youth Hostels Association and the Northern Ireland Youth Hostels Association). Inexpensive meals are available at most hostels and there are usually facilities for members to cook their own meals. Prices are kept low because members have to do a few household chores before departing. Accommodation is in single-sex dormitories although a few hostels have family rooms. The YHA offers tours and travel services to its members and a current membership card entitles the holder to use youth hostels throughout the world.

Journal: The Hosteller.

Youth Hostels Association of Northern Ireland 56 Bradbury Place, Belfast BT7 1RU. Tel. 0232–324733.

Aims: To help all, especially young people of limited means, to a greater knowledge, love and care of the countryside particularly by providing hostels or other simple accommodation for them in their travels, and thus to promote their health, rest and education.

There are seven hostels mostly situated in the eastern half of the Province (there are separate organisations for Scotland and England and Wales – see the Scottish Youth Hostels Association and the Youth Hostels Association). Most hostels are self-catering (though some provide meals and snacks) and there are facilities for members to cook their own meals. Prices are kept low because members have to do a few household chores before departing. Accommodation is in single-sex dormitories although some hostels have family rooms. A current membership card entitles the holder to use youth hostels throughout the world.

GLOSSARY

Anorak A thigh-length garment with a hood which is pulled over the head. It has a short zip and drawstrings and often a kangaroo pocket across the chest. Usually made of polyurethane-coated nylon or, less commonly, closely woven cotton.

AONB See Area of Outstanding Natural Beauty.

Area of Outstanding Natural Beauty (AONB) Regions of special landscape beauty which have been designated by the Countryside Commission in consultation with the local authority. AONBs have no special administrative arrangements but the local planning authority will usually pay particular attention to controlling development.

Avalanche A fall of rock, or more commonly snow, which occurs in mountainous areas.

Balaclava A woollen hat which can be fitted round the ears and chin. In good weather usually worn rolled up on top of the head.

Beck A mountain stream in the north of England.

Bench mark A mark made by surveyors on a permanent object such as a wall to indicate a known height above sea level.

Benighted Being stranded on a mountain after dark.

Bivouac sack (Bivvy sack) A simple plastic or nylon bag large enough to serve as a tent. It is carried for emergency use in bad weather in the mountains.

Bothy A simple structure provided for emergency shelter on mountains especially in Scotland.

Box quilting A method of sewing duvet clothing and sleeping bags so that there is always a layer of insulating material between two pieces of material holding the insulation in place. This eliminates the cold spots inevitable with simple quilting.

Bridleway A highway over which the public have a right of way on foot, on horseback and on a pedal bicycle. In Scotland there is no statutory right to use a pedal cycle on a bridleway.

Brocken spectre A combination of atmospheric conditions which results in the mountaineer seeing his own shadow cast on a wall of cloud or mist.

Burn A mountain stream especially in Scotland and Northumberland.

Byway More properly, a byway open to all traffic, is defined in the Wildlife and Countryside Act, 1981 as ' . . . a highway over which the public have a right of way for vehicular and all other kinds of traffic, but which is used by the public mainly for the purposes for which footpaths and bridleways are so used'.

Cagoule (Cag) A knee-length anorak.

Cairn A pile of rocks or stones to mark the summit of a mountain or the route of a path. Invaluable for route-finding in mist.

Clints The flat, smooth surface of limestone pavements.

Clitters The mounds of shattered granite found especially on Dartmoor.

Clough A ravine or valley with steep sides especially in the Peak District.

Col (See Pass).

Combe A narrow valley with grass covered slopes running into the side of a hill. Also used to describe a steep valley running in from the sea, especially in the west country, 'Coomb' and 'coombe' are variant spellings.

Common Land over which some members of the public (but not necessarily the public at large) have certain rights, e.g. the right to graze cattle or gather fuel. Common land always has an owner.

Contour Lines drawn on maps to indicate height and shape of land.

Cornice An overhanging lip of snow on a mountain ridge. Very dangerous to walkers on the ridge, as it can break and plunge down the ridge, carrying the walkers with it.

Corrie A Scottish name for a cwm (q.v.).

Crag A steep and rugged rock.

Crag-fast The condition of being unable to move on a crag or cliff. Walkers should never attempt to climb crags. No attempt should be made to rescue animals or climbers who are crag-fast but help should be summoned from the nearest point.

Crampons Claw-like metal objects strapped on the soles of boots to give better grip on ice and hard snow. Used only by the hardiest of walkers in mountainous country.

Cwm A rounded hollow in a mountain side forming a wall or cliff at one end and with a valley dropping away at the other end. Often there is a tarn or lake in the cwm which feeds a stream.

Definitive Map In England and Wales highway authorities have a legal-obligation to publish maps showing rights of way. The inclusion on the Definitive Map of a right of way is conclusive evidence in law of the existence of a right of way unless a diversion or extinguishment has been granted. This applies even if the right of way has been included on the map in error.

Down clothing Jackets, trousers, waistcoats etc, filled with down. Such clothing is exceptionally warm and comfortable but not really necessary in Great Britain except, perhaps, for winter mountaineering in Scotland.

Drove road A route used in times past for driving animals especially cattle and sheep to market.

Dubbin A leather preservative used on boots to keep them supple and water-resistant.

Duvet A down jacket.

Edge A term used particularly in the Peak District and Pennines to describe an outcrop of rock on a ridge forming a vertical face.

Emslie and English 2,000-footers 348 English summits which exceed 2,000 ft (608 metres) in height. The list was compiled by W. T. Emslie.

Escarpment A steep slope or inland cliff particularly in chalk country. The steepest part is the scarp and the more gradual slope is the dip.

Exposure The cooling of the body temperature caused by climatic conditions.

Fell Often used in the Lake District and Pennines to describe a mountain. Also used to describe a moor or mountainside.

Fell-walking A term used to describe serious walking in upland areas on the north of England.

Footpath A highway over which the public have a right of way on foot only.

Frostbite Frozen body tissue, especially of the extremities such as fingers, toes, ears and nose. A very serious condition.

Gaiters Knee-length waterproof garments that fit over the boots and protect the lower half of the legs from rain, snow and wet vegetation.

Ghyll A mountain stream or ravine, particularly in the Lake District and Pennines.

Gill (See Ghyll).

Glacier cream A cream used by walkers in snowy conditions to protect the exposed parts of the body from the harmful effects of ultra-violet radiation.

Glen A narrow valley, especially in Scotland.

Glissading A method of descending a snow slope by sliding. Not recommended unless properly taught.

Gorge A very steep-sided narrow valley.

Greasy rock Stones and boulders covered with lichen, moss and grass which is very slippery when wet.

Green roads Green roads have no statutory definition but they are usually unsurfaced public highways and are often classed as 'Roads Used as Public Paths' or 'byways open to all traffic'.

Grikes The deep fissures which are found in limestone pavements.

Grough A peat bog, especially in the Peak District.

Gully A ravine made by the action of water.

Hachures A form of shading on maps to represent the shape of the land.

Hag A peat bog.

Hanging valley A valley in a mountainside above the main valley. The stream from the hanging valley usually enters the main valley by a waterfall.

Headland path A path that follows a field boundary.

Helm wind The name of the strong north-easterly wind which blows over Cross Fell (893 metres), the highest point in the Pennines.

Hill A summit not exceeding 600 metres in height.

Hill-walking Another name for fell-walking.

Hoosier A crude gate made of barbed wire. One end is fixed to a post in the ground. The post at the free end has a loop of wire which can be attached to the fixed post thus allowing the wire to be opened and closed.

Ice axe Carried by experienced walkers in mountainous country in snowy conditions. It is used for cutting steps in hard snow and ice and as a walking stick for steadying the walker when crossing steep slopes.

Kissing gate A small gate hung in a U- or V-shaped enclosure.

Knott An outcrop of rock frequently found in the Lake District.

Ladder stile A stile over a wall or fence giving access by means of several ladder-like steps.

Lapse rate The rate of change in temperature caused by increased altitude. As a rule of thumb guide temperature decreases by 2°C every 300 metres of height gained.

LDP See Long-Distance Path.

Limestone pavements Large flat areas of limestone found particularly in the Yorkshire Dales National Park. The smooth surfaces are known as clints and the deep grooves caused by the action of water are grikes.

Long-Distance Path (LDP) A generic term for any named long-distance path.

Metamorphism The change in the structure and characteristics of snowflakes caused by atmospheric conditions. Metamorphism is one of the main causes of avalanches.

Moor High uncultivated ground usually covered in heather.

Mountain A summit over 600 metres.

Mountain rescue posts These are located in suitable places such as huts, hotels, police stations and farms. They are usually, but not always, on the telephone and contain first-aid equipment and a stretcher. Often marked on Ordnance Survey Maps.

Mountain rescue teams Volunteers who undertake rescue work. They are usually members of the walking and climbing fraternity living locally who give their services free.

Munro tables A list of Scottish mountains over 3000 ft compiled by Sir Hugh Munro.

Naismith's formula A method of calculating the time necessary to walk a certain distance in mountainous country. Allow one hour for every five kilometres covered, plus half an hour for every three hundred metres climbed.

National Park Areas of mountain, moor, heath, down, cliff or foreshore containing a high proportion of open country which have been designated as national parks by the Secretary of State for the Environment.

National Trail The Countryside Commission have designated 13 long-distance routes to be National Trails. Each is fully waymarked with the acorn symbol and the Commission pays for the creation of the route and towards its subsquent upkeep.

Needle A tall sharp rock or crag found particularly in the Lake District.

Outcrop A small cliff on a mountain.

Pack-frame A light-alloy frame carried on the shoulders and secured at the hips to which may be attached a sack for carrying kit and equipment.

Parka A fur-lined anorak.

Pass Low ground between two mountains which provides easy access to the next valley. Sometimes called a col.

Peak The summit of a mountain.

Peat Vegetable matter especially heather and bracken decomposed by water and often forming bogs and marshes.

Pike The name given to pointed mountains in the Lake District.

Ravine A pronounced cleft in a mountainside.

Ridge A narrow line with the mountainside falling steeply away on either side.

Road Used as Public Path (RUPP) 'A highway, other than a public path, used by the public mainly for the purpose for which footpaths or bridleways are so used' (National Parks and Access to the Countryside Act, 1949). Under the Countryside Act, 1968 RUPPs are to be reclassified as byways open to all traffic, bridleways or footpaths.

Rucksack A bag used for carrying kit and equipment. It is supported on the back by straps that pass over the shoulders. It may or may not be used with a pack-frame (q.v.).

RUPP See Road Used as Public Path.

Saddle A broad dip between two areas of higher ground in mountainous country.

Scar A cliff or rock face on a mountainside usually formed by a geological fault.

Scarp (See Escarpment).

Scramble Very easy climbing, without rope, on broken rocks.

Scree Areas of small stones on steep mountain sides found particularly in the Lake District.

Scree-running The art of running down a scree by digging the heels into the loose stone; rather similar to running down shingle on a beach. Most screes in the Lake District are now badly worn by constant use.

Sleeping bag An insulated bag used by campers instead of blankets.

Snow-blindness Temporary blindness caused by ultra-violet rays in mountainous country.

Snow goggles Special goggles worn in the mountains to protect the eyes from snow glare and ultra-violet rays.

Spot height Heights shown on Ordnance Survey maps.

Spur A projection from a mountain.

Stile A structure usually consisting of one or two steps giving access through a fence or hedge.

Tarn A mountain lake.

Tor A hill or rocky peak, particularly on Dartmoor and in Cornwall.

Triangulation pillar (Trig point) A stone or concrete pillar erected by the Ordnance Survey to mark an exact height established by surveying instruments.

Trig point (See Triangulation pillar).

Verglas A thin coating of ice on rocks which makes walking very dangerous.

Waymark A symbol indicating a path. Some waymarks indicate direction of path.

White-out Mist on a snow-covered mountain which makes it difficult to distinguish features on the ground.

Index

All Pan books are available at your local bookshop or newsagent, or can be ordered direct from the publisher. Indicate the number of copies required and fill in the form below.

Send to: **CS Department, Pan Books Ltd., P.O. Box 40, Basingstoke, Hants. RG21 2YT.**

or phone: 0256 469551 (Ansaphone), quoting title, author and Credit Card number.

Please enclose a remittance* to the value of the cover price plus: 60p for the first book plus 30p per copy for each additional book ordered to a maximum charge of £2.40 to cover postage and packing.

*Payment may be made in sterling by UK personal cheque, postal order, sterling draft or international money order, made payable to Pan Books Ltd.

Alternatively by Barclaycard/Access:

Card No.

Signature:

Applicable only in the UK and Republic of Ireland.

While every effort is made to keep prices low, it is sometimes necessary to increase prices at short notice. Pan Books reserve the right to show on covers and charge new retail prices which may differ from those advertised in the text or elsewhere.

NAME AND ADDRESS IN BLOCK LETTERS PLEASE:

....

Name————————————————————————————

Address————————————————————————————

————————————————————————————————

————————————————————————————————

————————————————————————————————